ALEKSANDR BLOK AND THE DYNAMICS OF THE LYRIC CYCLE

David A. Sloane

Slavica Publishers, Inc.

Slavica publishes a wide variety of scholarly books and textbooks on the languages, peoples, literatures, cultures, history, etc. of the USSR and Eastern Europe. For a complete catalog of books and journals from Slavica, with prices and ordering information, write to:

Slavica Publishers, Inc.
PO Box 14388
Columbus, Ohio 43214

PG
3453
.B6
279
1988

ISBN: 0-89357-182-2.

This book was published in 1988.

Text set by Sharon Nechis and Erica W. Townsend.

JUN 3 1991

FOR TIMOTHY

CONTENTS

ACKNOWLEDGEMENTS

While working on this book I often contemplated the debt I owe to excellent teachers. My interest in lyric cycles dates back to Professor Kiril Taranovsky's seminar on Blok at Harvard University in 1973. The paper I wrote for this course subsequently grew into a dissertation on "Strašnyj mir," written also under his expert guidance. From the dissertation emerged the idea for a much broader study, which this book finally embodies. The imperfections in it are my own, but whatever virtues it contains are due largely to the encouragement, advice and constructive criticism Professor Taranovsky gave me at various stages of my work on Blok. Professors Donald Fanger, Stephen Lottridge, Vsevolod Setchkarev and Jurij Striedter also contributed tangibly by listening to me and offering suggestions that made the writing immeasurably easier.

There are many others to whom I am sincerely grateful. Professor Arlene Forman, my colleague at Tufts University, discussed virtually every aspect of the book with me as it was being written and commented thoughtfully on the early drafts. Professor Gerald Pirog of Rutgers University gave invaluable advice in the initial stages of my research and later read the complete manuscript, making notes which were extremely useful in the final editing. Professor Alexander Levitsky of Brown University allowed me to consult his work on spiritual odes and, in private conversation, enriched my understanding of cyclization in the eighteenth century. A number of my students at Tufts helped by reacting to the "accidental cycles" discussed in the first chapter. Among my student assistants, I would single out Wendy Forgie, who tracked down abstruse references with uncommon skill; Gregg Gonzalvez, who read part of the book and made very sensitive suggestions; and Sharon Nechis, who typed the final draft, patiently incorporating my last-minute revisions.

Various institutions also contributed their support, financial or otherwise. The Andrew Mellon Foundation funded a semester of writing and research. The Tufts Committee on Faculty Research Awards generously helped pay for the book's preparation. And

Houghton Library at Harvard gave me access to its rare collection of Russian poetry, without which it would have been impossible to trace the history of the lyric cycle.

Finally, there is my family, who helped me through the hard times and shared with me the joys. Without their daily support this book could not have been written.

D.S.

PREFACE

One cannot approach Aleksandr Blok's poetry without asking some fundamental questions about the lyric cycle. Why did Blok organize virtually his entire lyric output into cycles? What information (if any) was he able to encode in the cycle that would have been absent otherwise? What need was there for him to create a cyclic construct unprecedented in Russian poetry—a "trilogy of incarnation"—out of nearly 800 separate lyrics and two poetic narratives? The more one tries to answer these questions, the more one is compelled to consider others which are at once more general but relevant specifically to the issue of Blok's poetics: What is a cycle? How do cycles "work"? What kinds of cycles are there? Is there a cyclic tradition in Russian poetry? If so, when did it begin and how long did it last?

Blok's contribution as a lyric poet cannot be understood unless one poses these questions and attempts to answer them. The problem one faces in doing so, however, is formidable since very little of the basic groundwork has been done. Only rather recently has the issue of cyclization begun to attract attention in the scholarly community, and the term "lyric cycle" does not even rate a separate entry in most poetic lexicons. To date most studies have been devoted to specific cycles by individual poets. The broader theoretical and historical issues have generally been neglected.

The present study is intended in part to rectify this circumstance. The first chapter is an elementary primer in the theory of the cycle; it addresses the problems of definition, semiotics and typology. The second provides a history of cyclization in Russian poetry up to Blok and investigates Blok's relation to this largely unknown heritage. In the concluding chapter, among other things, I consider what directions cyclization took after Blok and attempt to determine what influence his example had on his successors. In all of this I make no claim to ideal thoroughness, but hopefully my efforts will suggest avenues for further study.

The central chapters of the book deal with Blok's lyric "trilogy" itself and involve a different set of problems. Each of these chapters focuses on one volume of the "trilogy" and analyzes the cyclic dynamic that unifies it and is most characteristic of it. Here the essential task is not to fill gaps but to assimilate the lessons of an already voluminous literature on Blok's poetry and carry certain of its implications to new conclusions.

Since the 1960's Blok's cycles have received a great deal of critical scrutiny, most of which is at a very high level of scholarly expertise. Much of what has been achieved in understanding Blok as a cyclic poet can be attributed to the innovative methods of the Tartu semiotic school—particularly to the fine work of Z. Minc. Minc has done more than anyone else in recent years to focus attention on Blok's cyclic legacy, and thanks largely to her efforts the study of cyclization in Blok has been placed on a very firm footing. By now the discipline is well beyond the stage of generalities about the importance of context in his poetry; analyses now concentrate, for the most part, on the microstructural elements of Blok's cycles—especially words and motifs, which are the key to his poetic universe.

My own study derives a great deal from Minc, but it also differs substantively from her approach. Minc, it seems to me, sometimes oversimplifies the dynamics of Blok's cycles by ascribing to his imagery certain fixed symbolic values. The binary oppositions she employs to classify words and leitmotifs are extremely useful, but they are not absolutely infallible. What makes the word powerful in Blok is not its docile membership in one half of a binary construct, but its capacity to shift categories unexpectedly, its capacity (as D. M. Pocepnja observes) "to turn itself inside out," while still carrying the memory of its past associations.[1] Indeed, Minc provides the grounding for such a view, but her analytic strategies do not always accommodate the rich dynamics of Blok's cycles.

"Dynamics" is the appropriate word here because the lyric cycle, perhaps more than any other literary form, forces the reader to confront the ambiguities of esthetic structure and experience them as ongoing process. Every cycle is both a text and a group of separate texts, and these conflicting truths set in motion a dialectic that can never be fully reconciled. This is why, it seems, Edward Stankiewicz characterizes the lyric cycle as "the paradigm of all contemporary literature"[2]; in modern literature, as he points out, "the poetic text is . . . perceived as a voyage of discovery rather than one of attainment, a process in which the reader is expected to take an active part. It is precisely because the world appears to be disjointed and fragmented that the quest for integration is more keenly felt." [3]   Reading lyric cycles, especially Blok's cycles, makes one reflect upon this reality continually.

David A. Sloane
Tufts University
July 7, 1985

NOTES TO THE PREFACE

[1]D.M. Pocepnja, *Proza A. Bloka: Stilističeskie problemy* (L: Izd. LGU, 1976), 134.

[2]Edward Stankiewicz, "Centripetal and Centrifugal Structures in Poetry," *Semiotica*, No. 3/4 (1982), 231.

[3]Stankiewicz, 240.

ABBREVIATIONS

Blok's Cycles, Sections, and Poèmy

Volume I

AL	Ante Lucem
SPD	Stixi o Prekrasnoj Dame
RAS	Rasput'ja

Volume II

PZ	Puzyri zemli
NF	Nočnaja Fialka
RazSt II . . .	Raznye stixotvorenija
EP	Ee pribytie
G	Gorod
SnM	Snežnaja Maska
F	Faina
OL	Osennjaja ljubov'
ZOM	Zakljatie ognem i mrakom
VM	Vol'nye mysli

Volume III

StM	Strašnyj mir
PS	Pljaski smerti
ŽMP	Žizn' moego prijatelja
ČK	Černaja krov'
VOZ	Vozmezdie
JAM	Jamby
ISt	Ital'janskie stixi
VEN	Venecija
FLO	Florencija
RazSt III . . .	Raznye stixotvorenija
AS	Arfy i skipki
TP	Tri poslanija
MÈR	Mèri
ČDL	Čerez dvenadcat' let
K	Karmen
SS	Solov'inyj sad

ROD . . . . . Rodina
NPK . . . . . Na pole Kulikovom
OČPV . . . . . O čem poet veter

Other

AN . . . . . . Akademija nauk
L . . . . Leningrad
LGU . . . . . . Leningradskij gosudarstvennyj
                    universitet
M . . . . Moskva
MGU . . . . . . Moskovskij gosudarstvennyj universitet
Pb . . . . . . Peterburg
Pg . . . . . . Petrograd
SPb . . . . . . Sankt-Peterburg
TGU . . . . . . Tartuskij gosudarstvennyj universitet
ZK . . . . . . A. Blok, *Zapisnye knižki* (M: 1965)

NOTE ON ITALICS AND UNDERLINING

Throughout this book italics and underlining in any quoted text represents my own emphasis unless otherwise indicated.

D.S.

Пересмотрите также после меня и мои книги.
—Aleksandr Blok, diary entry from October 12, 1902

I

TOWARD A THEORY OF THE LYRIC CYCLE

> Any two pieces, placed side by side, are
> inevitably unified into a new concept.
>
> —Sergej Èjzenštejn, "Montaž 1938"

> I cannot make sense of a part without placing
> it in relation to a whole: that is common
> sense, and also a basic principle of
> interpretation theory.
>
> —Frank Kermode, *The Genesis of Secrecy*

Definition

"Lyric cycle," like much literary nomenclature, means different things to different people. A consensus exists that the term defines a group of separate lyrics which have a certain unity, but scholars disagree about the nature and degree of this unity.

According to one school of thought *any* grouping of lyrics indicated by their author as belonging together qualifies as a "cycle," regardless of the conceptual ties that may or may not exist between the member poems. This "inclusive" definition, which subsumes only the cycle's external form, is advocated cogently by Helen Mustard:

> Any student of the lyric cycle who approaches this form
> in its historical aspect must begin with a very liberal
> definition. He cannot assume that the cycle will
> conform to specific structural laws, for it is not a time
> honored genre that follows the prescriptions of a stylistic
> or aesthetic code. It is rather a structural device that
> admits of the most varied adaptations. . . . [It is]

sufficient to define it as a group of poems indicated by
their author as belonging together. . . . Since the cycle
is not an *a priori*, there is no criterion by which one
can dogmatically admit or exclude certain groups.[1]

V.A. Sapogov, a Soviet specialist, is essentially in accord with
Mustard:

> By lyric cycle is understood, usually, a collection of
> separate poems of some quantity which are connected
> more or less by a single theme.   Sometimes the
> collected poems of one genre (elegies, ballads) are called
> cycles.   Sometimes a cycle is understood simply as   a
> small collection of poems.
>   Apparently all these points of view (and not only
> these) are completely acceptable in the concept of the
> "cycle," in its etymological meaning so to speak, and
> are based on the cycle's external, "graphic" form, not
> the internal bonds which make a cycle an organic
> whole.[2]

Although Sapogov does not mention authorial intention here,
elsewhere he states explicitly that a cycle is "a group of works
consciously conjoined by their author."[3]
    According to a different view, which we might call
"restrictive," lyric cycles are limited to a smaller field by various
criteria of composition and content.   According to Joachim Müller,
genuine cycles must contain a central idea or concept (a "thematic
a priori") to which all the individual poems   are related,
notwithstanding their separate focuses:

> Beyond all the variations of motif there is always that
> which is itself varied . . . the central point to which
> the individual poems in their prodigious extensions refer
> back.   This I call the basic motif [Grundmotif], the
> basic experience [Grunderlebnis] or the experiential
> center [Erlebniszentrum]. . . .   I would call this the
> motivic, or better, the thematic *a priori* [thematische
> Apriori].   It is present from the outset   as the primary
> motivating force without necessarily being named.[4]

The "thematic *a priori*" of Shakespeare's first 126 sonnets, for
instance, is the poet's "love for a handsome man"; in Dante's *La
Vita Nuova* it is the poet's "love for Beatrice"; in Rilke's "Die

Sonette an Orpheus" it is the idea that "the divine nature of Orpheus exists above all else and continually manifests itself anew," and so on.[5] In Müller's view not every grouping of poems contains such an "*a priori*." He denies the designation "cycle," therefore, to poems unified only by similarity of "mood" [Stimmung] or by "concrete, tangible content" [konkret fassbarer 'Inhalt'].[6] Thus Schiller's "Antologie" and certain "books" of Goethe's do not qualify as "cycles."[7] L.K. Dolgopolov gives an equally restrictive definition, although unlike Müller he is not intent on devising a special terminology of cyclic analysis.   For him the essential property of a genuine cycle is simply its "internal unity" [vnutrennee edinstvo]—a unity manifest in more than just the generic identity or thematic similarity of the poems.   Using this criterion, he argues that the various sections of Fet's 1863 collection ("Èlegii," "K Ofelii," "Snega." "Melodii," "Antologičeskie stixotvorenija," "More") are not really "cycles."[8]

Different critical strategies underly these two types of definition.   The inclusive one aims at outlining a field of study within the broadest parameters.   In essence, it is concerned with cyclization as a formal *device* whose content is irrelevant.   The restrictive view presumes only a well-unified grouping and is concerned with the cycle as a *quasi-generic formulation* with specific determinants of content (whether this be an idea or concept or a kind of dramatic situation, a plot).

Neither definition is completely free of problems.   Calling any assemblage of poems (no matter how haphazard the author's selection) a "cycle" obviously opens the floodgates of theoretical endeavor to groupings of negligible unity—those made, for instance, purely on the basis of editorial expediency.   Such "cycles" could hardly be expected to offer much esthetic interest.   To require from cycles only specific degrees and types of unity, however, as do Müller and Dolgopolov, comes dangerously close to prescriptive poetics.   Those who adopt the restrictive definition are undoubtedly correct to look for internal rather than superficial principles of integration, but this criterion, after all, must be applied to any work of art—it does not create distinctions that help define the cycle per se.   Moreover to exclude from consideration groupings in which internal unity is apparently absent seems methodologically faulty—it precludes the possibility that the internal unity has simply not yet been discovered.   Indeed the reader may ultimately uncover what Proust only after the fact apprehended in his own *A la recherche du temps perdu*—"a unity that has been unaware of itself, therefore vital and not logical."[9]

The present study, therefore, adopts the inclusive definition but reserves the concept of internal unity advanced in the restrictive definitions as an evaluative criterion. Normally, when we read a novel or poem that does not hold together esthetically we are inclined to call it "unsuccessful" rather than ban it from the class of works to which it obviously belongs. Similarly, when we encounter a poorly unified cycle, we ought to characterize it as such but not strip from it the designation "cycle." At least as an initial hypothesis, such an approach is essential, as we shall see, for understanding the historical development of this form. If we were to limit ourselves from the outset only to ideal manifestations of the cycle, we would neglect the formative stages of its evolution.

It should be noted also that the present study is not concerned with non-authorial cycles, that is, groupings made by anyone other than the poet himself. It is not uncommon in literary scholarship for critics to speak about a particular set of poems containing a similar theme or image as a "cycle"—even where there is no evidence of the author's intent to cyclize them. We read about Puškin's "poet cycle," Žukovskij's "Protasova cycle" or Tjutčev's "Denis'eva cycle," although these poets never made any effort to group these lyrics together. To be sure, such critic's "cycles" are often of profound interest and sometimes contribute to a better understanding of a poet's oeuvre. One problem with them, of course, is that their precise contextual boundaries are moot; scholars often disagree about their exact composition (not to mention the question of their proper sequence). For present purposes we shall focus on a different phenomenon—namely how the poet generates meaning by creating a clearly delineated context within which separate poems interact.[10]

The very idea of delineating a context is inherent in the etymology of the word "cycle," which in Greek (*kyklos*) means "circle." This derivation is sometimes mistakenly construed by critics as an indication of structural circularity. Müller, for instance, employs an elaborate array of circular metaphors— "rounding out the circle," "architectonic center," "cyclic arches," "spirals" which "circle back" upon each other, and so on. He argues that every cycle has a "center of gravity" [Schwerpunkt] or "middlepoint" [Mittelpunkt] occupied by the "*a priori*." All of this, however, is just a complicated way of describing the unity of any work and tells us more about the richness of Müller's imagination than about structures specific to the lyric cycle. Granted, circular structures are present in many cycles but with no more frequency nor in any greater concentration than in other works of literature. Moreover introduction of the term "cycle" as a literary term had nothing at all to do with such sophisticated architectonics. The first use of the word to characterize a literary work occurred in reference to the so-called "epic cycle" of classical philology. The "epic cycle," to which Aristotle alluded in *Rhetorica* (1417^a 15) and which was later defined by Proclus (it has not been ascertained whether in the second or the fifth century A.D.) was a corpus of lays written after Homer so as to supplement the *Iliad* and the *Odyssey*. It was designed to provide an unbroken legendary history of the world from the age of the Titans to the final exploits of Odysseus.[11] The care with which these discrete epics were "stitched together" textually by the cycle's compilers demonstrates that they intended to make a single work out of separate ones—in a sense to embrace the whole with a contextual circle.[12] A circle, the traditional symbol of unity, represented the oneness or wholeness attributed to the final product. This, in essence, is the principle that underlies all cycles.

Context and Intertext: The Semiotics of the Lyric Cycle

Statements to the effect that a cycle means more than the sum of its parts or that meaning is generated not only within the separate lyrics of a cycle but also at the junctures between them—are truisms. Cyclic theory cannot content itself with repeating them, it must demonstrate what makes them valid.[13]

As separate texts all poems in a cycle are correlated intertextually. There may exist between them significant ties (e.g., a common motif, a reminiscence, a polemic), but to the degree that they are discrete compositions their interrelationship is no more privileged than that between any other texts. By selecting particular poems and enclosing them within a cycle, however, the poet changes the nature of their interrelationship. They can no longer be seen only as separate entities. They must also be perceived as members of a single text. Their interaction becomes contextual as well as intertextual.

The coexistence of these two competing modes of perception

and the resulting tension between them constitutes the precondition essential for generation of meaning in a cycle. On one hand, the conceptual boundary surrounding the poems and identifying them as one text produces the expectation of unity inherent in our apprehension of any esthetic work. On the other, the cycle's internal boundaries represent formidable impediments to contextual integration. Each poem insinuates itself on the reader as an independent system of meaning. For a cycle as a whole to mean something the tension between these conflicting premises must on some level be resolved. As Michael Riffaterre writes: "It is the mark of poetic discourse that whenever usage posits incompatabilities, they are reconciled."[14]

Reading a cycle as a contextual unit requires that one adopt as an initial strategy the hypothesis that the intracyclic boundaries are signs of segmentation rather than textual closure. Indeed, this strategy may ultimately prove unprofitable, but one cannot assume at the outset that a particular grouping is incoherent simply because its coherence is not immediately manifest.

To understand the signifying conventions of the lyric cycle it will be useful of consider procedures that occur in decoding any utterance. Semantic theory informs us that one function (perhaps the principal function) of context is to disambiguate the sign-vehicles in a given message.[15] To cite one example borrowed from Umberto Eco, the word "bachelor" has a number of different senses corresponding roughly to its dictionary definitions: 1) an unmarried man; 2) a person awarded an undergraduate degree; 3) a young knight who follows the banner of another; 4) a young male fur seal kept from the breeding grounds by the older males.[16] In ordinary speech, context will provide information sufficient to disambiguate the word "bachelor" in one of the above senses. On hearing the sentence "My husband is a *bachelor* of arts," for instance, we interpret the word in its second sense; if told "Victor is tired of being a *bachelor* and wants to get married," we understand it in its first sense. In a treatise about the sex life of seals we naturally select the fourth, and in an account of chivalric conventions we are likely to choose the third.

In the process of disambiguation the text "actualizes" (causes us to recognize as contextually relevant) certain of a word's semantic features called "semantic markers" or "semes." These are basic units of meaning which represent the virtual or implied properties of the word's referent. A dictionary definition generally designates only the "primitive" or "differentiating" semes, that is, those which distinguish one sense of a word from another.[17] Every word, however, possesses an almost limitless number of secondary or non-differentiating semes (whether denotative or connotative) which, though superfluous to the dictionary definition, are nevertheless objective or implied properties of the referent. Thus the word "bachelor" in its fourth sense contains, in addition to its primitive semes (young, male, seal, unmated), a lengthy catalogue of secondary ones (e.g., living, mammal, physical, having a circulatory system, able to swim, able to ingest, instinctual, frustrated, and so on). A given context may or may not actualize certain of these secondary semes. Hence a description of a bachelor's struggle with the older seals will actualize the semes "living," "physical," "instinctual"; an account of a cardiac operation on a seal will actualize the semes "having a circulatory system"; a study of the seal's psychology will, most likely, actualize the connotative seme "frustrated."

In a lyric cycle the phenomenon of "disambiguation" is analogous to what we just observed. The individual poem, like the word in a coherent utterance, belongs to a syntactic sequence that allocates meaning to its component parts. Just as the context of an utterance actualizes certain of a word's semes, the context of a cycle actualizes those features of the poem that are relevant to the dynamics of the whole. A cycle entitled "Spring," for instance, is likely to actualize in any given poem the motifs of growth, greenery, warmth, sunlight, perhaps even romantic love. A cycle in which the motif of night is dominant will tend to bring special attention to the motif of darkness, even in a poem which lacks a specifically nocturnal setting.

In the lyric cycle, however, the process of disambiguation is more complex. As an esthetic text, the cycle exploits ambiguity more consistently and more purposefully than the natural or practical language and requires that the reader exert greater effort in decoding its message. As in the apprehension of any work of art, the receiver of the message must in some sense "participate in the creation of its meanings," to quote Barbara Herrnstein Smith's apt formulation.[18] If the sentence "Victor is tired of being a bachelor and wants to get married" immediately and automatically actualizes the semes "unmarried"/"adult"/"male," the syntax of the lyric cycle actualizes its meanings more circuitously—via an intermediate stage I would call "forefronting."

By forefronting I understand that mechanism inherent in the syntax of every cycle that induces the reader to establish categories of comparability (equivalency) between the member poems in an effort to ascertain the semiotic system that unifies them. Forefronting corresponds to that stage in the reader's interaction with the text when he is still positing tentative interpretations and operating on the premise that "no part of the work can be declared *a priori* to lack signification" (Tzvetan Todorov).[19]   A cycle whose unifying principle is simple and superficial will not generally sustain forefronting beyond the first reading since the interpretive effort is not rewarded by further investigation.   By contrast, a rich, well-unified cycle—especially one whose unifying principles are elusive—may recommend a great variety of valid interpretations and continually offer new interpretive problems.   In this case the process of forefronting is, theoretically, unending.[20]

The concept of forefronting is based on the premise, articulated by Jurij Lotman, that literary semiosis occurs via the procedure of "comparing and contrasting" equivalent elements of a text ("so-protivopostavlenie èkvivalentnyx èlementov") and apprehending between them similarity and difference: "similarity is uncovered in different things, while differences are uncovered in similar things."[21]   In the following couplet from Lermontov's "Saška," for instance, the syntagmas "ščit varjažskij" and "syr gollandskoj" are equivalent inasmuch as both participate in a simile with "luna":

> Луна катится в зимних облаках,
> Как щит варяжский или сыр голландской.

To appreciate the humor of this passage the reader must recognize the semantic similarity of the two images (roundness) and at the same time their stylistic incompatibility.   Similarly the phrases "kak nebesa" and "kak poceluj" are syntactically and metrically equated in the following quatrain by Lermontov despite the fact that the nouns they contain belong to quite different semantic fields:

> Как небеса твой взор блистает
> Эмалью голубой,
> Как поцелуй звучит и тает
> Твой голос молодой.

According to Lotman the effect of this imagery derives largely from the fact that the semantic antithesis between "nebesa" and "poceluj" (which materializes along the axes "distant *vs.* close," "cold *vs.* warm," "inaccessible *vs.* accessible," "exterior-alien *vs.* interior-intimate," "nonhuman *vs.* human") is reconciled on a different semantic-emotive plane: "an image of a certain dual unity in earthly and heavenly beauty emerges."[22]

Lotman demonstrates that in an esthetic text structural equivalencies predicate semantic equivalencies specific to a given context and often quite uncharacteristic of the ordinary language. Semantic equivalency in this sense is a far cry from synonymy. Esthetic usage may equate two items which neither mean the same nor even belong to the same semantic field by suggesting (forefronting) a shared seme (e.g., "roundness") or a shared semic category (e.g., "distant *vs.* close") wherein they function in tandem. Theoretically, it is possible to find some semantic common ground between between any two members of the lexical encyclopedia.[23] "Peregrine falcon" and "Scotch Magic Transparent Tape," for example, are not synonyms, yet they are equivalent-similar via the shared semes "concrete," "non-amorphous," "clinging"; they are equivalent-dissimilar via the semic categories "organic *vs.* non-organic," "self-locomoting *vs.* inert," "feathered *vs.* unfeathered," "non-advertised *vs.* advertised."

Semiosis in a lyric cycle does not differ, essentially, from semiosis in other esthetic texts. Meaning is generated by the interrelationship of structurally equivalent segments (the individual poems). Comparing and contrasting these segments forefronts other categories of equivalency, whether formal (phonologic, strophic, rhythmic, grammatical) or thematic (motivic, temporal, spacial). Participation of successive poems in these categories produces chains of equivalency which allow the reader to define, tentatively, the cycle's central topics and begin formulating an interpretation. To the degree that these equivalency chains function as a coherent unit (a system), the cycle makes an esthetic "statement," that is, it *actualizes* certain of the forefronted items and categories. Not every equivalent element is necessarily meaningful; many prove incidental to the dynamics of the whole and only contribute to the "noise" which inevitably accompanies any message without constituting part of its meaning.

Puškin's "Lyric Cycle of 1836": A Semiotic Experiment

In 1954 Nikolaj Izmajlov advanced the intriguing hypothesis that Puškin, in the summer of 1836, composed a "lyric cycle" for publication in his new journal, *Sovremennik*. According to Izmajlov, the cycle consisted of the following poems:

I   "Ja pamjatnik sebe vozdvig nerukotvornyj . . ." (August 21)
II   "Otcy pustynniki i ženy neporočny . . ." (July 22)
III   "Prodražanie ital'janskomu" ("Kak s dreva sorvalsja predatel'-učenik . . .") (June 22)
IV   "Mirskaja vlast'" ("Kogda velikoe sveršilos' toržestvo . . .") (July 5)
V   "Kogda za gorodom, zadumčiv, ja brožu . . ." (August 14)
VI   "Iz Pindemonti" ("Ne dorogo cenju ja gromkie prava. . .") (July 5)[24]

The grouping is based partly on textual evidence (Puškin superscribed drafts of the second, third, fourth, and sixth poems with the Roman numerals II, III, IV, and VI) and partly on supposition (Izmajlov suggested I and V as the cycle's probable missing links, citing their affinity with the four other poems).

The initial response to Izmajlov's hypothesis was largely negative. Some of the most eminent Puškin specialists were sceptical about the nature of the grouping and the proposed reconstruction of its missing segments. It was "Pamjatnik" that stimulated the most controversy. Nikolaj Stepanov in 1959 chacterized "Kogda za gorodom . . ." (V) "an extremely convincing" choice for the fifth spot but objected to Izmajlov's choice for the first: "Including 'Pamjatnik' in a cycle of these verses seems to me unwarranted—this poem is too far from the others both in its theme and its artistic manner."[25] Rolf-Dietrich Keil's reaction in a 1961 article is puzzling in its equivocality: "Undoubtedly the thematic kinship (religion—death—freedom of the artist) and perhaps even the order of themes in the cycle is linked closely with 'Pamjatnik.' Nevertheless it seems to me that inclusion of 'Pamjatnik' as the first poem in such a cycle is unlikely."[26] Keil does not explain why "Pamjatnik" is unsuitable despite its "thematic kinship" with the other poems. The most vehement objection, however, came from Mixail P. Alekseev in a book on "Pamjatnik" (1967); he agrees [!] with Keil that there is "no thematic kinship" between this poem and the other five and calls the entire cycle "imaginary and concocted."[27] Alekseev argues that "many other poems by Puškin from 1835-1836 manifest common attributes of similarity," suggesting—apparently—that the proposed grouping lacks legitimacy because Puškin *could have* included any number of other poems from the same period as well.

It will be fruitful to scrutinize the objections to Izmajlov's hypothesis because they are grounded on commonly held but inaccurate assumptions about what a cycle is and how it functions esthetically. Alekseev is simply wrong, for instance, when he says the entire cycle is "imaginary." That Puškin numbered the poems indicates that he conceived for them a single context; only the inclusion of poems I and V is "concocted"—but Izmajlov himself admitted that their membership in the cycle is pure conjecture. The suggestion that other poems could have been chosen by Puškin is correct but irrelevant. As a point of historical fact it is worth noting that poets frequently performed surgery on their cycles—rearranging poems, excluding some, including others, renaming poems, amending the texts and so forth. Such operations have never precluded the possibility of calling specific groupings "cycles." Stepanov's objection that "Pamjatnik" does not belong in the cycle because it differs from the other poems in "artistic manner" is theoretically unsound (not to mention being factually incorrect). "Artistic manner" (style? tone?) may indeed be a unifying factor in a cycle, but it has never been a *sine qua non.* Would we disqualify the poem "Skazka" from the cycle "Stixotvorenija Jurija Živago," for instance, simply because its folk stylization contrasts with the Biblical intonation of many other verses?

Stepanov raises a more substantive issue when he speaks of "theme" (something paramount for Keil as well). If Stepanov means that we expect conceptual-ideational unity from a cycle, he is correct—we demand this of every text. If he means, however, that the main, ostensible theme of each poem (considered in isolation) must be matched in kind by every other poem, he is most certainly incorrect, because thematic unity in a cycle is often generated quite differently. To be sure, there are many cycles in which a single, easily recognizable theme runs through all the poems (e.g., the joys of spring, romantic love, the sea). Yet if such a superficial principle is all that binds them together, we are dealing with an esthetically impoverished grouping. The best

cycles manifest a more complex thematic structure that emerges
from subterranean levels of text.

   To illustrate this I propose to analyze Puškin's partially
hypothetical cycle.   The primary aim of this analysis is to
demonstrate what principles govern the semiotic potential of a lyric
cycle, and its secondary goal is to test Izmajlov's reconstruction of
the cycle's missing links. If Izmajlov was right, the questionable
poems (I and V) will contribute to the cohesiveness and efficacy of
the grouping. By analogy one can say that the best way to tell
whether a ship is seaworthy is to launch it and bring it to sea
trials.   Izmajlov himself lacked an analytic strategy grounded in
the semiotics of lyric cycles. This may be why he was unable to
persuade critics that his hypothesis was valid.

   Between the cycle's six poems there are a number of formal
equivalencies, the most conspicuous being prosodic. Five of the
poems (II-VI) are in standard Alexandrine verse (iambic hexameter
with paired rhyme and with caesura after the sixth syllable);
masculine and feminine clausulae alternate by couplets. Only poem
I departs somewhat from this norm, having the fourth line of each
stanza in iambic tetrameter and employing cross rhyme rather than
paired rhyme; the hexameter lines, however, have have caesura
after the sixth syllable like the other poems. Both V and VI have
a strong intonational break slightly beyond the midpoint of each,
and in each instance the break is marked by a step-verse
("lesenka"); the last lines of V and VI are abbreviated at the point
where caesura occurs in the other verses. The predominance of
iambic hexameter is potentially significant, since Puškin would
hardly have chosen such a weighty meter by accident.   The
Alexandrine is traditionally associated with solemn thematics (in
the eighteenth and early nineteenth centuries, for instance, it was
commonly used in elegies).

   There is also a relatively large number of lexical and
sublexical equivalencies, considering the cycle's diminutive size.
Lexemes (lexical as opposed to grammatical morphemes) that
appear three or more times in at least two different poems are
listed here in order of descending frequency: -*d/x*- (duša,
ravnodušno, dux, duše, dux, dxnul, vzdoxom, vdoxnoven'ja) (I, II,
III, V, VI); -*bog*- (božiju, božestvennyx, bože, božestvo, bogi, bog,
božestvennym) (I, II, IV, VI); *v(o)z*- (vozdvig, voznessja, vosslavil,
vozletat', vzvilsja, vzdoxom, vostorgom) (I, II, III, V, VI); -*živ*-
(pereživet, živ, oživi, žizn', živoj, životvorjašča, žil'cov) (I, II, III,

IV, V); -rod- (narodnaja, narodu, rod, narod, rodovoe, naroda, prirody) (I, IV, V, VI); -vlad- (oblasti, vladyko, vladyke, vlast', vladyku, vlasti) (II, III, IV, VI); -kr/v- (sokrytoj, kryl'ca, pokrovitel'stvom, pokrytyx) (II, IV, V); -ljub- (ljubezen, ljubonačalija, ljubvi, ljubo) (I, II, V); -prav- (pravitelja, prava, prava, prava) (IV, VI); -slov- (prazdnoslovija, slova, slova, slova) (II, VI); car' (carju, carej, carjam, carja) (IV, VI); vor (vorov, vorami, vor) (IV, V); -klad- (poklaža, kladbišče, kladbišče) (IV, V); žena (ženy, ženy, žen) (II, IV); -mil- (milost', umiljaet, umilen'ja) (I, II, VI); -mir- (mire, vsemirnogo, mirskaja) (I, III, IV); -m/r- (umru, mertvecy, mertvye)(I, V); -mysl- (mysli, zamyslax, pomyslov) (V, VI); -prazdn- (prazdnosti, prazdnoslovija, prazdnyx) (II, V); predaj- (predatel', predatel'skuju, predavšego) (III, IV); pri(n)jat' (priemli, primet, prijali) (I, II, III); svobod- (svobodu, svobodno, svoboda) (I, VI); -svjat- (svjaščennik, presvjataja, svjatyx) (II, IV); -slux- (slux, poslušna, poslušno) (I, IV); stolb- (stolpa, stolbiki, stolbov) (I, V); -tes/n- (potesnit', stesnennye, stesnjaet) (IV, V, VI).   Lexemic repetitions perform several potential functions.   On a purely formal level, they create phonologic cohesion within the cycle as do rhyme or assonance within a stanza.   As tangible equivalencies they indicate avenues along which comparison and contrast may prove fruitful. Moreover, given their semantic content, recurrence of the same lexemes already forefronts certain prominent thematic categories: religious faith, life–death, spiritual–moral concerns, social issues (rights, freedom, authority).   While conclusions are premature, it is worth mentioning that poems I and V each contain exactly half (13 out of 26) of the cycle's most frequent lexemes—a fraction which is not exceeded in any of the four other poems.

    As regards thematic equivalencies it is useful to make a distinction between those which are explicit and those which are embedded, not immediately apparent.   Several poems, for example, deal quite explicitly with the themes of state authority (I, IV, V, VI), death (I, III, IV, V), religion (broadly understood) (II, III, IV, V) and more specifically Christ's martyrdom (II, III, IV).[28]   The reader, however, must also consider embedded thematic indicators such as secondary and connotative semes, motifs of marginal prominence within any given poem and subtextual allusions.   As we shall see, it is largely at this level that Puškin's cycle functions as a semiotic system.

    A case in point is the central theme of the controversial first poem. "Pamjatnik" deals essentially with poetic creativity, a motif which appears again explicitly only in poem V, and there in just one obviously ironic image ("nadpisi . . . v *stixax*"); it is implicit in poem VI also as part of the larger theme of art ("sozdan'jami iskusstv i vdoxnoven'ja"). The apparent inconsequentiality of this motif, however, is deceptive. In poem II, for instance, where poetry is not mentioned, line 4 nevertheless alludes to the creation of "prayers" ("*Složili* množestvo . . . *molitv*"), forefronting an equivalency between poetry and prayer via the shared seme "verbal creativity." It is worth noting too, as does V. P. Stark, that the last seven lines of II paraphrase Éfrem Sirin's Lenten prayer and approximate the seven-line strophe which this church father of the fourth century popularized.[29] We are reminded that prayers were, at certain times in history and in certain cultures, virtually the only poetic form that was officially sanctioned. Pursuing the equivalency "poetry-prayer" further yields other similarities. Via the context of I and II, poetry and prayer share the connotative semes "transcendence" (I: "ves' ja ne umru"; II: "vozletat' vo oblasti zaočny") and "humility" (I: "Velen'ju božiju, o muza, bud' poslušna"; II: "dux smirenija, terpenija"). Poetry and prayer are also likened by the common supposition that they involve abstention from argument with others (I: "Xvalu i klevetu priemli ravnodušno/I ne osporivaj glupca"; II: "Da brat moj ot menja ne primet osužden'ja"). Finally, they are equated as channels of communication with the divine, although in poem I God is the "sender" of the message ("velen'ju božiju"), whereas in poem II God is the "addressee" (note the use of an archaic vocative: "*Vladyko* dnej moix!"). Thus the interaction of poems I-II seems to imply something of a dialogue between poet and heavenly spirit.

  Poem III, without mentioning poetry explicitly, clearly embeds this theme subtextually. It is difficult to read III without noticing that it echoes Puškin's famous lyric "Prorok" (1826). If in the earlier poem, however, an angel is sent to revive the poet-prophet and place him in service to God, in III a devil is sent to revive Judas and place him in Satan's employ. In both poems the motif of the mouth is extemely prominent—the protagonists in each case gain the power of speech through a kind of violent oral surgery ("Prorok": "I žalo mudryja zmei/V *usta* zamersie moi/Vložil desniceju krovavoj"; III: "I satana . . . naskvoz' prožeg *usta*"). In addition to "usta" other lexical auto-reminiscences are in evidence

("Prorok": "I on k ustam moim *prinik* . . . /Kak *trup* . . . ja
ležal"; III: "Dijavol . . . k licu ego *prinik*/ . . . /I brosil *trup* živoj
v gortan' geeny gladnoj"). Because of this subtext the poet (I)
and Judas (III) enter a relation of equivalency:

Poet (I) <---------------------> Judas (III) (anti–poet, anti–prophet)

                           ↑

                        "Prorok"

The equivalency, however, is mainly a contrastive one: genuine poet (I) *vs.*
false poet (III), divine inspiration (I) *vs.* demonic inspiration (III)
(note that the concept of "inspiration" is represented even
etymologically in III: "Dijavol . . . *Dxnul* žizn' v nego"). This
antithesis is sharpened by the joint implications of poems I-II,
which seem to suggest also the following oppositions: sacred speech
(poetry-prayer) (I-II) *vs.* blasphemy (profane poetry?) (III),
communion with God (I-II) *vs.* communion with Satan (III).

Poem IV contains no direct allusion to poetry or the poet,
although the theme is embedded there too at a much deeper level
which can be extrapolated from the other five poems. I shall
return to IV shortly.

Poem V, as indicated earlier, mentions "inscriptions in prose
and *in verse*" on the decaying tombstones of the city graveyard.
This detail receives no special emphasis nor is it a major theme in
V, but inasmuch as poem I likens great poetry to a timeless
"monument" the context of the cycle forefronts their thematic
equivalency. Once again the equation is more one of contrast than
similitude: "monument" (metaphoric, immaterial, great poetry,
permanent) (I) *vs.* monuments (literal, material, bad poetry,
transitory) (V). Comparing the content of poetry in I and V
suggests further antitheses (charity *vs.* selfishness, nobility *vs.*
vanity, sincerity *vs.* insincerity):

Что чувства добрые я лирой пробуждал,
Что в мой жестокий век восславил я Свободу
    И милость к падшим призывал.   (I)

Над ними надписи и в прозе и в стихах
О добродетелях, о службе и чинах;
По старом рогаче вдовицы плач амурный . . .   (V)

The lexemic repetition (I:"čuvstva *dobrye*"; V: "o *dobro*deteljax")
may be accidental, but in the context of the cycle it has a satiric

ring. At the end of V, in the description of the simple country
graveyard, there is a fleeting allusion to "prayer" which stands in
obvious contrast with the counterfeit sentiments on the city
tombstones ("Proxodit seljanin *s molitvoj i so vzdoxom*"). This
detail seems to enter into the relationships outlined above:

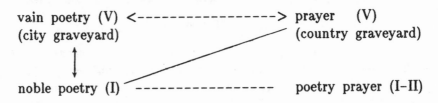

The central contrast in poem VI is between topical,
journalistic writing and genuine art. In the cyclic context it is
natural to ally the latter with real poetry (I), especially since the
correlation is encouraged by certain formal and thematic parallels.
Poems I and VI are locationally equivalent in that they mark the
cycle's physical perimeter; moreover there exist between them
certain striking lexical coincidences: "ne *osporivaj* glupca"
(I) — "*osporivat'* nalogi" (VI), "vosslavil ja *Svobodu*" (I) — "potrebna
mne *svoboda*" (VI), "ljubezen ja *narodu*" (I) — "zaviset' ot *naroda*"
(VI). One will note also the similarity in diction (I: "glupca"; VI:
"oluxov," "balagura"). In both, genuine art–poetry is seen as
something divine, quite distant from the petty squabbles of the
day.

The interaction of I and VI also forefronts a new category of
equivalency previously inconspicuous in the larger scheme:
accessibility. VI mocks censorship ("čutkaja cenzura") and
advocates unimpeded access to nature and to works of art; I deals
with the accessibility of the poet's legacy (his poetic "monument")
to the folk ("narod"). It is worth noting that in poem I every
reference to such access is in the future tense ("K nemu ne
zarastet narodnaja tropa," "*nazovet* menja," "dolgo *budu* tem
ljubezen ja narodu")—a detail which raises the possibility that the
poet's work is not presently accessible and will become so only
after his death. The words "moj žestokij vek," an obvious allusion
to the poet's own lifetime, tend to support this implication.

Tracing the category "accessibility–inaccessibility" through the
cycle yields other enlighting comparisons. Poem II, for instance,
carries "inaccessibility" as one of its latent semes ("Otcy *pustynniki*
i ženy *neporočny*"). While the attribute of monastic isolation

might at first appear irrelevant to the poet's situation, only one interpretive step separates the identification "poetry-prayer" from the equation "creator of poetry (poet)—creator of prayer (monk, nun)." And one can pursue this motif further. In poem III "accessibility" is relevant to Judas' interaction with his throng of admirers, the "demons" ("Tam besy, radujas' i plešča, na roga/Prijali . . . vsemirnogo vraga"). Since Judas is something of an anti-prophet, it is not difficult to visualize these "demons" as a sinister counterpart to the "narod " in poem I—the Judas-poet is depicted reaping an acclaim not unlike that desired by the genuine poet from future generations of his countrymen.[30]

The theme of accessibility is of central importance in poem IV. The folk's access to the crucifix is blocked ("puskat' ne veleno prostoj narod") by an arm of state authority ("dvux groznyx časovyx").[31] The text suggests that such access is the folk's lawful (Biblical) right inasmuch as the Virgin Mother and Mary Magdalene (both commoners) once occupied a position close to the cross ("po storonam životvorjašča dreva") and since the crucifix redeemed *all* mankind ("č'ja kazn' *ves' rod Adamov* iskupila"). Instead, only the idle rich ("guljajuščix gospod") are allowed to approach the altar. The situation lends credence to the implication in poem I that the folk's access to the poet is as yet unrealized and suggests an equivalency between the poet and Christ, between the poet's legacy (his "monument") and Christ's legacy (the crucifix). That this equation is based more on similarity than contrast becomes apparent when we consider that neither the poet's "monument" nor the crucifix are edifices in the conventional sense but rather Biblical symbols of eternal life. The crucifix is "životvorjašče drevo" (IV), that is, the "tree of life" ("Take also of the tree of life . . . *and live forever*")(Genesis 3:22); similarly "pamjatnik . . . nerukotvornyj" recalls Corinthians II 5:1 ("For we know that if our earthly house of this tabernacle were dissolved, we have a building of God, *an house not made with hands, eternal in the heavens*"). Moreover, the epithet "nerukotvorennyj" in the Bible is repeatedly ascribed to Christ's heavenly sanctum ("Xristos . . . prišed s bol'šeju i soveršennejšeju skineju, *nerukotvorennoju*"; "Xristos vošel *ne v rukotvorennoe* svjatilišče . . . no v samoe nebo, čtoby predstat' nyne za nas pred lice Božie") (Hebrews 9: 11, 24).

Poem V also treats the motif of accessibility, although outside the cyclic context one would hardly perceive it as one of the poem's major themes. "Grated fences" ("rešetki") bar visitors from

the ostentatious memorials of the well-to-do city dwellers—an
ironic analogue to the cordon surrounding the crucifix in poem IV.
Paradoxically, such barriers do not prevent thieves and vandals
from defiling the tombs, just as the gendarmes in IV do not
prohibit access to those least likely to appreciate the democratic
spirit of Christ's sacrifice.   Access to the graves in the village
cemetery, by contrast, is unblocked ("Tam neukrašennym mogilam
est' prostor").   They are approached not by thieves but by a
common villager who walks by, filled with sincere veneration ("Bliz
kamnej vekovyx . . . /Proxodit seljanin s molitvoj i so vzdoxom").
Taken by itself this scene is nothing more than an idyll, but in
the context of the cycle it seems to represents an enactment,
projected into the future, of the wish expressed in poem I ("k
nemu *ne zarastet narodnaja tropa*").

With regard to the theme of access poem VI is problematic.
It rejects outright the folk's authority over the poet, equating it
with that of the state ("Zaviset' ot carja, zaviset' ot naroda—Ne
vse li nam ravno?").   In this respect poem VI enters a contrastive
opposition with I and IV, where the folk's right of access (either to
the poet or to Christ) is to all appearances strongly affirmed.   If
one were writing Puškin's biography, one could account for this
inconsistency by referring to his long-standing ambivalence to the
"narod."   In an analysis attuned to the semiotics of the cycle,
however, one must either reconcile the discrepancy or acknowledge
it as one of the forefronted but unactualized cyclic equivalencies.

One solution to the problem is to recognize that the cycle in
fact posits two different images of the "narod" (one positive, the
other negative) and allocates them to two different time planes.
The positive "narod" is always depicted as something not yet fully
manifest, not contemporaneous with the object of its esteem but
existing after it and paying homage to its memory.   Hence in
poem I every positive reference to the folk is in the future tense.
In IV Christ is worshipped not so much by people of his own time
but by a "narod" which, centuries later, seeks to approach a
memorium to his sacrifice.   In poem V, the "narod," represented
metonymically by the passing villager, expresses veneration not for
the living but for the dead.   The negative "narod," by contrast, is
a contemporaneous phenomenon: it responds to topical issues in the
press (VI); it embraces in its midst the traitor-poet (III); but it is
fickle toward the genuine poet, giving alternately "praise and
slander" ("xvalu i klevetu")(I).   It is a "narod," however, which

the poet, in Christ-like humility and perhaps even in emulation of Christ, does not wish to blame for what it does ("Da brat moj ot menja ne primet osužden'ja") (II),

Another solution is that the common folk's right of access is to the poet's creation, his poetry—not to his creative process, which occurs via solitary communion with God. In poem IV the people's right is to the crucifix, a symbol of martyrdom, not to the mystery of Christ's death agony itself. Even the two Maries are located to the side ("po storonam"); they witness but do not participate in his private drama. Similarly, in VI the "narod" is denied access to the creative impulse, not its product. "Dependence" on the "narod" is pandering ("služit' i ugoždat'"), but poet and people are potentially equals as appreciators of art. The posture recommended at the end of VI, after all, is one any person can assume:

По прихоти своей скитаться здесь и там,
Дивясь божественным природы красотам,
И пред созданьями искусств и вдохновенья
Трепеща радостно в восторгах умиленья.

The responsibility for preserving a poet's legacy is one shared jointly by the folk and other poets. This is why literary citations (from Horace, Efrem Sirin, Francesco Gianni, Ippolito Pindemonte) play such an important role in this cycle.[32] This also helps demystify the cycle's most perplexing lines:

И славен буду я, доколь в подлунном мире
Жив будет хоть один пиит. (I)

Among the cycle's forefronted themes it is difficult to overlook "authority," especially since -vlad- is such a prominent lexeme. Poem I presents a dichotomy between state authority (symbolized by "Aleksandrijskij stolp") and heavenly authority ("velen'ju božiju"). The poet is unsubmissive to the former ("glavoju nepokornoj") but submissive to the latter ("o muza, bud' poslušna"). As the cycle progresses, this antithesis is expanded and diversified. Poem II deals with divine authority (" Vladyko . . . o bože") and implies retreat from earthly jurisdictions ("Čtob serdcem vozletat' vo oblasti zaočony")(note the etymology ob-(v)lad-t' > oblast'). Poem III introduces the motif of infernal authority ("satana," "prokljatomu vladyke"), contrasting it with the divine ("Xrista"); the cycle forefronts the equivalency satanic-earthly-state authority by virtue of their common opposition to divine sovereignty. Poem IV exploits the incompatibility of state and heavenly authorities for ironic effect, likening the crucifix to a "city manager's porch" and "state merchandise." Certain details in IV clarify Christ's relation to different types of authority and indirectly strengthen the identification between poet and Christ. Like the poet in I, Christ is superior to all earthly jurisdictions ("carju carej") but obedient to divine command; the image "predavšego *poslušno* plot' svoju" recalls his Biblical fealty to God the Father and echoes the phrase "o muza, bud' *poslušna*" (I). The first half of V is set outside the capital ("vse mertvecy *stolicy*"), the locus of state authority; the importance of this detail is underscored by the prominence of bureaucrats' shrines ("*činovnikov* usopšix mavzolei") and tasteless inscriptions about "service and ranks" ("o šluzbe i činax"). The imagery pleads for comparison with "Aleksandrijskij stolp" (I), especially since one type of memorial at the cemetery is "*stolbiki.*" Comparison yields difference (the bureaucrats' "columns" are smaller than the Tsar's) but also similarity (the petty fetish for material glorification). Indirectly, therefore, poem V further demeans Aleksandr's memorial, which had already suffered by contest with the poet's in I. In poem VI state and divine authorities are again contrasted in terms that recall the cycle's first poem. The poet's refusal to "bow his neck" ("ne gnut'. . .ni šei")(VI) reproduces his defiant posture in poem I ("Voznessja *vyše* on glavoju nepokornoj").

Another motif forefronted by cyclic context is the "tree":

III   Как с <u>древа</u> сорвался предатель-ученик . . .
IV   Тогда по сторонам животворяща <u>древа</u> . . .
V   Стоит широко <u>дуб</u> над важными гробами. . .

The "trees" in III and IV are antithetical: Judas' gallows, Christ's crucifix. The "oak" (V) does not participate directly in this contrast. If there is any common denominator in the treatment of this motif, it would seem to be the "tree's" association with the idea of life after death. The crucifix symbolizes resurrection-salvation; the gallows tree is the major prop in Judas' ressurrection-damnation; and the "oak" thrives ("kolebljas' i šumja") amid the graves of the dead, a perpetual reminder of life's continuity. The "oak" however, is contrasted not with another tree but with the monuments in the city cemetery ("Na mesto prazdnyx urn i melkix piramid") (V).   Recalling that Christ's "tree" (IV) and the poet's "monument" (I) are also equivalent, one might suggest that "trees" and "monuments" form a composite motif.

Exploring this possibility, one will note that "trees" and "monuments" share the seme "perpendicularity" and that their manifestations in the cycle are all unmistakably positive or negative: the poet's "monument," the "oak" and the crucifix-tree are emotively positive; Aleksandr's "column," the shrines of the rich and the gallows-tree are emotively negative.   Moreover the negative tree-monuments possess the common indicator *"down(ward)"* (Aleksandr's column is lower than the poet's; the bureaucrats' shrines are disintegrating, hence falling; Judas is removed from the tree and cast into Hell).   The positive tree-monuments, by contrast, are distinguished by the indicator *"up(ward)"* (the poet's "monument" is higher than Aleksandr's; crucifixion precedes Christ's resurrection and ascent to heaven; the "oak" towers over the graves in the village cemetery).   Finally, the negative tree-monuments are associated   with *decay* (III: "Dijavol vzvilsja . . . s svoej dobyčej *smradnoj*"; V: "Pod koimi *gnijut* vse mertvecy stolicy"), while decay is conspicuously absent in scenarios involving the positive tree-monuments (I: "Moj prax . . . *tlen'ja ubežit*"; IV: Christ's body does not decompose; V: "V derevne . . . *dremljut* mertvye").   Comparing and contrasting different manifestations of this motif in separate poems yields such a gold mine of information that the image of the tree-monuments emerges as the principal integrator of thr cycle's thematic content.   The results of such an effort are summarized below (implied items being bracketed):

Positive	*Negative*
Poet's "monument" (I)	Aleksandr's monument (I)
"not made with hands"	made with hands
immaterial	material
not decaying	[decaying?]
higher	lower
[inaccessible at present?]	accessible at present
divine authority	state authority
eternal	[transitory?]

humility	[vanity?]
"oak tree" (V)	shrines of rich (V)
natural	artificial
["not made with hands"]	["made with hands"]
eternal	transitory
not decaying	decaying
higher (towering)	lower (falling)
simplicity	ostentation
[humility?]	vanity
crucifix-tree (IV)	gallows-tree (III)
Christ	Judas
inaccessible to "narod"	accessible to demonic "narod"
not decaying	decaying
divine authority	infernal [state?] authority
salvation	damnation
upward movement	downward movement

Naturally, the context of the cycle encourages the reader to make tentative associations up and down the columns as well as experiment with different horizontal arrangements. It is tempting, for instance, to posit the semes "transitory," "decaying" and "vanity" under "Aleksandr's monument," even though they do not immediately come to mind on reading poem I in isolation. And redisposing "poet's 'monument'" alongside "shrines of the rich" or "gallows-tree" with an eye to the semantic oppositions their juxtaposition generates would not be a fruitless exercise. The more unified a cycle's connotative network, the more it opens the individual poems to interpretive insight, the more it emboldens the reader to project implications from one poem onto another. The poem within the well-integrated cycle is the quintessential "open" text.[33] This is why more than one critic views the lyric cycle as the poetic form most characteristic of the modern era—an era when intertextual play and enlistment of the reader as creative participant in esthetic communication have become more the rule than the exception.[34]

    At this point to linger on the plausibility of Izmajlov's hypothesis would be superfluous; his reconstruction of the cycle's missing links is not only believable, but inspired. The popular dictum "Puškin—èto naše vsë" acquires new truth in light of our experiment. Once again Puškin appears to have anticipated the practice of his successors without them even knowing it—in this case equaling the greatest cyclic achievements of the symbolist era. Indeed, one is unlikely to find in all of Russian poetry a lyric cycle that surpasses the genius of this hypothetical grouping.

Assuming Izmajlov was correct, one can only speculate why Puškin failed to number the first and fifth poems. The most likely explanation is that he foresaw the impossibility of publishing them as part of the cycle. Numbering lyric poems was an operation Puškin performed, as a rule, only in preparation for publication.[35] The numbered poems are all of earlier date (June 22, July 5, July 22); the hypothetical entries were written later, in mid-August. Puškin must have understood that including poems I and V would have made the cycle categorically unpublishable, given the severity of censorship at the time and his personal disfavor with Nicholas I. These poems are of course, even in isolation, dangerous indictments of the state apparatus; this is why they did not appear unexpurgated in Russia until 1881 and 1857, respectively. In the cyclic context, however, their impact (especially of poem I) is utterly devastating—precisely because of the interprojection of meaning that characterizes the dynamics of the lyric cycle.

"Accidental Cycles" and Reader Competence

One might well ask whether there ought to be some restrictions on creative reading. Given that a cycle is composed of words and that between almost any two words there exist categories of semantic equivalency whence one can derive comparisons, the semiotic potential of even the most random groupings of lyrics appears boundless. Every cycle becomes an unqualified masterpiece, a source of whatever untold meanings the reader's imagination might extrapolate.

The absurdity of this proposition points up an issue that cyclic theory must address, namely, how the reader determines that one set of poems is a "real cycle" full of latent meaning, while another is a meaningless agglomeration. The history of poetic collections, after all, abounds with stories of expediency. Poets sometimes grouped poems with little care or even delegated this responsibility to others. Fedor Sologub, for instance, a cyclist of no small merit, nevertheless gave Valerij Brjusov full proxy to compose his *Sobranie stixov* (Skorpion) as he saw fit. "I have nothing against the distribution of poems in whatever order you find best," he wrote Brjusov on August 31, 1903.[36] To compile his collections *Fimiamy* (1921), *Sobornyj blagovest* (1922) and *Nebo goluboe* (1922) Sologub enlisted his wife. Similar cases are attested in Tjutčev, Fet and even Mandel'štam. In such instances uncovering hidden meanings in a cycle passes from the province of interpretation into the area of contrivance. Yet the reader often cannot ascertain the conditions under which a cycle was formed, the degree of authorial intention or how important a role accident played in a cycle's compilation. Confronting a lyric cycle, therefore, is unique in literary experience in that the reader must entertain the possibility that the very text with which he is dealing may be the product of complete randomness. If he assumes that juxtaposing poems *can be* a meaningful device, he must also conclude that it *can be* completely meaningless. And even when there is clear evidence of intentionality, he cannot discount that certain inclusions may be motivated by non-esthetic concerns. For this reason acquisition of literary competence in lyric cycles requires that the reader develop an ability to gauge the value of his interpretive hypothesis against the chance that it may be pure fabrication, what Lev Šestov called "creation out of nothing "[37]

In this regard experimentation with "accidental cycles," created by pure random choice, can be instructive. Here the possibility that meaning is invested in the text is nil, and interpretation is only an exercise. As such, however, it allows us to compare the insights gleaned from meaningless cycles with those acquired from "real cycles," the aim being to determine whether and how the reader is able to distinguish the two.

Ideally, such an experiment would be carried out on a large scale, but a smaller sampling provided by my poetry students, all of whom had acquired some expertise in analyzing cycles, provides credible results. Different students were given "accidental cycles" and asked one of two questions: 1) Why did the author place these poems together? (Students were to assume that the grouping was intentional); 2) Is this cycle "intentional" or "accidental"? The same "cycles" were used for both questions, but different groups of students responded to each.

It is interesting that when asked Question #1, every student was able to fabricate a rationale for the creation of each "cycle," no matter how incompatible the poems. A plot was manufactured by one student, for example, to explain the juxtaposition of the following poems which I chose at random from *The Oxford Book of*

Russian Verse: Fet, "Teplym vetrom potjanulo. . ." (I); Polonskij, "Vstreča" ("Včera my vstretilis'. . .") (II); Bal'mont, "Utro" ("Na veršine gornoj. . .") (III); Axmatova, "Ty znaeš', ja tomljus' v nevole. . ." (IV). In this interpretation I depicts the location of an   anticipated rendezvous; II depicts the rendezvous itself and the lovers' parting; III is set the following morning—the male protagonist, saddened by separation from his beloved, is nevertheless comforted by her presence in his thoughts; in IV the poet, no longer believing that his love is requited, derives consolation from contemplation of their meeting place.

The following explication was contrived for a "cycle" containing 1) Lermontov, "I skučno i grustno. . ."; 2) Puškin, "Pir Petra Velikogo"; 3) Jazykov, "K Rejnu"; and 4) Krylov, "Osel i solovej" (I have amplified the student's remarks somewhat below). The first three poems contain the motif of *time's passage* (I: "gody proxodjat—vse lučšie gody"; II: "Godovščina li Poltavy/Toržestvuet gosudar'"; III: "Mogily/Tvoix bylyx bogatyrej. . .davno minuvšix dnej"). In IV the motif is embedded, in that aging is a biological reality of the animal participants in the fable. In the first three poems there is some conceptual unity in the treatment of this motif, since time past invariably evokes a feeling of nostalgia. The motif of *singing* occurs explicitly in the last three poems (II: "*pesni* družnye grebcov"; III: "pod zvučnym *peniem* plovcov"; IV "*pet'* velikij masterišče," "tvoe uslyšav *pen'e*"). In I the motif can be derived from the idea that all poetry (including this poem) is a type of "song." Here the common conceptual denominator is the inherent beauty of "song". All four poems are linked by the semic category *separation/distance* (I: "nekomu ruku podat'"; IV: "vsporxnul i poletel za tridevjat' zemel'"); in II the motif is embedded in the image of "ships" (which traverse distances), and in III the poet longs to see the distant rivers of his homeland. If any unity of concept exists here, it is simply that distances between things can sometimes be bridged, and sometimes not.

Such experiments seem to confirm Michael Riffaterre's thesis that an esthetic text posits "ungrammaticalities"—distortions of verisimilitude and violated expectations at the mimetic level—which the reader is compelled to restructure into "grammaticalities" on a secondary, semiotic level. The reader assumes that "his reading is wrong, his task unfinished, so long as the 'ungrammaticalities' are not removed."[38] He will search out whatever imaginative detours are necessary to arrive at the significance of the text. This is why Question #1, which presumes the existence of a text, invariably elicited strained but possible interpretations.

Question #2, which allows for the possibility of a non–text, however, usually elicited the conclusion that these same "cycles" were "accidental." Most commonly the reaction was that the groupings were unlikely or completely implausible.[39] One can only speculate why this is so. Judging from the students' responses, there is apparently a threshold beyond which imaginative reading is deemed unrewarding. If the reader must take convoluted "detours" to significance, the journey must somehow compensate for the inconvenience it involves. Interpretation justifies itself only when it gives what Barthes calls "the pleasure of the text"; when pain outweighs pleasure, the reader is likely to opt for a handy escape route.

Are there any objective criteria for evaluating this balance? Perhaps there are. If interpretation is elicitation of meaning from a text, then the interpretive effort is rewarded by the volume and richness of meaning that it yields. Meaning, in turn, is measured by the relative coherence and complexity of the reader's abductive schema. An interpretation with complexity but no coherence is worthless, as is one with coherence but no complexity.

Considering the interpretive constructs engendered by the accidental cycles, one notices that they are either extremely simple, as in the case where a trite plot line was invented to explain the grouping, or quite complex but incoherent. One can discern, for instance, equivalency chains in the second accidental cycle, but they remain conceptually isolated from each other, forming as if parallel rather than intersecting lines. This cycle does not interrelate the concepts "nostalgia for times past," "the beauty of song" and "distances can sometimes be bridged" in any coherent fashion, although there is no reason why they could not be in a meaningful cyclic context. In a meaningful cycle, by contrast, the equivalency chains continually intersect, they are mutually entailing, so that by tracing one of them through the cycle the reader inevitably encounters all or most of the others. Thus in Puškin's cycle the idea of the poet's situational likeness to Christ is suggested by the convergence of several equivalency chains (e.g., accessibility–inaccessibility, state *vs.* divine authority, the motif of the "tree–monument"). The well–integrated cycle, like any successful literary work, is a "self–focusing" semiotic system.[40] It continually leads the reader back to a core of textually related concepts, whereas the accidental cycle (or any cycle to the degree that its formulation is nonessential) tends to produce multiplication and diffusion of uncorrelated semic categories.

Jonathan Culler writes: "To read a text as literature is not to make one's mind a *tabula rasu* and approach it without preconceptions; one must bring to it an implicit understanding of the operations of literary discourse which tells one what to look for."[41] Only a reader who has assimilated the "grammar" of the genre or form with which he deals possesses the literary competence to understand it. Competence in reading lyric cycles involves a prodigious ability to integrate disjoined texts and, at the same time, a capacity to discriminate between what is significant and what is merely incidental. In every cycle there is at least a modicum of "accidentalness," coincidence. Many details that are meaningful within the individual poem are quite irrelevant to the dynamics of the cycle as a whole and only serve as reminders of the poems' irreducible separateness. Hence the view expressed by some theoreticians that every element of a text is meaningful cannot be applied to lyric cycles. Semic equivalences forefronted by cyclic context become significant only if and to the degree that they are actualized by a self-focusing system of meaning.

Typology

Literary competence involves not only an understanding of general theoretical principles, but an awareness of those conventions that govern literary practice. Appreciating a work depends in part on knowing to what class of works it belongs and to what degree it conforms or fails to conform to the norms of that class. The latter concern falls within the province of typology. If a study of semiosis in lyric cycles deals with things all cycles have in common, typology deals with ways of differentiating them.

Hypothetically, almost any criterion can be used to do so. The index to Mustard's *The Lyric Cycle in German Literature* lists sixteen different types, which subsume a variety of criteria: size ("larger lyric cycle"), theme ("love cycle," "nature cycle"), genre ("sonnet cycle," "epistolary cycle"), circumstances of composition ("arranged cycles," which are created *ex post facto*, as opposed to "composed cycles," which are created simultaneously with the member poems).[42] L. Ljapina proposes two others: 1) whether a cycle has one subject or many; 2) whether the poems are arranged according to temporal succession (as in narrative) or spacial sequence (as a series of simultaneous scenes).[43]

The criterion adopted here has been chosen for its ability to accommodate the great diversity of actual practice. Very simply, it is that factor which constitutes the cycle's most conspicuous unifying principle. Applying it with an eye toward the cycle's real historical manifestations, one can discern the following basic types:

1) *Generic cycles*, that consist of poems belonging to the same lyric genre (e.g., sonnets, elegies, spiritual odes, epistles, etc.).

2) *Thematic-motivical cycles*, whose poems are unified by at least one common theme or motif.

3) *Dramatic-situational cycles*, composed of poems that share the same situational premise. This need not be a concrete setting. It is, more commonly, an emotional or spiritual conflict that informs all or most of the poems and tends to objectify the poet as a dramatic persona, a lyric hero.

4) *Plot cycles* are the dynamic variant of the preceding type in that they depict not a stable dramatic situation, but one that evolves toward resolution of the central conflict.[44] Examples of this type are so diverse they will be examined below in a separate section.

The typology outlined above is not rigid. Many cycles exhibit characteristics of more than one type, so that hybridization is very common. These rubrics are to be understood, therefore, not as compartments into which all cycles must be pigeonholed but as poles toward which most cycles gravitate.

It should be noted also that the proposed order of types represents a gradation from lesser to greater complexity and intrinsicality, at least with regard to the most primitive examples in each category . Thus generic cycles, in their most elementary form, are unified only by a superficial principle, whereas thematic cycles always possess at minimum one internal unifying determinant. Similarly, we expect a more sophisticated correlation of poems in dramatic-situational and plot cycles than in cycles whose only integrating factor is genre or single motif.

It cannot be assumed, however, that membership in one of the four types is an indication of a cycle's esthetic value since the gradation applies only to a cycle's ostensible principle of organization, not to the wealth of interrelationships it may generate as a semiotic system. Naturally, in the absence of such a system any organizing principle is esthetically gratuitous. This is why one cannot generalize that all generic and thematic-motivical cycles are simpler, less subtle or less meaningful than cycles of the more "advanced" types.

Generic cycles, for example, can be extremely interesting. Mustard and Müller have demonstrated how rich and sophisticated a device the sonnet cycle can be in the practice of Petrarch, Shakespeare, Brentano and Rilke.[45] Sonnet cycles often have thematic unity, a dramatic situation or even the suggestion of a plot. This tendency of generic cycles to merge with "higher" types shows that many poets viewed such groupings as more than extrinsic formalities.

Apollon Grigor'ev's cycle "Dva soneta" (1845), for instance, is not at all the product of expediency:

I

Привет тебе, последний луч денницы,
Дитя зари, — привет прощальный мой!
Чиста, как свет, легка, как божьи птицы,
Ты не сестра душе моей больной.

Душа моя в тебе искала жрицы
Святых страданий, воли роковой,
И в чудных грезах гордостью царицы
Твой детский лик сиял передо мной.

То был лишь сон . . . С насмешливой улыбкой
Отмечен в книге жизни новый лист
Еще одной печальною ошибкой. . .

Но я, дитя, перед тобою чист!
Я был жрецом, я был пророком бога,
И, жертва сам, страдал я слишком много.

II

О, помяни, когда тебя обманет
Доверье снам и призракам крылатым
И по устам, невольной грустью сжатым,
Змея насмешки злобно виться станет!..

О, пусть тогда душа твоя помянет
Того, чьи речи буйством и развратом

Тебе звучали, пусть он старшим братом
Перед тобой, оправданный, восстанет.

О, помяни . . . Он верит в оправданье,
Ему дано в твоем грядущем видеть,
И знает он, что ты поймешь страданье,

Что будешь ты, как он же, ненавидеть,
Хоть небеса к любви тебя создали, —
Что вспомнишь ты пророка в час печали.

These poems have much more in common than sonnet form. The
reader will apprehend, for instance, distinct similarities in the
pattern of thought they trace: from belief, to disillusionment and
ultimately to reaffirmation. Moreover, certain lexical parallels
suggest a thematic kinship between the poems: "To byl liš'
son" — "Dover'e snam"; "s nasmešlivoj ulybkoj" — "Zmeja nasmeški";
"stradal ja" — "ty pojmeš' stradan'e"; "ja byl prorokom"
— "vspomniš' ty proroka"; "pečal'noju ošibkoj" — "v čas pečali." It
is not difficult to see that both poems are about disappointment in
love and that the addressee of both is the same; she possesses the
attributes "heavenly" (I: "luč dennicy," "Ditja zari"; II: "nebesa
. . .tebja sozdali"), "pure" (I: "čista"; II: "razvratom tebe zvučali")
and "inexperience" (I: "ditja"; II: "dover'e snam"). The "I" of
poem I and the "he" of II are clearly identified, since the word
"prorok" refers to both, and both have a sibling-like relationship
with the addressee ("Ty ne sestra duše moej"; II: "on staršim
bratom/Pered toboj . . . vosstanet"). The relationship between "I"
and "you" (I), however, belongs mainly to the past, while that
between "he" and "you" (II) belongs to the future. The fact that
many of the experiences attributed to "I" in poem I become the
addressee's in poem II ("sny," "nasmeški," "stradan'e," "pečal'")
seems to suggest that the addressee will undergo later the same
disillusionment the poet has already endured. A dramatic situation
emerges, a presentiment that the romantic union unrealized in the
past will be realized at some future time in the realm of memory
and feeling.

Like generic cycles, thematic-motivical cycles can be either
superficial or highly integrated groupings. Valerij Brjusov's
"Kartinki Kryma i morja" (*Tertia Vigilia*, 1900) is typical of the
former category in that its twenty-one poems have little in
common except that they are seascapes. A few motifs are repeated
(waves, rocks, water, etc.), but the bonds they create are

incidental. There is no real interaction between the poems and their only unifying concept is the general idea of the sea's exquisite beauty. A different case is Afanasij Fet's "More" (*Večernie ogni* I, 1883). These four poems also depict seascapes, but the first two poems are clearly paired, even as their titles suggest ("Burja," "Posle buri"), in a kind of temporal progression. They establish, moreover, a common emotive pattern—the threatening aspect of the stormy sea (I) *vs.* the salutory effect of the peaceful sea after the storm (II). The contrast is sharpest in the poems' final stanzas:

> Как будто бог морской сейчас,
> Всесилен и неумолим,
> Трезубцем пригрозя своим,
> Готов воскликнуть: "Вот я вас!"   (I)

> Освеженный лес прибрежный
> Весь в росе, не шелохнется. —
> Час спасенья, яркий, нежный,
> Словно плачет и смеется.   (II)

Poems III–IV ("Včera rasstalis' my s toboj . . .", "More i zvezdy") repeat the same pattern:

> Морская бездна бушевала.
> Волна кипела за волной
> И, с грохотом о берег мой
> Разбившись в брызги, убегала.   (III)

> Вдали затихавшие волны белели,
> А с неба отсталые тучки летели,
> И ночь красотой одевалася звездной.
> . . . .
> И с моря ночного и с неба ночного,
> Как будто из дальнего края родного,
> Целебною силою веяло в душу.   (IV)

The impression that the cycle consists of a pair of diptychs which mirror each other is reinforced by the similarity of imagery between I and III, II and IV. I and III depict the surf crashing against shore (I: "pena pleščet na *granit*"; III: "večnyj razdrobit' *granit*"); and in both the sea's anger takes the form of verbal

abuse (I: "bog morskoj . . . prigrozja . . . gotov voskliknut'"; III:
"bešenym uprekom"); in II and IV sleep is brought about by the
sea's rocking action (II: "spit, kidajas', čeln"; IV: "menja ubajukalo
more"), and in both recovery follows illness (II: "kak bol'noj . . .
čas spasen'ja"; IV: "celebnoju siloju"). In contrast to Brjusov's
cycle, each poem enriches the meaning of the others and
contributes to the "message" of the whole grouping.

A dramatic-situational cycle embodies an emotional conflict,
frequently a romantic relationship. Grigor'ev's "Dva soneta" is in
fact such a cycle, although on the basis of its form alone it belongs
to the generic type. Fet's "More" too has the rudiments of a
dramatic situation. Indeed, when generic or thematic cycles focus
on the poet and a particular circumstance, they begin to shade off
into the dramatic type. Puškin's cycle of 1836, for instance, is in
one sense thematic—it makes a statement about poetic creativity
and different kinds of authority. On another level, however, it
portrays the poet in conflict, striving to come to terms with
circumstances that surround him and threaten his poetic legacy.
In this sense the cycle is dramatic-situational. Fedor Sologub's
"Zvezda Mair" (1898-1900) resembles Puškin's to the degree that it
presents a poet in conflict with his immediate environment,
yearning to overcome its limitations. The cycle's six poems
contain an ideal vision of a mythical realm, the land of Ojle:

> На Ойле далекой и прекрасной
> Вся любовь и вся душа моя.
> На Ойле далекой и прекрасной
> Песней сладкогласной и согласной
> Славит все блаженство бытия.   (II)

The poet is physically confined to earth, the domain of all that is
most loathsome to him, while his soul seeks refuge on the
beautiful, holy and pure Ojle. Poems IV-V anticipate a potential
resolution to this dilemma in death:

> Мой прах истлеет понемногу,
> Истлеет он в сырой земле,
> А я меж звезд найду дорогу
> К иной стране, к моей Ойле.   (IV)

> Мы скоро с тобою
> Умрем на земле,—

Мы вместе с тобою
Уйдем на Ойле.   (V)

There is a suggestion of plot here, however minimal and
anticipatory, and in this respect Sologub's cycle begins to merge
with the following type.

Plot Cycles

The plot cycle proper is the most sophisticated and diverse of the
cyclic types. The concept overlaps to a certain degree with that of
the "lyric poèma," a term which of late has aquired some
popularity.[46] Generally, "lyric poèma" denotes a text of greater
continuity than we find in most plot cycles, and in fact it need
not even be composed of separate lyric poems. Brjusov's "Carju
Severnogo poljusa," Bunin's "Listopad," and Majakovskij's "Oblako
v štanax," for instance, may be called "lyric poèmas" but certainly
not "plot cycles." In cases where there is considerable plot
continuity and yet the segments are short enough and different
enough to be perceived as separate lyrics, however, it is fruitless to
quibble whether the work must be called by one name or the
other; it obviously belongs to both categories. Such, for example,
are Bal'mont's "Mertvye korabli," Blok's "Snežnaja maska" and
perhaps even "Karmen."[47]
    In practice one can discern three subtypes of the plot cycle,
depending whether the plot dynamic is episodic (sequential),
diaristic (attenuated) or archetypal (summational). Each of these
subtypes is treated separately below.
    The episodic plot dynamic manifests itself when a dramatic
situation evolves from poem to poem toward some resolution or
denouement.[48] The poems are arranged so as to suggest a definite
causal and temporal sequentiality of events, whether concrete or
psychological. A clear example is Brjusov's "Polden' Javy"
(1895),[49] where successive poems represent episodes in a romantic
liaison. Poem I introduces the cycle's erotic theme and outlines
the course of events that follows. Poems II–V form a neat
progression—from meeting (II: "Pod sen'ju pal'my—my dva
blednyx izvajan'ja"), to anticipation of a fateful rendezvous (III:
"Segodnja! Segodnja! odni i vdvoem!"), to sexual intimacy (IV:
"Sladostrastnye teni na temnoj posteli"), to parting (V: "My s

toboj razošlis' navsegda!'").

Konstantin Bal'mont's "Mertvye korabli" (*Tišina*, 1897) also contains an episodic plot, but its presentation is more problematic. The allegorical seafaring it depicts unfolds in linear sequence from beginning to end with the exception of the first poem, which predivines the tragic outcome of the journey ("spjat v tiši morej/Ostovy nemye mertvyx korablej"). Poem II pictures the journey's conception:

"На полюс! На полюс! Бежим, поспешим,
И новые тайны откроем!
Там, верно, есть остров—красив, недвижим,
Окован пленительным зноем!

Нам скучны пределы родимых полей,
Изведанных дум и желаний.
Мы жаждем качанья немых кораблей,
Мы жаждем далеких скитаний . . ."   (II)

Poem V depicts the journey itself ("My plyli—vsë dal'še—my plyli"), poem VI its stark conclusion ("Skripja bežit sredi valov/Gigantskij grob, skelet plavučij"), and poem VII serves as an epilogue wherein the seafarers are transmuted into the very elements that brought them ruin ("Da legkie xlop'ja [snega] letajut/I bezzvučnuju skazku pojut").

Poem III-IV, however, do not at first appear to participate in this sequence of events; Leonid Dolgopolov, who discusses the cycle at some length, calls them "lyrical digressions."[50] One can show, however, that both poems contribute to the unfolding action in a way that is quite characteristic of plot cycles. The poems are descriptive rather than narrative, and each juxtaposes a seascape and a landscape. The poet's perspective in III suggests that the seascape is in direct proximity, while the landscape (no doubt the "rodimye polja" referred to in II) is somewhere in the distance ("gde-to"):

В море приливы
Шумно растут.
Мирные нивы
Где-то цветут.

Пенясь, про негу
Шепчет вода.
Где-то к ночлегу

Гонят стада.   (III)

No event is narrated, in the strict sense, but the implication is that the seafarers have moved from inland to a point on or near the seashore ("prilivy . . . rastut").   The location of poem IV, however, is perplexing since the seascape now is less immediate, more distant than the rural setting ("gde-to" now refers to the marine environment):

Грусть утихает:
С другом легко.
Кто-то вздыхает—
Там—далеко.

Счастлив, кто мирной
Долей живет.
Кто-то в обширной
Бездне плывет.

Нежная ива
Спит и молчит.
Где-то тоскливо
Чайка кричит.   (IV)

One must conclude that the poet's pespective has reverted back to the "native fields"; this does not negate, however, the fact that the sea journey in IV is already in progress ("Kto-to obširnoj/Bezdne plyvet").   Thus poems III-IV, while ostensibly digressive, narrate a crucial event in the cycle's plot—the beginning of the sea journey.

Deriving a plot from this sequence of poems, even in the absence of overt story-telling, is not so different from reading a novel or watching a play as it might seem, except that the "decoding" occurs with more conscious effort.   As Seymour Chatman explains, every audience, when confronted with a narrative text, must interpret it by "filling in gaps," supplying unnarrated but essential events:

> Whether the narrative is experienced through a performance or through a text, the members of the audience must respond with an interpretation: they cannot avoid participating in the transaction.   They must fill in gaps with essential or likely events, traits and objects which for various reasons have gone unmentioned.   If in one sentence we are told that John

got dressed and in the next that he rushed to an airport ticket counter, we surmise that in the interval occured a number of artistically inessential yet logically necessary events: grabbing his suitcase, walking from the bedroom to the living room and out the front door, then to his car or to the bus or to his taxi, opening the door of the car, getting in, and so on. The audience's capacity to supply plausible details is virtually limitless, as is the geometer's to conceive of an infinity of fractional spaces between two points.[51]

Even in the relatively primitive operation of "decoding" the interrelationship between separate frames of a comic strip the reader is called upon to make such interpretive inferences. Essentially, this is what happens when we are given in poems II-IV the following sequence:

II: Desire to leave the "native fields" and go to the sea;
        Present location in the "native fields"

III: Sea is close; rural landscape ["native fields"] is far away

IV: "Someone" ("kto-to") is sailing at sea

By what convention, however, does the reader surmise that "kto-to" (IV) refers to the prospective seafarers of poem II? If just "some person" (any person) is sailing at sea, not our protagonists, then we are dealing with information which is not plot-significant. The sequence "Andrew fell ill. Peter was taken to the hospital. John recovered and was discharged from the hospital" does not constitute narrative because the actants in an otherwise coherent series of events are not the same.[52] In normal discourse such a "narrative" cannot tell a story. In a lyric cycle, however, it *can* tell a story because often what identifies the participants in an event series is not the noun or pronoun used to name them but the actantal role they perform. In some respects this phenomenon is analogous to what Vladimir Propp discusses in *Morfologija skazki*. According to Propp, the plots of Russian magical folk tales tolerate a great number of substitutions; a "grandfather" can substitute for a "tsar," a "princess" for a "sorcerer," provided their plot functions remain the same: "The names of the role-players change, but their roles do not change. . . . In studying the folk tale the question of *what* the tale's characters do is important, while the question *who* does something or *how* something is done—these are questions for secondary study."[53] The freedom of lyric and cyclic form makes it possible for participants to be "renamed" (via shifting perspective or via metaphor) without destroying the coherence of the narrative dynamic. We have already seen something similar in Grigor'ev's "Dva soneta" ("I" *vs.* "he," "I" = "he"). In "Mertvye korabli" the allusion to the seafarers as "kto-to" is an anomaly easily assimilated within this interpretive convention.

The second type of plot dynamic appears not in regular development from poem to poem but in attenuation amidst a great deal of purely descriptive or meditative "digressions." Progress toward resolution of the initial conflict is retarded since plot-significant events are dispersed, as they might be in a diary or chronicle. The difference between the episodic and attenuated dynamic can be understood in terms of Chatman's remarks about narrative "process" and "stasis":

> Discourse is said to "state" the story, and these statements are of two kinds—*process* and *stasis*—according to whether someone did something or something happened; or whether something simply existed in the story. Process statements are in the mode of DO or HAPPEN, not as actual words in English or any natural language (these form the substance of the expression), but as more abstract expressional categories. Both the English sentence "He stabbed himself" and a mime's plunging an imaginary dagger into his heart manifest the same narrative process statement. Stasis statements are in the mode of IS. A text that consisted entirely of stasis statements, that is, stated only the existence of a set of things, could only imply a narrative.[54]

In an episodic plot cycle "process statements" occur in most if not all the poems; almost every one represents a new stage in the plot's exposition. In a diaristic plot cycle "stasis statements" predominate; several or many successive poems represent essentially the same stage of plot development. The distinction can be visualized according to the following models:

Episodic (sequential) model

Plot–significant events	1	2	3	4	-	5	6	7
Stage of plot exposition	A	B	C	D	D	E	F	G
Poems in cycle	I	II	III	IV	V	VI	VII	VIII

Diaristic (attenuated) model

Plot significant events	1	2	-	-	-	3	-	-
Stage of plot exposition	A	B	B	B	B	C	C	C
Poem in cycle	I	II	III	IV	V	VI	VII	VIII

In diaristic plot cycles the central conflict is often an internal one, in which case the sense of plot development results more from the gradual evolution of psychological states than from presentation of concrete events. Here, as in a psychological novel, the plot manifests numerous peripeteia which cause the reader to readjust his "expectations in regard to an end."[55] Thus while the poet or lyric hero may advance toward a resolution of the psychological conflict, he may also revert back periodically to a meditative posture characteristic of an earlier stage in the plot, or he may, early on, anticipate a later stage. In such cases plot exposition may follow a pattern like the following: A A B B B B A B B B D C C C B C C C D D D. Here directedness toward some conclusion, a basic feature of any narrative, is present, but it is attenuated by various reversals and anticipations.

Nikolaj Ogarev's "Buch der Liebe (Otryvki iz avtobiografii)" (1841-1844) is an excellent example of the diaristic type. Of the cycle's forty-five poems, the first five trace an episodic plot—the poet falls in love (I-II), contemplates marriage (III) and finally bids farewell to his beloved and goes abroad (V). From here on, however, the plot becomes attenuated. Poems VI-XLV trace not so much a history of the poet's relationship with the beloved as a chronicle of the transformations of her image in his psyche; the entire drama is internalized. On this level, however, the dramatic conflict moves gradually towards a resolution. Through most of the cycle the the poet is obsessed with an illusory intimacy he achieves with the heroine with the aid of his prodigious fantasy—he recalls past meetings with her (VII, VIII, XIII, XXV, XXXVI); he contemplates her likeness in statues (XV, XVI, XXIV); he endeavors to paint her from memory (XXVII-XXIX); he visits places she once frequented in hopes of recreating a vision of her (XXXI, XXXIV); he goes to the opera to see a singer who reminds him of her (XXXIII-XXXV). In the first two thirds of the cycle this intoxication with her image is rarely balanced by a sobering awareness that the fantasy is potentially destructive; only on occasion does the poet step back and appraise his situation with detachment:

> Могу я видеть вещи холодно и ясно.
> Я вижу, что любовь моя есть бред,
> Который молодость мою погубит,
> Что носит смерть в себе, кто тщетно любит,
> Что б самом деле для меня длаженстби нет.
> Я вижу ход судьбы бесстрастной, ровной,
> Причины, следствия—все вижу я,
> Как будто человек другой в меня
> Взошел и судит безучастно, хладнокровно.   (XX)

Such musings anticipate a later stage in the plot's development. Beginning in poem XXXVII, the image of the beloved starts to slip into the dark recesses of forgetfulness:

> Уже давно я в книге этой
> Стихов в раздумье не писал;
> Молчала рифма; дух поэта
> В заботе праздной изнывал.
> Я тратил жизнь в порочной лени
> При буйном звуке пьяных чаш,
> И реже средь моих видений
> Являлся светлый образ ваш.   (XXXVII)

In the cycle's final poems there is something of a denouement in that the poet's preoccupation is overcome and the previous love is relegated to an important but modest place in his memory. Even near the end of the cycle, however, there are occasional flashbacks to the obsessive mentality of the earlier poems:

> Я возле вас сидел во сне:
> Моей любви прочли вы муку
> В дрожащем голосе — и мне
> Вы крепко, крепко сжали руку
> И говорили мне: люблю!   (XL)

   The archetypal (summational) plot dynamic differs from the preceding two in that it develops independently of the poems' sequence. We are speaking not of a narrative progression from poem to poem nor of a situation that evolves gradually toward some conclusion, but of a narrative archetype—a pattern of events which is repeated, whether in whole or in part, *within* the separate poems of a cycle.[56] Let us assume the following sequence of events: 1) Peter fell ill; 2) Peter was taken to the hospital; 3) Peter got well; 4) Peter was discharged from the hospital; 5) Peter went home. In an episodic plot cycle these events might be narrated in five successive poems; in a diaristic cycle their narration might be protracted over thirty or forty poems with the plot developing in gradual stages. In an archetypal plot cycle, by contrast, all five events might be "summed up" in one or several poems, while those remaining reproduce the sequence partially. Reading such a cycle does not produce the impression of progressive stages in the plot's exposition because all "stages" may be present in any single poem. The hypothetical model for this type of cycle might take the following shape:

Archetypal (summational) model

Plot-significant events							
2	1	1	2	1	1	3	1
4	3	2	3	2	2	4	4
5	4	3	4	4		5	
	5	4		5			
		5					
Stage of plot exposition							
–	–	–	–	–	–	–	–
Poem in cycle							
I	II	III	IV	V	VI	VII	VIII

Deriving a plot archetype requires that one choose a level of abstraction at which the various events in separate poems are perceived as analogous. A zero level of abstraction means not reducing the text at all, merely reproducing it verbatim as Tolstoj said he would have to do to summarize *Anna Karenina*.[57] The maximum level of abstraction means reducing the text to what all narrative has in common: "Something happened and then (consequently or contingently) something else happened" (according to Chatman) or "First there was equilibrium, then there was disequilibrium, and then there was a new equilibrium partially like the first" (according to Todorov).[58] At some level between these extremes it is sometimes possible to discern a recurrent event pattern just as Propp discovered a sequence of thirty-one invariant events or "functions" in 102 magical folktales from Afanas'ev's collection.[59] Propp showed that the "functions" "one of the family members becomes absent from the home," "a prohibition is placed upon the hero," "the prohibition is violated," and so forth always occur in the same order, although not every "function" will appear in every tale. Of course Propp could have carried abstraction still further and reduced his "functions" to fewer than thirty-one, but he operated at a level appropriate to the specific empirical task he had set.[60]

Andrej Belyj's "Zoloto v lazuri" (1904), in his book by the same title, is an excellent example of the archetypal plot cycle.[61] Two patterns recur, the first more common and more fully developed than the second:

Model #1 (Positive)
   1) The sky opens, giving sunlight. (The ideal light is golden, and it appears on a background of light-blue. Partial illumination of the sky at sunset, colored in hues of red, can also initiate this event sequence.)
   2) A "senior one" appears. (This may be God, an old man, a king, a priest, the poet or even the personification of eternity. Christ can be a "senior one" with respect to the people who worship him, but with respect to God the Father he is a "junior one.")
   3) The "senior one" speaks to the "junior one(s)" with an appeal, an invitation, a command or words of comfort.
   4) The "junior one(s)" experience joy or solace.
   5) The heavens (or, metonymically, God) provide affection.
   6) The "junior one(s)" fly (or anticipate flight) to the heavens (toward the sunlight).

Model #2 (Negative)
   1) The sky closes, giving darkness.
   2) Some "other one" appears (sometimes a personified natural phenomenon).
   3) The "other one" addresses the "junior one(s)" with disheartening words.

No single poem contains a complete and explicit version of the first model, although poem No. 5 (II in the subcycle "Zolotoe runo") is perhaps its fullest manifestation:

Пожаром склон неба объят . . .   (1)

. . . .
Зовет за собою   (2)(3)
Старик аргонавт:

. . . .
"За   солнцем, за солнцем, свободу любя,   (3)
умчимся в эфир
голубой! . ."

Старик аргонавт призывает на солнечный пир,   (3)
                                        (4?) (5?)

. . . .
Наш Арго,
готовясь лететь, золотыми крылами   (6)
забил.

Земля отлетает . . .
. . . .
И, блеском объятый,
светило дневное,
что факелом вновь зажжено,
несясь,
настигает
наш Арго крылатый.

The missing or implied elements of the first model are supplied in
other poems, for instance Nos. 11, 15 and 36:

           Пронизала вершины дерев
           желто-бархатным светом заря.   (1)
           И звучит этот вечный напев: (3)
           "Объявись—зацелую тебя. . ."   (5)

                      ———————

           Все тот же раскинулся свод   (1)
           над нами лазурно-безмирный,
           и тот же на сердце растет
           восторг одиночества пирный.   (4)

                      ———————

           Улыбнулись меж солнечных роз,   (1)
           в жемчугах ясных струй. . .
           Ветерок нам принес поцелуй.   (5)

Poem No. 4 (I of the subcycle "Zolotoe runo") contains a variation
of the second (negative) model:

Солнце село. Рыданий   (1)
полон крик альбатросов: (2)(3)

"Дети солнца, вновь холод бесстрастья!   (3)
Закатилось оно—
золотое, старинное счастье—
золотое руно!"

In many poems there is a mixture of the two archetypes, and
toward the end of the cycle, where the poet's attitude becomes
cynical, there are ironic perversions of each, as for instance in
poem No. 22 (IV of the subcycle "Ne tot"). Here the "senior one"
appears, but he presides over a chain of events that resembles
more the negative archetype:

	Model #1	*Model #2*
И он на троне золотом,		
весь просиявщий, восседая,	(1)	(2)
волшебно-пламенным вином		
нас всех безумно опьяняя,		
Ускорил ужас роковой.		
И хаос встал давно забытый.		
И голос бури мировой	(3?)	
для всех раздался вдруг, сердитый.		
И на щеках заледенел		
вдруг поцелуй желанных губок.	(5)	
И с тяжким звоном полетел		
его вина червонный кубок.		
И тени грозные легли		(1)
от стран далекого востока.		
Мы все увидели вдали		
седобородого пророка.		(2)
Пророк с волненьем грозовым		
сказал: "Антихрист объявился. . ."		(3)
И хаос бредом роковым		
вкруг нас опять зашевелился.		
И с трона грустный царь сошел,		
в этот час повитый тучей злою.		
Корону сняв, во тьму пошел		
от нас с опущенной главою.		

Constant repetition of the same archetypal patterns in Belyj's cycle makes it possible to reproduce them extremely compactly, since the reader learns to recognize them in the poet's metonymical shorthand. Individual words, especially names of colors, are symbolically allied with particular stages in the archetypes. "Lazur'" or "zoloto," for instance, can suggest the event "the sky opens, giving light," whereas "černyj" or "temnyj" can indicate "the sky closes, giving darkness." The word "vossedat'" can imply "the 'senior one' appears," and the epithet "bezzakatnyj" may suggest flight toward the sun—each can be interpreted as a "quotation" from the myth of the sun-journey. Hence the general contours of an entire archetype can be compressed within a single quatrain, as they are at the end of the poem "Starec" (No. 26):

> И все ярче рассвет
> золотого огня.
> И все ближе привет
> беззакатного дня.

The capacity of a lyric cycle to make a single word function as the sign of a plot archetype (that is, as a "mytheme") proved extremely important in the poetics of Russian symbolism. Indeed, judging from "Zoloto v lazuri" alone, Vjačeslav Ivanov's dictum "from symbol is born myth"[62] needs to be considered more than just symbolist sloganeering. The question of what ends the cycle served in the practice of particular movements and individuals, however, is a subject that properly belongs to the following chapter.

II

ALEKSANDR BLOK AND
THE CYCLIC TRADITION

> The critic need not answer the question
> "What did the poet wish to say?"; but he
> must try to answer the question "Whence did
> he come?"
> —Osip Mandel'štam, "Barsuč'ja nora"

Aleksandr Blok's achievement as a cyclic poet must be viewed within the context of a long-standing tradition. Blok did not introduce the lyric cycle into Russian poetry, nor was he the first to utilize it with conscious esthetic aims. His genius as a cyclist lies in his peculiar ability to exploit the information-carrying potential of his medium more consistently than any of his predecessors and on a much more monumental scale. Blok's lyric "trilogy," which organizes the bulk of his prodigious lyric output in a hierarchy of overlapping and interpenetrating contextual framings, is a cyclic phenomenon unequaled by any Russian poet before him in the magnitude and complexity of its design. But Blok's "trilogy," whose first version appeared in 1911-12, represents the logical extension of less ambitious efforts and the culmination of maturing historical trends that date back at least as far as the early nineteenth century and perhaps even to the middle of the eighteenth century. To understand the significance of Blok's achievement one must determine to what extent he conformed to pre-existing norms and to what extent he departed from them and developed a cyclic dynamic uniquely his own.

This task is extremely difficult, since there exists as yet no comprehensive history of the Russian lyric cycle. The studies presently available are not entirely adequate, in part because they are very brief but more importantly because they operate from what is an inaccurate premise—namely, that cyclization begins to

emerge only in the latter half of the nineteenth century and that
"genuine" cycles appear only at the turn of the century in the
practice of the Russian symbolists. This belief acquired general
acceptance in the 1960's, following the pioneering work of
Dolgopolov and Sapogov.

Dolgopolov, in his *Poèmy Bloka i russkaja poèma konca
XIX—načala XX vekov* (1964), was the first to outline a history of
the Russian lyric cycle, tracing its origins back to the small
thematic groupings of poems fashioned by Grigor'ev, Nekrasov and
Fet in the 1850's and 1860's:

> Namely in the poetry of the second half of the
> nineteenth century takes shape such a "synthetic" genre
> of lyrics as a cycle of poems. A series of poems is
> conjoined by the poet within a particular section [of a
> collection] which was supposed to represent a certain
> poetic unity. A cycle could carry within itself a more
> significant content than one poem taken in isolation.[1]

According to Dolgopolov, however, such groupings are only
marginally cyclic because their principle of unity is partially
generic, partially thematic; genuine cycles, which he characterizes as
"unified and independent poetic 'organisms'" possessing "internal
unity," do not appear until the 1890's in the symbolist era:

> Fet's sections do not possess the internal unity necessary
> for a cycle. The grouping of poems carries a partially
> thematic, partially generic character. . . .
>
> Only in poetry at the end of the nineteenth
> century and the beginning of the twentieth did
> examples of poetic cycles in the strict sense of the word
> appear. The section headings of all the major poetic
> collections of the 1890's through the 1900's were
> composed according to the same principle: they consist
> of the titles of cycles, under which are disposed the
> poems which comprise them. Cyclization became an
> immanent poetic tradition. . . .   The poetic cycle
> acquired all the features of a unified and independent
> poetic "organism". . . .[2]

Even the groupings of Bal'mont and Brjusov, Dolgopolov believes,
fall short of ideal unity, and he reserves the designation "the first
lyric cycle in Russian poetry in the proper sense of the word" for

Blok's first collection, *Stixi o Prekrasnoj Dame* (appeared 1904). [3]

Sapogov, in his dissertation "Poètika liričeskogo cikla A. Bloka" (1967), while not crediting Blok with the introduction of "genuine" cycles, does not expand the cycle's historical perimeter much beyond that established by Dolgopolov.[4]   He dates the Russian lyric cycle in its embryonic form from the mid-nineteenth century, citing Nikolaj Ogarev's "Buch der Liebe" (1841-44) as the first "attempt at conscious narrative cyclization"; Grigor'ev's "Bor'ba" (1843-1857) and "Improvizacii stranstvujuščego romantika" (1858) are mentioned as evidence of "the slowly maturing tendency toward lyric cyclization in Russian poetry."[5]   A special place in the history of the cycle is accorded Nekrasov's *Poslednie pesni* (1877), a collection which is "throughout exceptionally rigorous in its design and striking for its ideational monumentality."[6]   Like Dolgopolov, however, Sapogov argues that "combination of separate poems into more or less closed organic entities" occurred only at the end of the nineteenth and beginning of the twentieth centuries.[7] Groupings by genre, common in collections of the eighteenth and early nineteenth centuries, are dismissed as "mechanical" in that they do not yield the *"organic"* unity characteristic of cycles at a later stage of their evolution:

> It is possible to speak about poetic cycles in sentimentalist and romantic poets of the early nineteenth century only with strong reservations.   It is more accurate to speak about principles of constructing poetic collections.   For poets of the romantic school the traditional way of constructing poetic collections, dating back to the eighteenth century, was to distribute poems according to a generic principle.   K. Batjuškov's *Opyty v stixax i proze* (1817), for instance, is broken down into "Elegies," "Epistles," and "Miscellany" [Smes'], and to the last section are attached "Epigrams, inscriptions et cetera."   The number of such generic cycles could be much greater, as for example in the third edition of Žukovskij's works (volumes I-III, 1824).
>
> No significance was attached to the arrangement of poems under these rubrics.   The first collections of A. Puškin (1826) and E. Baratynskij (1827) are constructed according to the same generic principle.   This simplest of constructive principles for creating a lyric cycle was

predominant in [Russian] poetic practice during the first half of the nineteenth century. . . .

Generic combination of poems did not provide collections of poetry with the desired unity, since it was something mechanical and conventional.[8]

These views have not been directly challenged in Soviet scholarship, although the growing interest in Puškin as a cyclic poet in recent years indicates that a reassessment of them may well be overdue.[9]

Unquestionably, Dolgopolov and Sapogov are correct in arguing that grouping poems is an operation of no intrinsic interest if the only principle unifying them is superficial, "mechanical"; in such cases one might just as well study the esthetics of pagination or type faces. Creating a cycle entitled "Elegies" is esthetically meaningless so long as the poems contained therein have nothing in common but elegiac topoi; similarly, combining poems about "spring" is a gratuitous gesture if the only reason for doing so is their shared vernal theme. Genuine cycles, to borrow the metaphor used by Dolgopolov and Sapogov, are unified "organically" —they possess a conceptual unity, often a unity embedded inconspicuously in the substrata of the text.

While reliable for the period of cyclization they consider important, however, the studies of Dolgopolov and Sapogov dismiss too summarily the generic cycles of the eighteenth and early nineteenth centuries. Examination of poetic collections and smaller groupings of poems from this period reveals that, contrary to Sapogov's assertion, the inclusion of separate poems under generic or other ostensibly superficial rubrics was by no means always dictated solely by "mechanical" prescriptives. Nor was the arrangement of poems always (or even usually) arbitrary. Indeed, to be faithful to the criterion of organicity, the history of "genuine" cyclization must begin in the middle of the eighteenth century and perhaps even at the very inception of modern Russian poetry, with the publication of Trediakovskij's *Novyj i kratkij sposob k složeniju rossijskix stixov* (1735).[10] While highly unified cycles are still a relatively infrequent occurrence in the eighteenth century, the processes of cyclic evolution are already in evidence. Already there is a tendency for juxtaposed lyrics to form those conceptual bonds which render poems mutually informative, and poets became sensitive to this interaction. An analogy can be drawn to the primordial stages of evolving life.   Just as eons of molecular couplings and spontaneous manufacture of organic compounds preceded the appearance of DNA and the simplest organisms, so genuinely integrated cycles emerge gradually from modest beginnings, from combinative environments that sometimes generated unexpected possibilities.

To give a comprehensive history of Russian lyric cycle is a task that lies beyond the province of this study.   What follows is intended only as a preliminary outline of the cycle's historical development; hopefully, it will place Blok's contribution as a cyclist in perspective and suggest avenues for further investigation.

The Eighteenth Century

On the whole eighteenth century Russian poetry adhered to a strict genre system borrowed principally from the French neo-classicists but shaped to some degree by the older Ukrainian scholastic tradition whose influence was still felt even after the introduction of syllabo-tonic versification by Trediakovskij in 1735. Each of the three major literary figures of the mid-eighteenth century played an important role in codifying this system not only in practice but in their theoretical works as well: Sumarokov in his prescriptive "Èpistola o stixotvorstve" (1748), Trediakovskij in his translation of Boileau's "L'art poétique" ("Nauka o stixotvorenii i poèzii," 1752), Lomonosov in his genre-oriented theory of styles ("Predislovie o pol'ze knig cer'kovnyx v rossijskom jazyke," 1757). In this period virtually every collection of poetry is divided into sections by genre—the more monumental ("higher") genres gravitating toward the beginning of a collection, the smaller ("lower") ones gravitating toward the end.   Typically, an edition of lyric poetry was constructed as follows: 1) spiritual (or divine) odes, 2) panegyric odes, 3) elegies, 4) eclogues, 5) anacreontic odes (or songs), 6) fables, 7) epigrams, 8) inscriptions. Though the genre system became less regimented in the 1760's and 1770's, this way of organizing a poetic collection remained essentially unchanged even into the beginning of the following century.

Classical poetics was not especially condusive to the production of well-integrated cycles. The idea that every poem be designed to fit an abstract generic model tended to diminish the importance of a poet's individuality.   Genre determined subject,

style, mood and in essence the very posture and attitude of the
poet, so that apparent connections between lyrics resulted as a rule
not from any inherent bond linking them but from their common
relatedness to the model.   Therefore, while conceptual unities can
be discerned, they tend to be non-specific (e.g., admiration of
monarchs in panegyric odes, or peaceful contemplation of nature in
eclogues).   Moreover, the dominant lyric genre of the period, the
panegyric ode, was least suited to cyclization—in part because its
extraordinary length effectively precluded consecutive reading (one
ode after another), and in part because odes of this type were
written to commemorate specific occasions quite isolated from each
other and not reflecting a common experience (e.g., a military
victory, a coronation, a royal visit).

Despite these limitations, however, each genre tolerated some
thematic latitude, and poets were free to choose and arrange poems
more or less as they pleased under the different generic rubrics.
As a result there was an opportunity to create groupings wherein
poems were meaningfully interrelated, and eighteenth century poets
were sometimes quite sensitive to this possibility.

In groupings of spiritual odes, for example, there is a clear
tendency toward contextuality.   Alexander Levitsky writes that
spiritual odes, which are generally transpositions of psalms, "like no
other literary genre . . . lent themselves to the expression of
personal feelings and beliefs and became used for these purposes by
a number of poets."[11].   Unlike the panegyric variety, odes of this
type are of medium length (usually between thirty and sixty lines)
and therefore offer less resistance to consecutive reading; moreover,
they continually refer back to one basic set of circumstances: man
(the poet) in his relationship to God.   A grouping of spiritual odes
thus contains the rudiments of a dramatic situation and can with
proper emphases develop into a full-fledged dramatic-situational
cycle.

A case in point is Lomonosov's "Ody duxovnye" (*Sobranie
raznyx sočinenij v stixax i v proze*, 1751), which is a well-unified
and interesting cycle by any measure.   Seven transpositions of
psalms are followed by a translation from the Book of Job and two
original poems:

1)   Preloženie psalma 1
2)   Preloženie psalma 14
3)   Preloženie psalma 26

4)   Preloženie psalma 34
5)   Preloženie psalma 70
6)   Preloženie psalma 143
7)   Preloženie psalma 145
8)   Oda, vybrannaja iz Iova, glava 38, 39, 40 i 41
9)   Utrennee razmyšlenie o Božiem veličestve
10)   Večernee razmyšlenie o Božiem veličestve pri slučae velikogo severnogo sijanija[12]

Within this grouping there is a distinct thematic-conceptual development and the unmistakable imprint of authorial design. Poems Nos. 1-2 form an anthropological introduction, dividing mankind into categories of the righteous and the unrighteous. Here the image of man is generalized and the image of the poet as a separate lyric "I" is absent:

Блажен, кто к злым в совет не ходит,
Не хочет грешным в след ступать
И с тем, кто пагубу приводит,
В едином месте заседать . . .   (No. 1)

_____

Господи, кто обитает
В светлом доме выше звезд?
. . . .
Кто устами льстить не знает,
Ближним не наносит бед,
Хитрых сетей не сплетает,
Чтобы в них увяз сосед;

Презирает всех лукавых,
Хвалит вышняго рабов . . .   (No. 2)

In poem Nos. 3-6, which occupy a median position in the cycle, a dramatic situation emerges as well as a definite lyric persona. The poet repeatedly prays for deliverance from the ungodly who surround and persecute him:

Хоть полк против меня восстань,
Но я не ужасаюсь.
Пускай враги воздвигнут брань,
На Бога полагаюсь.   (No. 3)

_____

Суди обидящих, Зиждитель,

И от борющихся со мной
Всегдашний буди Покровитель,
Застунпник и Спаситель мой.   (No. 4)

———

Святою правдою твоею
Избавь меня от злобных мук,
Склонись молитвою моею
И сокруши коварных лук.   (No. 5)

———

Избавь меня от хищных рук
И от чужих народов власти:
Их речь полна тщеты, напасти;
Рука их в нас наводит лук.   (No. 6)[13]

Poems Nos. 7-8 are transitional in that they refocus the poet's attention away from the injustices which characterize his earthly condition. In poem No. 7, while still alluding to the "unrighteous," the poet contemplates momentarily the wonders of the heavens:

Блажен тот, кто себя вручает
Всесильному во всех делах
И токмо в помощь призывает
Живущаго на небесах.

Несчетно многими звездами
Наполнившаго высоту
И непостижными делами
Земли и моря широту.   (No. 7)

In No. 8, wherein the magnificence of God's universe is already the central theme, we find an exhortation to renounce complaints about one's immediate condition:

Сие, о смертный, рассуждая,
Представь Зиждителеву власть,
Святую волю почитая,
Имей свою в терпеньи часть.
Он все на пользу нашу строит,
Казнит кого или покоит.
В надежде тяготу сноси
И без роптания проси.   (No. 8)

Poems Nos. 9-10, which close the cycle, make no reference at all to earthly injustices; the poet is concerned only with the greatness of God as creator of the heavens and the insufficiency of man's intellect to comprehend the workings of the universe. Thus the dramatic conflict that surfaces in the median poems is resolved by way of transcendence: the poet, instead of reveling in victory over his malefactors, simply overcomes his earthly predicament in a gesture of humility and faith.[14]

Trediakovskij's "Ody božestvennye" (*Sočinenija i perevody, kak stixami tak i prozoju*, 1752) is also a well-integrated cycle but presents a quite different resolution of the psalmodic conflict. All but the last of the twenty-two poems in this grouping are renditions (Trediakovskij calls them "paraphrases") of Biblical texts. The first ten are from the Book of Psalms; the next eleven are prayers from various locations in the Old Testament; the final poem is an original composition:

1)   Parafrazis psalma 1
2)   Parafrazis psalma 6
3)   Parafrazis psalma 18
4)   Parafrazis psalma 42
5)   Parafrazis psalma 51
6)   Parafrazis psalma 78
7)   Parafrazis psalma 111
8)   Parafrazis psalma 136
9)   Parafrazis psalma 139
10) Parafrazis psalma 143
11) Parafrazis pervoj pesni Moiseevy. Isxoda glava 15
12) Parafrazis vtoroj pesni Moiseevy. Vtorozakonija glava 32
13) Parafrazis pesni Anny materi Samuila proroka.   Carstv, kniga 1, glava 2
14) Parafrazis pesni proroka Avvakuma. Avvakum glava 2
15) Parafrazis Isaiina proročija. Isaii glava 26
16) Parafrazis molitvy Ioniny. Iony glava 1
17) Parafrazis molitvy trex otrokov. Daniila glava 3
18) Parafrazis xvaly Bogu ot trex junoš. Daniila glava 3
19) Parafrazis pesni bogorodicy. Luki glava 1
20) Parafrazis proročeskoj molitvy Zaxarii otca predotečeva. Luki glava 1
21) Parafrazis pesni Devvoriny. Sudej glava 5
22) O nepostojanstve mira[15]

Placing the psalms first and the original composition last is a practice common in most eighteenth century collections and

therefore not especially noteworthy.   The order of poems Nos.
11-21, however, is interesting in that it does not correspond
precisely to the sequence of the original texts in the Scriptures; if
we were to adhere to the Biblical order, we would find instead the
following configuration of lyrics: Nos. 11, 12, 21, 13, 15, 17, 18, 16,
14, 19, 20.   What is striking here is that Trediakovskij, who is
generally fastidious about observing Biblical sequence, has displaced
poems Nos. 21, 16, and 14 from their "proper" order.   Yet these
three apparent misorderings are a function of the poet's deliberate
design.   In roughly the first two-thirds of the poems (Nos. 1-16)
the dominant theme is the poet's entrapment within a circle of
"enemies" (the unrighteous, the heathens).   The theme of the last
third of the poems (Nos. 17-21), by contrast, is the poet's joyous
deliverance, victory over his "enemies" and escape from a
threatening predicament.   The final poem, Trediakovskij's own
composition, is summational in that it argues the impermanence of
misfortune and reaffirms the poet's faith in the grace of God.
Clearly the selection of texts, the emphases Trediakovskij makes as
a translator and the arrangement of poems are not arbitrary—
Trediakovskij creates a lyric persona and a dramatic situation that
develops along the lines of an episodic plot.   The situation parallels
that in Lomonosov's "Ody duxovnye," except that here the poet,
instead of transcending the conflict with his malefactors spiritually,
gains victory over them as if in direct combat.

  With regard to rearrangement of Biblical texts, Sumarokov's
first cycle of spiritual odes (published in the journal *Ežemesjačnye
sočinenija*, 1755) is an even more striking specimen than
Trediakovskij's:

1)   Izo psalma 37 ("Bessmertnyj tvarej obladatel'...")
2)   Izo psalma 106 ("Tvoju Velikij Bože slavu...")
3)   Izo psalma 36 ("Ostav' zlodeev v ix delax...")
4)   Izo psalma 51 ("Čto sil'nyj xvalitsja zlodej...")
5)   Izo psalma 1 ("Blažen muž kto, merzja, ne vxodit...")
6)   Izo psalma 3 Siraxa ("Koliko budeš' voznesen...")[16]

Clearly, Sumarokov is not at all bound to scriptural sequence.

  The tone and emphasis of Sumarokov's grouping are entirely
different from Lomonosov's and Trediakovskij's, and one cannot
rule out the possibility of a polemic—especially since spiritual odes
had become an arena for competition between poets in 1743, when
these   three   writers   were   commissioned   to   produce   rival

transpositions of Psalm 143.[17]   In this case comparison suggests that Sumarokov may have deliberately created a cycle that was both more humble and self-effacing than those of his predecessors. In Sumarokov's six odes the notion of a poet's victorious struggle against "enemies" is virtually absent, and in fact there is no unifying dramatic situation at all.   Most of the poems are simply moral instructions or admonitions, and two of the poems (Nos. 3-4) conclude with parables.   Assuming that the arrangement is not purely whimsical, one can discern in it a progressive tendency toward concealment and withdrawal of the lyric "I."   Only in the cycle's first two poems is the lyric "I" prominent; but even here the lyric persona is quite unheroic.   In poem No. 1 he is weak and morally depraved, one of the unrighteous rather than one of the wronged:

> Во беззаконьи утопаю:
> Грехами я отягощен:
> От прав закона отступаю,
> Тщетою света восхищен:
> Достоин казни и мученья:
> Не вижу плоти излеченья.
> Мой дух перед тобой дрожит.
> Душа грехи всечасно множит
> И тишину мою тревожит,
> Спокойство от меня бежит.   (No. 1)

In poem No. 2 the "I" is dwarfed by the vastness of God's creation:

> Так мысль моя смятенна;
> Открывшаяся мне вселенна,
> Являет что конца ей нет.
>
> Я свет на свет постановляю,
> И милионы вображаю
> Их, в смутной мысли я своей.
>
> Толикож их взношу над оны
> И паки паки милионы:
> Пещинка то вселенной всей.   (No. 2)

Beginning in poem No. 3, the "I" effectively disappears as a separate persona and the focus shifts to a generalized "ty" or "on." Unlike Lomonosov and Trediakovskij, Sumarokov does not exploit the idea of a dramatic conflict in which the poet occupies center stage; rather the poet becomes the disembodied voice of conscience speaking equally to the condition of all men.

In 1795 Deržavin presented Catherine II with a manuscript volume of his own verses composed during her reign. As evidence that sequencing was of considerable importance to him, it is worth noting that Deržavin renounced the 1798 edition of his work in part because it violated the order of poems in the earlier manuscript;[18] hence in 1808, when he restored the volume to its original form, he prefaced the first part of *Sočinenija* with the following statement:

> Readers will now please observe the *first* part in the exact same order in which (excluding the drawings) it was presented personally by me to the deceased Sovereign Empress, hallowed be her memory. . . .[19]

On must wonder why Deržavin was adamant about this particular sequence. Was it merely because he wished to honor the sacred memory of his protectress by reproducing the volume exactly as he had presented it to her? Or was there some esthetic rationale? Indeed, the first eleven poems of part I are in the tradition of sacred verse and manifest a certain unity of concept. They are listed below with psalmodic sources and dates given parenthetically:

1)   "Bog" [No particular psalm; 1780-84]
2)   "Na osvjaščenie Kamennoostrovskogo invalidnogo doma [Psalms 107, 137, 140; 1778]
3)   "Vlastiteljam i sudijam" [Psalm 81; 1780]
4)   "Veličestvo Božie" [Psalm 103; 1789]
5)   "Pravednyj sudija" [Psalm 100; 1789]
6)   "Istinnoe ščastie" [Psalm 1; 1789]
7)   "Pobeditelju" [Psalm 90; 1793]
8)   "Pomošč' Božija" [Psalm 120; 1793]
9)   "Upovajuščemu na svoju silu" [Psalm 127; 1780]
10) "Sčastlivoe semejstvo" [Psalm 127; 1780]
11) "Uspokoennoe neverie" [No particular psalm; 1779][20]

It hardly seems accidental that the perimeters of this grouping are marked by two poems which have no particular psalm as their source and represent the most daring challenges to religious faith in all of Deržavin's work; each, however, ends with a painful reaffirmation of faith:

Но если славословить должно,
То слабым смертным невозможно
Тебя ничем иным почтить,
Как им к Тебе лишь возвышаться,
В безмерной разности теряться,
И благодарны слезы лить.   (No. 1)

Непостижимый сей Творец
Да будет мой покров, отец!
Он взором волны укрощает,
Он всей природой мне вещает:
"Испытывать судьбу забудь,
Надейся, верь—и счастлив будь!"   (No. 2)

Occupying a median position in the grouping are poems that challenge not godly but earthly authorities (or, more generally, the unrighteous), and in the cumulative impact of these verses there is a certain esthetic advantage:

Восстал Всевышний Бог, да судит
Земных богов во сонме их.
"Доколе", рек, "доколь вам будет
Щадить неправедных и злых?"
. . . .
Воскресни, Боже! Боже правых!
И их молению внемли:
Приди, суди, карай лукавых
И будь един царем земли!   (No. 3)

Но грешных племя и язык
Да истребит десница строга!
Хвали, душа моя, ты Бога:
Сколь Он премудр и сколь велик!   (No. 4)

Лжецы, мздоимцы, гордецы,
Отсюду мною изженутся
В дальнейшие земны концы,
Иль казнь повергнет их во гроб.   (No. 5)

Суда Всевидца не снесут

И не воскреснут нечестивы,
И грешники в совет правдивый
Отнюдь явиться не дерзнут.   (No. 6)

———

Господь . . . от сокровенных,
От хитрых сохранит сетей,
Спасет . . . от дерзновенных
И от зломышленных людей . . .   (No. 7)

———

Он кротких в милость принимает
И праведным дает покров;
Надменных власть уничтожает
И грешных низвергает в ров.   (No. 9)

In all fairness it must be said that Deržavin's grouping is not so meticulously organized that minor variations in the arrangement of poems is unthinkable, but nor is their order entirely arbitrary. It is interesting that poem No. 12 ("Felica"), which introduces a series of panegyric odes, has a unique impact when read after these first eleven lyrics; certainly the opening line of No. 12 ("*Bogopodobnaja* carevna. . .") carries a special resonance when it follows sacred verses that reaffirm the poet's faith in God.

Putting aside spiritual odes, one cannot overlook the efforts of at least two eighteenth-century poets to fashion contextually unified groupings of elegies. Although elegies did not occupy a hallowed place in the classicist pantheon of genres,[21] they provided excellent possibilities for cyclization because of their smaller size, their limited thematics (as conceived at that time) and the absence of any limitations on their arrangement. It is not altogether surprising, therefore, that Trediakovskij, in the very first manifesto of the modern Russian literary era, creates a full-fledged plot cycle consisting of two elegies. "Elegija I" ("Ne vozmožno serdcu, ax! ne imet' pečali...") and "Elegija II" ("Kto tol' bednomu podast pomošči mne ruky?..") are juxtaposed as examples of "eksametr" in his *Novyj i kratkij sposob* and prefaced by the following remark: "In the first [elegy] I have an imaginary spouse lament that he has been separated from his beloved and also fictitious mate Ilidara and that he already has no hope of seeing her because of the distance between them; and in the second he is in despair over the fact that he has learned of his Ilidara's death, although he cannot stop loving her even after her death."[22] As Grigorij Gukovskij points out, these two poems do indeed have "an internal thematic bond," and between them emerges "a semblance of plot movement" in accord with the author's intention.[23]

Sumarokov repeated Trediakovskij's experiment on a more ambitious scale in his collection *Raznye stixotvorenija* (1769). Section III of this edition contains nineteen elegies which manifest a definite design (albeit, not sustained with utmost consistency). The first ten poems in this sequence form a separate grouping with a single dramatic situation and attenuated plot development; all are love lyrics published separately in journals ten years earlier. It seems apparent that Sumarokov, in preparing the 1769 edition, rearranged the texts to enhance their narrative chronology, although for some reason this particular sequence was never repeated in any subsequent publication:[24]

1) "Prestan'te vy glaza dražaščeju prel'ščat'sja..."
2) "Drugim pečal'nyj stix rozdaet stixotvorstvo..."
3) "Dovol'no l' na tosku, o vremja ty vziralo!..."
4) "Naveki razlučen s toboju dorogaja..."
5) "Ty tol'ko dlja tovo ljubov' uničtožaeš'..."
6) "Vse radosti moi uxodjat ot menja..."
7) "Uže menja ni čto na svete ne prel'ščaet..."
8) "Uže ušli ot nas igranija i smexi..."
9) "Terpi moja duša, terpi različny muki..."
10) "Prestaneš' li moej dokukoj uslaždat'sja?..."[25]

Poem No. 1 depicts the lovers' parting; the poet recalls the joys and pains of love, vows faithfulness to his beloved and wishes the same constancy from her:

А ты любезная мя так же не забудь,
И в верности своей подобна мне пребудь!
Воспоминай союз всегда хранимый нами!

. . . .

И естьли буду мил тебе и по разлуке;
Так помни что и я в такойже стражду муке...   (No. 1)

In poem No. 2, set already after the parting, it becomes apparent that the poet's hope for requited love has been unrealized; the beloved refuses to renew their meetings:

Она бы всякой час со мной быть купно рада.
Сержусь, и думаю почто не изберет
К тому удобна дня, а ей в том воли нет.

Но как во многих днях, не сыщет дня такова,
Сулит увидиться, сулит не держит слова,
А я в обмане сем мучение терплю:
Сержусь, но гневом тем лишь пуще я люблю.   (No. 2)

In poems Nos. 3-7 nothing substantive changes in this basic situation, but we do encounter the psychological peripeties typical of a diaristic plot cycle—the poet vacillates between hope, resignation, hatred and love. He even entertains thoughts of suicide (No. 5). Finally, in poem No. 8, there is an effort to generalize the misadventure, to portray it as but one episode in an unhappy existence:

Мне кажется как мы с тобою разлучились,
Что все противности на мя вооружились:
И ото всех сторон, стесненный дух томя,
Случаи лютыя стремятся здесь на мя,
И множат серца боль в неисцелимой ране.   (No. 8)

In poem No. 9, as if carrying this train of thought further, the poet makes no specific mention of love or separation; the movement toward "generalizing" becomes complete:

Терпи, моя душа, терпи различны муки,
Болезни, горести, тоску, напасти, скуки,
На все противности отверзлось серце днесь,
. . . .
Веселой мысли нет, все радости сокрылись,
Все злые случаи на мя вооружились . . .   (No. 9)

This sentiment rounds off a well-formulated progression and would be, logically, the best place to conclude the cycle. The fact that poem No. 10 reverts back to the enamored manner of the earlier poems suggests that Sumarokov may not have intended it as part of this sequence, or that he had simply not mastered the technique of effective arrangement. The remaining nine poems in Section III all treat the theme of death; while their disposition is not entirely arbitrary, the interaction of these poems is unidimensional and relatively little is gained from their co-placement. The following century produced better and more interesting groupings of elegies, but Sumarokov's efforts in this medium may well have been noticed and appreciated by his successors.

The Early Nineteenth Century (to roughly 1840)

The early nineteenth century witnessed the progressive deterioration
of the classical genre system, and this development is reflected in a
movement away from the purely generic, hierarchical organization
of poetic collections.   Already in 1803 Nikolaj Karamzin publishes a
book of lyrics with no generic subdivisions (the first volume of his
Sočinenija),[26] and in 1808 Deržavin dispenses with such rubrics in
the first tome of his collected works (although in arranging the
poems he still follows to some extent the traditional classical
model).   The poets of Aleksandr Puškin's era vacillated between
generic organization of their collections and organization by some
other set of principles, but on the whole the trend was toward the
latter.   It is indicative, for example, that Puškin's first collection
(*Stixotvorenija*, 1826) contained the sections "Élegii," "Nadpisi i
èpigrammy" and "Poslanija" (traditional classical genres), while in
his second and final collection (*Stixotvorenija*, 1829-1835), Puškin
abandoned generic categories altogether and organized his poems
under chronological headings ("1815," "1816," "1817," etc.).
Similarly, Evgenij Baratynskij, whose first book of poetry was
divided into "Élegii" and "Smes'" (*Stixotvorenija*, 1827), discarded
even these minimal generic classifications in his second and third
collections (*Stixotvorenija*, 1835; *Sumerki*, 1842).   By 1829, perhaps
because Puškin had set a precedent, it becomes acceptable to
publish books of poetry with virtually no generic headings—such
are the collections of Dmitrij Venevitinov (1829), Anton Del'vig
(1829),[27] Pavel Katenin (1832) and Nikolaj Jazykov (1833).[28] The
significance of this development for the evolution of the lyric cycle
was dramatic—editorial convention relinquished the requirement of
grouping by genre and began to sanction experimentation with
other, more organic principles of arranging poems within a
collection.

The decline of the classicism as the dominant literary current,
however, signaled much more than the possibility of new
arrangements.   In a very fundamental sense it affected the function
of lyric poetry as an esthetic medium and created an environment
in which lyric cyclization could begin to flourish—not at the
margins of an esthetic system, but at its very core.   The romantic
esthetics that replaced classicism took a different view of the
individual lyric and enhanced the importance of the cycle as an
organic means of expression.

In this regard, it is of crucial significance that the romantic (or pre-romantic) poets of the early nineteenth century shifted the focus of lyric poetry from the surrounding world to the persona of the poet. In most basic terms, what distinguished romanticism from classicism was that it valued the poetic subject above all and had as its principal interest the poet's inner, emotional experience. As Gukovskij writes:

> Romanticism proposed the subject itself as the only object of analysis and description,—and the subject appeared before it both as an idea and as a complex, living and quite real psychological organism. . . . This discovery was directed against the discipline of classicism, which had ignored the concrete individual.[29]

Vasilij Žukovskij captured the spirit of the new movement in 1811, when he wrote for *Vestnik Evropy*: "The poet of the most recent time always depicts objects in relation to himself: he is not pervaded by them, nor does he surrender himself to it [*sic*] completely; he uses it in order to depict himself."[30] This view differs radically from that held by most eighteenth-century poets; for them, as a rule, the lyric experience had value only to the degree that it invested external phenomena with esthetic significance: expansive vistas, monarchs, military victories, the wonders of the heavens. The poet's own persona was not of intrinsic interest and justified its own presence only as a conduit to what lay beyond. Hence the opening lines of Lomonosov's "Oda na vzjatie Xotina" would serve as a fitting epigraph to a study of the dialectic operative in the imagination of the neo-classicist poet:

> Восторг внезапный ум пленил,
> Ведет на верьх горы высокой...

For the romantic poet the lyric impulse, by contrast, was narcissistic; its trajectory continually pointed back to the poet himself, who was, in essence, the only category of immanent consequence. This is why Konstantin Batjuškov could preface his volume of verse (*Opyty v stixax i proze*, 1817) with the following greeting:

К ДРУЗЬЯМ

> Вот список мой стихов,
> Который дружеству быть может драгоценен.
> Я добрым гением уверен,
> Что в сем дедале рифм и слов

Недостает искусства:
Но дружество найдет мои в замену чувства—
Историю моих страстей...

The statement that a body of poetry could comprise "a history of ones passions" was daring for Batjuškov's time—not because it was an idea unique to his esthetic method, but because it disclosed, apparently for the first time, a phenomenon that was maturing in the romantic era, namely the inherent cyclicality of a poetry whose only real subject was the personality and experience of the poet.   In effect Batjuškov was declaring the existence of his "lyric hero," whose image was the main integrating principle of his entire lyric output.[31]   As Lidija Ginzburg points out, the concept of the lyric hero develops as a concomitant to the dissolution of classical esthetics.[32]   For the classicist every genre had its traditional lyric "I"; the image of the poet changed as he moved from one genre to another. By contrast, "one of the main features of the romantic system in poetry is the absolute unity of the [lyric] hero's romantic personality."[33]   The lyric hero was the natural product of a method that attributed to the poet's image "certain consistent   features—biographical,   psychological,   narrative [sjužetnymi]."[34]

As Ginzburg suggests, creation of a lyric hero entailed the principle of "biographical" as well as "psychological" consistency —the poet could not just depict personality at one separate moment, he had to convey also a linkage of moments, a sense of "narrative" development.   Indeed it is true that poets who cultivated the image of a lyric hero (and virtually every important poet at this time does so to some degree) created the impression that a single life "story" underlies and unifies many of their separate lyrics.   In certain poets the sense of integral biography is more pronounced than in others.   Gukovskij is not unjustified, for instance, in perceiving Žukovskij's lyrics, taken *in toto*, as something approaching "a novel of the soul":

> The body of Žukovskij's work, which had created a
> character, is fused into a certain unity wherein separate
> works serve as elements, parts that complement each
> other, while all of them together emerge as a certain
> novel of the soul; this was the first sketch of the first
> psychological novel in Russian literature, without whose
> experience the realistic novel itself could not have been

constructed. Moreover, the novel, like the image of its
hero does not materialize simply as the sum of its
separate parts (the poems) but emerges as their organic
totality.[35]

To be sure, there is an element of exaggeration here, but also a
good deal of truth. Boris Èjxenbaum makes a similar observation
about the poetry of Denis Davydov, wherein the lyric hero is also
quite prominent:

Davydov continues the line of the epoch's small genres
. . . , but he does so in such a way that they are
combined into a single biographical cycle; they comprise
a certain kind of narrative poem [poèma] about routine
military life, at the center of which stands the author's
own portrait.[36]

It is of this same tendency that Puškin writes in *Evgenij Onegin*,
apropos of Jazykov's poetry:

Так ты, Языков вдохновенный,
В порывах сердца своего,
Поешь бог ведает кого,
И свод элегий драгоценный
Представит некогда тебе
Всю повесть о твоей судьбе.   (IV, xxxi)[37]

Here Puškin, as if echoing Batjuškov's "istorija moix strastej,"
ascertains quite accurately the inherent cyclicality running through
the separate lyrics of a romantic poet. Whether aware or unaware
of his poems' interconnection, he cannot do otherwise than write
"the whole tale of his own fate."

The presence of inherent cyclicality created the potential for
meaningful cyclization, but early in the century Russian poets did
not exploit this potential to its full degree. At this stage in its
development the lyric cycle is still emerging from and overcoming
the limitations of genre, and poets are only beginning to explore
ways of enhancing the interaction of their poems. Nor does such
enhancement always appear to be an important goal. Indeed, it is
often difficult to ascertain the rationale that underlies a particular
arrangement (rarely was chronology a significant factor, even when
poems were subscribed with their dates). At times poems seem to
be juxtaposed for no other reason than a common motif, mood or
addressee. Sometimes it even seems that poets (or their editors)
were striving to produce not meaningful juxtaposition, but variety,

so as not to bore the reader who chose to read the poems in sequence; here the ordering principle is not unlike that used today on popular record albums (slow song, fast song, instrumental, etc.). Even Puškin, who proved to be a cyclist of major importance, made a note to himself or to his editors (apparently apropos of the section "Smes'" in *Stixotvorenija*, 1826): "In general one ought to maintain *a certain variety* in the disposition of items."[38] With certain exceptions the precise ordering of poems did not become important for the romantic poets until the end of the 1820's; before that time there seems to have been an inclination to indulge the image of a romantic's whimsicality by dispersing poems in what would appear to be a careless manner. The only meticulous arrangements tend to be found at the very beginning or ending of a cycle, where it was the practice to place summational or programmatic statements. This explains why episodic and diaristic plot cycles are virtually non-existent in the first quarter of the century: poets were not arranging their lyrics to create a narrative dynamic.

We encounter, however, in certain instances an archetypal plot dynamic developing independently of the poems' sequence. Typically, these were cycles of elegies (or short elegiac pieces) that presented the lyric hero's pre-history in variations of one basic pattern.

An excellent example is the section "Romansy i pesni" in Žukovskij's *Stixotvorenija* (Volume I, 1815).[39] Most of the eighteen poems in this cycle are derived from a single biographical archetype that contains the following stages: 1) a period of joy and love (distant past); 2) an episode in which the above are lost (more recent past); and 3) a period of melancholy, hopelessness (present). "Mečty" ("Počto tak rano izmenila . . .") (No. 17), which is located perhaps deliberately near the end of the grouping, gives the archetype in full, but most of the remaining poems reproduce it only partially or represent one of its stages. It is interesting that in several instances the biographical prehistory is mediated through a first-person role player not strictly identifiable as the lyric hero.[40] Thus poem No. 1 ("Toska po milom") is the monologue of a maiden pining the loss of love and happiness; in No. 5 ("Pesn' Araba nad mogiloju konja") the archetypal pattern is represented in the history of a horseman's relationship with a beloved steed; No. 15 ("Uznik k motylku") dramatizes the situation of a prisoner who occupies the third stage of the archetype. These poems fit the established pattern so closely that they function not as deviations from but rather psychological projections of the lyric hero's dilemma. Admittedly, Žukovskij's biographical archetype is conventional to the extreme. It conforms to what R.V. Iezuitova calls "the fixed plot outline of the pre-romantic elegy": "recollection by the hero of bright, clear, but irrevocably forfeited days, languor over which alternates with awareness of the joyless present and future that in turn gives rise to a feeling of gloom and sadness."[41] This plot became so stereotyped that Vil'gel'm Kjuxel'beker would complain in 1824: "Judging by our Childe-Harolds who have barely emerged from their diapers, one might think that in Russia poets are already old men when they are born."[42] Nevertheless, Žukovskij's choice of poems and the psychological emphases he makes in them give his cycle a unique cumulative impact.

A richer and more original cycle of the same type is Batjuškov's "Èlegii" (1817), the first section of verse in his *Opyty*.[43] As noted earlier, these poems are immediately preceded by an allusion to "istorija moix strastej," but in "Èlegii" the sequence of poems does not in any way mimic narrative. Instead we find an archetypal history of the lyric hero in separate variations. The basic pattern differs little from Žukovskij's in that youthful happiness is followed by disillusionment, but Batjuškov's model is both more complex and biographically more concrete. There are in fact really two archetypes—one spiritual-emotional, the other biographical-topographical—that correspond to and complement each other:

Spiritual-Emotional	*Biographical-topographical*
A. *Ideal past* (a time of love, friendship, joy, passion and poetic inspiration)	(1) *Hero is in his homeland*
	(2) *Hero leaves his homeland and goes abroad* (to war or simply to travel in foreign lands)
B. *Time of disillusionment and spiritual trials*	(3) *Events threaten hero's life and possibility of return* (whether sickness, battle wounds or physical captivity)

C. *Time when happiness is* ————— *(4) Return to the homeland*
rediscovered (positive   (envisioned or actualized)
variant) or *lost irretriev-*
ably (negative variant)

The various stages or events in the biographical archetype correspond quite closely to real experiences in the life of Batjuškov, who participated in three military campaigns and was seriously wounded in 1807. Indeed, Batjuškov places less distance between himself and his lyric hero than Žukovskij, individuates him to a much greater degree and gives his experience more biographical immediacy.[44]   Moreover, the hero's emotional development, though it follows certain stereotypical stages, is ultimately open-ended. The final stage in the spiritual archetype is not entirely predictable: in some poems it is melancholic, in others it is optimistic, in still others it is a bittersweet combination of the two strains.   In reading Batjuškov's cycle one senses a unity of story line, but at the same time a certain incompleteness or ambivalence of the denouement.   While such ambiguity is not without esthetic effect, the cycle as a whole, despite what is a remarkable integrity for this time, does not really resolve the problem of the poems' separateness.   Had Batjuškov not gone insane in 1821, he might well have developed into an accomplished cyclic poet.[45]

The practice of grouping together poems that focus on the lyric hero's prehistory was apparently not unnoticed by poets whose collections appeared somewhat later.   The first five lyric poems in Nikolaj Gnedič's *Stixotvorenija* (1832) manifest a certain coherence of this type,[46] as do the first ten poems in Jazykov's *Stixotvorenija* (1833).[47]   In the case of Denis Davydov (1832), a series of eleven poems about military life even seem to be arranged with an eye toward episodic sequentiality; in them unfolds the life story of an aging hussar from his early carefree years to middle age and nostalgia for the past.[48]   It is interesting, moreover, that both Davydov and Jazykov create highly unified dramatic-situational cycles from three short poems about a romantic relationship—a genre cultivated later by Nekrasov, Grigor'ev, Blok and Axmatova.

Puškin occupies a curious place in the history of the lyric cycle.   On one hand, he was without question the foremost master of the cyclic form in his time, an innovator who anticipated many techniques of cyclization developed some sixty or seventy years later by the symbolists.   On the other hand, his influence as a cyclist appears to have been negligible—in part, perhaps, because his experiments were simply too far ahead of his time to be appreciated by his contemporaries; but more importantly because the bulk of his cyclic legacy was unknown to the public. Judging from editions of Puškin's poetry published after his death in 1837, he was the author of only two cycles—"Podražanija Koranu" and "Pesni zapadnyx slavjan"—the second of which cannot be considered a *lyric* cycle in the strict sense. Even those editions which appeared during his lifetime reproduce only partially the cyclic and quasi-cyclic groupings he made in the privacy of his creative workshop. This is why the discovery of Puškin as a cyclic poet is the doing not of other poets, but of academic researchers.

Most of the credit for this discovery belongs to Nikolaj Izmajlov, who in 1958 demonstrated that cyclization is a far more widespread phenomenon in Puškin than had previously been thought. According to Izmajlov, Puškin was constantly looking for "new principles of compiling lyric collections" and began very early, even in the 1826 collection, to arrange poems so as to enhance "their internal connection."[49] This principle becomes even stronger in 1829, when Puškin publishes the first two parts of his multi-volume edition and reaches its maximum manifestation in the third part (1832), where we find "definite thematic-ideational and at the same time (although not always) formally unified groupings that comprise more or less well-formulated 'cycles'."[50]

The problem with studying the arrangement of poems in Puškin's collections, however, is that the author played only a participatory role in their compilation (this fact is apparently overlooked by Izmajlov). In many instances Puškin left the choice and disposition of poems up to his editors, and when he did outline a particular order, his instructions were frequently overruled. Puškin sent the original plan for the 1826 edition, for example, to his brother Lev and to P. A. Pletnev, with the proxy "Print all this in the order that you wish" and "If other [poems] are found, print them."[51] Subsequently, he made certain emendations in the plan that was returned to him, which was already radically different from the design he had first outlined.[52] Even this revised list, however, which is apparently the one Puškin gave final approval, differs from the 1826 edition itself, so that further changes in the volume's formulation must have been made without consulting Puškin. Existing evidence suggests that compilation of *Stixotvorenija* (1829-1835) followed a similar pattern.

Puškin's printed collections, therefore, are not an entirely reliable guide to principles of cyclization Puškin may or may not have been developing. For this reason it makes sense to examine those groupings which we know for certain belong to Puškin. If we do so, it becomes apparent that the cycle was evolving in Puškin differently from his contemporaries—partially along paths traveled by his antecedents, partially in new directions which, ultimately, were blocked by his death.

In none of the lists prepared for the 1826 collection is there any grouping that contains an archetypal pre-history of the lyric hero, as we saw in Žukovskij, Batjuškov and others; there is however, "Podražanija Koranu" (1824), a cycle of nine poems which to some extent follow the eighteenth-century tradition of the spiritual ode. Here too there is a certain uniformity of theme and situation predetermined by the very nature of the genre (Allah communing with his prophet), but the grouping is unified on a more elemental level that no Russian poet before Puškin had ventured to explore. I am speaking not just of a conceptual unity that embraces all the poems at once, but of a unity that arises from conceptual interpenetration of separate poems and manifests itself as ongoing process. That is to say that the unifying principle of Puškin's cycle is not so much a summarizable theme or idea but the interprojection of meaning from poem to poem. The cycle enlists the reader's participation in a dynamic interplay.[53]

The mechanism that makes this possible is two-sided. On one hand Puškin provides a text whose conceptual unity is not readily apparent. The poems do not deal with one single theme; they do not have a common plot, nor even really a single concrete dramatic premise; nor are they derived from a common sura in the Koran.[54] Evidently, Puškin himself did not find the grouping easily tractable.[55] On the other hand, numerous thematic strands interlace the cycle, manifesting themselves on the level of a repeated lexeme, word or motif. In turn these equivalencies invite comparison and contrast of the textual segments to which they belong, the effect being that these segments become mutually informing. In a sense these equivalencies suggest ways in which the reader can construct new juxtapositions, new "texts" from the raw material available in a cycle. Hence a semantic gesture initiated in one poem can be completed in another:

А вы, о гости Магомета,
Стекаясь к вечери его,

Брегитесь суетами света
<u>Смутить</u> пророка моего.   (II)

———————

<u>Смутясь</u>, нахмурился пророк,
Слепца послышав приближенье:
Бежит, да не дерзнет порок
Ему являть недоуменье.   (III)

Moreover, repetition of a motif can give it contextual meaning. In
the passage about the "blind man" quoted above, one may
interpret the word "slepec" literally as in the Koran passage from
which it is derived, but the image acquires an additional,
metaphorical meaning from treatment of this motif elsewhere in the
cycle, where "blindness" is an attribute of imperfect faith:

Он милосерд: он Магомету
Открыл сияющий Коран,
Да притечем и мы ко свету,
И да падет с очей туман.   (V)

———————

И путник усталый на бога роптал:
. . . .
И зноем и пылью тягчимые очи
С тоской безнадежной водил он вокруг.   (IX)

The effect may be that the situation in one poem converges with
that in another, thus generating meaningful ambiguities.   This is
the case in poems I and IX, between which motivic and lexical
equivalencies are especially prominent:

I	IX
Кого же в <u>сень успокоенья</u> Я ввел, главу его любя, И <u>скрыл</u> от зоркого гоненья	Он жаждой томился и <u>тени</u> <u>алкал</u>. . . . . И кладез <u>под</u> <u>пальмою</u> видит он вдруг
<u>Стезею</u> правды бодро следуй. . .	И <u>путник</u> усталый. . . . . И с богом он дале пускается в <u>путь</u>.
Не я ль в день <u>жажды напоил</u> Тебя?	Он <u>жаждой</u> томился. . . И <u>жадно холодной струей освежил</u> Горевшие тяжко язык и зеницы.
Дрожащей твари проповедуй	Рыдая, <u>дрожащей</u> главою поник.
. . . <u>главу</u> его любя . . .	. . . . .главою поник.

Клянуся <u>утренней</u> звездой.

. . . <u>пустынными</u> <u>водами</u>.

. . . . . . .уж солнце высоко
На <u>утреннем</u> небе сияло вчера!
С <u>утра</u> я глубоко проспал до <u>утра</u>.

В <u>пустыне</u> блуждая. . . . .
. . . .
Иссяк и засохнул в <u>пустыне</u>
    <u>безводной</u>.

This convergence is significant because it suggests that the traveler who forsakes Allah in IX is not just an allegorical everyman but, more specifically, the alter ego of the prophet. This in turn affects the resonance of the whole cycle, since it forefronts all intimations that the prophet's faith is less than secure. It is impossible to agree with S. A. Fomičev, therefore, that "the lyric hero of Puškin's cycle does not waver for an instant in his motives, which are from the outset righteous."[56] To the contrary, the cycle is perhaps foremost a confession of spiritual vacillation if we consider that poem I, in retrospect, carries the effect of a divine reprimand addressed to a prophet who has just expressed discontent (the words "Net, ne pokinul ja tebja" must be in answer to the unstated accusation "Ty menja pokinul"); the prophet can easily be distracted from Allah's work ("Bregites' suetami sveta/Smutit' proroka moego") (II); he is too proud to bring Allah's words to the "blind man" (III); he includes himself among the spiritually "blind" ("Da pritečem i my ko svetu,/I da padet s očej tuman") (V); and he is subject to evil dreams ("prorok, udali. . .Lukavye sny")(VII). Even poem IV, wherein the prophet's voice is thoroughly righteous, indirectly supports the idea that "Podražanija Koranu" is in essence about the prophet's own malecontent:

С тобою древле, о всесильный,
Могучий состязаться мнил,
Безумный гордостью обильный;
Но ты, господь, его смирил.   (IV)

Within the context of this poem the image of the rebellious "mogučij" cannot possibly apply to the prophet, who is the speaker; but in the larger context of the cycle it applies perhaps to him above all others. Similarly, every other poem in the cycle can be read in two ways—either as closed text, or as text whose meaning is a function of cyclic interaction. The precarious balance between these different, but equally valid approaches constitutes the cycle's principal esthetic dynamic.

The other groupings Puškin made in anticipation of the 1826

edition are purely generic in nature ("Èlegii," "Èpigrammy i nadpisi," "Podražanija drevnim," "Poslanija").[57] In preparing the 1829-1835 edition, Puškin still followed a generic principle in the groupings "Tri soneta" and "Èksametry,"[58] but more characteristically his approach is thematic. As Izmajlov noted, the first five poems in a list made (evidently) in September 1831 ("Brožu li ja vdol' ulic šumnyx," "Ja vas uznal, o moj orakul," "Primety," "Čto v imeni tebe moem?", "Kogda tvoi mladye leta") are thematically related, as are three poems closer to the end of the list that Izmajlov calls the "farewell cycle" ("Proščanie," "Zaklinanie," "Dlja beregov otčizny dal'noj").[59]

None of these, however, is as interesting estetically as the so-called "Caucasian Cycle," whose precise formulation Puškin arrived at only gradually, over a period of seven years (1830-1836). The final version, outlined in a list prepared in 1836 for an unrealized collection of poetry, contains nine poems entitled "Stixi sočinennye vo vremja putešestvija (1829)": 1) "Dorožnye žaloby"; 2) "Kalmyčke"; 3) "Na xolmax Gruzii ležit nočnaja mgla. . ."; 4) "Monastyr' na Kazbeke"; 5) "Obval"; 6) "Kavkaz"; 7) "Iz Gafiza"; 8) "Delibas"; 9) "Don."[60] As Izmajlov indicates, the order of poems parallels Puškin's journey to the Caucasus as related in "Putešestvie v Arzrum." In this regard, the cycle resembles a travel diary and represents, apparently, the first example of such a cycle in Russian literature. More interesting, however, is the degree of contextuality, particularly in the median poems (Nos. 4-6), which form something of a triptych. As in "Podražanija Koranu," interpenetration of meaning occurs via repetition of certain motifs which acquire contextual significance. In this case a number of words and lexemes appear in all three of the poems: *b(e)reg, gora, nad,* and *pod* (preposition or prefix). Others appear in two of the three: *veršina* (poems 5, 6); *vys-* (4, 6); *mčat'sja* (5, 6); *nebo* (4, 5); *obval* (5, 6); *orel* (5, 6); *parit'* (4, 6); *svirep-* (5, 6); *smir-* (5, 6); *tesn-* (5, 6); *uščele* (4, 6) and *šum-* (5, 6). To be sure, not all of these are equally significant, but quite prominent among them are those motifs which belong to the semantic field "height" and, more generally, the semantic category "up vs. down" (*gora, nad, pod, veršina, vys-, nebo, parit',* and perhaps *orel*). This is important because in the first of the median poems this category carries symbolic significance:

МОНАСТЫРЬ НА КАЗБЕКЕ

Высоко над семьею гор,
Казбек, твой царственный шатер
Сияет вечными лучами.
Твой монастырь за облаками,
Как в небе реющий ковчег,
Парит, чуть видный, над горами.

Далекий, вожделенный брег!
Туда б, сказав прости ущелью,
Подняться к вольной вышине!
Туда б, в заоблачную келью,
В соседство бога скрыться мне!..   (No. 4)

The symbolic connotations of the lofty monastery (salvation, freedom) carry over into the next two poems, where the image of the river Terek becomes an unmistakable analogue to the poet's yearning for spiritual emancipation. Poems Nos. 5 and 6 provide as if conflicting resolutions to the poet's dilemma; if in No. 5 the river escapes confinement, in No. 6 its efforts to do so are thwarted:

Вдруг, истощась и присмирев,
О Терек, ты прервал свой рев;
Но задних волн упорный гнев
Прошиб снега...
Ты затопил, освирепев,
Свои брега.   (No. 5)

Играет и воет, как зверь молодой,
Завидевший пищу из клетки железной;
И бьется о берег в вражде бесполезной
И лижет утесу голодной волной...
Вотще! нет ни пищи ему, ни отрады:
Теснят его грозно немые громады.   (No. 6)

It would appear too that the associations of the river with the poet's aspiration for freedom are not lacking in the cycle's last poem ("Don"):

Блеща средь полей широких,
Вон он льется!.. Здравствуй, Дон!
. . . .

Отдохнув от злой погони,
Чуя родину свою,
Пьют уже донские кони
Арпачайскую струю.   (No. 9)

Such resonances contribute to the impression that Puškin's cycle is
not so much a travel diary as a spiritual journey whose landmarks
are symbolic encounters.

Puškin's "Lyric Cycle of 1836," which was analyzed in depth
in the preceding chapter, is a cyclic achievement without equal in
the nineteenth century and perhaps in all Russian poetry. There is
no need to recapitulate what was said before. It will suffice to
point out that it represents, even if one were to discard its
hypothetical segments, an advanced stage in the development of
techniques which are manifest already in "Podražanija
Koranu" —namely, contextual enrichment of the word's connotative
aureole and creation of a semantic system unique to the individual
grouping. Neither this cycle, nor the "Caucasian Cycle," however,
were published in the precise configuration designated by the poet.
This circumstance severely limited the influence Puškin had as a
cyclist on his contemporaries and successors.

The only poet of Puškin's time who rivals his cyclic
achievement, albeit in a quite different way, is Baratynskij.[61] He
at least lived long enough to insure that his greatest contribution
to cyclization (*Sumerki*, 1842) reached the public eye, and for this
reason he was more influential than Puškin on the development of
the cycle in the latter half of the nineteenth century. Baratynskij,
of course, was a poet of much narrower range than Puškin.
Throughout his career he focused on a small body of themes, most
notably poetic creativity, the human condition (from a broad
philosophical perspective) and man's relation to nature (in the
spirit of Schelling's *Naturphilosophie*). Even his love poetry, like
Tjutčev's, is often refracted through the prism of his philosophical
concerns. What was, however, in one respect the poet's limitation,
in another respect opened new possibilities. As might be expected
when a poet develops and reworks the same core of ideas over a
period of many years, Baratynskij's lyrics possess a certain intrinsic
cyclicality. In and of itself this does not create lyric cycles but
may, as in Baratynskij's case, provide the esthetic rationale for
doing so.

Even in Baratynskij's first collection (*Stixotvorenija*, 1827) the arrangement and grouping of poems clearly has an artistic function. Still adhering to the generic tradition, Baratynskij divides the volume into two sections, "Èlegii" and "Smes'," the first of which is subdivided into three "books" (Kniga pervaja, Kniga vtoraja, Kniga tret'ja).[62] The first "book," containing eight poems, focuses on a set of related philosophical problems which are left unresolved or, more accurately, are resolved contradictively in different poems, so that while not making a coherent philosophical statement, it poses a coherent existential question. What emerges is the image of a poet wrestling with certain choices: passion *vs.* emotional detachment, glory *vs.* obscurity, living life with abandon *vs.* life sobered by awareness of death, agitation *vs.* peace, hope *vs.* despair. All of these can be summarized under the semantic opposition "activity *vs.* inactivity," which is the central issue of Baratynskij's oeuvre. The best indication that this issue is left unresolved in the cycle is that its last two poems ("Dve doli" and "Burja") are polemically juxtaposed; they advocate diametrically opposite world-views. The second "book" is the least unified of the three and offers little interest as a cycle. The third, however, is integrated by an episodic plot line which traces a generalized romantic relationship through various stages and ends with abnegation of erotic love. The title of the last poem ("Èpilog") suggests the grouping's narrative character. Significantly, the outcome of the love drama is directly related to the existential dilemma outlined in the first "book"; in renouncing love, the poet also gives preference to "inactivity":

> Охота петь уж не владеет мною,
> Она прошла, погасла, как любовь.
> Опять любить, играть струнами вновь
> Желал бы я, но утомлен душою?
> Иль жить нельзя отрадою иною?
> С бездействием любезен мне союз...
>
> ("Эпилог")

This final gesture, which is prepared in preceding poems by echoes of the philosophical questions in "book one," is particularly noteworthy because it represents the first instance in Russian poetry of conceptual interaction *between* cycles—a phenomenon which became common only in the symbolist era.

Baratynskij's *Stixtvorenija* (1835) contributed little to cyclization that was new,[63] but his *Sumerki* (1842) is a landmark

in the history of the cycle.   This collection of twenty-six poems
(twenty-seven in the uncensored manuscript) is the best integrated
book of poetry published in Russia to date, and in this respect it
anticipates the symbolists' demand for unities that embrace whole
volumes of lyrics.   The very title is an innovation.   To be sure,
descriptive titles had appeared before (Fet's *Liričeskij panteon* and
Nekrasov's *Mečty i zvuki* in 1840), but Baratynskij's was the first
to suggest the unique mood of an entire collection.   Moreover, the
subtitle "Sočinen*ie*" held forth the promise that together the poems
constitute a single "composition."   This promise is very nearly
fulfilled.

Essentially, what unifies *Sumerki* is its sustained focus on the
themes of time and the poet and the way it consistently manages
to correlate the two.   The correlation is perhaps most conspicuous
in those poems that trace the lyric hero's spiritual development;
there we find basically one degenerative pattern: the poet's early
days are characterized by animation, hope and friendship, while his
later years give way to spiritual paralysis and social alienation.
Different variations of this pattern occur in "Bokal," "Byli buri,
nepogody...", "Na čto vy dni!.." and the in diptych created by the
juxtaposition of "Zdravstvuj, otrok sladkoglasnyj!.." and "Čto za
zvuki?..." These last two poems (Nos. 20-21) depict, respectively, a
budding poet producing his first ecstatic melodies and an aged poet
whose song evokes ridicule from the surrounding crowd.   Reading
Sumerki, one is inclined to recall the words "istorija moix strastej"
in Batuškov's *Opyty*, and it may not be accidental that the first
poem in Baratynskij's collection seems to echo his predecessor's
phrase:

> Вам приношу я песнопенья,
> Где отразилась жизнь моя...

Unlike Batjuškov, however, Baratynskij is as much concerned
with the "biography" of civilization as he is with the life history of
the poet.   As E. N. Kuprejanova observes, the title "Sumerki"
"referred to the 'twilight' of the poet's own life and creative career.
But at the same time it contained a suggestion of something
greater—the sunset of spiritual life for all humanity, first and
foremost of its esthetic culture."[64]   Indeed, many poems deal with
the obsolescence of poetry in an age of enlightened materialism; for
the cycle as a whole, therefore, the opening lines of "Poslednij
poèt" carry programmatic significance:

Век шествует путем своим железным,
В сердцах корысть, и общая мечта
Час от часу насущным и полезным
Отчетливей, бесстыдней занята.
Исчезнули при свете просвещенья
Поэзии ребяческие сны,
И не о ней хлопочут поколенья,
Промышленным заботам преданы.

Here and elsewhere in *Sumerki* historical time continually acts to the detriment not only of the poet, but of poetry and esthetic values in general. Hence in "Snačala mysl', vološčena..." (No. 18) the subtlety and spareness of poetry are replaced by prose's wordiness and the vulgarity of polemic journalism:

Сначала мысль, воплощена
В поэму сжатую поэта,
Как дева юная, темна
Для невнимательного света;
Потом, осмелившись, она
Уже увертлива, речиста,
Со всех сторон своих видна,
Как искушенная жена
В свободной прозе романиста;
Болтунья старая, затем
Она, подъемля крик нахальной,
Плодит в полемике журнальной
Давно уж ведомое всем.

In the broadest sense, *Sumerki* is a requiem for Russian poetry's Golden Age, which by 1842 (the year Gogol's *Dead Souls* appeared) had most certainly come to an end. All of the poems in *Sumerki*, whether or not they treat directly the themes of time and the poet, are allied implicitly to them via this contextual aim.

The Middle and the Latter Half of the Nineteenth Century (to the early 1890's)

By the end of Puškin's era, the practice of grouping poems by genre, while not disappearing entirely, had become all but obsolete. Puškin and his contemporaries, however, despite the steps they took toward contextualizing separate lyrics, had not produced a body of cyclic techniques that was widely accepted and consistently applied. While ending the strangle hold of a rigid genre system, they had not canonized a new set of cyclic principles to take its place. This task was undertaken by the generation of poets that followed.

The 1840's witness a rapid growth in the popularity of the lyric cycle and an almost spontaneous proliferation of cyclic types and subtypes, many of which were hitherto unknown in Russian poetry. By the 1850's there is already a well-defined cyclic repertoire that remains fairly constant until the end of the century.

By far the most prominant place in this repertoire is occupied by dramatic-situational cycles and plot cycles of the episodic or diaristic type. To the former category belong Apollon Grigor'ev's "Dva soneta" (1846), examined in the preceding chapter, and two cycles by Nekrasov which, despite their generic titles are masterpieces of dramatic cyclization. The first, "Poslednii èlegii" (published for the first time in his *Stixotvorenija*, 1856), is remarkable for the way it revitalizes the traditional metaphor of the poet's path ("put'") and conveys the subtle conflict of emotions experienced by the poet in anticipation of death. The second, "Tri èlegii" (1874), focuses on a romantic relationship and derives from the poems' interaction a unique expression of anguish at the loss of a beloved woman. Turgenev's "Variacii" (1845) also dramatizes the hopeless separation of lovers; one indication of its contextuality is that the last poem ("Utro tumannoe, utro sedoe..."), which has been made into a popular song and is frequently anthologized, loses much of its impact when extracted from its cyclic environment. In more or less the same vein is Apollon Majkov's "Iz prošlogo" (*Stixotvorenija. Kniga vtoraja*, 1858), which portrays in vivid detail a tender, loving relationship between the poet and his beloved without suggesting any development of plot.

Without doubt the outstanding acheivement in this period with regard to the plot cycle is Grigor'ev's "Bor'ba" (1857). This grouping of eighteen poems approaches narrative in the sequential arrangement of its segments: it is not difficult to trace the story of love from its initial stages to a denouement in which the lyric hero is rejected for a rival. In itself, however, the episodic plot is not the most significant feature of Grigor'ev's cycle, since such a dynamic is manifest in many cycles of this period.[65] What makes "Bor'ba" remarkable is the depth and unity of characterization; in this respect it is rivaled within this period only by Aleksej

Apuxtin's "God v monastyre" (1886).

A subtype of the dramatic-situational cycle that became quite popular in the middle of the nineteenth century might perhaps best be called the *memory cycle*. Memory cycles contain two dramatic premises, one framed inside the other. The outer or framing situation is a function of the present, while the inner or core situation is an experience (usually a love affair) recalled from the past. Typically, there is a dynamic interrelationship between the two, and the cycle chronicles the lyric hero's effort either to resurrect or to suppress a reminiscence which is partially obscured by the passage of time. In Grigor'ev's "Starye pesni, starye skazki" (1846), for instance, the recollection of a painful romantic relationship is triggered by contemplation of an "old book," apparently a forgotten album of poems:

> Книга старинная, книга забытая,
> > Ты ли попалась мне вновь—
> Глупая книга, слезами облитая
> В годы, когда, для любви не закрытая,
> > Душа понимала любовь!
> . . . .
> Что бы то ни было, — книга забытая,
> > О, не буди, не тревожь
> Муки заснувшие, раны закрытые...
> Прочь твои пятна, годами не смытые,
> > И прочь твоя сладкая ложь!   (No. 1)

In the cycle's median poems this wish to suppress memory is unrealized; the poet reexperiences the pain of love and separation. In the last poem, the poet acknowledges regretfully his inability to forget and sees potential relief from his memories only in universal annihilation:

> Или за миром призрачных явлений
> Нам тщетно суждено, бесплодно жизнь губя,
> > Искать себя, искать тебя,
> О разрушения зиждительного гений?
> Пора, пора тебе, о демон мировой,
> > Разбить последние оплоты
> И кончить весь расчет с дряхлеющей землей...
>
> Уже совершены подземные работы,
> Основы сущего подкопаны давно...

Давно создание творцом осуждено,
        Чего ж ты ждешь еще?..   (No. 6)

Apuxtin's "Vesennie pesni" (1860) is similar in concept and design
to Grigor'ev's cycle and may even be a conscious polemic with it.
Here the painful reminiscence is triggered by the onset of spring,
but the ending is optimistic; in the final poem, personified spring
offers consolation for the very memories it stirred up:

Я знаю: любовь незабвенна...
Но слушай: тебе я верна,
Моя красота неизменна,
Мне вечная юность дана!

. . . .

Приду я... На душу больную
Навею чудесные сны
И язвы легко уврачую
Твоей безрассудной весны!   (No. 6)[66]

By contrast, positive reminiscences are the subject of Ogarev's
"Vospominanija detstva" (1854-59).   Here the poet strives to
preserve in his memory and make part of the present a series of
enchanting scenes from a long-forgotten childhood; the framing
situation is mentioned only at the very perimeters of the cycle:

Мне детство предстает, как в утреннем тумане
Долина мирная . . . .   (No. 1)

О! погодите же, вживитесь в жизнь мою—
Давно минувшего приветливые тени!..
Но вы уноситесь... И я один стою
И слышу вечных волн тоскующие пени.   (No. 7)

The cyclic repertoire also includes a wide assortment of
thematic-motivic groupings, the most popular among them being
those unified by a particular setting or series of locales encountered
on a journey.   The *locale cycle* is the favorite genre of Majkov,
whose "Očerki Rima" (1847), "Neopolitanskij al'bom" (1862), "V
stepjax" (1870) and "U Mramornogo morja" (1888) are the most
typical, though not the most successful representatives of this type.
To the same category belong Jakov Polonskij's "Zakavkaz'e"
(1846-51), Aleksej Tolstoj's "Krymskie očerki" (1867) and
Konstantin Slučevskij's "Murmanskie otgoloski" (1889), although

these groupings too are only modest achievements in terms of their contextual unity.   More successful in this regard are Turgenev's "Derevnja" (1847) and Apuxtin's "Derevenskie očerki" (1859), which, unlike most of those mentioned above, have as their setting the native landscape of central Russia.

By far the most interesting grouping of this kind is Karolina Pavlova's "Fantasmogorii" (1863), which represents a fusion of the locale cycle and the memory cycle.   In one sense "Fantasmogorii" is a realistic diary of the poet's travels abroad (Constantinople, Venice, Dresden, Marseilles), but on a deeper level the journey is symbolic.   Movement forward is at first seen as a means of achieving oblivion:

> Так бы нестись, обо всем забывая,
> В споре с насилием вьюги и вод,
> Вечно к брегам небывалого края,
> С вечною верой, вперед и вперед!   (No. 2)

Ironically, however, the journey continually serves a mnemonic function, causing the lyric heroine to refocus on the painful experiences she seeks to forget.   Thus movement forward becomes symbolically ambiguous—geographically it signals progress, but on an emotive level it continually signals regress.   The paradox is captured most effectively in the cycle's last poem:

> Бегут вдоль дороги все ели густые
>   Туда, к рубежу,
> Откуда я еду, туда, где Россия;
>   Я вслед им гляжу.
> . . . .
> К чему же мне слушать, как шепчутся ели,
>   Все мимо скользя?—
> О чем мне напомнить они б ни сумели,—
>   Вернуться нельзя!   (No. 13)

The road forward, away from Russia is simultaneously a spiritual path backward to memories which, contrary to the poet's original hope, can never be left behind.   Therein lies the dramatic paradox of this cycle, which has few equals in the period under discussion.

In some cycles the unifying principle is seasonal as well as locational.   In Turgenev's "Derevnja," for instance, the poet's return to and departure from a rural habitat is chronicled along a time coordinate from early summer to late autumn.   Majkov's

"Mgnovenija" (1858), at least the first two-thirds of it, is structured in much the same way. The poet most closely associated with *season cycles* proper, however, is Afanasij Fet. "Snega," a collection of winter scenes, first appears in his *Stixotvorenija* (1850) and is republished in each subsequent edition of his poetry, although the choice of poems is not always identical. A cycle entitled "Vesna" is included in Fet's *Stixotvorenija* (1863) and in *Večernie ogni I* (1883). In a list prepared just before his death for what was to be the final, authoritative edition of his poetry, Fet introduced two new sections, "Leto" and "Osen'," thus providing a full complement of seasonal groupings.

The cyclic repertoire contains a number of other important, but less common types: 1) philosophical meditations, such as Ogarev's "Monologi" (1856) and Fet's "Èlegii i dumy" (1883); 2) socio-ethnographic portraits reminiscent of the "physiological sketch" in prose—Nekrasov's "Na ulice" (1863), "O pogode" (1865) and Majkov's "Žitejskie dumy" (1858); 3) "mood cycles," that is, groupings unified neither by theme, situation or plot, but by a particular quality of feeling or impressionistic concept—the section "Melodii" that appears in all of Fet's collections or the section "Fantazii" in Majkov's *Stixotvorenija* (1850).

How do we account for this sudden, widespread interest in cyclization at mid century? Undoubtedly, part of the explanation lies in the extraordinary popularity of Heinrich Heine, whose *Buch der Lieder* (1827) and *Neue Gedichte* (1844) had a powerful influence on Russian poetry from the 1840's through the 1870's.[67] These two collections form a kind of lyric diary, a poetic autobiography that contains models of almost every cyclic type prominent in Russia at the time. In the absence of a well-established native tradition, Russian poets apparently turned to Heine's poetry as a primer of cyclic technique.[68] It is indicative that most of the poets who actively developed the lyric cycle were also translators of Heine (e.g., Ogarev, Grigor'ev, Majkov, Pavlova, Fet); Majkov even created a cycle out of his own renditions of Heine ("Roman v 5-i stixotvorenijax," 1866).

Heine's example, however, would probably have been overlooked if Russian poetry had not reached a stage where the cycle fulfilled certain inherent esthetic needs. Dolgopolov is correct, therefore, when he argues that the proliferation of cycles is linked to the decline and effective disappearance of the romantic *poèma* in the middle of the century.[69] The *poèma* provided a large context for lyric expression, both in the digressions and in the very fabric of the narrative, which is typically interwoven with the author's subjective intonations.[70]   According to Dolgopolov, the lyric cycle filled a gap left by the obsolescence of the *poèma*:

> The emergence and formation of cycles of poems was caused in all likelihood by the fact that poetry continued to "require" larger poetic genres although given the degeneration of the *poèma* into a story in verse, it was forced to make do with the resources of lyric.   The lyric cycle often turned out to be just such a *poèma*, only of an extremely lyrical variety.[71]

Carrying Dolgopolov's observation a step further, one might note that the popularization of the lyric cycle and the emergence of the realistic novel occur almost simultaneously—a circumstance which may not be purely accidental. To some degree, both these forms have a common genealogy in the romantic *poèma*.   Puškin's *Evgenij Onegin*, which gave birth to the realistic novel, [72] was in the author's initial conception a monumental "*poèma*."[73]   The ongoing counterpoint between digression and narration, the continually shifting focus between author and hero, and the fragmentary mode of exposition were features Puškin's "novel in verse" inherited from the romantic *poèma*. As the novel evolved later in the nineteenth century, however, the tendency was toward elimination of these conventions of romantic style—the digressive element was suppressed, the authorial persona was concealed, and the fabric of narrative was smoothed out so that its textual seams became less obtrusive. Puškin's successors strove to vacuum out of the novel blatant manifestations of authorial subjectivity and whimsicality—above all, the lyric digressions.   By way of compensation, the digressive, subjective element of romantic narrative seems to have found a new home in the lyric cycle, an environment where it truly flourished. Moreover, just as the novel sublimated lyricism in nature description and the idiosyncratic perceptions of its individual characters, the lyric cycle sublimated the narrative element (the episodic plot) in what was ostensibly a non-narrative medium.

The interrelationship between the lyric cycle and the novel (or other prose narrative) in the mid-nineteenth century is too complex to treat exhaustively here. It is worth noting, however, that the existence of the genealogic tie between these two forms

helps explain why they manifest a certain syncretism.   It seems
not accidental, for instance, that the realistic novel, at least in its
early stages of development, resembles a cycle of fragments (e.g.,
Lermontov's *Hero of Our Time*) or a series of loosely bound
vignettes (e.g,, *Dead Souls*).   At the same time, cyclic poets of this
period often mimicked novelistic conventions quite consciously.
Grigor'ev originally subtitled his cycle "Bor'ba" "Liričeskij *roman*,"
and Majkov labeled five translations of Heine "*Roman* v 5-i
stixotvorenijax."   Ogarev   gave   the   subtitle   "Otryvki   iz
avtobiografii" to his "Buch der Liebe," and Apuxtin appended the
characterization "Otryvki iz *dnevnika*" to his "God v monastyre."
There is some truth, therefore, in K. G. Isupov's remark that the
cycle is not so much a genre per se as a form that models itself
after other genres.[74]   For the period under consideration at least,
this observation carries much validity.

Despite   the   cycle's   widespread   popularity   in   the   mid
nineteenth century, not all poets went along with the trend.   Fedor
Tjutčev, for instance, who must be ranked with Fet and Nekrasov
as one of the three great poets of this era, never cyclized his
poems, nor did he take part in compiling the only collection of his
lyrics published in his lifetime.[75]   Ivan Nikitin, a poet of lesser
stature, also abstained from cycles in both of his lyric collections
(1856, 1859).   The majority of poets used the device consistently
but sparingly, leaving the larger body of poems in any given
collection uncyclized and grouping only a smaller percentage of
them under cyclic rubrics.   Of the major poets, only Majkov
employs what might be called unbroken or continuous cyclization,
that is, the disposition of *all* poems under descriptive headings.
This practice is adopted in his third collection (1858) and adhered
to in all subsequent editions.   Fet's collections of 1850, 1856, and
1863, as well as the first volume of his *Večernie ogni* (1883) come
close to continuous cyclization, but in each there is a section of
"Miscellaneous poems" ("Raznye stixotvorenija"), whose function is
clearly non-cyclical.

The mere popularity of the cycle, however, and even the
diversity of cyclic types are not in themselves indications that
cyclization   always   served   important   esthetic   aims.   Indeed, it
frequently produced contextuality of the most superficial kind and
in many instances proved little more than an editorial convenience.
Even Majkov, the most cyclic poet of the era (judging from the
format of his collections), produced few cycles of genuine unity.

There is evidence too that Fet did not become aware of the cycle's esthetic potential until late in his career and even then was inconsistent in exploiting it.   By his own admission, he took no active part in compiling his first three collections, and in the preface to the third issue of *Večernie ogni* he wrote: "Until recent years we left the problem of preserving and grouping our works to literary friends.   Thus, all the poems in *Liričeskij panteon* [1840] and the 1850 edition were gathered and arranged by Apollon Grigor'ev, to whom belong the very titles of the sections also. . . . The 1856 edition was compiled exclusively according to the selection and insistence of my former circle of Petersburg friends."[76] Even the 1863 edition, though compiled by Fet himself, differed little from the 1856 version; clearly Fet was still relying on the tastes of his "Petersburg friends" (principally, Turgenev).   None of these collections, as Dolgopolov indicated, provide much basis for discussion of genuine cyclization.   The poems are arranged, for the most part, impressionistically, with little apparent effort to create apt juxtapositions.   Only in the first issue of *Večernie ogni* (1883) did Fet begin to experiment seriously with this possibility, and as a result he produced two genuinely unified cycles ("Èlegii i dumy" and "More"), both of which have been mentioned earlier.   In the cycle "Vesna" too one can sense a certain authorial design.   Fet, however, did not carry his experiments much further, and in the plan prepared in 1892 for the definitive collection of his poetry he disposed the poems, for the most part, in the same order thay had appeared in previous editions, beginning with *Stixotvorenija* (1863). In this plan, for instance, the cycle "More" is simply a combination of the 1863 and 1883 versions in the precise order the poems had appeared earlier.   Essentially, the same is true of "Vesna," "Snega" and other groupings.   It is clear, therefore, that Fet took interest in the cycle as an esthetic device only in his declining years and that this interest wained without producing a body of lasting acheivements.   Fet's apparent contribution to the development of the cycle belongs in fact more to his editors.   That they structured his collections according to a partially thematic, partially impressionistic principle provided a model which Symbolists borrowed at the end of the nineteenth century.

The Era of Symbolism (1895-1910)

In the Symbolist era the lyric cycle becomes something of an obsession. Beginning with Konstantin Bal'mont's collection *V bezbrežnosti* and Valerij Brjusov's *Chefs d'oeuvre*, both of which appeared in 1895, nearly every major volume of lyric poetry is composed of cyclic groupings from cover to cover, and the rubric "Miscellaneous Poems" all but disappears. Continuous cyclization, which had before been the exception to the rule, now becomes common practice and leads, on the one hand, to a more consistent exploitation of the cycle for esthetic aims. On the other hand, the sheer popularity of the cycle carried the potential for its overuse—something certain symbolists began to perceive shortly after the turn of the century.

Unbroken cyclization affected the very concept of a poetic collection, which now came to be seen as an artistic whole whose cycles were but individual parts. This is apparent from the fact that most symbolists chose descriptive titles for their collections instead of the conventional "Sobranie stixotvorenij" and often introduced them with an epigraph or a programmatic lyric. It is not uncommon, moreover, to find direct statements at the beginning of a volume about its unity of concept and design. In a preface intended for *Gorjaščie zdanija* (1900), for instance, Bal'mont writes: "This book was written almost completely under the force of a single mood, which for many weeks turned my life into a fairy tale."[77] Andrej Belyj speaks at length about the thematic unity of his collection in prefatory remarks to *Pepel* (1909) and states specifically that "the cycles . . . are bound into a single whole: this whole is an immaterial expanse, and in it is Russia's disappearing center."[78] An equally ambitious, though less outlandish statement is found in Brjusov's preface to *Urbi et Orbi* (1903):

> A book of poetry ought to be not a random *collection* of heterogeneous poems, but namely a *book*, an enclosed whole unified by a single idea. Like a novel, like a treatise, a book of poetry unveils its content continuously from the first page to the last. A poem, torn out of this common bond, loses as much as a separate page removed from a unified argument. The sections in a book of poetry are no different from chapters which explain each other and cannot be

comprehended in an arbitrary context.[79]

One should of course approach such pronouncements, like any statement of authorial intent, with caution, recalling Frank Kermode's warning that "the first person to misunderstand the content of Mark was the man who wrote it."[80] That Brjusov's claims are exaggerated is apparent from subsequent editions of *Urbi et Orbi*, where poems are rearranged, extracted, and some new ones added—operations that would be impossible were Brjusov's statement unimpeachable. What makes assertions like Brjusov's important is not that they are literally verifiable, but that they indicate a more conscious striving for contextuality than was evident in Russian poetry before. Moreover, they underscore the symbolists' effort to make the cycle serve a larger, supra-cyclic function.

To account for the symbolists' fascination with the lyric cycle one must consider two important features of their poetics, namely the impressionistic character of the movement in its early stages (especially as regards Bal'mont and Brjusov) and the mythopoetic world-view of the so-called "younger generation" of symbolists (Blok, Belyj and Vjačeslav Ivanov).

From the outset Russian symbolism was closely allied with the artistic method of impressionism. Dmitrij Merežkovskij, in what was the first manifesto of the movement ("On the Causes of the Present Decline and the New Currents of Contemporary Russian Literature," 1893), identified the "three principal elements of the new art" as "mystical content, symbols and a broader *sensitivity to impressions*."[81] He traces the last trend back to Turgenev, whom he calls "the greatest Russian artist-*impressionist*,"[82] and discovers Turgenev's stylistic legacy in Garšin and Čexov: "Čexov, like Garšin, has no need for painting a whole canvas. In fleeting moods, in microscopic nooks, in life's atoms the poet reveals whole worlds."[83] In 1894 Brjusov wrote that the symbolist's aim was "to hypnotize the reader, to evoke in him a particular mood,"[84] and he described the style of symbolism as follows:

> The poet conveys a series of images which have not yet taken the form of a complete picture, sometimes combining them as if into a single whole . . . , sometimes simply enumerating them one after another. The bond connecting these images is always more or

less coincidental, so that they must be perceived as landmarks along an unseen path open to the reader's imagination. Thus Symbolism can be called . . . "a poetry of indirect suggestion [poèzija namekov]."[85]

A few years later Brjusov said poetry's function was to eternize "fleeting moods" which last but an "instant" and never recur.[86] For Bal'mont too the poet's role was to fix the momentary experience:

> . . . художник создает свою картину,
> Закрепляя мимолетное событий . . .
>
>   ("Kak pauk v sebe roždaet pautinu...")

In *Gornye veršiny* (1904) he wrote that symbolism was the poetry of "unfinished phrases" and that it was "inextricably tied to two other variants of modern art . . . 'decadence' and 'impressionism'."[87]

Without mentioning the cycle specifically, such pronouncements are directly relevant to its dynamics. The essence of the impressionistic method—its use of momentary, apparently disjoined images to create a coherent effect—closely parallels the dialectic of intertextuality and contextuality in the lyric cycle. The fact that an individual poem expresses only an "indirect suggestion" or represents an "unfinished phrase" potentially activates the capacity of the cycle to disambiguate the implications of its component parts. In theory at least, cyclization provided one means of conveying a poetic thought and still honoring Tjutčev's famous dictum that was the cornerstone of symbolist esthetics: "Mysl' izrečennaja est' lož'" ("The spoken thought is a lie"). The individual poem could remain a cryptic utterance, a "suggestion," whose "unspoken" meaning was interpreted via the cyclic context.

Theory and practice, however, are different, and the symbolists did not always achieve what they set out to do. Their insistence that the poem represents a unique, "fleeting" experience did not jibe easily with the idea of contextuality. Zinaida Gippius, the best woman poet of the movement, recognized this in 1904, when she wrote in the preface to her first lyric collection:

> A book of poems—even by an author who is not entirely "isolated"—is a tiresome thing. After all, every poem corresponds to the complete sensation of a given moment; the poem emerges and it is finished; the next

poem belongs to the next moment, already a different
one; they are separated by time, by life; the reader goes
from page to page, only exhausting his eyes and ears
with the passing transitions.[88]

These remarks are aimed against cyclization (especially continuous
cyclization) and, more specifically, against Brjusov's statement at
the beginning of *Urbi et Orbi.* Moreover, the very design of
Gippius' book is a tacit polemic — it is entitled simply "Sobranie
stixov," it contains no cycles, and it disposes the lyrics in
chronological order. Thus even within the symbolist camp the
notion of lyric contextuality was not universally accepted. That
Merežkovskij's 1904 collection and Fedor Sologub's collections of
1896 and 1904 were uncyclized suggests Gippius was not alone in
her reservations.[89]

Within the "older generation" of symbolists, the most ardent
cyclists were not accidentally those who defined their method as
impressionistic — Bal'mont and Brjusov. These two poets were the
most important figures in Russian poetry at the turn of the
century, and their collections established norms of cyclic technique
both for their contemporaries and for the generation that followed.

Bal'mont's cycles are as uneven in quality as his poetry.
Despite a prodigious natural gift, Bal'mont was often unable to
evaluate his own work critically, to determine what was appropriate
and successful in a given context. As a consequence, he tended to
include in his collections poems that were either inferior by
themselves or only marginally relevant to the groupings he created.
Many of his collections, therefore, give the impression of being
almost amorphous is design, unhoned and capriciously edited.
Often his cyclic rubrics denote a metaphoric concept which is
elusive at best and at worst requires a stretch of the imagination
incommensurate to the quality of poems it embraces. Bal'mont's
contemporaries, even those who valued him as a poet, were
cognizant of these failings. Brjusov wrote in 1903 that Bal'mont
"doesn't know how to make a selection of verses. All his books
are a disordered combination of poems."[90] Blok, who cherished
Bal'mont's *Budem kak solnce* (1903), nevertheless described those
collections which appeared several years hence with disdain:

This is . . . simply gibberish, no other word can be
found. At best it resembles some kind of delirious
rambling, in which one can with great effort discern (or

invent) some indefinite lyric meaning; but in most cases
it is just an agglomeration of words.[91]

Similarly, Innokentij Annenskij called Bal'mont's *Pticy v vozduxe*
(1908) "one of his latest lyric conglomerations."[92]

In light of these appraisals it is tempting to dismiss Bal'mont
as a cyclist and proceed further, but examination of his more
successful collections reveals that despite his inconsistency he was
capable of remarkable contextuality and even a certain elegance of
design.   What distinguishes Bal'mont's best cycles is their
concentrated system of imagery—typically, a group of related
motifs will be repeated to the point of saturation and acquire
contextual meanings which unify the various poems.   One might
even speak of "symbols," although their connotations are so stable
from   poem   to   poem   and   the   reality   they   present   so
conventionalized, as a rule, that "allegory" seems the better term.

This technique is most evident in Bal'mont's nature cycles,
beginning with "Za predely" in *V bezbrežnosti*.   Here the sun,
moon, sea, wind and other elements continually appear in contexts
that lend each image a certain fixed emotive and conceptual value.
The sun, for example, is associated with activity, striving and
life—the moon with inactivity, peace and death.   Other imagery
participates in and reinforces this basic duality.   Hence the
turbulent surface of the sea, the brook, wind and daylight are
allied with "activity," while the bottom of the sea, ice, cliffs and
night connote "inactivity."   In Bal'mont the allegorical significance
of such motifs is fairly constant—not only from poem to poem,
but from cycle to cycle and even volume to volume.   Cycles in
Tišina (1898), *Tol'ko ljubov'* (1903) and *Budem kak solnca* (1903),
therefore, develop the system of imagery in "Za predely" without
altering it substantively.   *Budem kak solnce*, for instance, opens
with the macrocycle "Četveroglasie stixij," Bal'mont's most
ambitious nature allegory.   The poems are arranged to form a
series of intracyclic subgroupings devoted respectively to the sun
(Nos. 1–13), the moon (Nos.   14–23), water (especially the sea)
(Nos. 24–26), the wind (Nos. 38–44), cold climates and winter
(Nos. 45–46), warm climates and spring (Nos. 47–57).   Underlying
this meticulous, strictly architected design is a rather fluid,
impressionistic orchestration of motifs, which are less signs of
objective realia than emotive gestures.   Like musical chords in
major and minor keys, whole complexes of imagery accumulate

around the cycle's thematic dominants—the sun and the moon. The sun is strength, passion, bright colors, movement, exuberance, loudness, heat, and it is specifically a masculine element:

> Вездесущий Огонь, я тебе посвятил все мечты,
> Я такой же, как ты.
> О, ты светишь, ты греешь, ты жжешь,
> Ты живешь, ты живешь!
> В старину ты, как Змей, прилетал без конца
> И невест похищал от венца.
> И, как огненный гость, много раз, в старину,
> Ты утешил чужую жену.   (No. 11)

The moon is tranquility, quiet, subdued tones, passivity, cold, and it is specifically a female element:

> Наша царица вечно меняется,
> Будем слагать переменные строки,
>   Славя ее.
> Дух мой дрожащий любит, склоняется,
> В лунном сияньи—мы грезы, намеки,
>   Счастье мое.
>
> Наша царица, бледная, ясная,
>   Светит сияньем зеленых очей.
> Как же люблю я тебя, о прекрасная,
> Вечно-нежданная, стройная, властная,
> В самом бесстрастии пламенно-страстная,
>   Тайну познавшая лунных лучей.   (No. 19)

The other elements, and indeed all of the natural world are a constant intermingling of these two basic principles, which, as we have seen, originate in Bal'mont's early lyrics.

The allegorical cosmology that interconnects Bal'mont's different books is the index of a larger, supracyclic design which the poet envisioned for his work. The first volume of his *Sobranie stixov* (1904-1905) opens with a self-analytic, almost confessional pronouncement:

> I love all the Elements and my creative work is alive with them.
> It began—this protracted creative work whose outlines have only now become apparent—with sadness, depression, darkness. It began under the Northern Sky,

but by virtue of an internal inevitability it moved
through yearning for limitlessness and boundlessness,
through long wayfarings over the deserted planes and
troughs of Silence, and finally approached the joyous
Light, the Fire, the victorious Sun.

As is quite evident to the attentive eye, there is a
link spanning the interval from each of my books to the
next, and I know that as long as I am on this Earth, I
shall not lose the strength to forge more and more
links, and the bridge which my imagination creates will
disappear ahead in the open and beckoning distance.[93]

This statement is a truly momentous event in the history of
Russian poetry because it marks the first occasion a Russian poet
characterizes his own lyric collections as metaphorical landmarks
along a "creative path." To decode Bal'mont's meaning is not
difficult if one considers the titles of his books in chronological
sequence: *Pod severnym nebom, V bezbrežnosti, Tišina, Gorjaščie
zdanija, Budem kak solnca.* Subsequently both Blok and Belyj
made similar assertions, signaling an effort to expand lyric context
to the boundaries of an author's entire poetic oeuvre. In Bal'mont's
case the intention is at least partially realized. The dominant
mood of his first collection, as he says, is "sadness";[94] its central
idea is summarized in the first poem:

> Живи, молись — делами и словами,
> И смерть встречай, как лучшей жизни весть.
> *(Pod severnym nebom)*

His second and third books, despite their hopeful conclusions, are
generally gloomy in tone. Bal'mont's fourth and fifth collections
are entirely different in emphasis; as Vladimir Orlov writes:

> These two books indeed reflected a sharp break in the
> poet's general attitude and world-view—a break which
> marked a change in the whole tonality of his work.
> The pale colors, the nuances, the shaded brush strokes
> of his first collections are replaced by bright colors,
> blinding bursts of light, sinister reflections in deep red;
> his lyric whisper is replaced by loud, shouted
> "dagger-like words."[95]

Bal'mont's summary of his creative path is oversimplified, but
correct in its general outline.[96] Of interest too is the fact that his

books themselves occasionally allude to other volumes. The poem "Iz-pod Severnogo neba" in *V bezbrežnosti*, for instance, is an unmistakable polemic with his preceding collection:

> Из-под северного неба я ушел на светлый Юг,
> Где звучнее поцелуи, где пышней цветущий луг.
> Я хотел забыть о смерти, я хотел убить печаль,
> И умчался беззаботно в неизведанную даль.

And the poem "Kinžal'nye slova," which appears at the beginning of *Gorjaščie zdanija*, is obviously aimed against the style of *Tišina*:

> Я устал от нежных снов,
> От восторгов этих цельных
> Гармонических пиров
> И напевов колыбельных.
> Я хочу порвать лазурь
> Успокоенных мечтаний.
> Я хочу горящих зданий,
> Я хочу кричащих бурь!

The idea of a contextuality that bridges the gaps between cycles and volumes of poetry is one which the symbolists actively cultivated, and Bal'mont's gestures in this direction are among its first indications.

By comparison with Bal'mont's cycles, Brjusov's appear to be more deliberately formulated, architected from beginning to end as if according to a well-defined structural principle. Brjusov, in composing his cycles, seems to have adhered closely to the esthetic credo he expressed in *Tertia Vigilia* (1900):

> Люблю я линий верность,
> Люблю в мечтах предел.

Brjusov's analytic tendency, which characterizes his creative method in general, is a far cry from Bal'mont's largely unregulated spontaneity, and it emanates from a quite different poetic gift.[97] Whereas the integrity of Bal'mont's most successful cycles is on the level of motif and mood, in Brjusov it is usually an the level of theme, sometimes style or genre. One might say that the typical cycle of the former resembles a musical tone poem, while that of the latter is more like a theme and variations. If Bal'mont's cycles sometime seem amorphous and unfocused, Brjusov's err in the opposite direction, becoming at times almost schematic.[98]   To

illustrate this it will be instructive to examine the composition of
Urbi et Orbi (1903), which is generally recognized as Brjusov's best
and most influential collection.[99]

On the surface, *Urbi et Orbi* bears a remarkable resemblance
to nineteenth century lyric collections. Certain of the cycles' titles
are borrowed directly from the classicists and early romantics:
"Èlegii," "Ody i poslanija," "Antologija," "Ballady," "Sonety i
terciny." Others—"Dumy," "Kartiny. Na ulice"—sound as if they
were lifted from Fet ("Èlegii i *dumy*"), Majkov ("Žitejskie *dumy*,"
Kartiny"), Nekrasov ("*Na ulice*") or Slučevskij ("*Dumy*").[100]
Despite the warning in Brjusov's preface that the generic titles are
not to be understood in their "normal meaning," [101] it is clear that
he is allying himself with pre-symbolist traditions, not least of all
the neglected cyclic practice of Puškin's era. This is indicative, on
the one hand, of Brjusov's evolution in these years away from the
excentric manner of his early poetry toward a classical, "Puškinian"
clarity,[102] and, on the other hand, of his incessant passion for
experimentation, for new means of poetic expression. As is often
the case, new possibilities are discovered by re-exploring what is
old and largely forgotten.

The unity of *Urbi et Orbi*, as is typical of Brjusov's
collections, is based on the summarizing effect of certain
programmatic cycles, whose thematic breadth is great enough to
accommodate conceptually the other, subordinate groupings. In
this instance, "Dumy. Predčuvstvija" and "Dumy. Iskanija"
(Sections I and III) serve as "umbrella cycles" and provide the
collection with its central theme—the poet's creative path or, more
accurately, his search for a creative path. The other cycles
represent, metaphorically speaking, different avenues open to the
poet—hence their very diversity is a function of the larger design.
The "umbrella" principle makes for neat subordination, but it also
gives Brjusov's collection a certain schematic quality. Like a
well-organized argument, it presents its theme, then illustrates and
documents it; in this respect Brjusov's comparison of *Urbi et Orbi*
to a "treatise" (cited above) is perhaps more apt than his
comparison of it to a "novel."[103]

The term "novel," however, is not irrelevant to the two
"umbrella cycles," which contain the suggestion of an episodic plot.
Both trace a pattern of departure, traveling and wandering, and
finally return "home"; "home," moreover, is not identical to the
point of departure, so that the implication of circularity is only

partial.   Thus the first poem of "Dumy. Predčuvstvija" introduces the idea of the poet's "departure" from his creative past:

Я песни слагал вам о счастьи, о страсти, о высях,
границах, путях,—
О прежних столицах, о будущей власти,
о всем распростертом во прах.

. . . .

Довольно, довольно! я вас покидаю! берите и сны
и слова!
Я к новому раю спешу, убегаю, мечта неизменно жива!
Я создал и отдал, и поднял я молот,
чтоб снова сначала ковать.
Я счастлив и силен, свободен и молод, творю,
чтобы кинут опять
(No. 1) ("Po ulicam uzkim . . .")

The next several poems develop this same theme, either as movement "upward" (No. 2: "Lestnica") or movement from "inside" to "outside," that is, escape:

И вот опять как алчный узник,
Смотрю на волю из окна.
(No. 3)("Poslednee želanie")

Ты ждешь меня у двери, посох!
Иду! иду! со мной—никто!
(No. 4)("U sebja")

Бегу от пышного алькова,
Безумный, вольный и нагой!
(No. 5)("Pobeg")

In the median poems the path is uncertain:

Пришел я в крайние пустыни,
Брожу в лесах, где нет путей.
(No. 7)("Iskatel'")

And loss of "Ariadne's thread" makes backtracking through the labyrinth impossible:

. . . воздух был все ядовитей
И гуще тьма... Вдруг нити—нет.

И я один в безвучном зале.
Мой факел пальцы мне обжег.
Завесой сумерки упали.
В бездонном мраке нет дорог.

(No. 8)("Nit' Ariadny")

The cycle's last three poems ("Bludnyj syn," "U zemli," "V otvet")
trace the poet's return "home" to his native "soil." The plot of
the other "umbrella cycle" closely parallels that of the first, and
interaction between the two expands the implications of both. In
"Dumy. Iskanija" the theme of the path allegorizes the poet's effort
to escape his own self, his past, his artistic calling:

Желал бы я не быть "Валерий Брюсов".
Не пред людьми—от них уйти легко,—
Но пред собой, перед своим сознаньем . . .
. . . .
О, если б все забыть, быть вольным, одиноким,
В торжественной тиши раскинутых полей,
Идти своим путем, бесцельным и широким,
Без будущих и прошлых дней. . . .

(No. 1) ("L'Ennui de vivre...")

Here too the path is circular in that it brings the poet back to his
own past, to reminiscences of childhood (No. 6: "Mir"), and causes
him ultimately to rediscover the self and reaffirm the creative
impulse (No. 7: "In hac lacrimarium valle"). The circularity,
however, is not absolute; the poet's new "home" is not identical to
the one he abandoned:

И я иной, чем прежде, но все же это—я,
И песнь моя другая, но это—песнь моя.

(No. 7)

The suggestion of this cycle, whose impact affects the way one
reads its companion piece, is that the poet is transmuted by his
creative odyssey, revitalized and changed by reestablishing spiritual
contact with a distant and forgotten past. This idea is related to
the very design of *Urbi et Orbi*, its assimilation of pre-symbolist
cyclic models.

Most of the remaining cycles—even those whose unity is
strictly thematic, generic or stylistic—can be seen as illustrations of
stages in the spiritual-creative metamorphosis outlined above.
Thus section II ("Pesni"), a series of stylized folksongs about life in

the lower classes, exemplifies the poet's return to the "soil," his escape from decadent elitism. Section VII ("Kartiny. Na ulice") also signifies an interest in life's mundane realities. These two cycles, which at times recall the poetic manner and civic consciousness of Nekrasov, stand in contrast to sections IV and V ("Ballady," "Èlegii"), which are allied with the poet's decadent strain, that is, the point of departure in his creative journey. Even sections VI, VIII, and IX ("Sonety i terciny," "Antologija," "Ody i poslanija"), which themselves produce no unity of concept, contain many poems that relate back to the dominant theme of the path and are, in a sense, taken under its wing. At times the "umbrella" principle operates *within* a cycle as well. "Antologija," for example, concludes with the famous poem "Nekolebimoj istine...," an expression of Brjusov's belief in the multiplicity of artistic truth:

И все моря, все пристани
Люблю, люблю равно.

This credo provides a rationale for the very diversity of the poems that precede it.

With regard to contextualization of the separate lyric, Brjusov's *Urbi et Orbi* is a formidable achievement, and certain of its sections are masterpieces of cyclization. The same can be said, less enthusiastically, about his *Me Eum Esse* (1897) and *Tertia Vigilia* (1900) which are architected in similar fashion. Yet *Urbi et Orbi* falls short of ideal organic integrity, as Brjusov must have sensed, judging from subsequent re-editing of the collection. His fellow symbolist, Sergej Solov'ev, was correct when he qualified his praise of this book with the reservation that there remains in it a certain unassimilated "sediment."[104] Indeed, Brjusov exploited the constructive potential of arrangement and grouping to its esthetic limit. What is lacking is a more elemental, verbal organicity—something Bal'mont possessed naturally but failed to utilize in full measure.

Like Bal'mont, Brjusov conceived a correlation between his separate collections, although the nature of this correlation was different from that visualized by his elder contemporary. In Brjusov's formative years, when his poetic craft was maturing, he viewed each successive book as a creative laboratory for testing new artistic possibilities. Significantly, the edition of his collected works published in 1908-1909 bears the title *Puti i pereput'ja*,

which the poet explicates as follows: "If my work deserves
attention at all, then it deserves it for those 'paths and crossroads'
I traveled before coming forth upon the present road."[105] The idea
of multiple creative "paths," rather than a single "path," is
essential to understanding the interrelation of Brjusov's early
collections.   As we have seen, *Urbi et Orbi* begins with a
disavowal of his previous poetic method, a "departure" in search of
new techniques and themes.   Similar gestures demarcate his
preceding collections.   The preface to *Me Eum Esse* differentiates
"the character of my new poetry," and in the book itself we find
the auto-polemical lyric "Po povodu *Chefs d'oeuvre*":

> Верь мне: давно я считаю ошибкой
> Бедную книгу мою . . .

Similarly, in *Tertia Vigilia* the poet distances himself unequivocally
from *Me Eum Esse*:

> "О, эти звенящие строки!
> Ты сам написал их когда-то!"
> —Звенящие строки далеки,
> Как призрак умершего брата.

("Po povodu Me Eum Esse")

Brjusov's belief in experimentation led him to emphasize wherever
possible the novelty of each new book and to look upon each
previous collection as an extinct stage in the evolution of his poetic
technique.   It is largely this attitude that shaped the image of the
poet in Brjusov's lyrics, an image Victor Erlich accurately terms
"the maker," that is, the poet-craftsman.[106] The emphasis on craft
rather than experience and the tendency to focus on discontinuities,
"departures," make it difficult to see Brjusov's poet as an integral
personality whose biography spans a lyric oeuvre.   As Dmitrij
Maksimov observes, "for Brjusov his spiritual development was not
so important . . . as the sheer striving 'further onward' toward
novelty and perfection, primarily of a purely literary nature. . . .
Brjusov . . . did not think of his development   as something
natural, predetermined, unified, and organically integrated."[107]   In
this respect, as we shall see, Brjusov differed radically from Blok.

The lyric cycle was ideally tailored to fit the impressionistic
esthetics of Bal'mont and Brjusov—it provided a way of organizing
the multiplicity of unique "moments" into a coherent picture, like
ceramic tiles in a mosaic.   The cycle's kaleidoscopic unity balanced
the essential pluralism of their world-view.   For the "younger

generation" of symbolists, whose world-view was monistic and quasi-religious, the appeal of the cycle lay elsewhere—in its capacity to mimic the inherent relatedness of all experience. Central to the artistic method of Vjačeslav Ivanov, Andrej Belyj and Aleksandr Blok is the Nietzschean concept of "eternal return," the repeatability of historical and spiritual events, whose apparent uniqueness is illusory.[108]   The individual "moment" had no value by itself, but was important only to the degree that it reflected recurring patterns in life and in the eternal scheme of the universe.[109]   For these poets the contextuality of the cycle represented less a whimsical creation of unity from separate lyric experiences than an approximation of the unity all experience possessed as revelation of a common mystical truth.

All symbolists believed art was an expression of intuitive, rather than intellectual knowledge.   For Brjusov "art is comprehension of the world by other than rational means."[110] Characteristically, however, only the "younger generation" viewed artistic creativity as something approaching sacred ritual.   In this they were encouraged by the prediction of their teacher, Vladimir Solov'ev, that art would become the vehicle of a "religious idea."[111] Solov'ev's works, which the "younger" symbolists read with the reverence of disciples, undoubtedly inspired the following statement of Ivanov, the group's principal theoretician:

> True symbolist art adjoins the realm of religion since
> religion is above all the feeling of that tie which binds
> all things and the meaning of all types of life.   This is
> why one may speak of symbolism and religious art as
> entities which are in a certain sense interrelated.[112]

For Ivanov, genuine symbolism, which he distinguished from the impressionistic, "idealistic" symbolism of Bal'mont and Brjusov,[113] strives to return poetry to its primitive union with religious rite, to its beginnings in the dithyrambs of the Dionysian chorus.[114]   The key to this union lay in the very nature of the symbol, which possessed the capacity to generate myth:

> Like the first shoots of spring grass, the buds of myth
> have sprouted from symbols, the first signs of myth
> creation.   The poet has suddenly recalled that he was
> once a "myth-creator." . . . From symbol is born
> myth. . . .   What is poetry destined to become?
> Universal, infant-like, myth-creating.[115]

Later Belyj echoed Ivanov's formula: "the word gave birth to myth; myth gave birth to religion."[116]

The aspiration to create "myth" was partially realized within the context of the cycle. As Z. G. Minc points out, the cycle became in some cases "the functional equivalent of a 'poèma-myth'."[117] The most cogent explanation of this lies in the cycle's potential for generating plot, that is, for mimicing myth's narrative dynamic. In this regard archetypal plot cycles proved a suitable vehicle, since their design approximated mythic narrative. The very repetition of essentially the same event pattern from poem to poem simulated the consecration of myth through ritual.

Of the "younger" symbolists the closest adherent to archetypal plot patterns is Andrej Belyj. As we have seen, the first cycle in his collection *Zoloto v lazuri* ritualizes the myth of the "sun journey." Allied with this myth, an original product of Belyj's imagination, is a second, more traditional one that is derived from the Biblical Apocalypse. The book's last cycle, "Bagrjanica v ternijax," effects a fusion of the two mythological constructs in that it alludes both to the "sun journey" and the second coming of Christ. Belyj's next collection, *Pepel* (1909), consists entirely of episodic and diaristic plot cycles—a fact hinted at already in the dedication of the book to Nekrasov. Indeed, certain of the cycles, especially "Derevnja," adhere so closely to plot that they approach the continuity of stories in verse.[118] Here too, as in the preceding collection, one can discern a recurring event archetype or, more accurately, two archetypes—one involving escape from confinement (whether from a stifling urban setting, a grave or imprisonment), the other involving a romantic triangle wherein the more unsavory of two rivals always emerges victorious. These patterns are repeated from cycle to cycle with little variation and give the collection a certain schematic quality. As Pavel Gromov observes:

> The plots differ only in individual details of story or genre, but their basic skeleton is uniform; consequently, we are left with a recurring, largely illusory plot. . . . Belyj is unable to conceive anything poetically except in terms of schemata.[119]

Vjačeslav Ivanov, despite his call for "myth-creation," was less an inventor of myth than Belyj. Typically, Ivanov did not generate his own myth, but borrowed it from classical or Biblical sources, often from their most obscure recesses. This is why Annenskij, an accomplished classical scholar in his own right, complained of Ivanov's "inaccessibility" and "pedantry."[120] Ivanov's abstruseness is evident in *Kormčie zvezdy* (1903), his first collection, which is eclectic in its mythological allusions and quite modest as an achievement of cyclicality. Here the closest Ivanov comes to unifying poems around a single mythological plot is the cycle "Dionisu," but even this grouping does not gel organically. Subsequently, Ivanov produced some genuine cyclic masterpieces—most notably the small collection *Eros* (1907), and several cycles in *Cor ardens* (1911-12) (e.g., "Solnce-serdce," "Godina gneva" and "Zolotye zavesy"). In his best cycles, however, Ivanov's artistry still lies in his ability to utilize existing myth rather than manufacture his own. The reason for this may be his belief that while symbolism opened the path to a new mythology, the era of "myth-creation" was only on the horizon. In 1909 he wrote: "The efforts of poetry in our time to approach myth are, of course, still far away from that theurgical goal to which we have given the name 'myth-creation'."[121] To reach this goal, according to Ivanov, the artist must first uncover myth in his own personal experience:

> The first prerequisite of that myth-creation we are discussing is an act of spiritual heroism on the part of the artist himself. . . . Myth, before it can be felt by everyone, must be experienced as an internal event, personal in scope, but suprapersonal in content.[122]

In several respects, Aleksandr Blok came closest to fulfilling Ivanov's "first prerequisite" by making his own spiritual biography into a "personal" and "suprapersonal" myth. He was able to do so, to a large degree, by his mastery of the lyric cycle.

The Cycle in Blok and the Concept of the Lyric "Trilogy"

Cyclicality is the very essence of Blok's creative method. There is hardly a poem in his poetic legacy that is not at once a whole in and of itself and at the same time an index of other poems, whether in the immediate context or elsewhere in his far-flung lyric oeuvre. In this sense Blok's poetry is the extreme manifestation of what Edward Stankiewicz has called the "centrifugal structure" of modern literature—the tendency of texts to "depend for their interpretation on a knowledge of other texts of the same or different temporal order that constitute as it were, their underlying, subtextual, or implicit dimension."[123] Vjačeslav Ivanov was apparently the first to recognize this, when in November 1904 he reversed his initial disapproval of Blok after seeing his poems cyclized in *Stixi o Prekrasnoj Dame* (1904),[124] the young poet's first collection: "Unexpectedly, I have come to love Blok. . . . I am even ashamed to admit that until I saw his poems in their aggregate I doubted both his originality and his spontaneity."[125]

To regulate the interaction of his poems Blok devised an elaborate system of contexts which he called a "trilogy of incarnation." Separate lyrics are grouped in cycles; small cycles are often incorporated into larger ones; large cycles are in turn conjoined to form volumes, which possess a certain compositional integrity; and the volumes themselves comprise what Blok termed "a novel in verse"—a mythologized biography of his lyric hero. The "trilogy" underwent several redactions, from its initial version in *Sobranie stixotvorenij* (1911-12) to the revised version in *Stixotvorenija* (1916), and ultimately to the so-called "canonical" variant published after the Revolution (1918-22).[126] Russian poets before Blok, though they spoke about the interrelatedness of their various collections, never succeeded quite to the degree Blok does in organizing the bulk of their lyric output into such a monumental cycle of the whole.

Blok's achievement as a cyclist, however, lies not just in the monumentality of his design. What distinguishes Blok most from his antecedents is that interrelatedness of separate lyrics is always an organic feature of his poetics from his earliest serious efforts in 1898 to the end of his literary career. It is not something "learned" so much as an intrinsic disposition of his poetic gift.

At the same time, Blok's cyclic legacy emanates from trends manifest earlier in Russian poetry, and Blok assimilates the lessons of his predecessors. The roots of his method lie in that inherent cyclicality characteristic of some romantic or pre-romantic poets who constantly reworked a single biographical archetype, and it is no accident that Blok calls Žukovskij "my first inspiration" (VII, 12). In a real sense, his "trilogy" is the ultimate realization of the romantics' desire to make separate poems "tell a story of a whole life," as Puškin said of Jazykov's elegies. There is no question either that Blok learned the architectonics of the cycle from his more immediate antecedents, not least of all—his fellow symbolists. The best indication of this is the fact that Blok introduced no new cyclic types, but rather expanded the potential of existing ones. In this regard he was a student-prodigy who grasped the possibilities of the device more intuitively than his teachers and applied them with greater esthetic effect.

Evidence that Blok drew from existing tradition in formulating his own principles of cyclization is largely circumstantial, since statements by him about the cycles of other poets are not numerous and they occur, for the most part, rather late in his career, when his cyclic technique was already established and therefore less subject to external influences.[127] According to Blok, his formative years before entering Petersburg University (fall 1898) were spent in an environment that kept him ignorant of the so-called "new poetry," so that his earliest poetic endeavors, to the degree they are derivative, are connected with models from the pre-symbolist era.[128] Among the poets who had the strongest influence on him at this time were (in addition to Žukovskij) Puškin, Lermontov, Polonskij, Majkov, Fet and Apuxtin—most of whom, as we have seen, left their mark on the history of the lyric cycle. Quite possibly Blok was familiar with Baudelaire's *Les Fleurs du mal* at this time too, since his mother, an accomplished translator of French, collaborated with him in April 1898 on a parody of "L'Albatros (from the cycle "Spleen et Idéal").[129]

It is also known that Blok had developed a taste for Heine in these early years, reading him in translation,[130] and perhaps also in the original German.[131] It is possible, however, that Heine's impact as a cyclist was not felt by Blok until 1908, when he received an authoritative edition of the poet and had the opportunity to read his cycles in their full complement.[132] At that time Blok announced his intention to translate *Buch der Lieder* in its entirety (an advertisement to this effect appeared in Blok's *Zemlja v snegu*, 1908), although subsequently he abandoned this project. He translated only twelve poems from the cycle "Die Heimkehr and placed them alongside his own cycle "Na rodine" in *Nočnye časy* (1911). This is the only occasion Blok integrated translations into the design of his own lyric collection—a fact which underscores the importance of Heine to him. At the end of his life Blok spent three years (1918-21) editing a multi-volume translation of Heine for the publishing house "Vsemirnaja literatura," roughly at the same time he was compiling the final version of his "trilogy." Judging from Blok's diary and notebook entries from this period, Evgenija Knipovič is justified in saying that editing Heine was less a task of obligation for Blok than "communion with a living person, infinitely close in one respect, exasperatingly distant in another."[133] On the evidence of this exceptional, one might even say "loving" interest in Heine, which spans Blok's entire career, one is inclined to trace Blok's cyclic genealogy back to Heine no less directly than other antecedents. Like Blok, Heine is a poet of multiple contexts (the cycle, the subcycle, the volume), which affect the apprehension of his individual lyrics. And through these contexts, Heine generated the image of a lyric hero whose biography unfolds with remarkable continuity from poem to poem, cycle to cycle, and volume to volume. Blok, who ultimately came to see his lyric poetry as a kind of "diary" (VII, 15), could hardly have found a precedent closer to his own conception of an oeuvre than Heine's.

Another of the pre-symbolist poets who undoubtedly helped shape Blok's concept of the cycle is Apollon Grigor'ev. As with Heine, Blok's fascination with Grigor'ev began early, in the protective environment of the maternal home, and persisted throughout his life. Grigor'ev was a favorite of Blok's grandmother (who knew Grigor'ev personally) and his mother, both of whom were most influential in forming the young boy's literary tastes. It is likely, therefore, that Blok knew Grigor'ev before the turn of the century, although serious study of him began apparently only in June 1902, when Blok acquired his *Stixotvorenija* (1846) and made copious notes about his impressions (ZK, 28-30). Direct indications that Grigor'ev was important for him as a cyclist, however, appear only much later, in 1914-15, when Blok was preparing a new edition of Grigor'ev's poetry for the publishing house of K. F. Nekrasov.[134] Therein Blok is scrupulous about preserving the exact composition of Grigor'ev's cycles, even to the point of reproducing the 1846 collection in its original form; in Blok's words, this is "the order . . . chosen by the poet himself" and there is no reason to "disturb the integrity of the book."[135] In the preface Blok mentions the cycle "Gimny" (also in the 1846 collection), calling it a work "underrated" by critics (V, 516), and in commentaries to this edition he insists on the importance of preserving the cycle "Bor'ba" as an integral unit.[136] Such remarks establish Blok's admiration for Grigor'ev but do not ascertain the nature of the kinship between them. In this regard, Pavel Gromov's remarks are enlightening:

> Blok personifies his lyric hero. In his poetry the lyric "I" is given, so to speak, a dramatic "personality" . . . . Here again Blok relies on the precedent of Grigor'ev, on his search for a new type of lyric hero—concretized and objectified. Blok not only personifies his lyric hero, turning him into a concrete persona—he also cyclizes his poems, combines them around a certain unified "narrative theme" . . . . Here too Blok, in his own way, is continuing the artistic search of Grigor'ev, who tried to create a single, integrated lyric novel.[137]

Undoubtedly, the subtle characterization of protagonists in Grigor'ev's cycles must have had great appeal for Blok.

After 1898 Blok begins to take serious interest in the "new" or "decadent" poets, and after the turn of the century their influence on him becomes dominant. The watershed date is spring 1901, when Blok is introduced, almost simultaneously, to Vladimir Solov'ev's *Stixotvorenija* (1900) and the first issue of the miscellany *Severnye cvety* (1901); the latter contained poems by Brjusov, Bal'mont, Sologub and other Symbolists of the "older generation." These events mark the beginning of new relationships which had an effect on the development of his cyclic technique.

There is no need here to review Solov'ev's profound importance for the young Blok. That Blok adapted Solov'ev's worship of the "Eternal Feminine" to his own cult of the "Beautiful Lady" hardly requires further documentation. What interests us here, specifically, is how Blok's contact with Solov'ev may have directed him toward kinds of contextuality that are characteristic of his lyrics. There are in fact two sides to this issue—Solov'ev's poetry and Solov'ev's philosophical writings, both of which Blok read with fascination.

At first it might appear fruitless to consider Solov'ev as a poet in this regard because he produced no cycles, except in one obscure instance that could hardly have been known to Blok.[138] Acknowledging this, however, Minc argues persuasively that Solov'ev's poetry is inherently cyclic:

> Two aspects of Solov'ev's lyric poetry allow us to discern in it the first artistic steps toward the

specifically symbolist genre of the lyric cycle. It is
Solov'ev's profound fidelity in the course of many years
to a single circle of thoughts, moods and means of
esthetic apprehension of the world. . . . It is [also] the
inevitable appearance (as a result of the correlation
between Solov'ev's lyrics and his mythopoetic
philosophy) not only of recurring motifs, but of
something resembling "lyric characters."[139]

Indeed, Solov'ev's focus on the poet and his relation to the Divine
Sophia gives his poetry a certain unity which, even in the absence
of cycles, could not help but leave a strong impression on Blok.

Solov'ev's prose, however, may have had an even greater
impact. Its central theme, which runs through almost all his
essays regardless of their individual topics, is "synthesis" — a
concept related directly to the dynamics of the lyric cycle and
more generally to the world view of the "younger generation,"
Solov'ev's disciples. According to Solov'ev, there exists in the
world "a moulding force which brings together the most varied
substances into the unity of a living organism," what he calls
"pan-unity [vseedinstvo]."[140] This "force," however, manifests itself
at different times with varying intensity, so that in history
"pan-unity" or "synthesis" is only the final stage of a dialectic
reminiscent of the Hegelian formula: "thesis" (monolithic unity — a
positive phenomenon), "antithesis" (diversity, multiplicity — a
negative phenomenon), and "synthesis" (unity derived from
diversity and multiplicity — a maximally positive phenomenon). In
"Čtenija o bogočelovečestve" ("Readings about God-manhood"), for
instance, Solov'ev applies this scheme to man's religious
development:

> Religious truth, emerging from a single root, developed
> in man into a multiplicity and variety of different
> branches. To cut off all these branches, to leave a
> single, bare, dry and sterile trunk . . . this is the aim
> sought by the rationalistic purification of religion. A
> positive religious synthesis, however, a genuine
> philosophy of religion must embrace the totality of
> religious development, not excluding a single positive
> element, and it must seek religious unity in
> integration.[141]

Solov'ev's triadic formula acquired the significance of myth for

Blok,[142] and it underlaid the very concept of his lyric "trilogy," as we shall see.

Solov'ev's essay "Žiznennaja drama Platona" ("Plato's Life Drama"), which appeared first as a preface to *Tvorenija Platona* (1899), may also have carried special import for Blok's conception of his own oeuvre. The copious marginalia in Blok's copies of this essay indicate that the young poet read it with considerable interest and introspection.[143] Here Solov'ev, faced with the task of editing a Russian translation of Plato, advances the unusual thesis that the philosopher's works ought to be arranged not in the chronology of their writing, which in any case is difficult to ascertain, but according to the chronology of his *"life drama"*:

> For Plato philosophy was above all a life task. Life for him was not a tranquil succession of days . . . but a profound and complex drama embracing his entire being. The development of this drama . . . was reflected and immortalized in the dialogues. Therefore Plato himself, as the hero of his own *life drama*—here is the true unifying principle of Plato's creations, the order of which is determined naturally by the development of this drama.[144]

The idea that real-life chronology is less important than the chronology of life as esthetic construct may well have had a major impact on Blok when he, even in his formative years, contemplated the task of organizing his lyrics into a quasi-autobiographical narrative.

Among the symbolists, Brjusov occupied in Blok's eyes a hallowed place in the pantheon of cyclic poets. Blok's reaction to *Urbi et Orbi*, which he began reading in mid November 1903, is nothing short of ecstatic. On November 20, he writes Belyj:

> The book has me under its sway; it stings, caresses and winds itself around me. Its appearance, its content are a series of unbelievable revelations, illuminations approaching genius. . . . I will spend yet a great deal of time with it, and I can boast and do a dance around the room because I haven't yet finished reading it, haven't smoothed out all its pages. (VIII, 69)

Six days later he writes Sergej Sokolov, editor of the miscellany *Grif*, that he is "tormented" by Brjusov's book, that "this is something completely surpassing the limits of possibility, so unexpected and monumental that it is difficult to get control over it."[145] Early in December he confesses to his friend and fellow symbolist, Sergej Solov'ev, that he is "beside himself from *Urbi et Orbi*" and vows to write verses which "will duplicate Brjusov's."[146] The cause of Blok's rapture, which can hardly be determined from these initial, impressionistic remarks, is apparent in the two reviews he wrote of the book—the first of which Brjusov himself rejected for being too effusive in its praise.   What appealed to Blok was, precisely, its contextuality.   In the earlier review we read: "This is above all something integral [celostnoe], no less synthetic spiritually than the motto of the ancient metaphysician: 'unity in multiplicity,' the simplest thing in the most complex" (V, 532).[147] The second review opens by quoting Brjusov's preface to *Urbi et Orbi*, which, as mentioned above, likens the book to a "treatise" or "novel"; following the quotation, Blok comments:

> These lines . . . at first seem superfluous and place upon the author an apparently impossible task.   They sound like a mathematical formula.   It is hard to imagine that one could raise on the tip of this formula alone the weight of such various poems, the product of three years work. . . .
>
> But the promise is fulfilled.   Before us is a book like a song, from which not a word can be extracted, enclosed within its ten parts and leaving only a narrow channel from one part to the next—as if from one chapter to the next. (V,541)

Brjusov's words left such an indelible imprint on Blok that he paraphrased them eight years later in the preface to the first edition of his "trilogy":

> Many [of the poems], taken in isolation, are of no value; but each *poem* is essential to the formation of a *chapter*; from several chapters is compiled a *book*; each book is part of the *trilogy*; the whole trilogy I can call a "novel in verse." (I, 559) [148] [Blok's emphasis.-D.S.]

Blok's indebtedness to Brjusov has been discussed elsewhere and need not be belabored here.[149]   One ought not assume, however, that Brjusov's insistence on contextual integration of separate lyrics was an epiphany, a totally new concept for Blok.

In fact, Brjusov's example only confirmed and helped define views which Blok was developing independently of Brjusov before he encountered *Urbi et Orbi.* One indication of this is that Blok characterizes Brjusov's collection as "synthetic," as "a unity in multiplicity"—concepts with which he was familiar from ancient Greek philosophy as well as Vladimir Solov'ev's prose, and qualities which he had earlier begun to perceive in the poetry of both Fet and Solov'ev. The criterion of "integrality [celostnost']" was not new to Blok. Already in November 1902 he wrote Mixail Solov'ev, the philosopher's brother, of his intention to edit a collection of Vladimir Solov'ev's "humorous verses"—a task he believed must be performed "in integral fashion [cel'no]."[150]   Blok applied this criterion to Bal'mont's collections *Budem kak solnce* and *Tol'ko ljubov'* even before he picked up *Urbi et Orbi.*[151]   He comments on the "integrality" of Bal'mont's books (V, 528), although he finds this quality lacking in certain largely superficial respects:

> One cannot help but fault Bal'mont for the cover of his collection *Budem kak solnce.* It runs contrary to the content of the book and gives not the slightest hint of its essence. . . . The cover of the book *Tol'ko ljubov* is much better, but it does not merge with the melody of the book, whose central idea is still more delicate and transparent than *Budem kak solnce.* Moreover, the contents of both books are distributed not entirely evenly, and certain items need rearranging. (V, 530)

Reading *Urbi et Orbi after* writing these lines, Blok perceived it via comparison with Bal'mont's books as a more complete realization of that unity he had come to demand of a poetic collection. Brjusov's book was more a fulfillment of an anticipation than a genuine revelation, despite Blok's ecstatic reaction to it. One should not exaggerate, therefore, Brjusov's influence on Blok as a cyclist—especially since the contextuality Brjusov created in his collections is essentially different from that in Blok's. As Minc accurately observes, "Brjusov's idea proved extremely dear to Blok, although subsequently it was filled with a new content."[152]

The cyclicality of Blok's lyrics lies not so much in the consistent development of one or several themes, but in the semantic enrichment of the word.[153]   Certain words or motifs acquire symbolic significance from their repeated use in similar contexts and begin to carry the weight of these associations from poem to poem, cycle to cycle, and even volume to volume. Blok's word-motifs have the capacity to "recall" their own past in each new textual environment, to evoke metonymically the other texts that inform them. They are not merely recurring images, but semantic interpretants, whose acquired "memory" allows the reader to decode new and frequently cryptic poetic messages. The concept of word as integrator of Blok's cyclic contexts and indeed, ultimately, of his entire poetic universe is the subject of the following chapter and need not be treated here in exhaustive detail. It will suffice to point out that this dynamic came quite naturally to Blok and is manifest from the outset of his career. Already in a cycle of fifteen poems published in the miscellany *Grif* (1904) and mailed to the editor on October 1, 1903 (more than a month before Blok's encounter with *Urbi et Orbi*)[154] the most typical feature of his cyclic technique is quite prominent. Here, repetition of certain motifs serves not merely as a formal link between the poems, but as an index of textual segments that can be meaningfully juxtaposed. Like Puškin's "Podražanija Koranu," Blok's cycle calls upon the reader to construct, so to speak, new poems out of the raw material provided. By way of example, one could cite the leitmotif of the "stairs" ("*stupeni*") or "stairway" (*lestnica*), which runs through several of the poems:

> Я просыпался и всходил
> К окну на темные ступени. (I, 219)   (No. 6)

- - - - - - -

> Там—в улице стоял какой-то дом,
> И лестница крутая в тьму водила.
> . . . .
> Там гул шагов терялся и исчез
> На лестнице—при свете лампы жолтом.
> . . . .
> По лестнице над сумрачным двором
> Мелькала тень, и лампа чуть светила. (I, 192) (No. 7)

- - - - - - -

> Мне страшно с Тобой встречаться.
> Страшнее Тебя не встречать.
> . . . .
> Прильнув к церковной ступени,
> Боюсь оглянуться назад.   (I, 237) (No. 13)

И молча, как по знаку, двинулись вниз.
На ступеньках шорох белых женских риз.   (I, 284)
(No. 14)

Here the "stairway" is a place of mystical anticipations and some
fateful meeting, whether with the Lady, with death or both
simultaneously.   But repetition of the motif serves not just to
infuse it with contextual meaning; the effect, more significantly, is
that different lyric situations cannot be seen as entirely
discrete—they are superimposed upon each other like
transparencies, so that it is impossible to contemplate one without
discerning the others in the background.   Thus the image of the
"stairway" in the poems just cited is projected upon the brief
scenario which unfolds in "Po gorodu begal černyj čelovek . . ."
(No. 8); the other texts act as interpretants of this cryptic lyric:

По городу бегал черный человек.
Гасил он фонарики, карабкаясь на лестницу.

Медленный, белый подходил рассвет,
Вместе с человеком взбирался на лестницу.

Там, где были тихие, мягкие тени—
Желтые полоски вечерних фонарей,—

Утренние сумерки легли на ступени,
Забрались в занавески, в щели дверей.

Ах, какой бледный город на заре!
Черный человечек плачет на дворе.   (I, 278)

The textual "memory" of the motif helps decode the symbolic
significance of the "little man's" ritual and demystifies his strange
behavior at the end—here the "stairs" do not in fact prove the
place of anticipated meeting.

The importance of repetition in Blok was not universally
understood by his contemporaries.   It is indicative of the disparity
between them as cyclists, for instance, that Brjusov felt the
constant recurrence of the same motifs and situations in Blok was
simply tedious.   In 1905 he wrote condescendingly: "Like . . . Boris
Musatov . . . Blok copies from himself, repeats devices that were
once successful, images that were once original."[155]   Even in 1922,
long after Blok was acknowledged as the greatest Russian
symbolist, Brjusov again commented: "From the same cliche Blok

. . . reproduces dozens of poems which are hardly distinguishable from one another. Five-six themes, three-four devices he dispersed over hundreds of pieces, not bad ones but monomorphic: again and again about one and the same thing."[156]　Sergej Gorodeckij, an important poet who was at first allied with Blok before moving to the Acmeist camp, wrote disapprovingly in 1910: "[Blok] does nothing except retell his own verses."[157]　Among Blok's contemporaries, Kornej Čukovskij and Viktor Žirmunskij were the first to discern that Blok's repetitions were essential to the semantic overcoding of his motifs,[158] but only since the appearance of Lidija Ginzburg's *O lirike* (1964) has this aspect of Blok's poetics come under serious scrutiny.[159]　Ginzburg points out that the meaning of Blok's symbols "is born from the total context of his oeuvre and in turn . . . transforms every individual context."[160] Already in Blok's first collection "context is accumulated from poem to poem, and from it emerge those . . . symbols which will pass through his whole oeuvre."[161]

Ultimately, it is acquisition of contextual meaning that allows amalgamation of Blok's lyrics into something resembling "a novel in verse" and gives his poetry the quality of myth. Each of his recurrent symbol-motifs (e.g, door, window, sword, stairs) traces a path through his poetic oeuvre, preserving within itself the memory of its past textual environments. These environments are assimilated by every new text in which the image appears and are essential to its decoding. Understanding Blok's poetry, therefore, requires constant backtracking through the previous work—a recurring odyssey to the source and initial symbolification of his imagery.　This orientation toward origins is something that resembles myth. As E. M. Meletinskij observes:

> The cardinal feature of myth, especially primitive myth, consists in the reduction of the essence of things to their genesis: to explain the structure of a thing means telling the story of how it came into being. . . . The mythic epoch is an epoch of *original objects* and *original actions*: the first fire, the first spear, the first house, and so forth. . . . Since the essence of things, to a significant degree, is equated with their origin, knowledge of origin is the key to the application of the thing, and knowledge of the past is equated with wisdom.[162]

Similarly, "wise" reading of Blok's mature poetry, specifically that contained in the third volume of his "trilogy," always subsumes knowledge of his earlier lyrics—particularly the first volume, where the lyric hero's deepest and most lasting aspirations are in sharpest relief.

Blok first mentions his "trilogy" while compiling the first volume of his collected poetry for the publishing house "Musaget" in November or early December 1910: "Volume I—strictly chronologically (300 chapters of part I of the *trilogy*)" (ZK, 173). The word appears also in the preface to this edition written January 9, 1911 (I, 559) and again in the afterword drafted in June 1911 (ZK, 182). Blok's most informative statement about the design of the "trilogy," however, occurs in his letter to Belyj from June 6, 1911:

> I am firmly convinced that all my verses together are a *"trilogy of incarnation in human form"* [*"trilogija vočelovečenija"*] (from the instant of too-bright light —through the unavoidable marshy wood—to despair, deprecations, "retribution" and . . . to the birth of a "social" man and artist who looks the real world steadfastly in the face). (VIII, 344) [Emphasis is Blok's.—D. S.]

There is no doubt that the primary inspiration for this tri-partite formula (suggested by the strategic placement of the prepositions "from"—Volume I, "through"—Volume II, and "to"— Volume III) was Vladimir Solov'ev, especially since the word "vočelovečenie" is a direct borrowing from Solov'ev's prose, where it signifies incarnation of the divine element in the figure of Jesus Christ.[163] Admittedly, Blok's summary of the "trilogy's" plot is eccentric (note the reduction of the whole first volume to an "instant"), and one might prefer the popular version, which alleges that Blok's Beautiful Lady (Volume I) is transmuted into the Incognita (Neznakomka) (Volume II) and ultimately into personified Russia (Volume III)—an interpretation of the myth that Blok himself sanctioned.[164]   Minc offers perhaps the most reliable precis of the plot, which she calls "the invariant 'myth of the path':"

> 1) the primordial bliss of original existence; 2) the loss of "paradise" and descent into "the terrible world" of material, historical reality; 3) the discovery of "new life" which combines the lofty values of spiritual being with

material incarnation of the earthly.[165]

The question must be asked, however, to what extent is one
justified in speaking of Blok's three volumes (in any of their
redactions) as a "trilogy," as a unified work. The mere fact that
Blok characterized them as such is hardly adequate proof. It was,
after all, typical of the symbolists to make claims about the unity
of their lyrics, and such pronouncements can never be taken
entirely at face value. Moreover, there are unities, continuities in
the development of any poet. The biographer commonly discovers
an evolution in the poet's interests, themes and style, world view,
maturation of talent and so forth—all those things we associate
with the poet's "creative path" or "periodization" of the poet's
work. Is Blok's poetry any different in these respects?

The answer to this question must be equivocal. To create a
single, unified work from hundreds of separate lyrics is an
impossible task, no matter how many eloquent prefaces argue
otherwise. All those poets, including Blok, who urged the
contextual reading of their verses were all well aware of this.
They exaggerated contextuality in order to counterbalance the
ingrained tendency to view poems as separate texts—a reading
strategy that made cyclization meaningless. What distinguished
Blok from other cyclists was that contextuality was a more
inherent element of his creative method, so that he was able to
exploit the balance of separateness and integration more successfully
than any of his contemporaries. Thus when he speaks of his
lyrics as a "trilogy" there is an element of overstatement, but also
a greater element of truth than in similar statements by his fellow
symbolists.

To a large degree, what gives the "trilogy" the semblance of
a single work (more specifically, a kind of narrative) is that its
general design is present from the outset; as in any well-plotted
story its middle and ending are prefigured by its beginning. There
is much validity to Blok's remark from August 1907, long before
the "trilogy" is first mentioned, that "everything I wrote serves as
an organic continuation of the first [book]—*Stixi o Prekrasnoj
Dame*" (VIII, 190).[166] Indeed Blok's first volume establishes a
dramatic conflict that develops in the volumes that follow—the
poet's romance with the Beautiful Lady is in a real sense the
subject of all his lyrics, and his early polemic with Del'vig could
well stand as an epigraph to his entire lyric production:

Ты, Дельвиг, говоришь: минута — вдохновенье,
Оно пройдет... А я тебе скажу:
Оно горит всю жизнь— . . .[167]

(February 8, 1899)

The first volume is essentially a book of anticipations,
fortune-telling, and in predivining his future—his "path"—the lyric
hero envisions a multiplicity of different scenarios, all of which
involve, essentially, the possibility of union with the Lady, an
eventuality that is the poet's strongest and most sacred wish.   In
the context of the "trilogy" these scenarios take on the quality of
prophecy, and nearly all of them are either realized on some level
in the succeeding volumes or return to haunt and inspire the lyric
hero as he strives to redefine his destiny in light of his past.   The
central event of the second volume, the poet's fall from grace, for
instance, is presaged in the programmatic lyric "Predčuvstvuju
Tebja. Goda proxodjat mimo..." (June 4, 1901):[168]

Весь горизонт в огне, и близко появленье,
Но страшно мне: изменишь облик Ты,

И дерзкое возбудишь подозренье,
Сменив в конце привычные черты.

О, как паду — и горестно, и низко,
Не одолев смертельныя мечты!   (I, 94)

Some poems in the first volume clearly anticipate the poet's tragic
romance with the Snow Mask, the crucial episode of volume II (in
the "trilogy's" 1916 and "canonical redactions"):[169]

"Двери тебе отопру
В сумерках зимнего дня".   (I, 140)

_____

Деву в снежном инее
Встречу наяву.   (I, 144)

_____

Будет день, и распахнутся двери,
Вереница белая пройдет.

Будут страшны, будут несказанны
Неземные маски лиц...   (I, 233)

Many of the ominous expectations that abound in the first volume
are fulfilled in the second.   On occasion the first volume also

points ahead to the third, which in some ways represents a return
to ideals forfeited earlier:

> Ты смотришь, тихая, строгая,
> В глаза прошедшей мечте.
> Избрал иную дорогу я,—
> Иду,—и песни не те...
>
> Вот скоро вечер придвинется,
> И ночь — навстречу судьбе:
> Тогда мой путь опрокинется,
> И я возвращусь к Тебе.   (I, 196)

Such verses suggest that the biography of Blok's lyric hero, at
least in some indefinite and general outline, was conceived during
the period of his first volume, during the period of his greatest
fascination with Vladimir Solov'ev. Already in 1900 Blok had in
mind the lessons of Solov'ev's essay about Plato's "life drama," and
one year later, as he pored over "Readings about God-manhood,"
the following words must have lodged deeply in the young poet's
soul: "In the performance of a drama every actor . . . has his own
particular role, but could he perform it well if he did not know the
whole content of the drama?"[170] Very early on, Blok knew if not
"the whole content of the drama," then at least the principal
turning points of its plot. Already in June 1902 he writes his
closest friend and confidant, Aleksandr Gippius: "Is it really
possible to reach 'the light' without first passing through 'the
darkness'? I personally . . . will not surrender a single iota of my
'life drama' . . ." (VIII, 37). And in June 1903 he confessed to
Belyj that "scepticism . . . lies like a stone in the road, and it is
impossible to ride around it."[171] Both these remarks suggest that
Blok then visualized the "events" of his second volume as an
inevitable stage in his spiritual passage; they imply also that Blok
already saw the "life" of his lyric hero as a tri-partite structure
with a beginning, middle, and ending. A notebook entry from
April 1904 tends to confirm this: "To sense Her [the Lady]—only
in early youth and just before death" (ZK, 63). By October 1905,
still five years before he mentions the "trilogy," the ternary
formula seems firmly established; again in a letter to Belyj he
writes: "The 'first heroic task' I performed in insurmountable
anguish, as if predivining that after the first there would be (there
had to be) a second and third—the conquest of the dragon and
death" (VIII, 140-141).

To the first edition of his "trilogy" Blok appended the comment that his verses from 1901 constitute "that 'magic crystal' through which I first discerned, however 'indefinitely', the whole 'free expanse of the novel'" (I, 560). The sense of this statement, in light of what has just been discussed, hardly requires clarification, but one must wonder whether the reminiscence from *Evgenij Onegin* (Chapter VIII, stanza 50) carries deeper significance. Here I mean not only that Blok's hero, like Puškin's, typifies a whole class of his contemporaries; in this sense Blok's "trilogy" is, as Ivanov said all myth must be, "suprapersonal in content." I have in mind, more specifically, what Sergej Bočarov cites as the crucial and dynamic contradiction of Puškin's novel:

> The knot is tied already in the second stanza, where Onegin is introduced to the reader. "With the hero of my novel/Without prefaces, right away/Let me acquaint you:/Onegin, my good friend,/ Was born on the banks of the Neva..." . . .Here also is the indispensable third member of the relationship—the reader, to whom this is addressed and who appears in the following lines just as ambiguously, as the reader of the novel and at the same time on common ground with the hero: "Where, perhaps, you were born,/Or shone, my reader:/ There I once walked myself. . ."
> . . .The relationship "author—hero" is identified with the relationship "I—friend": like four persons from two, the world is squared, two series paradoxically converge into one. In fact the reality in which the author, hero and reader come together is a fantastic reality, even though it is geographically located "on the banks of the Neva" and it is discussed in a matter-of-fact, colloquial vein. This reality is hybrid: the world in which the novel is being written and read is intermingled with the "world" of the novel; the frame, the boundary separating the worlds has disappeared; *the depiction of life has been mixed up with life itself.*[172]

Significantly, Bočarov draws a direct parallel between this phenomenon and Blok's concept of artist and man:

> At a different time in Russian literature and life Blok will say in his speech about the crisis of Russian

symbolism: "The artist must be timid in his very
brazenness, knowing what the cost of mixing art and
life has been, and remaining in life a simple human
being." This credo of the poet originates in our literary
tradition with Puškin.[173]

What Bočarov calls a "credo", however, might just as well be
called a curse, because the fusion of art and life, to the degree that
it was unregulated, was something Blok viewed with trepidation.
This is why he speaks of the "cost of mixing art with life" and in
the same essay describes the anguish of his predicament:

I stand before the creation of my art, and I do not
know what to do. In other words, what am I to do
with my own life, which from this moment on has
become art; my creation, after all, *lives* beside me—not
alive, not dead, a blue phantom. . . . (V, 430-431)

Blok, like Puškin, preferred not a pure and stable "fusion" of art
with life, but a dynamic interrelationship between the two—an
interrelationship regulated by the creative persona of the author.
For Blok real life, empirical life was always prey to the randomness
of non-esthetic experience; to the degree that art merely recorded
this life without transforming and ordering it, art too risked
becoming random and chaotic. The function of the artist,
particularly the artist as cyclist, was to fashion life as esthetic
construct by uncovering a singleness of design beneath the
accidents of real experience. Hence at the beginning of the *poèma*
"Vozmezdie" he writes:

Жизнь — без начала и конца.
Нас всех подстерегает <u>случай</u>.
Над нами — сумрак неминучий,
Иль ясность божьего лица.
Но ты, художник, твердо веруй
В начала и концы. Ты знай,
Где стерегут нас ад и рай.
Тебе дано бесстрастной мерой
Измерить всё, что видишь ты.
Твой взгляд—да будет тверд и ясен.
Сотри <u>случайные</u> черти—
И ты увидишь: мир прекрасен.

This abhorrence of *slučaj* (chance) predicated all Blok's efforts to shape his lyric oeuvre into a unified whole.   In a sense, his "trilogy" is a kind of exorcism of *slučaj*, since it attempts to validate the interrelatedness of lyric "moments" and prove their conformity to the poet's esthetic design.

III

"MIGRATORY WORDS"
VERSES ABOUT THE BEAUTIFUL LADY
AND COMPANION CYCLES OF
BLOK'S FIRST VOLUME

> This morning visions flocked to me
> Like wild swans, and lifted me on their
>   broad wings.
> —Henrik Ibsen, "Brand" (Act II, scene 2)

In some respects the three cycles of Blok's first volume—"Ante Lucem" (AL), "Stixi o Prekrasnoj Dame" (SPD) and "Rasput'ja" (RAS)—call to mind a poetry of bygone times. SPD, the largest of the three, sets the tone of the volume as a whole and establishes its principal concern—the poet's relationship with an ideal beloved whose image is inseparable from the heavenly signs. An ethereal creature whose earthly counterpart is Blok's real-life sweetheart and wife-to-be (Ljubov' Dmitrievna Mendeleeva), the Lady continually appears like a divine revelation on the backdrop of the sky's rosy glow at dawn or dusk. She is infinitely pure, all-knowing and inaccessible—an embodiment of the "Eternal Feminine" principle celebrated in the closing lines of *Faust* ("Das Ewig-Weibliche/Zieht uns hinan"). The poet is the Lady's knight, seeking Her gracious attention, or Her seer and oracle, striving to comprehend Her mysteries. This is a poetry which elicits comparison with that of Goethe, Novalis, Dante, and Petrarch; in a spirit it belongs more to the era of German romanticism or to the Italian Renaissance than to the turn of the twentieth century, when it was written.

With regard to the kind of interaction it invites between reader and text, however, Blok's cycle belongs very much to the new era and in fact epitomizes the esthetics of symbolism. In SPD Blok communicates not by naming things, but by suggesting

them, as Mallarmé advocated, and he realizes more fully than any
of his contemporaries Verlaine's wish for an idiom

> Plus vague et plus soluble dans l'air,
> Sans rien en lui qui pèse ou qui pose.

("Art poétique")

The language is "vague" to the extreme and "soluble in the air" to
the degree that it defies paraphrase. It is so elusive that no single
sense of a poem can impose itself from the outset, and the diligent
reader is invariably drawn deeper into the web of the text, whose
latent meanings he strives to divine or decode. This is not to say
that the poems resist esoteric interpretations (indeed these insinuate
themselves in abundance), but that their real subject is always
shrouded in a dream-like indefiniteness. As in a dream realia from
waking experience are present, but their significance is always
unclear.

Let us consider, for instance, SPD #150 ("Pri žoltom svete
veselilis'..."):

> При жолтом свете веселились,
> Всю ночь у стен сжилмался круг,
> Ряды танцующих двоились,
> 4 И мнился неотступный друг.
>
> Желанье поднимало груди,
> На лицах отражался зной.
> Я проходил с мечтой о чуде,
> 8 Томимый похотью чужой...
>
> Казалось, там, за дымкой пыли,
> В толпе скрываясь, кто-то жил,
> И очи странные следили,
> 12 И голос пел и говорил...

(SPD #150)(I, 224)

The poem depicts a ball at which the poet discerns, apparently, his
double amidst (or perhaps behind?) the dancers, but the
implications of this already quite shadowy situation are, to say the
least, uncertain. To begin with, what need is there for the
concrete detail "*yellow* light" (line 1) in such an unrealistically
presented scene? Perhaps "yellow" carries some symbolic meaning?
Of what "miracle" does the poet speak in line 7? Why does the
double "sing" and what is the content of his speech in the last

line?   The poem ends precisely at the point where its implications
are haziest.   Even the identity of the double, who is familiar to
the poet at the beginning ("neotstupnyj drug"), acquires obscurity
in the closing stanza ("kto-to," "oči strannye").   One might even
wonder whether this is the same figure who appeared earlier.

In SPD #64 ("Vosxodja na pervye stupeni...") we find a
similar phenomenon:

> Восходя на первые ступени,
> Я смотрел на линии земли.
> Меркли дни — порыву исступлений
> 4 Гасли, гасли в розовой дали.
> Но томим еще желаньем горя,
> Плакал дух, — а в звездной глубине
> Расступалось огненное море,
> 8 Чей-то сон шептался обо мне...

(SPD #64)(I, 137)

Here too certain concrete details are evident—the sunset, the stars,
the steps.   From the outset, however, there is a disturbing spacial
perspective: the poet is only on the "first steps" of some edifice,
yet he already occupies a vantage point which allows him to see
into the remote distance ("linii zemli").   The steps apparently have
some symbolic importance which, however, is not explained in the
poem.   Going on, one must ask whose "spirit" is mentioned in line
6 and why the "spirit" yearns for "grief" (line 5).   Whose "dream
whispered" at the end, and what did it say?   This poem too ends
with its vaguest utterance (note the indefinite pronoun "čej-to" in
the last line), at precisely that point where we might expect some
clue to the meaning of its strange imagery.

These poems are typical of SPD and the first volume as a
whole in that they leave in obscurity much basic information which
would be customary in texts of an earlier era.   They insist on
raising questions to which they supply no answers, as if to imply
that incomprehensibility is one of their essential features.   They
seem laden with symbolic meaning, but they do not in themselves
provide any key for deciphering the symbolic code.   In SPD Blok
has clearly mastered the technique of speaking in the "confuses
paroles" to which Baudelaire refers in his famous poem
"Correspondances."

Readers both sympathetic and unsympathetic to Blok have
spoken about the bewilderment these early verses generate.   One

reviewer of the ten poems which made Blok's literary debut (March 1903) characterized them as "versified nonsense,"[1] while another called them "a collection of words insulting to common sense."[2] Even long after Blok's reputation was well-established, critics and scholars continue to disparage what they see as the excessive obscurity of the first volume.   L. I. Timofeev, for instance, writes:

> Blok's poetry acquired an exceptionally complex, unintelligible form within which, beyond its apparent meaningfulness and difficulty, lay hidden a quite limited content.[3]

Similarly, A. Gorelov, speaking of SPD #29 ("Segodnja šla Ty odinoko...") and other verses of the first volume, suggests that the reader's encounter with such cryptic poetry is frequently unrewarding:

> Verses like these . . . become such complex puzzles [rebusami] that efforts expended deciphering their dark and highly coded meaning are not always compensated esthetically.[4]

By contrast, Kornej Čukovskij saw the "dark" and "coded" aspect of Blok's early poetry as its principal asset; in his view the style of these poems, which he calls "cryptograms," serves a distinct esthetic function:

CRYPTOGRAMS

> He [Blok] was the singular master of vague, inarticulate speech.   No one else knew how to be so unintelligible. . . .   To speak unintelligibly is not an easy art, it is accessible to few. And who among the symbolists in those years . . . did not try his hand at this most difficult of arts. Only Blok, however, was successful at it.   The others are sphinxes without riddles,—no matter how hard they tried, they always remained comprehensible, while Blok possessed a multiplicity of devices for clouding his poetic speech. Frequently he hid from his readers the very subject of his discourse and subsequently was compelled to write commentaries to these clouded verses.

. . . .

SECRETS

All these devices and mannerisms were perfectly
suited to making speech obscure. Only in such a
disjointed, diffuse language could he tell about that
secret which for many years was his only theme. This
language was as if created for secrets. . . . Only that
elusive, disjointed, inarticulate, unintelligible, drowsy
speech which Blok mastered with such superlative skill
at twenty or twenty one years of age could be used to
express this theme. . . . If Blok had not possessed the
gift of speaking unintelligibly, his theme would have
killed his Beautiful Lady. But he always talked about
her as if beyond the bounds of human speech. . . .[5]

Whether or not one agrees with Čukovskij's positive appraisal,
there is no question but that his remarks capture the most salient
feature of this poetry: it is encoded speech designed to secret
mysteries. One can only fault Čukovskij's implication that Blok
always understood these mysteries and that he was able to explain
their meaning via commentary when and if he chose to do so. It
is worth recalling Paul Valéry's wise observation: "When we are
perplexed . . . an appropriately vague language comes to our aid,
[and] masks our helplessness . . ."[6]

The fact is that Blok himself groped to understand his own
early verses and was often at a loss to decipher them. A number
of anecdotal reports confirm this. When asked by his close friend
Evgenij Ivanov, for example, to identify the rider in the lines

И стало ясно, кто молчит
И на пустом седле смеется,   (SPD #142) (I, 215)

Blok did not know how to reply; his answer was uncertain: "Most
likely, the Antichrist" (I, 610). Aleksej Tolstoj, the novelist,
reports asking Blok the meaning of a cryptic line in a somewhat
later poem and receiving the response: "I assure you, I myself do
not know."[7] Such reactions are not vain posturing, as one might
surmize from Tolstoj's tasteless caricature of Blok in *Xoždenie po
mukam*,[8] but rather a genuine failure to understand his own words.
Similar remarks from Blok's correspondence, where there can be no
question of public posturing, offer ample evidence of his sincerity.[9]

The most revealing incident, however, is Blok's aborted
attempt in August-September 1918 to supply prose commentaries

to SPD. His stated purpose was to explicate the cryptic verses of his first book in much the same way Dante interpreted his lyrics about Beatrice in *La Vita Nuova*; verses were to be juxtaposed with prose exegesis:

> I felt lost in the forest of my own past until I got the idea to make use of the device Dante chose when he wrote *The New Life*.
>
> Eliciting aid and quiet counsel from Her, about whom this book is written, I hope I shall succeed in supplementing it with words simple enough to help others understand its only really essential content. (I, 561)

Blok did not complete this project, but there remains in his diary a preliminary draft of the commentaries. They are divided, like those in Dante, into two general categories: 1) biographical background (VII, 338-345), and 2) textual interpretation (VII, 346-350).

Careful examination of this draft reveals why Blok abandoned the idea. The biographical reminiscences are informative and coherent enough, although there are lapses in Blok's memory and some blatant inaccuracies;[10] if Blok had had access to Ljubov' Dmitrievna's diaries, which were apparently lost at Šaxmatovo (ZK, 424), he might well have ironed out these difficulties. Where Blok turns to interpretation of the poems, however, he experiences serious problems. The text is peppered with confessions of perplexity; words such as "apparently" ("vidimo," "očevidno," "po-vidimomu") and "perhaps" ("možet byt'") appear repeatedly and with growing frequency as the commentaries unfold. Parenthetical queries are numerous: "Are the doubles already looking to be hired?"; "Where is the idea about the curse of time?"; "Her 'mutable' soul (!?)"; "A mad man—who is this? Is he in me?" (VII, 348-349). It is hard to imagine that such commentaries would be useful to the average reader; instead of "simple words," as promised, we usually find verbatim quotation of the poems, and this practice becomes more persistent as the commentaries near their abrupt end. One of the last poems Blok discusses, SPD #15 ("Vse bytie i suščee soglasno..."), is treated as follows (verbatim or almost verbatim quotations from the poem are italicized):

The preceding absence of an answer forces [me] to put

> on armor, and this is expressed in the sensation of
> myself as a microcosm, in which are located *the whole
> universe,* the whole *past and future* and *in
> overabundance—all the lights with which she is aglow;*
> therefore *there is neither weakness nor strength;* her
> *compassion* or *indifference* does not affect me [because]
> *a seer* does not require *sympathy. I have* already *crossed
> the boundary line* and *I am only waiting for another
> pre-arranged vision in order to fly away into another
> empty space* (which does not frighten me either). (VII,
> 349)

Such an "explication" would undoubtedly receive a failing grade in
freshman literature class.   Even if it only reiterates what was
written seventeen years earlier, however, it is enlightening for its
implications.   As a reader of his own poetry, albeit a privileged
one, Blok seems to have experienced the same perplexity as others,
and somehow simple repetition of words proved more acceptable to
him than paraphrase or exegesis as a means of grasping its
significance.   Critics have suggested that Blok abandoned this
project because it was "too complex"[11] or because "he did not have
time."[12]   Neither of these explanations is very plausible since Blok
was always extremely generous with his energy and time whenever
he re-edited the first volume, his sentimental favorite.[13]   More
likely, he realized that in contrast to *La Vita Nuova* the first
volume succeeded to the degree that it evoked interpretive
speculation in the reader (Blok himself included) and that to
extract this dynamic from the book was to deprive it of whatever
esthetic value it did have.   Moreover he seems to have understood
intuitively that the most effective cipher or key to the poems'
encoded meaning lay somewhere in the poems themselves, in the
words they contain.

About a week before he began the Dante-style commentaries
Blok made the following entry in his notebook:

> At night I awoke in horror ("again all the old rubbish
> [to go] into my books").   But what sort of "retribution"
> is this?   Among other things—[retribution] for
> incomplete utterances, for half-clarities, for slow
> deterioration.   Whoever wishes to understand will
> understand better by reading it all carefully one thing
> after another.   (ZK, 422)

By abandoning the commentaries, Blok seems to have reverted back to this precedent—allowing the poems themselves, in their interaction, to clue each other's meaning.

What Blok wrote in fall 1918 provides a rare glimpse of a poet applying various ciphers to his poetry, much in the same way a literary critic does. He uses, primarily, a "biographical cipher" (alluding to real events and persons in his life as well as the psychological context of the imagery). To a lesser degree, he employs a "subtextual cipher" (indicating the source of a borrowed word or phrase); specifically, he cites several reminiscences from Vladimir Solov'ev.[14] Another to which he only refers in the notebook entry from August might be called a "cyclic cipher"—the capacity of one poem (or several poems) to act as another's interpretant.

The discussion that follows treats each of these ciphers but focuses specifically on the last, which is, properly speaking, the one directly relevant to the broader subject of this study. The cyclic cipher, as we shall see, operates via the mechanism of recurring words and images which in a sense "migrate" from poem to poem, creating conceptual ties and indicating which poems (or textual segments within poems) may interrelate meaningfully. This dynamic is the key not only to the first volume but to Blok's esthetic method in general; the word in its various "migrations" is the basic integrator of the "trilogy" and, indeed, of Blok's entire poetic universe.[15]

To demonstrate the importance of the "migratory" word-image it will be instructive to examine each of the several ciphers separately and consider how useful each is as a device for decoding the early Blok.

The Biographical Cipher

The interrelationship between poetry and life is a complex one which varies from poet to poet. While lyric tends to translate life experience into esthetic fact more directly than most literary modes, many poets can be understood without knowledge of their biographies. As Edward J. Brown points out, the love poems of Catullus "lose very little through the reader's ignorance of particulars, since these poems are lyric verbalizations of widely experienced and immediately recognized emotional states."[16] The

same could be said for the philosophical poetry of Tjutčev and
Baratynskij, or for most of Bal'mont's and Sologub's lyric output.
Most Russian poets of the twentieth century, however, moved
toward a more intimate connection between biography and lyric.
The poetry of Axmatova, Majakovskij, late Mandel'štam and
Cvetaeva, for example, is highly autobiographical. Indeed much of
Cvetaeva's verse is incomprehensible without at least some clue to
the realia underlying it.[17]

Blok occupies a position somewhere between these two
extremes. As mentioned earlier, his "trilogy" represented an effort
to regulate the interrelationship of life and art without severing the
ties between them. Following and developing more fully a
tendency of the romantic poets on whom he was nurtured, Blok
created an idealized autobiography, a legend about his own fate
which guided both his choice of poetic detail and his selection of
poems for inclusion in the "trilogy." When Blok wrote in 1915
"the stronger the lyric poet, the more fully his fate [sud'ba] is
reflected in his verse" (V, 514), he meant not that a poet ought to
give a documentary account of his life, but that he ought to
present a coherent "life drama" derived from real experience while
at the same time mediated by the concept of esthetic inevitability.
Blok himself succeeded so well in this endeavor that his poetic
personality overshadowed the real man in the eyes of his
contemporaries. Hence Boris Èjxenbaum remarked immediately
after Blok's death that his "poetry became for us a tragic actor's
emotional monologue, and Blok himself became this very actor
made up to resemble himself."[18] This observation was echoed by
Jurij Tynjanov:

> Few people knew Blok. As a person he remained
> a riddle for the broad literary circle of Petrograd, not to
> mention all of Russia.
> But all over Russia people "know" Blok as a
> person, believe firmly in the definiteness of his image,
> and if anyone should happen to see his portrait even
> once, he already feels that he knows him inside and
> out.[19]

The intimate relationship between poet and lyric hero in Blok
suggests that knowledge of his biography is not irrelevant to an
understanding of his poetry; this is especially true of the first
volume, where certain of life's realia are quite conspicuously given

the status of esthetic fact. Though all the poems of Blok's
"trilogy" are subscribed by their date of composition, only those in
the first volume are arranged in strict chronological order, giving
AL, SPD, and RAS the quality of a single, continuous diary.[20]
Life's chronology governed the disposition of poetic material.
Moreover SPD and RAS are demarcated by a purely biographical
event; the poems in SPD, with exception of its opening lyric, were
written before November 7, 1902 (when Ljubov' Dmitrievna
accepted Blok's marriage proposal), while those in RAS were all
written after this date. Geographical realia are also important.
The titles of the six sections of SPD contain the place of
composition (whether Šaxmatovo or Petersburg), and beneath the
poems Blok frequently placed more specific topographical
indications, e.g., "Selo Boblovo" (the Mendeleev estate), "Cerkovnyj
les" (a wooded area between Šaxmatovo and Boblovo), "Selo
Dedovo" (the estate of Mixail Solov'ev), "Bad Nauheim" (the
German spa where Blok's family vacationed). There are also
dedications to the persons unknown to the general public, as for
instance a to certain "N. Gun" (Blok's university companion) or to
"K.M.S." (Ksenija Mixaijlovna Sadovskaja—Blok's first, adolescent
love).

Private circumstances are indisputably important in the first
volume, and one cannot dismiss outright even rather simplistic
biographical readings of SPD like Nikolaj Gumilev's:

> There has been much conjecture about Blok's Beautiful
> Lady. People have wanted to see in her either the
> Woman Clothed with the Sun, or Eternal Femininity, or
> a symbol of Russia. But if we accept that this is
> simply a girl with whom the poet was first in love,
> then it seems not a single poem in the book would
> contradict this opinion, and the image itself, closer as a
> consequence, would become even more wondrous and
> gain infinitely from an esthetic perspective.[21]

In a similar vein Čukovskij comments:

> If one delves attentively into his first book, one sees
> that this is a genuine tale about a certain young man
> who fell so ecstatically in love with his neighbor that he
> made her into a Luminescent Maiden and transformed
> the whole rural landscape surrounding her into an
> unearthly habitat. . . . When you read in Blok's first

book about the red icon lamps glowing in the princess's
tower, about the doves alighting on her intricately
decorated door, about the lofty hill on which her tower
stands, and so forth, and so forth,—behind all this
majestic imagery you discern an unimposing Russian
provincial setting: an estate of gentlefolk nestled on a
hill, a dovecote, a rosy-cheeked girl-next-door, a little
stream, a young birch grove. In this way it is possible
to decipher all the most high-sounding imagery in
"Verses about the Beautiful Lady," so that one is left
with a true-to-life (and entirely realistic) account.[22]

While such pronouncements suffer from exaggeration and perhaps
even critical naiveté, they accurately signal Blok's encoding of real
events and settings in a highly periphrastic symbolic idiom. And
as Čukovskij indicates, awareness of the underlying realities can
often serve as a cipher to the cryptic utterance.

The reader who encounters the poem "Tam—v ulice stojal
kakoj-to dom..." (SPD #119) without knowing the circumstances
that inspired it, for instance, might be at a loss to explain why the
poet takes such intent interest in "a certain house" and the
"jingling glass" of the door on the stairway:

Там — в улице стоял какой-то дом,
И лестница крутая в тьму водила.
Там открывалась дверь, звеня стеклом,
Свет выбегал, — и снова тьма бродила.

Там в сумерках белел дверной навес
Под вывеской "Цветы", прикреплен болтом.
Там гул шагов терялся и исчез
На лестнице — при свете лампы жолтом.

Там наверху окно смотрело вниз,
Завешанное неподвижной шторой,
И, словно лоб наморщенный, карниз
Гримасу придавал стене — и взоры...

Там, в сумерках, дрожал в окошках свет,
И было пенье, музыка и танцы.
А с улицы — ни слов, ни звуков нет, —
И только стёкол выступали глянцы.

По лестнице над сумрачным двором
Мелькала тень, и лампа чуть светила.
Вдруг открывалась дверь, звеня стеклом,
Свет выбегал, и снова тьма бродила.

(SPD #119) (I, 192)

Though this poem is rich in concrete detail, it is impossible to determine from the immediate context whether the building described is a private residence, a house of prostitution, some kind of live-in florist shop, or something else entirely.   From Blok's private diaries and correspondence, however, we know that it is the home of the actress Marija Čitau on Gagarin Street in Petersburg. Dame Čitau gave drama classes there which Ljubov' Dmitrievna attended in the winter of 1901-02, and Blok waited daily outside the door in the courtyard for his sweetheart to exit (VII, 345). His diary contains an unsent letter to Ljubov' Dmitrievna that explains the significance of the "jingling" door glass:

> I used to wait one hour, two hours, three.   Sometimes you weren't even there.   But God, if you were!   The the hallway door that I cherished would suddenly jingle and make banging sounds as it was opened and slammed shut.   Light would race down from the dim yellow lamp.   (VII, 55)

The letter he sent to Ljubov' Dmitrievna on May 1, 1903 gives further insight into the poem's symbolism:

> When in the upstairs apartment there were laughter and cries, I stood below underneath the yellow lamp. . . . To this day I approach these steps and listen for the rustle of your dress, and I bow down to the ground, and I kiss the grey steps. . . .   Much of my heart remains within the walls of this staircase beneath the yellow lamp.   There was too much genuine, non-human trembling and joy of suffering there to leave this behind.[23]

With these biographical ciphers much that was cryptic in the poem becomes clear—it is not difficult to visualize the lovelorn poet listening and watching anxiously for signs that his beloved is about to descend the staircase.

Such "quotations from the text of life," as Minc calls them,[24] abound in Blok's first volume, and frequently knowledge of their source unlocks the mystery of a cryptic utterance. In SPD #105 ("Žizn' medlenaja šla, kak starja gadalka..."), for instance, we encounter an allusion to the "jagged-edged forest" whose significance cannot be discerned from the immediate context:

> Остановясь на перекрёстке, в поле,
> Я наблюдал зубчатые леса.
>
> . . . .
>
> И вспомнил я сокрытые причины
> Плененья дум, плененья юных сил.
> А там вдали — зубчатые вершины
> День отходящий томно золотил...
>
> (SPD #105) (I, 178)

If we know, however, that this image refers to the forest surrounding Boblovo, the summer estate of Ljubov' Dmitrievna, the poet's fascination with it becomes clear.[25] Similarly, the poet's fixation on the "fur coat" in SPD #161 ("Ego vstrečali povsjudu...") is decoded if we know that in the fall of 1902, before Blok's marriage proposal was accepted, Ljubov' Dmitrievna continually wore this coat as Blok followed her through the streets of St. Petersburg:

> Ему дивились со смехом,
> Говорили, что он чудак.
> Он думал о шубке с мехом
> И опять скрывался во мрак.
>
> (СПД #161)(И, 235)

Moreover knowledge of the circumstances that gave rise to a particular poem frequently provides insight into the poet's creative experience. Avril Pyman, for instance, points out that the poem "Ja šel — i vsled za mnoju šli...") (SPD #82) was inspired by an evening of New Year's fortune-telling at the Mendeleevs' after which Blok walked home alone from Vasilevsky Island opposite Petersburg.[26] Indeed these events helped produce the macabre imagery of this poem:

> "Я шел — и вслед за мною шли
> Какие-то неистовые люди.
> Их волосы вставали под луной,
> И в ужасе, с растерзанной душой

Зубами скежетали, били в груди,
И разносился скрежет их вдали.
(SPD #82) (I, 155)

The biographical approach, however, has its limitations. Real-life circumstances, while they are important for the creative process, are by no means an infallible key to a poem's significance nor are they always relevant to the poem as an esthetic object. The reader who knows of Blok's activities on the night of December 31, 1901, for example, does not really appreciate SPD #82 as poetic artifact any more deeply than a reader who remains ignorant of them. He understands better the poem's embryology but has no greater insight into the poem's meaning.[27]

Moreover, even where biographical information helps decipher a cryptic poem or image, knowledge of it is hardly ever essential. The most perplexing verses of the first volume, including those already cited, yield very few secrets to the biographical cipher that they would not also yield to the subtextual or cyclic ciphers. The phrase "jagged-edged forest" ("zubčatyj les") in SPD #105, for instance, can be explicated simply by allusion to other lyrics in the first volume; this image is quite clearly identified as the wood which rings the Beautiful Lady's abode:

Сегодня шла Ты одиноко,
Я не видал Твоих чудес.
Там, над горой Твоей высокой,
Зубчатый простирался лес.

И этот лес, сомкнутый тесно,
И эти горные пути
Мешали слиться с неизвестным,
Твоей лазурью процвести.
(SPD #29) (I, 102)

Similarly the significance of the "fur coat" in SPD #161 is no mystery to the reader who recalls the image of the beloved's "silvery-black fur" in SPD #147 ("Ona strojna i vysoka..."):

И я, невидимый для всех,
Следил . . . .
Ее сребристо-черный мех...
(SPD #147) (I, 221)

In these and most other instances biographical information is useful but superfluous to the conscientious reader, especially to the reader for whom it is more important to understand Blok the artist than Blok the man. Thus the effort to comprehend Blok's first volume as esthetic object is likely to confirm the author's own prediction, quoted earlier, that "whoever wishes to understand will understand better by reading it all . . . one thing after another."

It is quite apparent too from the composition of the volume in its "canonical" form that Blok was guided in his selection of poems by the principle that the most cryptic among them be accessible to some cipher other than the purely biographical. In choosing 314 poems out of the more than 800 lyrics he wrote from 1898 to June 1904, he discarded many which, though not inferior to others esthetically, were incomprehensible without knowledge of the biographical realia. He did not include, for example, the excellent poem "Pjat' izgibov sokrovennyx..." (I, 468), which by his own admission was "encoded" (VII, 348) and whose meaning could be grasped only by one who knew the real-life circumstances underlying it. In general, Minc's observation that "Blok did not include [in AL] . . . those early works in which the intimate-lyric thematics proved to be only intimate"[28] holds true not only for the cycle AL, but for SPD and RAS as well. Thus if one agrees with Gorelov that Blok's first volume often reads like "poetic hieroglyphics,"[29] one must acknowledge too that Blok did not wish that his biography be the only other text on the Rosetta stone.

The Subtextual Cipher

Blok has not usually been regarded as a poet for whom reminiscences from the works of other poets are so widespread or important a phenomenon as they are, for instance, in the poetry of Osip Mandel'štam or Vjačeslav Ivanov, who characteristically required of their readers a willingness to unearth multiple and often highly obscure subtexts. In recent years, however, it has become apparent that Blok's poetry too is rich in quotations,[30] whether they be conscious or unconscious.[31] Blok's "orientation toward 'the word of another [čužoe slovo'],'" as Minc calls this tendency, is already quite strong in the period of the first volume and becomes even more distinct in his mature poetry.[32]

Borrowing words from another text, however, is not necessarily an esthetically significant act—the mere presence of a reminiscence is not always an indication that the source text (or subtext) holds any clue to a poem's meaning. As Kiril Taranovsky explains apropos of Mandel'štam, there are different kinds of subtext with different implications:

> There are four kinds of subtext: (1) that which serves as a simple impulse for the creation of an image; (2) *zaimstvovanie po ritmu i zvučaniju* (borrowing of a rhythmic figure and the sounds contained therein); (3) the text which supports or reveals the poetic message of the latter text; (4) the text which is treated polemically by the poet. The first two do not necessarily contribute to our better understanding of a given poem.[33]

Abbreviating somewhat the above distinctions, one might say that there are reminiscences which are incidental or non-productive with regard to interpretation of a given poem and others which are significant or productive in this regard. In Blok's case it is useful to distinguish between those borrowings which are simple quotations (non-productive) and those which are true reminiscences (productive) in that they set in motion a meaningful interaction between the two texts, whether this interaction be mutually supportive or polemical. In the latter category, as we shall see, there are indeed many which provide a key to a cryptic image and thus serve as ciphers.

The majority of borrowings in AL, which contains Blok's earliest poetry, are non-productive. As might be expected from a young poet who is still learning his craft and has not yet found his own distinct voice, he often imitates the phrasings of his favorite predecessors, his "great teachers" as he called them (VII, 29), without bringing into play the larger implications of the source texts:

Светит месяц ночь ясна...
(Puškin, "Poxoronnaja pesnja
Iakinfa Maglanovica")

Пусть светат месяц, ночь темна ...
(AL #1) (I, 3)

Ленивой грядою идут облака...
(Puškin, "Sražennyj rusar'")

Лениво и тяжко плывут облака...
(AL #34) (I, 37)

К востоку, всё к востоку
Летит моя душа...
(Žukovskij, "Pesnja")

Мой дух летит туда, к Востоку...
(AL #36) (I, 39)[34]

Lexical echoes of this type are still encountered in SPD and RAS:

И тайный вздох немеющей любви... (Vl. Solovĕv, "Začem slova...")	Моя любовь — немеющая тень (SPD #59) (I, 132)
Чтоб без мысли и без речи Верный счёт вести часам... (A. Grigor'ev, "Zimnij večer")	Она без мысли и без речи На том смеется берегу... (SPD #131) (I, 204)
Её спасали от насилья Бессмертной пошлости людской... (Tjutčev, "Čemu molilas' ty...")	Ах, если б мог я научиться Бессмертной пошлости толпы... (RAS #41) (I, 281)
Вся жизнь моя — в веках звенящий стих... (Bryjusov, "Kleopatra")	Поставлю на страже звенящий стих... (RAS #46) (I, 286)

In these instances virtually nothing is gained from knowing the source of Blok's quotations.

In other cases, however, comparison of text and subtext may prove fruitful. As Konstantin Močul'skij points out, Blok's "Medlitel'noj čredoj nisxodit den' osennij..." (AL #31) recalls the imagery, tone and metric structure of Fet's poem "Opavšij list drožit ot našego dvižen'ja":[35]

ФЕТ

Опавший лист дрожит от нашего движенья,
Но зелени еще свежа над нами тень,
А что-то говорит средь радости сближенья,
Что этот желтый лист — наш следующий день.

Как ненасытны мы и как несправедливы:
Всю радость явную неверный гонит страх!
Еще так ласковы волос твоих извивы!
Какой живет восторг на блекнущих устах!

Идем. Надолго ли еще не разлучаться,
Надолго ли дышать отрадою? Как знать?
Пора за будущность заране не пугаться,
Пора о счастии учиться вспоминать.

БЛОК

Медлительной чредой нисходит день осенний,
Медлительно кружится желтый лист,
И день прозрачно свеж, и воздух дивно чист —
Душа не избежит невидимого тленья.

Так, каждый день стареется она,
И каждый год, как желтый лист кружится,
Всё кажется, и помнится, и мнится,
Что осень прошлых лет была не так грустна.

(AL #31) (I, 34)

In both poems the "yellow leaf" symbolizes death, and in both the poets contemplate the past and future. However, the optimistic upbeat of Fet's ending (so typical of his late poetry) is reorchestrated by Blok into an unrelieved pessimism. Here Blok engages in a friendly polemic with the older poet and by doing so, already begins to find his own lyric voice, the characteristic inflections that remain with him throughout his career.

In the first volume it is not uncommon to encounter a single poem informed by several subtexts simultaneously—a phenomenon given the name "poligenesis" in recent scholarship.[36] Even in the lyric just cited there are productive reminiscences from not only Fet's poem, but Puškin's "Osennee utro"[37] and Tjutčev's "Kak vesel groxot letnix bur'...". Another example is SPD #128 ("Probivalas' pevučim potokom..."), where the Beautiful Lady manifests herself in the visage of Death:

Пробивалась певучим потоком,
Уходила в немую лазурь,
Исчезала в просторе глубоком
4   Отдаленным мечтанием бурь.
Мы, забыты в стране одичалой,
Жили бедные, чуждые слез,
Трепетали, молились на скалы,
8   Не видали сгорающих роз.
Вдруг примчалась на север угрюмый,
В небывалой предстала красе,
Назвала себя смертною думой,
12   Солнце, месяц и звезды в косе.
Отошли облака и тревоги,
Всё житейское — в сладостной мгле,
Побежали святые дороги,
16   Словно небо вернулось к земле.
И на нашей земле одичалой
Мы постигли сгорания роз.
Злые думы и гордые скалы —
20   Всё растаяло в пламени слез.

(SPD #128) (I, 201)

As Minc observes, the image "Solnce, mesjac i zvezdy v kose" (line 12), is a reminiscence from Puškin's "Skazka o care Saltane," where the words "*Mesjac* pod *kosoj* blestit,/A vo lbu *zvezda* gorit" appear three times in reference to the fairy princess who emerges from enchanted form (a swan) to marry Prince Gvidon.[38]   The situational parallel—Prince Gvidon, like the "we" in SPD #128, languishes forgotten in a remote locale until rescued by a beloved female spirit—enhances the image of the death-goddess in Blok's poem and helps explain the joyous mood of reunion Blok describes. The words "Solnce, mesjac i zvezdy v kose," however, are at the same time derived from the Biblical Apocalypse: "And there appeared a great wonder in heaven; a woman clothed with the *sun*, and the *moon* under her feet,   *and upon her head a crown of twelve stars*" (The Revelation of St. John the Divine 12:1).   Via this subtext the ethereal heroine acquires another dimension and is seen from a different perspective. Still other locutions in SPD #128 recall Dmitrij Merežkovskij's lyric "Esli rozy tixo osypajutsja..." (1883), wherein Death is personified as a beautiful female.   These different subtexts coexist in Blok's poem and interact dynamically, complicating the image of the heroine and illuminating her countenance from various angles.

In the cases above appreciation of Blok's verses is enriched by knowledge of their subtext, but awareness of it is hardly essential for apprehension of their basic message.   There are instances, however, where the subtext can serve as a genuine cipher to the cryptic utterance.   The poem "Tam, v sumrake sobora..." (SPD #86), for example, closes with the following enigmatic couplet:

И смутно чуется познанье
И дрожь голубки и змеи.

(SPD #86) (I, 159)

One cannot grasp the meaning of these lines without knowing Vl. Solov'ev's lyric "Pesnja Ofitov," wherein Solov'ev, following the example of the Gnostics, employs the allegorical symbolism of the "dove" and the "snake" to represent the spiritual element and the material element of the universe, respectively; their union symbolized the mystical "synthesis" of spirit and flesh, heaven and earth.

On occasion Blok himself provides in an epigraph the subtext which unlocks the meaning of a cryptic poem.   Such is the case, for example in SPD #131 ("Ja otrok zažigaju sveči...")

> Имеющий невесту есть жених; а друг
> жениха, стоящий и внимающий ему,
> радостью радуется, слыша голос жениха.
>
> От Иоанна III, 29

Я, отрок, зажигаю свечи.
Огонь кадильный берегу.
Она без мысли и без речи
4   На том смеется берегу.

Люблю вечернее моленье
У белой церкви над рекой,
Передзакатное селенье
8   И сумрак мутно-голубой.

Покорный ласковому взгляду,
Любуюсь тайной красоты.
И за церковную ограду
12   Бросаю белые цветы.

Падет туманная завеса.
Жених сойдет из алтаря
И от вершин зубчатых леса
16   Забрежжит брачная заря.

(SPD #131) (I, 204)

The pertinence of the epigraph has been elucidated by Taranovsky: the "bridegroom" ("ženix") is Christ, the bride ("nevesta") is Christ's Church, and the "bridegroom's friend" ("drug ženixa") is John the Baptist.[39]   By analogy the mysterious woman on the "other shore" is identified with the "bride," and the poet-"novice" who sanctions the marriage by strewing "white flowers" is identified with the "bridegroom's friend."   The epigraph, however, does not exhaust the relevant subtexts.   "Belyj," "goluboj," "sumrak," "tumannyj," "zarja" belong to a fund of symbolic catchwords employed by   Dmitrij Merežkovskij's philosophical circle at the turn of the century.   For those initiated into the mysteries of his "White Synthesis" (a quasi-religious concept of absolute perfection), using these words invoked a body of canonical texts which included Merežkovskij's own novels and poems, the poetry of Z. Gippius (Merežkovskij's   wife,)   and   the   writings   of   Solov'ev.   Blok assimilated this symbolic shorthand in the summer of 1902, when

SPD #131 was written and when his fascination with the
Merežkovskijs reached its peak.[40]

Unlike Belyj, however, Blok never became a member of the
Merežkovskijs' inner circle, and being adogmatic in his poetic
method, he avoided slavish attachment to its symbolic jargon.[41] As
Ginzburg observes, Blok employed "the signs of a shared Symbolist
code," but he made it into something "individually Blokian."[42] He
almost never relies entirely on the code of any particular group or
movement, but rather creates his own code with its own decoding
mechanism.   The images mentioned above ("belyj," "goluboj,"
etc.), for example, are used so consistently and their symbolism is
so well-established in Blok's early cycles that reference to
extra-textual sources is not a *sine qua non* for understanding their
significance.   Here and elsewhere in the first volume knowledge of
subtext can open new perspectives and may even help decipher
some cryptic verse, but a cipher far more basic to the semiotic
dynamic of these poems is the "migratory word."

The Cyclic Cipher: The "Migratory Word"

The essence of Blok's gift as an artist lies in his extraordinary
ability to make the poetic word serve new semantic functions.
This fact has long since been acknowledged in Blok scholarship,
beginning with Viktor Žirmunskij's seminal essay "Poèzija Bloka"
(1921):

> The poet as if disregards the normal meaning of words
> and creates for himself a special metaphoric speech, a
> second level of language over the first or normal level;
> he uses this symbolic language to designate experiences
> which are inexpressible in prose speech. . . .   Reading
> Blok's works, we can compose a whole dictionary of
> such allegories [inoskazanij]: "night," "evening,"
> "darkness," "mists" (especially "sky-blue mists"),
> "haze," "twilight," "wind". . . .[43]

The following year Čukovskij partially fulfilled Žirmunskij's behest,
offering in *Kniga ob Aleksandre Bloke* (1922) an essay which at
times resembles a "dictionary" of Blok's favorite motifs. The book
is extremely impressionistic and lacks the systematic thoroughness
of a lexicon, but by focusing on the recurrence of certain words

(e.g., "tuman," "son," "sumrak," "strogij," "rab," "veter")
Čukovskij suggests by example that these repetitions are the key to
understanding Blok as a poet. Čukovskij's aim was to ascertain
the special meaning these words derive from the context of Blok's
verse.

Žirmunskij and Čukovskij laid the groundwork for more
in-depth studies of Blok's semantics which have appeared in more
recent times. Among these L. Ginzburg's remarkable essay
"Nasledie i otkrytija" (1964) occupies a place of special importance.
Ginzburg was the first to evaluate the exceptional role of context
and cyclization in the semantic enrichment of Blok's poetic word.
She points out that Blok's poetic vocabulary, for the most part, is
borrowed from the nineteenth-century romantics, but that he puts
words to an entirely different use. Words in Blok acquire their
meaning from the context of his "trilogy":

> From poem to poem context grows in increments and
> with it . . . emerge those Blokian symbols which run
> through his whole oeuvre, undergoing constant change.
> They develop from poetic imagery which had long been
> commonplace, such as azure, star, sunset, darkness, fog,
> wind, snowstorm— words which belonged to the
> inexhaustible and therefore impersonal unity of the
> romantic style. Very early on, Blok transformed these
> words into perpetually active elements of context,
> something distinctive to the highest degree. . . . Basic
> to Blok's method is the creation of recurring, fixed
> verbal symbols which draw their meaning from the
> common interrelatedness of his separate works and
> introduce this meaning into each new text. Blok's fund
> of symbols, which is formulated already in "Verses
> about the Beautiful Lady," does not disappear in his
> subsequent poetry. Their meaning, however, undergoes
> change as old symbols intersect with new ones which
> are assimilated into the circle of Blok's poetic imagery.[44]

These observations form a landmark in Blok scholarship and helped
determine the future course of investigations into Blok's poetics,
which have focused more and more since the mid 1960's on the
questions of cyclization and semantics.

Almost simultaneously with Ginzburg's essay there appeared
two articles in *Blokovskij sbornik I* (1964) which suggested avenues

of research very close to the one outlined by Ginzburg.   In
"Kritičeskaja proza Bloka" D. E. Maksimov emphasized the
polisemantic quality of Blok's language,[45] and in "Poètičeskij ideal
molodogo Bloka" Minc performs what is essentially a
context-oriented semantic analysis of Blok's first volume— albeit
on a rather small scale.[46]   Subsequently both scholars expanded
their efforts in this area and supplied their original observations
with fuller theoretical grounding.   The importance of Maksimov's
"Ideja puti v poètičeskom soznanii Aleksandra Bloka" (1972), in
this regard, can hardly be overestimated.[47]   Maksimov traces the
theme of the "path" through its various permutations in Blok's
prose and verse, citing this idea as one of the principal
"integrators" of Blok's poetic world; he argues that such
"integrators," which are in essence words or clusters of semantically
related words, cannot be fully understood without awareness of
their whole history in Blok's oeuvre, that is, without awareness of
their broadest authorial context.[48]   Since 1964 Minc has pursued
semantic analysis of Blok in a most ambitious way, most notably
in her four-volume study *Lirika Aleksandra Bloka* (1965-75).
Allied with these impressive efforts are two frequency dictionaries
of Blok's early verse produced by Minc jointly with other
researchers.[49]   One of the most enlightening observations she makes
about the way words function in Blok occurs in an article
co-authored with Jurij Lotman about the problem of deciphering
the image of "fire" (ogon', požar):

> In the lyrics of the mature Blok the symbols' meanings
> are uncovered not only in the immediate context (part
> of a text or one poetic text), but also in considerably
> broader contexts (cycle, volume, and in the extreme—
> the whole oeuvre), since *every concrete mention of
> "fires," "conflagrations" etc. potentially contains all those
> meanings previously itemized.*[50]

The principle that every use of a word in Blok's poetry
potentially implicates other texts in his oeuvre, from which it may
derive quite different, perhaps even contrastive meanings conditions
what D. M. Pocepnja aptly calls the "inner contradictoriness," the
"explosiveness" of Blok's poetic semantics:

> One and the same word (image) can enter into
> contrasting esthetic categories of Blok's world-view.   In
> this the characteristic feature of Blok's word becomes

manifest—its inner contradictoriness, its explosiveness, which reflects a dialectic understanding of life's phenomena, each of which can turn itself inside out.[51]

Indeed, Blok discovered a means of unlocking the word's "explosive" semantic potential, and he did so, one might add, very early in his career—in some respects too early, before he had acquired the wisdom and mastery to channel it and mold it to his own esthetic needs. Like a child who naively rubbed the magic flask and did not know how to make the jinni return, Blok—as we shall see—was not fully prepared at first to contain the chaos that this new verbal dynamic unleashed. This is why the first volume, though it remained for him the one he cherished most, was a constant frustration for him in later years when he had gained complete control of his artistic gift. This is why too, if—as Čukovskij says—Blok's contemporaries were "Sphinxes without riddles," the young Blok was often a Sphinx without solutions.

Blok's genius derived largely from his paradoxical attitude toward the poetic word. On the one hand, he shared the symbolists' belief that the word in its referential, denotative function (and even in its conventional connotative function) was an inadequate vehicle for expressing the poet's inner experience. For Blok, as for Tjutčev ("Silentium"), silence was in some respects preferable to the distortions generated by words, and it was no doubt with this in mind that he copied into his notebook in June 1902 the following verses of L. Vil'kina (Minskaja):

Слова

Безмолвное отрадно мне признанье.
Храню его. Я говорю без слов:
. . . .
О, полюби и ты моё молчанье!
Слова мертвы и тяжелей оков.
Слова — души обманчивый покров,
В словах — любви с угрозой сочетанье.

(ZK, 30)

Initially, Blok's Muse, the Beautiful Lady, is a purely musical presence that speaks to the poet in a non-verbal (or perhaps pre-verbal) medium; hence Blok was to write in his Dante-style commentaries, as he contemplated his early verses from the vantage point of poetic maturity: "To the end of January [1901] SHE [the Lady] is not mentioned in verse, there is only HER music. . . .

[My] psychology at that time . . . was *against words*" (VII, 346)
Similarly, in 1910 he characterized his earliest perceptions of the
Lady as "musical sounds, appeals, whispers, *almost words*" (V,
427). As the Lady's oracle, the poet seems to have envied Her the
capacity to communicate in a wordless idiom; the word threatened
to dissolve the mystery with which She entrusted him:

> Из отголосков далекой речи,
> С ночного неба, с полей дремотных,
> Всё мнятся тайны грядущей встречи,
> Свиданий ясных, но мимолетных.
>
> Я жду — и трепет объемлет новый,
> Всё ярче небо, молчанье глуше...
> Ночную тайну разрушит слово...
> Помилуй, боже, ночные души!
>
> (SPD #35) (I, 108)

Blok alluded to this same frustration in a diary entry from July
1902: "I want not words. There were words before and there will
be in the future; words are infinitely mutable, and there is no end
to them in sight. . . . I want *something beyond words* [Ja xoču
sverz-slov]" (VII, 52–53).

Blok knew, however, he could not escape the reality that
"poetry is made with words," as Mallarmé once said,[52] and he
sought to overcome their inherent limitation—to let words remain
words and at the same time transform them into "something
beyond words," to invest them with new content and significance.
Already in a rather early poem, SPD #41 ("Ne poj ty mne i
sladostno, i nežno...")(July 25, 1901), he invokes the "word" as the
carrier of transcendental knowledge and a certain mystic spell over
the beloved:

> Одни слова без песен сердцу ясны.
> Лишь правдой их над сердцем процветешь.
>
> (SPD #41) (I, 114)

This belief in the word's incantational power is evident also in the
titles Blok chose for two separate sections of SPD in the 1916
edition: "Vorožba" ("Fortune-telling"), "Koldovstvo" ("Sorcery").
It appears as a topic in his correspondence with Ljubov'
Dmitrievna as well: "I shall discover for You sacred *words* and
sounds" (November 10, 1902); "Some day I shall find for You an
unforgettable *word* or sensation, or something outside the customary

bounds. . . . Then something unexpected will be revealed suddenly, and we will comprehend completely" (December 15, 1902).[53] Blok also developed an attachment to the word's very "mutability," about which he had complained earlier; such is the implication of SPD #113 ("Dnem veršu ja dela suety..."), where the epithet "perelivčatyj" ("iridescent") embraces ambiguously the nouns "kraski" ("colors") and "slova" ("words"):

> Я люблю, и любуюсь, и жду
> Переливчатых красок и слов.
>
> (SPD #113) (I, 186)[54]

Blok's seems to be alluding to the word's capacity to proffer multiple meanings simultaneously—something which for him constituted the essence of the "symbol," as a notebook entry from July 1902 suggests:

$\sigma\upsilon\mu\text{B}\acute{\alpha}\lambda\lambda\omega$ ($\Sigma\acute{\upsilon}\mu\text{Bo}\lambda o\nu$)—

соединяю ⎫
спаиваю ⎬ символ есть слияние смуслов.
сливаю ⎭

(ЗК, 31)

It is this aspect of the poetic word, the "symbol" in Blok that prompted Gumilev to write: "No one knows how to unite two themes in one like Blok without contrasting them, but rather fusing them chemically."[55]

This capacity to combine meanings results from the tendency of the word in Blok's poetry to function not only as a referential sign, but as an index of other texts. The poetic word accumulates the implications of the texts which contain it, and when it reappears in a new text, in a new poem, it retains the memory of those other environments as part of its esthetic potential. Like a migratory bird, Blok's word tends to remember its previous habitats.

Curiously, the image of the "migratory word" is supplied by Blok himself in the poem ("Net konca lesnym tropinkam..."):

> Нет конца лесным тропинкам.
>   Только встретить до звезды
>   Чуть заметные следы...
> 4   Внемлет слух лесным былинкам.

Всюду ясная молва
Об утраченных и близких
По верхушкам елок низких
8   Перелетные слова...

Не замечу ль по былинкам
Потаенного следа...
Вот она — зажглась звезда!
12   Нет конца лесным тропинкам.

2 сентября 1901. Церковный лес.
(SPD #51) (I, 124)

This lyric is, among other things, about poetic creativity. At the beginning, the poet wanders through the "forest paths" (might this be Baudelaire's "forêt de symboles"?),[56] straining his senses and anticipating the onset of inspiration. First there are hardly any stimuli, then suddenly he hears distinct "speech" ("molva"), which carries the recollection of things (or persons?) "lost" ("utračennyx") and "cherished" ("blizkix"). Finally "words" arrive like "migratory" creatures (the only logical possibility being—"birds"). At the end the poet contemplates again the endless "paths," as if sensing a certain disorientation or even enclosure (this is perhaps an early indication of Blok's growing feeling of entrapment in the echo-chamber of his own early poetry). Whence the "words" emanate is uncertain, but the possibility that they originate in Blok's own lyrics cannot be ruled out, since in the first volume autoreminiscences are frequently the starting point of a new poem. As Čukovskij remarked: "One [poem] flows over into another, one as if grows out of the other";[57] in a similar vein Blok himself wrote in January 1902: "A lyric mood exists when very inspired echoes [otkliki] fly out of very inspired verses" (VII, 22). It is remarkable too that Blok's angel of inspiration, unlike Puškin's ("Prorok") and Lermontov's ("Angel"), not only reveals sounds to the poet, but echoes back to him the poet's own words:

Какой-то вышний серафим
Принес мне чудных звуков море.
Когда я был везде гоним, —
Я шел к нему — поведать горе;
А он речам моим внимал,
Моим словам он вторил страстно,
И этим мне познать давал,

Что в мире зло и что прекрасно.

(I, 436) (September 23, 1899)

This unusual statement captures vividly the essence of the creative impulse in the early Blok: the poet hears "sounds" ("čudnyx zvukov"), he speaks ("moim rečam"), and his words are "repeated" ("moim slovam on vtoril strastno"). To a large degree, gaining access to Blok's first volume means tracking down these repetitions, retracing the flight of his favorite "bird-words," so to speak, and experimenting with the new textual couplings they suggest.

To illustrate this let us examine the recurring image of "smykanie kruga" (closing the circle), which first appears in an enigmatic couplet at the end of SPD #8 ("Ty otxodiš' v sumrak alyj..."):

Ты ль смыкаешь, пламеная,
Бесконечные круги?

(SPD #8) (I, 81)

Subsequent usage of this image (or imagery almost identical to it) provides clues to its symbolic meaning:

И вдруг, в преддверьи заточенья,
Послышу дальние шаги...
Ты — одиноко — в отдаленьи,
Сомкнешь последние круги...

(SPD #14) (I, 87)

Тебя не вижу я, и долго бога нет.
Но верю, ты взойдешь, и вспыхнет сумрак алый,
Смыкая тайный круг, в движеньи запоздалый.

(SPD #36) (I, 109)

Холодная черта зари —
. . . .
. . . верный знак, что мы внутри
Неразмыкаемого круга.

(SPD #135) (I, 208)

Сомкнулись царственные дуги,
Душа блаженна, Ты близка.

(RAS #6) (I, 244)

From comparison of these verses it becomes evident that "smykanie kruga" is associated with accessibility or inaccessibility of the Lady (who is characteristically located inside the circle).   The poet may find himself on one or the other side of this magical boundary of inclusion-exclusion, whether *with* the Lady inside the circle (as in SPD #135, RAS #6 and, apparently, SPD #36) or *apart from* Her outside the circle (as in SPD #14 and, apparently, SPD #8). This symbolism is operative also in the image of "les, *somknutyj* tesno"—the forest which surrounds the Lady and makes Her inaccessible in SPD #29 (I, 102).

Ultimately, it is acquisition of such contextual meaning that allows Blok to amalgamate his lyrics into something approaching a "novel in verse," because the semantic memory of certain words spans the entire "trilogy."   Hence a word can become a mythologeme, a quotation from the mythic biography of the lyric hero; the path such a word traces through the lyric oeuvre becomes a metonym for the myth as a whole.   This occurs, for instance, with the word "meč" (sword), one of the most persistent motifs in Blok's poetry.   Originally, in the period Blok called the "thesis," the sword is a symbol of chivalric service to the Lady; it is associated with the concepts of fidelity, purity and spiritual strength.   Such are the dominant associational ties of the word "meč" in the first volume:

> Придвигается мир
> Моего обновленья.
> Воскурю я кадило,
> Опояшусь меч́ом
>
> Завтра с первым лучом
> Восходящего в небе светила.

(AL #67) (I, 70)

———

> Ныне, полный блаженства,
> Перед божьим чертогом
> Жду прекрасного ангела
> С благовестным мечом.

(SPD #6) (I, 79)

———

> Я стерегу Ее ключи
> И с Ней присутствую, незримый,

Когда скрещаются мечи
За красоту Недостижимой.

(SPD #157) (I, 230)

Светлый меч нам вскроет двери
Ослепительного Дня.

(RAS #56) (I, 297)

Depreciation of the sword represents detriment to the sacred values; hence appearance of the "wooden sword" (already in the first volume) suggests ridicule of the original Ideal and reversal of sword's primary emotive associations:

Он — мечом деревянным
Начертал письмена.
Восхищенная странным,
Потуплялась Она.

Восхищенью не веря,
С темнотою — один —
У задумчивой двери
Хохотал арлекин.

(SPD #137) (I, 210)

In the poetry of 1905-07, which comprises the core of Blok's second volume and represents the period he characterized as the "antithesis," the sword is symbolically lowered or lost—a sign of the poet's fall from grace:

Вот рассыпался меч, дребезжа.
щит упал . . . .
. . . .
Больше нет королевских венцов...

("Nočnaja fialka") (II, 33)

И в руке твой меч железный
      Опусти.

(SnM #8) (II, 220)

Меч мой железный
Утонул в серебряной вьюге...
Где меч мой? Где меч мой?

(SnM #15) (II, 233)

At the beginning of the third volume, Blok alludes to the history of the "sword" in words which would be incomprehensible without the context of the "trilogy":

> Вот <u>меч</u>. Он—был. Но он—не нужен.
> Кто обессилил руку мне? —
>
> . . . .
>
> <u>Меч</u> выпал. Дрогнула рука...
> (StM #16) (III, 29)

Later in the third volume the lyric hero seeks to regain the "sword," rededicate himself to the old Ideal and rediscover the spiritual vigor he once possessed as the servant of the Beautiful Lady. As a symbol the "sword" is now enriched with new meanings, while retaining all those contextual associations it accumulated earlier. It now becomes allied with the poet's anticipations of the Revolution, as it is in the cycles "Jamby" (JAM) and "Na pole Kulikovom" (NPK):

> И всем — <u>священный меч</u> войны
> Сверкает в неизбежных тучах.
> (JAM #12) (III, 96)

> И, к земле склонившись головою,
> Говорит мне друг: "<u>Остри свой меч</u>,
>
> Чтоб недаром биться с татарвою,
> За святое дело мертвым лечь!"
> (NPK II) (III, 250)

In this way the word "meč" distills the myth of the entire "trilogy." Many other motifs perform a similar function, among them such recurring images as "ogon'," "koster," "sneg," "zarja," "dver'," "car'," "put'," and certain colors (especially "sinij," "belyj," and "krasnyj"). Some of these will be examined in detail on subsequent pages.

Symbolic meanings are frequently acquired not only by the individual word or lexeme as above, but also by motivic groupings—clusters of words belonging to the same semantic field. Within such clusters many of the same contextual meanings are shared, and one word can borrow from the fund of connotative associations belonging to the cluster as a whole. The words "zabralo" and "stjag," for instance, each occur only once in the entire first volume and therefore develop no contextual meaning of their own. Where they do appear, however, they derive symbolic significance from the semantic cluster of martial imagery associated elsewhere with chivalric service to the Lady ("meč," "ščit," "znamja," "boj," etc.):

Но я вблизи — стою с мечом,
Спустив до времени забрало.

Души кипящий гнев смири,
Как я проклятую отвагу.
Остался красный зов зари
И верность голубому стягу.

(RAS #48) (I, 289)

This is not to say that whenever a word belonging to a given semantic cluster appears it automatically and invariably draws from the connotative fund of that grouping—the word's capacity to do so is only a potential. In the verses above, "zabralo" and "stjag" indeed draw from this fund, but only because the poem itself clearly sanctions such an extrapolation.

The inventory of associations a word (or semantic cluster) accumulates in its "migrations" sometimes undergoes what might be called *perversion*—that is, a given symbol appears in a context which simultaneously evokes its primary or usual connotations but reverses their emotive content. This tendency is especially prevalent toward the end of SPD and in RAS, where the poet's faith in the Ideal is undercut by a growing skepticism. We have already seen an example of perversion in the image of the "wooden sword" (SPD #137) (I, 210).

Let us consider another example. The word "*sveča*," has a primary symbolic connotation that is maximally positive. This image belongs to a semantic cluster containing words such as "lampada" (icon lamp), "ikona" (icon), "kadilo" (censer), "obraz" (in the sense "icon"), "altar'" (altar), "amvon" (pulpit), "cerkov'" (church) and "sobor" (cathedral)—all of which are allied with sacramental worship of the Lady. Such is the symbolism of "sveča" in SPD #86 ("Tam, v polusumrake sobora...") (I, 159), SPD #131 ("Ja, otrok, zažigaju sveči...") (I, 204), SPD #158 ("Vxožu ja v temnye xramy...") (I, 232) and RAS #72 ("Moj ljubimyj, moj knjaz', moj ženix...") (I, 315). But the image of "sveča" in SPD #114 ("Ljublju vysokie sobory...") at once evokes recollection of the candle's positive symbolism and at the same time subverts its customary implications:

> Люблю высокие соборы,
> Душой смиряясь, посещать.
> . . . .
> И тихо, с измененным ликом,
> В мерцаньи мертвенном свечей,
> Бужу я память о Двуликом
> В сердцах молящихся людей.
> Вот — содрогнулись, смолкли хоры,
> В смятеньи бросились бежать...
>
> (SPD #114) (I, 187)

Here the devotional "candles" recall an attitude of piety and reverence, while at the same time they are allied more directly with sacrilege.   The following poem, SPD #115 ("Ja znaju den' moix prokljatij..."), enacts a similar reversal by depicting the poet's sinister double beckoning the poet with this customary artifact of religious devotion:

> Он манит белою русалкой,
> Он теплит издали свечу...
>
> (SPD #115) (I, 188)

In this instance, not only the word "sveča," but the words "belaja" and "izdali" — both of which are allied with the Lady's benign aspect — also undergo perversion since they are associated in the immediate context with portents of evil and doom.   Virtually any of Blok's positive symbols can be such perverted. Even the image of "smykanie kruga," which, as we saw, is associated with the Lady's beneficence, can be used in a context which nullifies its positive meaning and recasts in it a negative mold:

> Явился он на стройном бале
> В блестяще сомкнутом кругу.
> Огни зловещие мигали,
> И взор описывал дугу.
>
> (SPD #153) (I, 227)

Here the poet's wicked double is included in the magical "closed circle," usurping the role normally reserved for the devout servant of the Lady.   This capacity of the word to "turn itself inside out," as Pocepnja aptly observed, constitutes one of the most important aspects of Blok's semantics.

As we have seen, the word in the first volume tends to become the carrier of ever larger structures of meaning. Ultimately, the word can even become a shorthand notation of certain archetypal, symbolic situations. To illustrate this it will be useful to examine the motif or the *"door"* (*"dver"*) in conjunction with the other members of its semantic cluster ("vorota," "kryl'co," "seni," "preddverie," "porog," "vxod," and "papert'"). This image is one of the most prominent "migratory" motifs in Blok's early poetry, and its importance (as we shall see in subsequent chapters) does not diminish in his second and third volumes.

In the first volume the door most commonly represents a boundary which separates the poet from an ideal space and acts as a barrier to it. This is the primary symbolic meaning of the door. The concept is already manifest in the cycle AL:

> Сама судьба мне завещала
> С благоговением святым
> Светить в преддверьи Идеала
> Туманным факелом моим.
>
> (AL #18) (I, 21)

> С холодной жаждой искупленья
> Стучался я в господний дом.
> . . . .
> Стучусь в преддверьи идеала,
> Ответа нет . . . .
>
> (AL #62) (I, 65)

In SPD, where ideal space is specifically identified with the Lady's realm, the door motif acquires even more prominence. It is significant, for instance, that the first poem of SPD begins and ends with the image of the poet at the "gate" ("vorota") to the Lady's tower-chamber:

> Отдых напрасен. Дорога крута.
> Вечер прекрасен. Стучу в ворота.
>
> Дольнему стуку чужда и строга,
> Ты рассыпаешь кругом жемчуга.
>
> . . . .
> Ты ли меня на закатах ждала?
> Терем зажгла? Ворота отперла?
>
> (SPD #1) (I, 74)

Here the closed (or locked) gate at the beginning suggests the Lady's inaccessibility, while the open (or unlocked) gate at the end connotes Her accessibility. Obviously, passage through the door, though not realized in this poem, represents fulfillment of the poet's most cherished goal— meeting with the Lady.

The circumstances in SPD #1, wherein the poet is located outside the door and the Lady resides within, are repeated in a seemingly limitless number of variations as the first volume unfolds:

Передо мной закрыта дверь
В таинственный приют.

(SPD #75) (I, 148)

Я медленно сходил с ума
У двери той, которой жажду.

(SPD #108) (I, 181)

Я стоял один у дверей.
. . . .
Я один не ушел от двери...

(SPD #132) (I, 205)

Подходя к золотому порогу,
Затихал пред Твоими дверьми.

(RAS #15) (I, 254)

И откроет белой рукою
Потайную дверь предо мною
Молодая, с золотой косою,
С ясной открытой душою.

(RAS #33) (I, 273)

Сторожим у входа в терем,
     Верные рабы...

(RAS #73) (I, 316)

Since the image of the door occurs repeatedly in contexts depicting in essence the same set of circumstances, the door itself can serve as an emblem of this archetypal situation. The situation becomes part of the word's connotative fund, from which each reference to a "door" can potentially draw. To this fund also belong two possible minimal scenarios of meeting: one involving entrance of the poet through the door, the other involving exit of the Lady. In SPD #1, SPD #75, RAS #15, and—apparently—RAS #33, which are quoted above, the former scenario is envisioned; the latter is subsumed in a series of poems, including SPD #62 ("Skripnula dver'. Zadrožala ruka..."), SPD #85 ("Vysoko s temnotoj slivaetsja stena..."), and SPD #119 ("Tam — v ulice stojal kakoj-to dom..."), to which earlier we applied a biographical cipher. (How much richer in meaning this poem proves to be when we apply the "migratory" cipher—in this instance, the door image—and the many texts it accumulates!)

The circumstances just described (poet outside, Lady inside), however, represent but one of several variations involving the door. If we designate the first Situation A, its converse—Situation B—presents the poet inside his abode with the heroine arriving or seeking entry from without:

> Встану я в утро туманное,
> Солнце ударит в лицо.
> Ты ли, подруга желанная,
> <u>Всходишь ко мне на крыльцо?</u>
>
> (SPD #54) (I, 127)

> Будет день, словно миг веселья.
> Мы забудем все имена.
> <u>Ты сама придешь в мою келью</u>
> И разбудишь меня от сна.
>
> (SPD #160) (I, 234)

A third—let us call it situation C—involves entrance or exit through the doors of a church. Unlike the Lady's abode, the church is an edifice to which access is typically unimpeded:

> Входите все — в открытые <u>брата</u>.
> Там—в глубине—Мария ждет молений,
> Обновлена рождением Христа.
>
> (SPD #110) (I, 183)

As such it represents a common ground between the earthly and the divine, a logical meeting place for the poet and the Lady:

> Вхожу я в темные храмы,

Совершаю бедный обряд.
Там жду я Прекрасной Дамы
В мерцаньи красных лампад.

В тени у высокой колонны
Дрожу от скрипа дверей.
(SPD #158) (I, 232)

———

Ты сказала сама: "Приду".
У входа в сумрак молений
Я открыл мое сердце. — Жду.
(RAS #14) (I, 253)

It is apparent that the first volume endows the word "door" (and words of the same semantic cluster) with a rich symbolic meaning by making it the metonym for a number archetypal situations or scenarios. To enumerate *all* the meanings this image acquires, however, is an impossible task because they are, in effect, the mnemonic traces of a great many texts. To itemize them fully would be to reproduce these tests in their entirety. At best one can make certain generalizations: that the "door" is firmly associated with accessibility of the Lady (or the Ideal), that the open (or unlocked) door is maximally positive, while the closed (or locked) door connotes the negative. These implications are intrinsic to all the archetypal scenarios outlined above.

It must be remembered, however, that the meaning of the word "door" in any given context can never be equated entirely with its meaning in other texts. This is sometimes overlooked by those who, in an effort to systematize the symbolic values of Blok's imagery, are not sufficiently attentive to the function of the word in the poem itself.[58] No matter how unified Blok's cycles are, they remain cycles, that is, they do not fully achieve the status of a single text. This is why, when we speak of contextual meanings and the word as index of other texts, we are speaking only of its potential.

What makes Blok's first volume exceptional is that this potential is activated so often. On those occasions where the door image appears, for instance, it nearly always implicates in some way its usage in other texts. This is true even when none of the archetypal situations is explicitly indicated:

Жду я холодного дня,

Сумерек серых я жду.
Замерло сердце, звеня:
Ты говорила: "Приду, —

Жди на распутьи — вдали
Людных и ярких дорог,
Чтобы с величьем земли
Ты разлучится не мог.

Тихо приду и замру,
Как твое сердце, звеня,
<u>Двери</u> тебе отопру
В сумерках зимнего дня.

(SPD #67) (I, 140)

Мы тогда откроем <u>двери</u>,
И заплачем, и вздохем...

(SPD #92) (I, 165)

Светлый меч нам вскроет <u>двери</u>
Ослепительного Дня.

(RAS #56) (I, 297)

In the cases above the immediate context signals none of the archetypal situations specifically, yet one can hardly appreciate the symbolism of the open (unlocked) door without alluding to them.

It is quite common, moreover, to encounter perversions whose effect subsumes awareness of the archetype. SPD #81 ("Noč' na novyj god"), for instance, involves perversion of archetypal Situation A:

```
      За воротами смеются,
 8    Дальше — улица темна.
      Дай взгляну на праздник смеха,
      Вниз сойду, покрыв лицо!
      Ленты красные — помеха,
12    Милый глянет на крыльцо...
      Но туман не шелохнется,
      Жду полуночной поры.
      Кто-то шепчет и смеется,
16    И горят, горят костры...
      Скрипнет снег — в морозной дали
```

Тихий крадушийся свет.

Чьи-то санки пробежали...

20   "Ваше имя?"   Смех в ответ...

Вот поднялся вихорь снежный,

Побелело всё крыльцо...

И смеющийся и нежный

24   Закрывает мне лицо...

(SPD #81) (I, 154)

This poem is informed by certain subtexts—most notably, Žukovskij's ballad "Svetlana" and Puškin's *Evgenij Onegin* (V. ix), and more generally by the folk custom of New-Years-Eve fortune telling, during which young girls, before retiring, perform various rituals to divine their fated mate.   Typically, the girls will ask passers-by their name in the belief that the response will reveal the name of their bridegroom-to-be; this custom underlies the central episode in Blok's poem.   At the same time one cannot read SPD #81 in the context of the first volume without recognizing the similarity of this scene with the situation wherein the Lady resides inside her abode while the poet seeks entry at Her door; the prominence of the door motif in these verses tends to corroborate this inference ("Za *vorotami* smejutsja," "Milyj gljanet na *kryl'co*," "Pobelelo vsë *kryl'co*").   But if the circumstances recall an archetypal scenario of meeting the Lady, they also give this event an ironic and ominous cast.   The ridiculing laughter ("*Smex* v otvet," "*smejuščijsja* i nežnyj"),   which would be inappropriate to the solemnity of the genuine meeting, and the fact that the visitor is not the poet but a ghostly phantom (perhaps the spectre of death) gives the whole picture a disturbing tinge.   The oxymoron in the poem's final lines ("Duša zadumčivoj Svetlany/*Mečtoj čudesnoj smuščena*") underscores the unsettling effect of the perverted scenario.

In SPD #104 ("Gadaj i ždi. Sredi polnoči...") the archetype undergoes a similar reversal:

Гадай и жди. Среди полночи

В твоем окошке, милый друг,

Зажгутся дерзостные очи,

4   Послышится условный <u>стук</u>.

И мимо, задувая свечи,

Как некий Дух, закрыв лицо,

С надеждой невозможной встречи

8   Пройдет на милое крыльцо.
                    (SPD #104) (I, 177)

The arrival of a ghostly intruder, who is unmistakably a messenger
of death (note the traditional symbolism of the extinguished
candles), resembles the archetypal door situations and recalls them
by certain familiar allusions ("uslovnyj *stuk*," "Projdet na miloe
kryl'co"). Whether the model is Situation A, B or C, however, is
immaterial; what matters is that image of meeting the Lady is
evoked in a context which converts the joy of this event into a
macabre fantasy. Such sentiments are in keeping with the growing
ambivalence the poet feels toward the Lady, especially toward the
end of SPD, where Her appearance often conjures up deep-seated
fears and forebodings—anticipations which are allied with the
Lady's "transmuted countenance" (SPD #21) (I, 94). From this
perspective the various perversions of the door's primary symbolic
meaning seem to acquire a status of normalcy or even
predictability. One is not surprised, for instance, when through the
open door passes not the Lady, but a coffin:

> Целый год не дрожало окно,
> Не звенела тяжелая дверь;
> Всё забылось — забылось давно,
> И она отворилась теперь.
>
> Суетились, поспешно крестясь...
> Выносили серебряный гроб...
>   (RAS #19) (I, 258)

Or when the idea of the open door evokes not ecstasy, but
trepidation:

> И тщетно замыкают двери
> Досель смотревшие в окно.
>   (SPD #146) (I, 220)

———

> Дрожу от скрипа дверей...
>   (SPD #158) (I, 232)

Or when the lyric hero, in a gesture of frustration, abandons
entirely the search for the door:

> Пускай другой отыщет двери,
> Какие мне не суждены.
>   (SPD #149) (I, 223)

Or when the poet in the guise of his double, Harlequin, makes attendance at the door an act of mockery rather than devotion:

У задумчивой двери
Хохотал арлекин.

(SPD #137) (I, 210)

The point to be made here is not that the meaning of "door" is identical in these different poems, but that in each case its meaning is derived at least in part from the various contexts through which it has "migrated." The memory of these other habitats creates a dynamic which conforms to certain recognizable patterns but is ultimately unique in each individual poem.

So far our discussion has focused on ways the word acquires contextual meaning; attention was paid to the single word (or semantic cluster) and its enrichment by a multiplicity of texts. The converse of this phenomenon is equally important: how the individual poem is enriched by a multiplicity of "migratory words" which converge within its boundaries. One cannot help but think that Blok had this in mind when he wrote in December 1906: "Every poem is a veil spread out over the sharp points of a few words. These words shine like stars. It is because of them that the poem exists" (ZK, 84).

My analysis of Puškin's "lyric cycle of 1836" demonstrated how repetition of words in a cyclic context can create meaningful links between poems and encourages comparison-contrast of the textual segments that share the same lexeme. In the first edition of SPD (1905) Blok disposed his lyrics in such a way as to forefront these links, placing closely related poems together whenever possible. In subsequent editions, where chronology determined arrangement, coplacement of such poems greatly diminished, although it did not disappear entirely.

In the final version of SPD we still encounter a tendency to pair two poems, each of which echoes the other and develops its imagery. Interrelated in this way, for instance, are the two lyrics which open the section "St. Petersburg. Spring 1901":

Я вышел. Медленно сходили
На землю сумерки зимы.
Минувших дней младые были
Пришли доверчиво из тьмы...

Пришли и встали за плечами
И пели с ветром о весне...

Ветер принес издалёка
Песни весенней намек,
Где-то светло и глубоко
Неба открылся клочок.

В этой бездонной лазури,
В сумерках близкой весны

И тихими я шел шагами,
Провидя вечность в глубине...

О, лучших дней живые были!
Под вашу песнь из глубины
На землю сумерки сходили
И вечности вставали сны!..
(СПД #2) (И, 75)

Плакали зимние бури,
Реяли звездные сны.

Робко, темно и глубоко
Плакали струны мои.
Ветер принес издалёка
Звучные песни твои.
(СПД #3) (И, 76)

The second poem essentially restructures the idea of the first, using many of the same lexical-morphemic building blocks; one will note that both poems share the lexemes "sumerki," "zima" or "zimnij," "vesna" or "vesennij," "t'ma" or "temnyj," "veter," "pet'" or "pesn'," "glubina" or "gluboko," and "sny," as well as the prefix "pri-" ("prišli," "prines"). Both have the same rhyme structure, and both are designed according to a circular model (the first and the last couplets in each being nearly identical). The two poems, however, differ in emphasis. The central contrast in SPD #2 is between past ("zima") and future ("vesna"), old ("minuvšix dnej") and young ("mladye byli"); its primary opposition is temporal. The central contrast in SPD #3, while it operates also within the categories above, is between far ("izdaleka") and near ("blizkoj vesny"), cosmic-external ("gluboko," "bezdonnoj lazuri") and intimate-internal ("struny moi"); its primary opposition is spacial. In both poems these antitheses are bridged—in #2 by the concept of "eternity" ("večnost'"), in #3 by the agency of sound or "song" ("pesni tvoi"). The interaction between these poems is not unproductive; each tends to reinforce the other.

On occasion the paired poems, instead of reinforcing each other, are mildly autopolemical; such is the juxtaposition of SPD #27 and #28, which are also linked by a concentration of shared lexemes (underlined below):

В бездействии младом, в передрассветной лени
Душа парила ввысь, и там Звезду нашла.
Туманен вечер был, ложились мягко тени.

4   Вечерняя Звезда, безмолвствуя, ждала.

Невозмутимая, на темные ступени
Вступила Ты, и, Тихая, всплыла.
И шаткою мечтой в передрассветной лени

8   На звездные пути Себя перенесла.

И протекала ночь туманом сновидений.
И юность робкая с мечтами без числа.
И близится рассвет. И убегают тени.

12   И, Ясная, Ты с солнцем потекла.

(SPD #27) (I, 100)

——————

Какому богу служишь ты?
Родны ль тебе в твоем <u>пареньи</u>
<u>Передрассветное</u> волненье,
4   <u>Передзакатные</u> <u>мечты</u>?
Иль ты, сливаясь со <u>звездой</u>,
Сама богиня — и с богами
Гордишься равной красотой, —
8   И равнодушными очами
Глядишь с нездешней <u>высоты</u>
На пламенеющие <u>тени</u>
Земных молитв и поклонений
12   Тебе — царица чистоты?

(SPD #28) (I, 101)

Certain of the shared lexemes are common enough not to arouse special interest (e.g., zvezda, mečta), but the words *parit', paren'e*, and *peredrassvetnyj* are fairly rare in the first volume and in fact do not appear in SPD at all with the exception of these two poems. This suggests that their repetition here may predicate some meaningful interaction. Indeed, the second poem seems to act as a commentary upon the first, whose language is more ambiguous. If read alone, for example, SPD #27 does not make clear whose "soul soared upward" ("Duša parila vvys'") (line 2). One's first inclination might be to identify it as the poet's, in which case the second stanza of #27 implies an ethereal spiritual meeting between poet and addressee; or one might conclude that the "soul" belongs to the addressee, in which case its passage to the "star" (line 2) and the action of the second stanza only isolate the heroine from the poet. The words "v tvoem paren'i" (line 2) in #28 tend to sustain the latter reading; in this respect the second poem supplies a kind of interpretation of the first (though not necessarily the only valid one). At the same time #28 is intoned somewhat polemically toward #27. One will observe, for example, the switch in #28 to an uncapitalized pronoun ("ty" instead of "Ty"), the contrast between "peredrassvetnoe *volnen'e*" (here obviously the poet's)(#28) and the addressee's "peredrassvetnaja *len'*" (#27), and perhaps also the heroine's disconcerting indifference ("*ravnodušnye* oči") (#28). It is possible to detect in #28 a note of distress (perhaps even vexation) that was completely absent in the reverent, self-effacing poem that precedes it.

Paired poems, like those above, are encountered intermittently throughout SPD and RAS, but beginning with the second section of SPD there is a growing tendency on the one hand for mutually informing poems to be dispersed and, on the other hand, for individual poems to interact meaningfully with not one but several poems simultaneously. Put differently, Blok's poetry in time becomes increasingly autoreminiscential, and the individual poems function more and more as accumulators of Blok's own texts. At the same time, and to a large degree as a result of this tendency, the poetry becomes more cryptic, so that autoreminiscences become the principal (if not sometimes the only) available ciphers to the coded utterance.

To illustrate this, let us examine a particularly cryptic poem from the cycle RAS:

Все кричали у круглых столов,
Беспокойно меняя место.
Было тускло от винных паров.
Вдруг кто-то вошел—и сквозь гул голосов
5   Сказал: "Вот моя невеста".

Никто не слыхал ничего.
Все визжали неистово, как звери.
А один, сам не зная отчего, —
Качался и хохотал, указывая на него
10   И на девушку, вошедшую в двери.

Она уронила платок,
И все они, в злобном усильи,
Как будто поняв зловещий намек,
Разорвали с визгом каждый намек,
15   И окрасили кровью и пылью.

Когда все опять подошли к столу,
Притихли и сели на место,
Он указал им на девушку в углу
И звонко сказал, пронизывая мглы,
20   "Господа! Вот моя невеста".

И вдруг тот, кто качался и хохотал,

Бессмысленно протягивая руки,
Прижался к столу, задрожал, —
И те, кто прежде безумно кричал,
25   Услышали плачущие звуки.

25 декабря 1902

(RAS #13) (I, 252)

What makes this poem cryptic is the absence of any plausible motivation for the actions as they appear in sequence, although each in isolation (e.g., "kto-to vošel," "uronila platok," "podošli k stolu") is completely feasible.   Clearly some cipher must be brought to bear on this text if the events, in their interrelationship, are to make any sense.   The hypothesis advanced by Vladimir Orlov, that the poem expresses Blok's fear of introducing Ljubov' Dmitrievna, to whom he was only recently engaged, into the salon of the Merežkovskijs is persuasive, especially since Blok at this time repeatedly refused Gippius's requests that he do so.[59]   There is also evidence that this poem is one of many veiled lampoons Blok aimed at these former mentors in late 1902, early 1903.[60]   The biographical cipher, however, while it provides a rationale for the general situation depicted in the poem, does not go very far toward explaining its specific imagery.   A subtextual cipher can also be applied.   Avril Pyman's insightful observation that the scene recalls Tat'jana's dream in *Evgenij Onegin* (V. xi-xxi) directs us to the poem's only really important subtext.[61]   Indeed the lexical parallels with Puškin are striking, and there are a number of situational affinities: the noisy patrons in Blok's poem and the demon-like revellers in Puškin, the "bride" at the door in Blok and Tat'jana (or Ol'ga) at the door in Puškin, the "girl" in the corner and Tat'jana in the corner with Onegin, Blok's bridegroom and Onegin (or Lenskij).   Moreover the rivalry between Lenskij and Onegin is not irrelevant to the relationship between the bridegroom and the mocking figure in Blok's poem.   These subtextual allusions, however, still leave much that is unexplained, and it will be fruitful to consider what ciphers RAS #13 accumulates from elsewhere in the first volume.

One will note, for instance, that RAS #13 contains the word "dveri" ("devušku vošedšuju v *dveri*") (Line 10) and quite obviously involves perversion of the archetypal door scenarios symbolic of the poet's anticipated meeting with the Lady.   Here we have, specifically, perversion of Situation B (the Lady entering the abode of the poet): the bride comes not alone, but already with the bridgegroom; her arrival evokes ridicule; and in her willingness to betray the bridegroom, she proves quite unworthy of either reverence or respect. Other key words provide clues to the puzzling behavior of the figure who first ridicules the engaged couple ("kačalsja i xoxotal") (lines 9, 21) and then, making plaintive gestures ("protjagivaja ruki") (line 22), weeps pitifully at the poem's end ("Prižalsja k stolu, zadrožal . . . plačuščie zvuki") (lines 23, 25).[62]   One familiar with Blok's first volume will recognize that this chameleon-like creature resembles, alternately, the poet's two antithetical doubles, Harlequin and Pierrot. These stock characters from the Commedia dell'arte—the first a cynical scapegrace who by conniving invariably wins the beautiful but fickle Columbine, the second a faithful sad sack who always loses the beloved to his rival—are in a sense the bathetic counterparts of Onegin and Lenskij. The key words here are "*Kačalsja*," "*xoxotal*," "*zadrožal*," and "*plačuščie*." The former two are allied with the image of Harlequin (and, more generally, with the irreverant, mocking or sinister double), although instead of "kačat'sja" we usually encounter in the first volume the synonym "šatat'sja":

Неотвязный стоит на дороге,
Белый — смотрит в морозную ночь.
Я — навстречу в глубокой тревоге,
Он, <u>шатаясь</u>, сторонится прочь.
(SPD #74) (I, 147)

———

Свет в окошке <u>шатался</u>,
В полумраке — один —
У подъезда шептался
С темнотой арлекин.
. . . .
С темнотою — один —
У задумчивой двери
<u>Хохотал</u> арлекин.
(SPD #137) (I, 210)

———

И, <u>шатаясь</u>, вторил тот самый —
Незнакомец с бледным лицом.
(RAS #24) (I, 263)

———

Я был весь в пестрых лоскутьях,
Белый, красный, в безобразной маске.
Хохотал и кривлялся на распутьях,
И рассказывал шуточные сказки.

(RAS #37) (I, 277)

———

В роще хохочет над круглым горбом
Кто-то косматый, кривой и рогатый.

(РАС #65) (И, 306)

By contrast, "zadrožal" and "plačuščie" are verbal signatures of Pierrot (or, more generally, the faithful lover-servant of the Lady). "*Drož'*," for instance, is an attribute of the participants in the anticipated meeting with the Lady:

И полны заветной дрожью
    Долгожданных лет,
Мы помчимся к бездорожью
    В несказанный свет.

(SPD #96) (I, 169)

———

Ты сама придешь в мою келью...
. . . .
По лицу, объятому дрожью,
Угадаешь думы мои.

(SPD #160) (I, 234)

———

В церкви станешь ты, бледен лицом,
И к царице небесной придешь, —
Колыхнусь восковым огоньком,
Дам почуять знакомую дрожь...

(RAS #72) (I, 315)

———

The same is true for the verb "*drožat*":

. . . жду я Прекрасной Дамы.
. . . .
Дрожу от скрипа дверей.

(SPD #158) (I, 232)

———

Я здесь один хранил и теплил свечи.

Один — пророк — дрожал в дыму кадил.

(RAS #1) (I, 239)

On two occasions this attribute is ascribed unambiguously to Pierrot:

Наверху — за стеною —
Шутовской маскарад.

Там лицо укрывали
В разноцветную ложь.
Но в руке узнавали
Неизбежную дрожь.

(SPD #137) (I, 210)

———

. . . за бледной Коломбиной
Бежал звенящий Арлекин.

А там — в углу — под образами,
В толпе, мятущейся пестро,
Вращая детскими глазами,
Дрожит обманутый Пьеро.

(SPD #153) (I, 227)

The opposition "drož'" vs. "lož'" (SPD #137) and the location of the "trembling" Pierrot "under the icons" (SPD #153) underscore the association of this image with genuine love and piety. The verb *"plakat"* (and sometimes its synonym "rydat'") develops in the first volume essentially the same connotations, as is evident for example in RAS #24 ("Potemneli, pobleki zaly..."):

У дверей затихнувшей спальни
Я плакал, сжимая кольцо.
. . . .
У дверей Несравненной Дамы
Я рыдал в плаще голубом.

(RAS #24) (I, 263)

From the comparisons above it is clear that the mocking figure at the beginning of RAS #13 is the poet's alter ego in its irreverent Harlequin-like aspect, ridiculing the sacred love which elsewhere is the most cherished subject of his verse. At the end of the poem the same figure metamorphoses into a Pierrot-like character, lamenting the loss of his beloved. Moreover the poem reenacts the

traditional episode of Columbine's infidelity; such is the implication
of the "dropped handkerchief" ("uronila platok") (line 11)—a sign
that the "bride" is still receptive to other partners.   From a
different perspective, the episode of the dropped handkerchief,
bloodied in the fray of unfamiliar suitors, is an allegory for rape so
transparent that it hardly requires external ciphers.   In the context
of the first volume, however, this event acquires deeper significance.
The handkerchief is a metonymy for the Lady's "devičij narjad" (I,
186), Her "beloe plat'e" (I, 194) and Her other "white"
accoutrements ("belye cvety," "lilii," "belye strany," "belyj xram,"
"belaja cerkov'" "belyj ogon' Kupiny")—all symbols of her chastity
and the Ideal She represents.   To ravish, to violate the Lady or to
bloody her accoutrements was tantamount to desecrating the Ideal;
such is the implication of the poet's words to his double in SPD
#79 ("Dvojniku"):

> Ты совершил над нею подвиг трудный,
> Но, бедный друг! О, различил ли ты
> Ее наряд, и праздничный и чудный,
> И странные весенние цветы?..
>
> . . . .
> И знал ли ты, что я восторжествую?
> Исчезнешь ты, свершив, но не любя?
> Что я мечту безумно-молодую
> Найду в цветах кровавых без тебя?
>
> . . . .
> Твой подвиг — мой, — и мне твоя награда:
> Безумный смех и сумасшедший крик!
>
> (SPD #79) (I, 152)

The nature of the double's crime (ironically called his "podvig") is
unclear—whether deflowering or murder it is left as if deliberately
ambiguous, implying that the two are symbolically equivalent.[63] In
either case, one cannot help but conclude that this very crime is
reenacted in RAS #13, as the reminiscences from SPD #79 suggest
(SPD #79: "v cvetax *krovavyx*," "*bezumnyj smex*," "*sumasšedsij
krik*"; RAS #13 "vse *kričali*," "okrasili *krov'ju*," "*xoxotal*," "*bezumno
kričal*").

Among the "migratory words" that inform RAS #13 is
"*zveri*" in line 7: "Vse vizžali neistovo, kak *zveri*." Curiously, *all*
the other occurrences of this word in the first volume equate
"zveri" and "ljudi" ("Utaju ot *ljudej* i *zverej*"; "stolpilis' v kuču

ljudi, zveri"; "Tam Kolombina! O, *ljudi*! O, *zveri*!") (SPD #11 and #146, RAS #47) (I, 84 220, 228).[64] It is worth examining the context of the earliest usage:

В непрестанной молитве моей

. . . .

Я хранилище мысли моей
Утаю от <u>людей</u> и <u>зверей</u>.

(April 1, 1901)

Underlying these verses is the belief characteristic of the first volume that the poet's knowledge of the Lady is too sacred to be shared with others; revealing it is tantamount to defiling Her. It is significant that at the end of 1902, when RAS #13 was written, Blok's literary debut (March 1903) was imminent. This momentous event was anticipated by him, however, with more apprehension than joy, as certain of his lyrics from early 1903 attest:

Я к людям не выйду навстречу,
Испугаюсь хулы и похвал.

. . . .

Я выйду на праздник молчанья,
Моего не заметят лица.
Но во мне — потаенное знанье
О любви к Тебе без конца.
(RAS #21) (January 14, 1903) (I, 260)

———

Никому не открою ныне
Того, что рождается в мысли.
(RAS #22) (January 27, 1903) (I, 261)

Sometimes one can detect veiled allusions to these same fears:

Равнодушные лица толпы,
Любопытных соседей набег...
И кругом протоптали тропы,
Осквернив целомудренный снег.
(RAS #19) (January 6, 1903) (I, 258)

With this in mind one can see RAS #13 as a nightmarish allegory for "going public," for revealing the Lady (and the innermost recesses of the poet's own soul) to the unappreciative and blasphemous "crowd."[65]   Such a reading is consonant with the implications of the "dropped handkerchief" and with Blok's reluctance to introduce his fiancée to the Merežkovskijs, whose private soirees he already viewed with abhorrence.

The discussion of RAS #13 demonstrates how a cryptic poem in Blok's first volume accumulates other texts (mostly Blok's own) which act as the poem's interpretants. The more cryptic the poem and the more texts it accumulates, however, the more open it is to different readings. In the case of RAS #13 these various readings complement each other: the "migratory" ciphers help transform what at first appears to be nonsense into a statement with multiple layers of meaning.

Many poems in the first volume, however, present a more formidable interpretive problem, since the relevant subtexts suggest not just different but contradictory, even mutually exclusive readings. The analogy might be drawn to a stereoscopic postcard, which reveals completely different pictures depending on the angle at which it is held; the viewer can discern one picture or the other, but not both simultaneously. In such cases the reader is faced with the dilemma of either resolving the contradictions on some level or acknowledging that the boundary between ambiguity and unintelligibility is nowhere to be found. The elusiveness of boundary is the most alluring and frustrating feature of Blok's first volume.

To illustrate this point, let us examine another extremely cryptic poem, SPD #132 ("Govorili korotkie reči..."):

Говорили короткие речи,
К ночи ждали странных вестей.
Никто не вышел навстречу.
4   Я стоял один у дверей.

Подходили многие к дому,
Крича и плача навзрыд.
Все были мне незнакомы,
8   И меня не трогал их вид.

Все ждали какой-то вести.
Из отрывков слов я узнал
Сумасшедший бред о невесте,
12   О том, что кто-то бежал.

И, всходя на холмик за садом,
Все смотрели в синюю даль.
И каждый притворным взглядом

16   Показать старался печаль.

     Я один не ушел от двери
     И не смел войти и спросить.
     Было сладко знать о потере,
20   Но смешно о ней говорить.

     Так стоял один — без тревоги.
     Смотрел на горы вдали.
     А там — на крутой дороге —
24   Уж клубилось в красной пыли.

                              (SPD #132) (I, 205)

Of this lyric Boris Solov'ev wrote: "Here one incomprehensible detail follows the other, so as to create a strange, confused and completely incoherent picture."[66] To unscramble this "picture" one can try applying our "migratory" ciphers.

The poem seems to involve an archetypal door situation (poet outside, Lady inside); that the poet remains beside the door and does not leave ("Ja odin ne ušel ot *dveri*") (line 17) is a conventional sign of his fidelity. The reference to the "bride" (line 11) is in keeping with this situation, and the poet seems to play the role of best man ("družka"), who typically enters the bride's home before the wedding together with the bridegroom. The guests (wedding guests?) are present, only the bridegroom is still missing. The circumstances are remarkably similar to these in the poem immediately preceding it, SPD #131 ("Ja, otrok, zažigaju sveči...") (I, 204), which we examined earlier, and it is fair to see these two poems as a mutually informing pair. Indeed the parallels between them are striking: the presence of a "bride" (SPD #131:"imejuščij *nevestu*"), anticipation of a "bridegroom" and the attendance of the poet as a third party. Moreover there is a likeness between the closing lines of each poem:

Жених сойдет из алтаря   Смотрел на горы влали.
И от вершин зубчатых леса   А там — на крутой дороге
Забрежжит брачная заря.   Уж клубилось в красной пыли.
          (SPD #131)   (SPD #132)

These parallels suggest the possibility that the "bridegroom" of #131—Christ—is the absent bridegroom in #132, and that he is in fact approaching from the distant hills, "descending" at the twilight hour at the end of #132, as anticipated in #131. His steps (or perhaps the gallop of his horse)[67] stir up the dust in the road, which takes on a reddish hue in the dawn light ("Už klubilos' v *krasnoj* pyli"). Hence the poet stands "without anxiety" ("bez trevogi"), as if certain of the bridegroom's imminent arrival. The suggestion that the "bride" may be dead ("Podxodili mnogie k domu,/*Kriča i plača navzryd*") is not an impediment to the joyous outcome, since the Second Coming implies resurrection and eternal life.

This reading is entirely plausible, if we interpret the poem's last line as an indication of an approaching traveller. The poem is ambiguous, however, and if we conjecture that the billowing dust signals instead a departing traveller ascending the road, other texts in the first volume insinuate themselves as keys to the riddle. It will be recalled, for instance, that the Lady's abode is on a high, not infrequently on top a "mountain":

> Там, над <u>горой</u> Твоей высокой,
> Зубчатый простирался лес.
>
> (SPD #29) (I, 102)

> Ты горишь над высокой <u>горою</u>,
> Недоступна в своем терему.
>
> (SPD #47) (I, 120)

Thus one scenario of meeting involves the poet's ascent to the Lady's divine heights. Indeed the image of the "steep road" ("na *krutoj doroge*") at the end of SPD #132 may well be an autoreminiscence of the cycle's first poem ("Otdyx naprasen. *Doroga kruta*") (SPD #1) (I, 74), where the scenario of ascent and approach is clearly outlined. With these subtexts in mind one can interpret the dusty mountain road not as the Second Coming, but as the cherished meeting with the Lady far off in the distance. Other texts tend to support this interpretation, particularly SPD #90 ("Uxodit den'. V pyli dorožnoj. ."), where red dust on the road is the locus of the poet's fulfillment:

> Уходит день. В <u>пыли</u> <u>дорожной</u>
> Горят последние лучи.
> Их <u>красный</u> отблеск непреложно
> Слился с огнем моей свечи.
> . . . .
> И всё, что было невозможно
> В тревоге дня, иль поутру,

Свершится здесь, в пыли дорожной,
В лучах закатных, ввечеру.[68]

(SPD #90) (I, 163)

Such a reading involves suspension of ordinary perspective (the poet cannot be ascending the mountain and watching himself do so in the distance simultaneously), but spacial detachment from the self is common enough in the first volume not to offer an interpretive obstacle.

Nor are these the only speculations the text encourages. If one focuses on the words "kto-to *bežal*" (line 12) and "*gory* vdali" (line 22), one is struck by the affinity of this imagery with the opening lines of the poem which immediately follows:

Сбежал с горы и замер в чаще.
Кругом мелькают фонари...
Как бьется сердце — злей и чаще!..
Меня проищут до зари.

(SPD #133) (I, 206)

One might well conjecture that the "red dust" on the road at the end of #132 is stirred up by the run-away bridegroom moving farther into the distance, perhaps *down* the mountain slope as in #133.   Or perhaps the bridegroom will never return, as in SPD #155:

Ушел он, скрылся в ночи,
Никто не знает, куда.
. . . .
Он был обручен с Женой.
. . . .
Вот брежжит утренний свет,
Но дома его всё нет.
Невеста напрасно ждет,
Он был, но он не придет.

(SPD #155) (I, 229)

The imagery above is so close to that in SPD #132 ("ušel . . . v noči . . . nevesta . . . ždet . . . brežžit utrennij svet"), it seems to offer yet another clue to the puzzle.

What is problematic about SPD #132 is its receptivity to not only different, but quite antithetical interpretations, each of which, no matter how hard one might try to reconcile them, ultimately cancels the others out.   For one who has mastered the code of

Blok's first volume such verses (of which there are many) cannot help but evoke frustration. To be sure, re-tracing the flight of the "migratory words" allows one to enter an enchanted world of tiny revelations whose supply sometimes seems bottomless. This is indeed an entrancing experience. Yet the very multiplicity of such insights, especially where none of them acquires the weight of finality, often thwarts the reader's natural desire to savor the fruits of the interpretive effort. One cannot help but think that Blok was aware of this dynamic and at times hid behind it, comforting himself with the knowledge of his own unintelligibility. He may well have had this in mind when he confessed his fear of "being found" in the verses from SPD #133, quoted earlier. The continuation of this poem, which as we saw contributes to the ambiguity of SPD #132, seems to convey this very sentiment:

> Пускай бегут за мною следом
> Среди запутанной травы.
>
> Мое болото их затянет,
> Сомкнется мутное кольцо,
> И, опрокинувшись, заглянет
> Мой белый призрак им в лицо.

(SPD #133) (I, 206)

Even here, however, while gloating over his own inaccessibility, there is evidence that Blok felt creative isolation had extracted too high a price. Already in May 1902, he had complained about a sense of entrapment in his own verse:

> Пою я, серый соловей,
> В моей темнице многоцветной.

(SPD #124) (I, 197)

Later, in correspondence with Ljubov' Dmitrievna, he grumbled that his poetry had become "an apparatus for repetition."[69] One receives the impression from Blok's poetry of late 1902-1903 that he felt himself enclosed in a chamber of echoes. RAS #47 ("Dvojnik"), for instance, suggests that the young poet, dressed in the guise of Harlequin, is struggling to break free of the repetitious ramblings of the old, tired poet who follows him:

> Злобно кричу я: "Мне скучно! Мне душно!"
> Он повторяет: "Иди. Не пущу".

(RAS #47) (I, 287)

Years later Blok confirmed this when he remarked apropos of his first volume that he had "confined the youth who was in [his] breast to a prison of sweet harmonies" (VIII, 385).

In RAS Blok is already taking the first uncertain steps toward escape from this "prison." This is evident in poems about the life of the urban lower classes ("Fabrika," "Iz gazet") (RAS #61, #67) (I, 302, 308-310) and about the social unrest that led to the Revolution of 1905 ("Staruxa gadala u vxoda..." "—Vse li spokojno v narode?..") (RAS #25, #29) (I, 264, 269). Poems such as these are a prelude to the fantastic realism of the second volume, especially the cycle "Gorod" (G). Evident also are strident satirical thrusts aimed at the mysticism of the Solov'evists:

И мне смешно, что я поэт...
Устал я верить жалким книгам
Таких же розовых глупцов!
Проклятье снам! Проклятье мигам
Моих пророческих стихов!

(RAS #41) (I, 281)

This element of self-parody is present also in RAS #53 ("Sižu za širmoj. U menja...") (I, 294), a grotesque portrait of an idealist walled off from the world and engrossed in contemplation of his own "little hands" and "little feet." In RAS the ridiculing voice of Harlequin gradually begins to drown out the reverent intonations of the Lady's devotee.

In *The Genesis of Secrecy* Frank Kermode recalls that when asked by the twelve disciples to explain the parable of the sower, Jesus answered: "To you has been given the secret of God, but for those outside everything is in parables; so that they may indeed see but not perceive, and may indeed hear but not understand" (Mark 4: 11-12).[70] Kermode then draws an analogy to the parable "Before the Law" in Kafka's *The Trial*: all his life a man seeks admittance to the Law; he cajoles and bribes the doorkeeper incessantly to let him in, but to no avail; finally, near death and too old to move, the man sees an immortal radiance streaming through the door; the doorkeeper rises and shuts the door. The man is not given admittance to the Law, he is permitted only to view its light momentarily from the outside. For Kermode, the Law is like the secrets of a parable (or indeed any literary text to the degree that its meanings are never fully manifest)—the

interpreter is given to see a radiance, to become in his mind's eye
an insider to the work, to witness for a moment a secret it
contains before the door is shut again.[71]   Nor is this door, as we
are told in Kafka's fable, the only door—there are many others
elsewhere.

The reader of Blok's first volume experiences something akin
to Kafka's supplicant.   Meanings are hidden within a language
designed, it would seem, to shroud a mystery—a language, as
Čukovskij said, "created for secrets."   To gain access to these
secrets the reader searches for ciphers or clues—whether in Blok's
life, in the literature he knew, or in the cyclic context.   The cyclic
clues, the only ones Blok ordinarily provides the reader, are the
poems themselves—the poems are the "doors" to each others'
mysteries.   At the same time the cycle produces its own mysteries.
There are, so to speak, many different "doors" and no clear
indications as to which ones lead to the most fruitful interpretive
insights.   There is, after all, no better place to hide a door than
with hundreds of doors just like it.   Thus the cycle, while
providing a mechanism for disclosing its secrets, does not reveal
them to the casual reader.   It demands of the reader, like the
mysteries of the Lady, an arduous rite of initiation:

> Моя сказка никем не разгадана,
> И тому, кто приблизится к ней,
> Станет душно от синего ладана,
> От узорных лампадных теней.
>
> Безответное чуждым не скажется,
> Я открою рекущим: аминь.
> Только избранным пояс развяжется,
> Окружающий чресла богинь.

(I, 531)

And even those who enter the sacrarium are confronted by a maze
of criss-crossing corridors, many of which only disguise the
impenetrable obscurity which lies at the core of the young Blok's
poetic universe.

Blok himself was not only the keeper of secrets, but the
seeker of their radiance—not only the doorkeeper, but the
petitioner in Kafka's parable.   As we have seen from the perplexed
lapses in the Dante-style commentaries, Blok struggled to
understand the mysteries of these early verses, and there is little
doubt that the constant reformulations of the first volume represent

attempts to uncover them. One will recall that in 1916 he wrote that he chose and arranged his lyrics so as to show his creative path *to the degree that I understand it* at any given time" (VIII, 457). The selection and disposition of the poems was, therefore, an act of interpretation.

In some respects the different roles Blok played vis-á-vis his own poetry parallel the distinction he makes in AL between the "singer" and the "poet":

Хоть всё по-прежнему певец
Далеких жизни песен странных
Несет лирический венец
В стихах безвестных и туманных, —

Но к цели близится поэт,
Стремится, истиной влекомы,
И вдруг провидит новый свет
За далью, прежде незакомой...
(AL #40) (I, 43) [Blok's emphasis—D.S.]

The "singer," by the very spontaneity of his gift, is a keeper of the mystery—his "strange" songs and "cloudy" verses reproduce the inarticulateness of the inspirational moment. The "poet," more conscious and deliberate, strives to understand the truth that lies beyond the songs and gain access to their secret meaning. While the "singer" is perhaps the principal creative agent within the individual lyric, the "poet" alone is the architect of cycles. He alone fashions a meaningful design from the cryptic visions of the "singer." It is of this collaboration that Blok speaks near the end of his first volume, as he looks forward to a new creative impulse:

Этой повестью долгих, блаженных исканий
Полна моя душная, песенная грудь.
Из этих песен создал я зданье,
А другие песни — спою когда-нибудь.
(RAS #43) (I, 283)

IV

THE BURGEONING OF PLOT:
"THE SNOW MASK" AND OTHER
CYCLES OF BLOK'S SECOND VOLUME

> Пели ясные бури
> из пространств дорогую поэму.
> —A. Belyj, "Svjaščennyj rycar'"
> (*Zoloto v lazuri*)

In several respects Blok's second volume, which spans that
portion of his career he later characterized as the "antithesis"
(1904-08)(V, 429-434), represents a radical departure from the first.
To begin with, there is a marked tendency, evident even from the
most perfunctory examination, toward shorter cycles. The smallest
cycle of the first volume (excluding the tiny groupings "Religio"
and "Molitvy") contains seventy poems (AL), while even the
largest cycle of the second, "Gorod" (G), contains only forty-five.
The decrease in size, moreover, is but one symptom of a
fundamental difference in cyclic technique—namely a movement
toward more tightly unified groupings of poems, toward cycles
whose thematic and stylistic limits are more clearly defined. The
smaller cycles bring interaction between the separate lyrics into
sharper focus and eliminate the atmospheric diffuseness which
characterized the first volume.[1] Allied to this development is
introduction of "Miscellaneous Poems" ("Raznye stixotvorenija")—a
section absent in the first volume; this provided a separate,
non-cyclic repository for poems whose membership in any given
cycle would have diminished its unity and cohesiveness.[2] The
crucial distinction between the two volumes with regard to
cyclization, however, is the emergence of plot as the primary
organizing principle. In the second volume, Blok's "migratory
words" become the carriers of plot.

The plot dynamic of SPD (and the first volume as a whole) is of the most attenuated sort. In essence, SPD presents a single dramatic conflict (the poet's separation from the Lady) that develops in depth and complexity but draws no closer to resolution as the cycle unfolds. Union with the Lady is not realized, and the last poem of SPD offers little hope that it will ever be achieved ("Ty, Orfej, *poterjal nevestu...*") (SPD #164) (I, 238). The following cycle opens with a counterfeit "denouement"—the wondrous meeting appears to have taken place, the poet seems to become the Lady's consort ("I vot—Ona . . . /I v Onyj Den'—odin učastnik *Vstreči*—/Ja ètix *vstreč* ni s kem ne razdelil") (RAS #1) (I, 239). But subsequently it becomes apparent that no genuine union has occurred, and at the end of RAS the Lady, shrouded in a deathly slumber, is as far out of reach as ever:

> Спи ты, нежная спутница дней,
> Залитых небывалым лучом.
>
> Ты покоишься в белом гробу.
> Ты с улыбкой зовешь: не буди.
>
> (RAS #80) (I, 323)

If one can speak of plot in the first volume, therefore, it is most certainly one of character and thought rather than one of action and fortune. What movement there is charts a trajectory not from separation to meeting but from hope to disillusionment. The Lady's image acquires in the poet's imagination progressively more frightening features, and anticipation of Her is increasingly intertwined with expectations of doom. At the same time, the lyric hero undergoes ominous changes (particularly emergence from within him of his cynical doubles), all of which place his original aspirations further and further out of reach. While expressions of disenchantment and apprehension increase quantitatively as SPD unfolds, however, the plot line "hopeful anticipation → despair" traces a highly aberrational path. Hopeful lyrics still appear near the end of SPD (e.g., "Ljubil ja nežnye slova...", "Bezmolvnyj prizrak v teremu...", "Vxožu ja v temnye xramy...") (I, 230-232), and gloomy premonitions are not uncommon at the beginning (e.g., "Predčuvstvuju Tebja. Goda proxodjat mimo...", "I pozdno i temno. Pokinu bez želanij...") (I, 24-25); the same is true of the cycle RAS. Swings of mood and attitude are so widespread that they very nearly neutralize the sense of plot movement in these cycles.[3] For this reason most discussions of SPD's "plot" (sjužet)

are based on the original 1905 version,[4] where the ninety-three
poems are arranged non-chronologically and in such a way as to
enhance the illusion of narrative development. In the "canonical"
version, where the poems are disposed in strict chronological
sequence, the plot dynamic is considerably weakened. No doubt
this is why some Blok scholars have spoken of the first volume's
"poetic inertia,"[5] its lack of "action."[6] In their final form AL,
SPD and RAS belong to a hybrid cyclic category—they lie
somewhere along the continuum between the dramatic-situational
and the diaristic plot cycle.

        Full-fledged plot cycles appear only in the second volume,
and they are but one sign of the poet's general turn toward
narrativity in the years of the "antithesis." Brjusov was perhaps
the first to discern this when he wrote in a review of *Nečajannaja
Radost'* (1907), Blok's second collection, that "Blok is more an epic
poet than a lyric poet."[7] Indeed one of the distinguishing features
of the second volume is the prominence of plot in its various
manifestations. It is significant, for instance, that Blok made
"Nočnaja fialka" (NF), his first complete *poèma*, an integral part of
this book. He also included, particularly in the section "Raznye
stixotvorenija" (RazSt II), a number of lyrics that might be called
"summational" —narrative lyrics that give in essence a conspectus
of the poet's creative biography, whether in whole or in part (e.g.,
"Angel-Xranitel'," "Syn i mat'," "Začatyj v noč', ja v noč'
rožden...") (II, 102-103, 108-109, 130-131).[8] Such poems
synthesize various plot lines from Blok's lyric oeuvre and act as
catalysts to the gradually emerging myth of the "trilogy." There
is, moreover, in the very design of the second volume a supracyclic
narrative structure manifest in the disposition of the various cycles.
To this point we shall return in the chapter's conclusion. The
central focus of the discussion that follows will be the dynamics of
"Snežnaja Maska" (SnM), Blok's most remarkable achievement in
the genre of the episodic plot cycle and that cycle which is most
emblematic of the second volume's role in the design of the
"trilogy." Like SPD in the first volume, SnM is the pivotal cycle
in the second.

        Blok's first episodic plot cycle was "Ee pribytie" (EP), a
series of seven fragments originally planned as "chapters" in the
unfinished *poèma* entitled "Pribytie Prekrasnoj Damy" (II, 392).[9]
The cyclic interrelationship of these fragments is evident in the
relative independence of each piece—a circumstance underscored by

the fact that they all appeared, originally, in separate publications. They were reunited in the first edition of the second volume (appeared January 1912), and in the "canonical" edition are included in the section RazSt II (II, 50-56). EP has been treated elsewhere at some length,[10] and there is no need to discuss it comprehensively here—especially since it is, by Blok's own admission, "weak" (II, 392).   It will be fruitful, however, to examine the cycle's episodic structure, which in certain respects is typical of the genre as practiced by Blok's predecessors, while in others hints at innovations Blok will employ with much greater esthetic impact in SnM.

In order to understand where Blok's technique coincides with that of his antecedents and where he departs from them, it will be useful to consider briefly the distinction between story-sequence (the order of events as they occur in actuality) and discourse-sequence (the order in which these events are presented in the narrative medium).   The dichotomy is essentially the same as that made by the Russian Formalists between "fabula" (story) and "sjužet" (plot).   As Seymour Chatman points out, "discourse can rearrange the events of the story as much as it pleases, provided the story-sequence remains discernible."[11] Otherwise the narrative loses coherence.   In most episodic plot cycles story-sequence coincides with discourse-sequence.   As a rule, we encounter relatively few "anachronies"—flashbacks and flashforwards ("analepses" and "prolepses" in Gérard Genette's terminology).[12] The likely reason for this is that the cycle already contains a number of inherent impediments to narrative coherence: the absence of connective text to define the temporal interrelationship of the separate poems, the absence of a narrator per se, and the relative independence of the verb tense system in each poem. Moreover, as we observed in Bal'mont's "Mertvye korabli," there may be a shifting narrative perspective and a certain flexibility in identification of the cycle's actants.   Anachronies only further complicate the already formidable task of reconstructing a coherent story and, for this reason (it would seem), are usually avoided.

EP is typical of the genre in that anachronies, at least on the level of the cycle's macrostructure, are relatively few and not especially difficult to accommodate.   Thus the first and second poems narrate the ships' departure from port and the anxious contemplation of their passage from the perspective of those on shore:

Далеко за полночь — в дали
Неизведанной земли —
Мы печально провожали
Голубые корабли.

        (EP I) (RazSt II #15) (II, 50)

———

Ночи укрывали
От очей бессонных
Всё, что совершалось
За чертой морей.

Только на закате
В зорях наклоненных
Мчались отраженья,
Тени кораблей.

        (EP II) (RazSt II #16) (II, 51)

EP III depicts essentially the same event as EP I—the beginning of the sea journey—but now from the perspective of the sailors:

Ветер, ты, вольный,
Раздуй паруса!

        (EP III)(RazSt II #17)
        ("Pesnja matrosov")(II, 52)

EP IV narrates events unknown to those on shore—the stranding of the sailors in a distant, inhospitable land and their appeal to the elements to help them return to port, despite the raging storm at sea. EP V, which is narrated from alternate perspectives (first from the home port, then from the ships), depicts the return journey in progress:

Мы сквозь зимнюю вьюгу ведем корабли.
Мы заморские тайны несем...

        (EP V) (RazSt II #19) (II, 54)

EP VI-VII picture the final event, the safe arrival of the ships at home port (now from a more generalized point of view coinciding more or less with the perspective of those on shore):

Злые бури отошли.
В час закатный, в час хрустальный
Показались корабли.

        (EP VI) (RazSt II #20) (II, 55)

———

Стали на рейде и ждали рассвета,
Ночь возвращенья мечте уделя.
(EP VII) (RazSt II #21) (II, 56)

In its gross design, therefore, EP provides a fairly conventional exposition of a simple allegorical plot—from initiating action (zavjazka) to denouement (razvjazka).

On the microstructural level, however, there are a number of anachronies which do not yield easily to interpretive scrutiny. EP I, for instance, depicts already the return of one of the ships, "Ptica Pen"—an event which cannot logically precede their departure (still the subject of EP III):

"Птица Пен" ходила к югу,
Возвратясь, давала знак:
Через бурю, через вьюгу
Различали красный флаг... (EP I)

The appearance (reappearance?) of the ship's "flag" is recounted again in EP II:

В час, когда являлся
Первый светлый флаг. (EP II)

Since in both cases above this event (apparently the *same* event) is depicted as anterior to discourse time (that is, it is narrated in the past tense) and since discourse-sequence and story-sequence elsewhere coincide, the reader is left with several interpretive choices: 1) "Ptica Pen" departed with the other ships but returned before them; 2) "Ptica Pen" made the round-trip *once*, separately and prior to the departure of the other ships; 3) "Ptica Pen" used to make this journey *repeatedly* regardless of what the other ships do (the imperfective verbs "xodila," "različali," "javljalas'" can be understood in the iterative sense); or—what involves a suspension of conventional narrative logic—4) "Ptica Pen" remains with the bevy of ships but its return is narrated anticipatorily via poetic license (its *future* arrival is conveyed in the *past* tense). It is difficult to determine which of these (or perhaps other) possibilities is most plausible. More significant is the very presence of ambiguity in construction of story-sequence. Such ambiguities, as we shall see, gain greater prominence in SnM, where they serve a crucial esthetic function.

It is worth noting also the coexistence in EP of two different plot lines (one negative, the other positive), neither of which prevails to the exclusion of the other, despite the fact that they are logically incongruent. On the one hand, the cycle's denouement is maximally beneficent—the ships return, fulfilling the most cherished hopes of those on shore and insuring the sailor's salvation from the dangers of the stormy sea. The ships carry a priceless cargo (EP V: My zamorskie tajny nesem/. . ./Trjumy polny sokrovišč"), and they are greeted with unrestrained joy:

> Буйные толпы, в предчувствии счастья,
> Вышли на берег встречать корабли.
>
> Кто-то гирлянду цветочную бросил,
> Лодки помчались от пестрой земли...   (EP VII)

On the other hand, a catastrophic plot line develops and persists from beginning to end despite its progressive subordination. In fact this plot line contains two variant endings: 1) the ships return, bringing cataclysmic tidings; 2) the ships sink and the sailors perish. In EP I, it will be recalled, the dock workers express apprehension about the cargo they unload, fearing that it may contain not "gold ingots" ("zolotye slitki") or the "magnificent bird" ("čudesnaja ptica") but the "black tsarina" ("černaja carica"):

> Золотые ль слитки плыли
> В наши темные кули?
> Не чудесная ли птица
> В клетке плечи нам свели?
>
> Или черная царица
> В ней пугливо замерла?   (EP I)

And at the perimeters of EP II there are ominous presentiments of the sailors' death and a catastrophe of universal proportions:

> Жизнь была стремленьем.
> Смерть была причиною
> Не свершенных в мире
> Бесконечных благ.
> . . . .
> Бледная планета,
> Разрывая мраки,
> Знала о грядущем
> Безнадежном дне.   (EP II)

The last word in EP II ("*dne*") is ambiguous, alluding simultaneously to the sailors' doom (their location at the "*bottom*" of the sea) and to the unhappy outcome of the entire enterprise ("the *day*" when hopes will go unfulfilled). In EP V there is again a premonition of the sailors' death:

> Утро скажет: взгляни: утомленный работой,
>   Ты найдешь в бурунах
>   Обессиленный труп,
>   Не спасенной твоею заботой...   (EP V)

In the final poem, notwithstanding the outpouring of joyous emotion, there is still a distinct undercurrent of loss and disillusionment:

> Что-то безмерно-печальное есть.
> Там — в океане — в земном водоеме —
> Бродит и плещет пугливая весть...
> . . . .
> Смерть или жизнь тяготает над морем...
> . . . .
> Кто не проснулся при первом сияньи —
> Сумрачно помнит, что гимн отзвучал.
> Чует сквозь сон, что утратил познанье
> Ранних и светлых и мудрых начал...   (EP VII)

What is at issue here is not merely the presence of a bitter-sweet ending but the coexistence of two mutually exclusive denouements. The sailors have survived, yet their life paradoxically remains in the balance ("Smert' ili žizn' tjagoteet nad morem"). They bring precious cargo (V: "trjumy polny sokrovišč"), but their arrival signals the loss of something precious ("utratil poznan'e/Rannix i svetlyx i mudryx načal"). It is as if at the conclusion of EP Blok does not wish (or is unable) to resolve the ambiguities generated by the conflicting plot lines, and instead of eliminating one in favor of the other he chooses to leave both of them intact.

EP was written in December 1904, on the eve of the 1905 Revolution. The lack of resolution at the end of the cycle no doubt reflects Blok's ambivalence toward this impending historical event.[13] Originally, when the work was conceived as a *poèma* rather than a cycle, Blok had intended to conclude it with the disembarkation of the Beautiful Lady—an idea he discarded and later ridiculed in the self-parody, "Poèt":

> Ему хочется за море,
> Где живет Прекрасная Дама.

. . . .
— Так зачем же она не приходит?
— Она не придет никогда:
Она не ездит на пароходе.

(RazSt #31) (II, 69-70)

The non-appearance of the Lady and the questionable significance
of the ships' arrival at the end of EP reflect the poet's uncertainty
about the Revolution's meaning and its impact on his poetic
method. Through most of his early period Blok had maintained an
elitist disdain for the "crowd," and only recently had he begun to
reappraise his ethereal Ideal, seeking for it some earthly, social
application.

Indeed the plot of EP mirrors this reappraisal. The
allegorical sea journey, unlike that in Bal'mont's "Mertvye korabli"
and unlike the sun journey in Belyj's *Zoloto v lazuri*, is a
departure and a return—a wayfaring in search of distant,
fantastical lands (symbolizing the world of the old Ideal) and a
coming home to earth, to the soil and to the people
(*narod*)(symbolizing the new Ideal).

It is noteworthy that the outlines of this plot materialize
along a set of motivic sequences. Primary among these is the
image of a female, erotic figure who continually interacts with the
sailors, whether beneficially or detrimentally. Upon their departure
she is identified with the sea and characterized metaphorically as
the "bride" (an image suggesting her purity and exclusivity):

Подарило нам море
Обручальное кольцо!
Целовало нас море
В загорелое лицо!
Приневестилась
Морская глубина!   (EP III)

In EP V the female role is assumed by the "night," which is
characterized as a "harlot" ("bludnica"), suggesting the theme of
deceipt ("nevesta" → "bludnica"). In EP VI, as the ships
approach the home port, the seamen are lured on by a new
beloved ("krasavica"), who is identified with the "land" ("zemlja"):

А уж там—за той косою—
Неожиданно светла,
С затуманенной красою
Их красавица ждала...

То—земля, о, дети страсти,

Дети бурь,—она за вас!—   (EP VI)

The major episodes in the cycle's plot crystallize around these related motifs, which in sequence outline the following pattern:

old ideal(+)→deceipt/disillusionment(-)→new ideal(+?)

| "nevesta" (III) | "bludnica" (IV) | "krasavica" (IV) |
| "more" (III) | "zemlja odičalaja" (IV) | "zemlja [rodnaja]" (VI) |

To this scheme we may add also the transformational series "zarja" (heavenly light) (OLD IDEAL) → "majak" (earthly light) (NEW IDEAL), which like the others undergoes an intermediate, "deceptional" phase:

Ты нам мстишь, электрический свет!

Ты — не свет от зари, ты — мечта от земли,

Но в туманные дни ты пронзаешь лучом

Безначальный обман океана...   (EP V)

Blok is experimenting here with a technique he will use more daringly in SnM—the "migratory" motif (if not precisely the "migratory word") is already becoming the integrator of a plot dynamic.

"Snežnaja Maska"

SnM, Blok's most ambitious and inspired effort in the genre of the episodic plot cycle, contains thirty poems written over the phenomenally short span of sixteen days (December 29, 1906 through January 13, 1907). Twenty-seven of the thirty were written during a total of six calendar days—January 3-4 (eleven poems), January 8-9 (nine poems), January 12-13 (seven poems). On only two other occasions did Blok pen lyrics with such compulsive abandon—once in March 1914, when he wrote the cycle "Karmen" (K), and once in January 1918, when he produced the bulk of his *poèma* "Dvenadcat'."[14]   Nor is it accident that Blok sensed a common bond between these three feverish spurts of creative energy; in "Zapiska o 'Dvenadcati'" he remarked that "in January 1918 I surrendered myself . . . to the natural elements [stixii] no less blindly than in January 1907 or March 1914" (III, 474).   On each of these occasions Blok felt possessed by the unbridled force of the elements.

Immediately prior to starting SnM Blok read Nietzsche's "The Birth of Tragedy," making a detailed conspectus of the essay and characterizing it in his notebook as a "revelation" (ZK, 84). Blok was fascinated by Nietzsche's views on the spontaneity of the lyric impulse, its grounding in the uninhibited and irrational side of the human temperament, its likeness to music and its origin in the ecstatic frenzies of the Dionysian chorus. For Nietzsche lyric poetry achieved its purest condition when it approximated the unregulated music of the dithyramb, when it reproduced the chaotic feeling of the inspirational moment—that is, when it was furthest from manifestations of Apollonian clarity, form and structure. There is little doubt that in SnM Blok experienced something akin to the enthusiasm of the bacchanalian reveler. Indeed, by his own admission, SnM was for him a kind of poetic access route to Dionysus: "Soon this new, fresh cycle of mine will come. And Aleksandr Blok is on his way to Dionysus" (ZK, 86).[15]

In truth, SnM is very much imbued with the Dionysian spirit and its attendant inclination toward "lyric disorder." In manuscript Blok subtitled the cycle "liričeskaja poèma" (II, 426), and in some respects the stress ought to be placed on the word "liričeskaja" rather than "poèma" since SnM in almost every way frustrates the effort to see it as narrative. All narrative, after all, subsumes the "Apollonian" requirement that the reader be able to reconstitute from the discourse a coherent story with an identifiable beginning, middle and ending. So much of what the reader encounters in SnM, however, works against this principle and undercuts narrative coherence. It is extremely difficult, for instance, to reconstruct from SnM a logical sequence of story-events since events in the separate poems (or even within the same poem) so often seem unrelated or they follow irregular patterns hardly identifiable from real experience. Often it is uncertain whether an event occurs once or a multiplicity of times. Spacial categories (far—near, up—down, forward—backward) often seem to be juggled in an entirely unpredictable manner. Even the identity of the drama's protagonists is frequently unclear. SnM is an eccentric metaphoric fantasy that achieves its effect by shattering all the expectations one normally brings to narrative and atomizing the customary elements of narrative in an apparently chaotic medium. At the same time, or more accurately later in the reader's receptive process—after the initial shock of confusion, SnM offers the reader the basic building blocks of its story and points the way toward deciphering their interrelationship.

The key to deciphering the cycle as narrative is provided in the second poem ("Snežnaja vjaz'"):

> . . . тайно сплетая вязь,
> Нити снежные тку и плету.

(SnM #2) (II, 212)

The metaphor of "weaving" "snow threads" accurately captures the narrative structure of SnM. Plot is uncovered by scrutinizing the minutest verbal detail ("snowflakes," as it were) that "thread" their way from poem to poem, acting as accumulators of the narrative dynamic. Initially, one is more likely to get a sense of plot development by tracing the repeated word (and its contextual environments) through the cycle than by attempting to ascertain more general transitions between larger segments of the text.[16] Plot emerges first and foremost at the level of the microtext. Moreover, as Blok "weaves" his plot "threads," one becomes aware that the fabric of the text ("vjaz'") is multilayered—there is not one summarizable story but rather a multiplicity of stories closely interwoven with each other, so that no one way of abstracting the plot is adequate to the complexity Blok has devised. To this point we shall return, but first let us examine the ways in which SnM impedes the apprehension of its plot. Some of these, as mentioned earlier, are evident in the cycle EP as well.

One such obstacle is the proliferation of anachronies. One will note, for example, the logical impossibility of the following event sequences:

И как . . . . Твои не вспомнить поцелуи На запрокинутом лице.	(SnM #1) (Hero and heroine are intimitely aquainted.)
Да. Я с тобой незнаком.	(SnM #2) (Hero and heroine are not aquainted.)
———	
И гордость нового крещенья Мне сердце <u>обратила</u> в <u>лёд</u>.	(SnM #5) (Action completed.)
И душа <u>леденела</u>. . . . . . .сердце <u>застывающее</u>...	(SnM #6) (Action still in process.)
———	
И приветно глядят на меня: "Восстань из мертвых!"	(SnM #28) (Hero is dead.)
Убей меня, как я убил...	(SnM #29) (Hero is still alive.)

Anachronies also occur within the same poem (e.g., "Ja s toboj neznakom./. . ./Ty ne pervaja mne predalas'") (SnM #2). In all these cases it is not merely the existence of anachronies that hinders the reconstruction of story-sequence (anachronies are prevalent, after all, in many kinds of conventional narrative) but the fact that the text provides few reliable indications (e.g., tense, temporal adverbs) as to the real order of events. Often the reader can rely on analogy with common life experience (verisimilitude) to decode the order of events (e.g., two people must meet before they become intimately acquainted),[17] but where events are metaphorical (e.g., "the soul froze") real life hardly provides a useful decoding model.

Another problem involves what narratologists call "frequency." According to Genette, there are a number of possible relations between story and discourse with regard to this category: 1) narrating once what happened once (singulative), 2) narrating n times what happened once (repetitive), and 3) narrating once what happened n times (iterative).[18] What concerns us here is that discourse normally provides some indication whether a story event occurred once or was repeated. Moreover we can assume that certain events by nature can happen only once to the same individual (e.g., birth, death) or to a pair of individuals (e.g., first meeting). Ostensibly, SnM chronicles a romantic liason that ends tragically for the poet-hero. In order to formulate a coherent story we must assume that certain key events occur only once at a particular point in time: first meeting—>first intimacy—>hero's death. In the cycle, however, these events are presented in such a way as to create some doubt about their singularity. There is some question, for example, even as we have seen from verses quoted earlier, whether Blok's cycle begins with the inception of a new relationship (SnM #2: "Ja s toboj neznakom") in which case "meeting" is a singular event, or with the resumption of a relationship begun in the past (SnM #1: "vspomnit' pocelui") in which case "meeting" is an event with multiple occurrences. There are suggestions, moreover, especially early in the cycle (where Blok seems most intent on disconfirming our conventional expectations), that the poet is narrating not so much a single liaison as a whole class of similar liaisons:

> Ты не первая мне предалась
> На темном мосту.   (SnM #2)

———

Он видит все мои измены...
. . . .
И канет темная комета
В пучины новых темных встреч. (SnM #5)

Hence the poet can view the course of events, even before they occur, as something entirely predictable; narration of the new becomes synonymous with re-reading the old:

О, стихи зимы среброснежной!
Я читаю вас наизусть.   (SnM #2)

If we disregard SnM #1-#2, which in any case anticipate much of the cycle's plot (giving the reader a forehand glimpse of things *in medias res*), the first real "meeting" with the heroine occurs in SnM #5 ("Vtoroe kreščen'e"), but even here there is a suggestion that meetings have occurred before ("Ja tak ustal ot lask podrugi/Na zastyvajuščej zemle").   The idea that each singular event may be but a metonymy for a whole series of the same is enhanced by the prominence of leitmotif "vnov'"/"opjat'"—words which appear seventeen times in the cycle (and once even in the cycle's opening line:"I *vnov'*, sverknuv iz čaši vinnoj..."). Later in the cycle, where "first meeting" is no longer at issue, it is curious how often the poet causes the hero to re-experience his own "death":

Она
Расстанься с долнею жизнью!

Он
Прости! Прости!   (SnM #15)

———

И холодными призорами
Белой смерти предала...   (SnM #27)

———

И взвился костер высокий
Над распятым на кресте.   (SnM #30)

Presumably, these are multiple narrations of the same metaphoric event, but given the unsettled boundary between singularity and multiplicity elsewhere in the cycle, there remains even here a modicum of ambiguity (one might recall the opening line of the poem "Perexožu *ot kazni k kazni...*") (II, 274).

In the first chapter it was pointed out that for narrative to be coherent the actants in an event sequence must remain the same ("Peter fell in love with Paula, Andrew married Felicia, William and Mary lived happily ever after"—does not constitute a plot). The plot cycle, however, can tolerate a certain flexibility in naming the actants without sacrificing coherence, provided the actantal roles remain essentially the same. This is the case in SnM, where the heroine (to a greater extent than the hero) appears under a variety of metaphoric guises. Thus she is identified with the snow storm and assumes the designations "metel'," "v'juga," "snežnaja ptica," "veter," "vixrej snežnaja doč'"; her image is also inseparable from the nocturnal elements ("noč'," "kometa," "zvezda," "luna," "mrak,"). The hero's appelations are less varied ("rycar'," "poèt," perhaps "car'"). These different "names," however, do not generally produce incoherence—they are assimilated under the pronominal designations "ty" and "ja." To be sure, on one occasion (SnM #9) ("Kryl'ja") it is virtually impossible to determine the identity of the speaker and addressee (whether the poet and the Snow Mask respectively or vise versa), but this is the exception rather than the rule.[19] What is more problematic is the the heroine's symbolic identity, which (even as the cycle's title indicates) is "masked," not completely fathomable. This is why it is difficult at first for the poet to determine on the one hand whether the heroine is singular or multiple, and on the other hand whether she represents something new or something from his distant past. This ambiguity initially inhibits narrative coherence, but, as we shall see, its gradual resolution constitutes one important layer of the cycle's plot.

Given these formidable obstacles to reading SnM as narrative, it is remarkable that the cycle has elicited quite a number of plot summaries, the first of which was contained in Brjusov's May 1907 review:

The content of the book is defined in the quatrain:

Тайно сердце просит гибели.
Сердце легкое скользи...
Вот меня из жизни вывели
Снежным серебром стези...   [SnM #27]

The history of this "annihilation" [gibeli] is indeed narrated in the thirty poems of "The Snow Mask". . . .

Before the reader unfolds an affair between the Knight-Poet and the Woman in the snow mask—from its inception, when the poet believes he

> Вдыхает, не любя,
> забытый сон о поцелуях,   [SnM #1]

to the final tormented cries:

> Возврати мне, маска, душу!   [SnM #26]

Or:

> Убей меня, как я убил
> Когда-то близких мне...   [SnM #27]

. . . The affair ends in the book with the annihilation of the hero. He "goes of his own will to the bonfire" [SnM #29] and she sings "above the one crucified on the cross" [SnM #30].[20]

This and most other summaries treat SnM on the level of its larger structural units—they map the general contours of its plot as manifest at certain critical stages represented by individual poems or groups of poems. The apprehension of plot, however, as pointed out earlier, must proceed initially from consideration of much smaller structural units. Before examining ways SnM synthesizes a summarizable story, therefore, one must examine the "stories" told by its most minute units—its word-motifs. In this regard it is worth noting that the "migratory word," which toward the end of the first volume becomes in Blok's perception a mechanism of creative entrapment, in SnM (and in the second volume as a whole) becomes a vehicle by which Blok escapes "the prison of sweet harmonies." When the "migratory word" acquired plot, it gained the means to overcome its own inertia.

There are essentially two types of narrative dynamic on this level of the word-motif: 1) the symbolic-connotative meaning of the motif remains unchanged, but its manifestation, non-manifestation or degree of manifestation is plot-significant; 2) the motif's symbolic-connotative meaning undergoes a plot-significant change. We may call the above types "stable" and "unstable," respectively.

Motifs that function in a "stable" mode belong either to a positive or to a negative emotive sphere (world of ideal faith vs. world of betrayal) and do not shift from one category to the other.

The following motifs, for instance, are generally "stable" in SnM:

World of Ideal Faith (+)	*World of Betrayal* (−)
korabl'	lad'ja
solnce	luna, kometa
vesna	zima
sledit', stereč'	dremat', spat'
pomnit'	zabyt'
žizn'	smert'
meč	absence of "meč"
car', geroj	
	voda, sneg
vverx=vverx	vverx=vniz
blizko=blizko	blizko=daleko
	oprokinut'

In the "stable" mode a plot dynamic is signaled by an incremental or decremental pattern in the treatment of a given motif. In SnM there is generally a progressive ascendancy of motifs in the negative sphere and a declining manifestation of the positive motifs. The image of the "ships" ("korabli"), for instance, which is allied with the world of the Beautiful Lady (and perhaps also the social aspirations of the *narod* as evident in the cycle EP) follows a progressively declining pattern:

> . . . в дали невозвратные
> Повернули <u>корабли</u>.
>
> Не видать ни мачт, ни паруса,
> Что манил от снежных мест.   (SnM #3)

> И покинутые в дали
>   <u>Корабли</u>.
> И какие-то за мысом
>   Паруса.   (SnM #9)

> Не надо <u>кораблей</u> из дали...   (SnM #11)

> И за тучей снеговой
> Задремали <u>корабли</u>.   (SnM #14)

И корабль закатный
  Тонет.   (SnM #16)

И на вьюжном море тонут
  Корабли.   (SnM #20)

The "ships," which are at first only distanced from the hero(#3), become progressively more inaccessible—they are "abandoned" (#9), they become "unnecessary" (#11), and finally they are lost entirely when they "sink" (#16, #20). The pattern is one of "manifestation → decreased manifestation → non-manifestation."

There is a similar trend in Blok's treatment of the motif "solnce," although in SnM #13 there is a temporary resurgence of this positive symbol:

. . . бредет за дальним полюсом
Солнце сердца моего.   (SnM #6)

И опять открыли солнца
Эту дверь.
И опять влекут от сердца
Эту тень.   (SnM #13)

Где ты, солнце?   (SnM #15)

Верь мне, в этом мире солнца
  Больше нет.   (SnM #20)

Negative motifs, by contrast, are in progressive ascendance. "Forgetfulness" (–), for instance, ultimately wins out over "memory" (+):

И как . . . .
. . . не вспомнить поцелуи...   (SnM #1)

Ты сказала: "Глядись, глядись,
Пока не забудешь
Того, что любишь".   (SnM #6)

И нет моей завидней доли —
В снегах забвенья догореть.   (SnM #11)

———

Вам забвенью и потере
Не помочь!   (SnM #13)

———

Тихо. Сладко. Он не вспомнит,
      Не запомнит, что теперь.
Вьюга память похоронит...   (SnM #24)

———

Я всех забыл, кого любил,
Я сердце вьюгой закрутил...   (SnM #29)

"Wakefulness"/"Vigilance" (+), an attribute of the poet's guardian angel in SnM #4 ("On ne smežit upornyj vzor./On *sterežet* vse poselui..."), eventually yields to "sleep" (-). In the treatment of this motif one will note a gradation from minimal manifestation ("dremat'") to complete manifestation ("spat'"):

"Кто ты? Кто ты?
Скован дрёмой,
Пробудись!

От дремоты
Незнакомой
Исцелись!..   (SnM #13)

———

Задремали корабли...   (SnM #14)

———

А в шкапу дремали книги...   (SnM #17)

———

Это—сны твоей дремоты...   (SnM #22)

———

И на снежных постелях
Спят цари и герои...   (SnM #28)

In each of these motivic sequences, of which we have examined only a few, the final event or "denouement" so to speak occurs at different points in the cycle. For the motif of the "ships" it occurs in SnM #16, for the "sun" in #20, for "forgetting" in #29 and for "sleep" in #28. In a sense each motif has its own separate subplot whose rate of development is peculiar to it alone. This circumstance produces an unusual relationship between discourse time and story time: the individual poem isolates a particular discourse NOW, but the story NOW is variable—at different points simultaneously, depending on which motif is chosen to identify it.

In the "unstable" mode, plot movement occurs when a particular motif assumes a connotation or symbolic value different from the one it had originally. More accurately, it might be said that the motif acquires a *new* connotation that is superimposed on the old, since in Blok the word tends to "remember" its previous history. In many instances this involves simple perversion (ironic usage), examples of which were examined in the preceding chapter. Even some more or less "stable" motifs are occasionally subject to this kind of reversal. In SnM #8, for instance, the "evil heroine" (the one belonging clearly to the "World of Betrayal") expropriates the positive motif "korabli," equating it deceptively with her own negative symbol "lad'ja":

> Душу вверь <u>ладье</u> воздушной—
> <u>Кораблю</u>.   (SnM #8)

Sometimes motifs familiar from the first volume and allied with the myth of the Lady are perverted by their location in contexts suggesting betrayal. This occurs, for example, when chivalric imagery appears in the description of the masquerade:

> Он рассказывает сказки,
> Опершись на <u>меч</u>.
> И она внимает в маске.   (SnM #18)

> <u>Дамы</u> с шлейфами, <u>пажами</u>,
> В розовых тенях.
>
> <u>Рыцарь</u> с темными цепями
> На стальных руках.
>
> Ах, к походке вашей, <u>рыцарь</u>,
> Шел бы длинный <u>меч</u>!
>
> Под <u>забралом</u> вашим, <u>рыцарь</u>,
> Нежный взор желанных встреч.   (SnM #21)

The word "kel'ja," formerly a symbol of monastic devotion to the Lady, is perverted when it designates the location of the hero's infidelity:

Стерегут мне <u>кельью</u> совы...

. . . .

У меня в померкшей <u>келье</u>
Два меча.

. . . .

То горят и дремлют маки
Злых очей.   (SnM #13)

Such perversions are plot–significant because they indicate progressive usurpation by the Snow Mask of accoutrements belonging to the "World of Ideal Faith."

Significant also are those occasions where the symbolism of a motif undergoes a more substantive and permanent change not ascribable to irony or perversion (which are in essence temporary dislocations of a word's primary symbolic value). The motif of the "cross," for example, is initially a conventional emblem of ideal faith. When it first appears, the "cross" is associated with the "ships," and the disappearance of both is symbolically correlated:

Не видать ни мачт, ни паруса,
Что манил от снежных мест.
И на дальнем храме безрадостно
Догорел последний <u>крест</u>.   (SnM #3)

Unlike "korabli," however, "krest" follows a trend of *increased* manifestation as the cycle unfolds. SnM #5, which sublimates the lexeme "krest" in its title ("Vtoroe *kreščen'e*"), suggests that the image of baptism (and therefore metonymically—the "cross") is to play an important role at each stage of the hero's fate:

ВТОРОЕ КРЕЩЕНЬЕ

Открыли дверь мою метели,
Застыла горница моя,
И в новой снеговой купели
Крещен вторым крещеньем я.

И, в новый мир вступая, знаю,
Что люди есть, и есть дела.
Что путь открыт наверно к раю
Всем, кто идет путями зла.

Я так устал от ласк подруги
На застывающей земле.

И драгоценный камень вьюги
Сверкает льдиной на челе.

И гордость нового крещенья
Мне сердце обратила в лед.
Ты мне сулишь еще мгновенья?
Пророчишь, что весна придет?

Но посмотри, как сердце радо!
Заграждена снегами твердь.
Весны не будет, и не надо:
Крещеньем третьим будет—Смерть.   (SnM #5)

The implied "first christening" undoubtedly alludes to worship of
the Lady. The "second christening" is a metaphor for the hero's
initiation into the world of the Snow Mask. And the "third
christening" (Death) will be the final stage in their liason. By
implication, therefore, the "cross," which is present both
morphologically ("kreščen," "kreščen'e") and metaphorically
("dragocennyj kamen' v'jugi . . . na čele"), is a symbol that will
survive passage from the "World of Ideal Faith" to the "World of
Betrayal," although its meaning will be transmuted. The nature of
this transformation is two-fold and paradoxical. On one hand, the
"cross" continues to be allied with the old ideal but becomes a
symbol of retribution, not faith. In the "crossed swords" of SnM
#10, for instance, it is not difficult to recognize the agency of the
angelic figure who earlier (SnM #4) threatened to extract payment
from the hero for his sins:

Он стрежет все поцелуи
Паденья, клятвы и позор.

И Он потребует ответа,
Подъемля засветлевший меч.   (SnM #4)

Ангел, гневно брови изламывающий,
Два луча — два меча <u>скрестил</u> в вышине.   (SnM #10)

It is undoubtedly this threatening "cross" that the poet implores
the Snow Mask to help him destroy in SnM #12:

Птица вьюги
Темнокрылой,
Дай мне два крыла
. . . .

> Чтоб огонь зимы палящей
> Сжег грозящий
> Дальний <u>крест</u>!   (SnM #12)

On the other hand, however, the "cross" itself is annexed by the world of the Snow Mask and becomes part of its symbolic inventory:

> Вьюга строит белый <u>крест</u>,
> Рассыпает снежный <u>крест</u>...
> . . . .
> И вздымает вьюга смерч,
> Строит белый <u>крест</u>,
>   Земетает твердь...   (SnM #14)

———————

> (Вьюга вздымает белый <u>крест</u>)   (SnM #15)

Clearly the "cross" is an extremely menacing image, whether allied with the world of the old ideal or with that of the Snow Mask. This is born out in the cycle's final poem, where the poet is impaled and immolated on the "cross" in a pose of Christ-like martyrdom:

> И взвился костер высокий
> Над распятым на <u>кресте</u>.
>
> Вейся, легкий, вейся, пламень,
> Увивайся вкрыг <u>креста</u>.   (SnM #30)

The event sequence just outlined indicates that on a certain plane the "World of Ideal Faith" and the "World of Betrayal" function in coalition with each other, bringing about the hero's demise together.   Hence the cycle's last poem contains a double-edged denouement—a sadistic conclusion to the liaison with the Snow Mask (who speaks the words in SnM #30) and, simultaneously, a just retribution for that liaison.[21]

   In addition to the two narrative modes just discussed, there are instances in which a particular word-motif, while not belonging either to the "World of Ideal Faith" or to the "World of Betrayal," nevertheless accumulates a certain plot dynamic. Tracing the image of the "door" through the cycle, for example, produces an outline of events that approaches conventional narrative in its logicality and is in effect free of anachronies:

> Я не открою тебе <u>дверей</u>.

Нет.
Никогда.   (SnM #2)

_____

Открыли <u>дверь</u> мою метели,
Застыла горница моя.   (SnM #5)

_____

И опять открыли солнца
Эту <u>дверь</u>.
. . . .
Ты кому открыла <u>двери</u>,
Задремав, служанка-ночь?   (SnM #13)

_____

Тихо вывела из комнат,
     Затворила <u>дверь</u>.
. . . .
Вьюга память похоронит,
     Навсегда затворит <u>дверь</u>.   (SnM #29)

Considering these fragments together, one can draw connective inferences with relative ease: the poet at first refuses to admit the Snow Mask (#2), but she enters anyway (#5); representatives of the old ideal enter the poet's abode and attempt to reclaim his spirit (#13); the poet finally leaves his former sanctuary and recognizes the impossibility of return to it.[22]   A different scenario emerges when we trace the motif of "catching up" through its various manifestations:

Ты встаешь за мной вдали...   (SnM #3)

_____

Ты меня настигла...   (SnM #6)

_____

Он
Ты влечешь меня к безднам.
. . . .
Она
О, настигай! О, догони,
. . . .
Оставь тревоги,
Метель в дороге
Тебя застигла...

. . . .
Ты — в лунном круге.   (SnM #15)

From this perspective the cycle narrates a certain reversal: first the heroine "catches up" with the hero, then the hero pursues the heroine to her lunar realm.

From the discussion above it is apparent that each synopsis of SnM's plot, inasmuch as it condenses at the most elemental level around separate motifs, will vary depending on which motif is chosen as its basis.   Plot summaries, however, can amalgamate many motifs and generalize story development at more abstract levels, and one can hardly make the argument that SnM is a coherent narrative unless one is able to recapitulate its story in a way that demonstrates the poems' collective impact.   It goes without saying that different persons will summarize the same plot in non-identical ways, and Tsvetan Todorov is correct that "to write about a text is to produce another text."[23]   This warning, however, did not prevent Todorov himself from summarizing plots,[24] and it is fair state that this enterprise can be useful as a means of interpretation.   While no plot summary exhausts the information any narrative contains, each reveals truths about it. We shall consider below, therefore, a number of ways to restate the plot of SnM in summary form, acknowledging that each is only partially sufficient.

I. *TRAGIC LOVE STORY* (The hero falls in love with the Snow Mask; he betrays his former beloved; ultimately he is destroyed or abandoned by the Snow Mask.)

This, the most conventional account of what "happens" in the cycle, corresponds closely to Brjusov's summary, quoted earlier. Irene Masing gives a slightly different rendering:

> The poet decides to conquer a woman.   He thinks it will be easy, but it proves that he has met a femme fatale, who causes him much suffering, mocks and teases him, and finally leaves him when she has achieved his destruction.[25]

Masing, however, prefers what she calls a "philosophical" summary which focuses on the dynamic of sin and retribution:

> What begins as a temporary and partial deviation from what the poet has hitherto considered the "right path" (I, II) leads to his annihilation on the cross and

in "snow fire" (XXX).   One act of rebellion against divine order (IV) leads to a series of events—the "second christening". . . , the cosmic experiences. . . , the pursuit of erotic adventures (XVII, XVIII, XIX), the search for comfort in "*skazki*" (XX, XXI) and ultimately to the realization that the loss of set values and beliefs leads to "confusion" (XXVI), alienation from life (XXIX), and to secret suffering under a "mask of snow" (XXX).[26]

The cycle can also be read as an esthetic transsubstantiation of Blok's biographical liaison with the beautiful actress Natal'ja Nikolaevna Voloxova, who was the principal real-life prototype of the Snow Mask (though not the only one).[27]   This approach is adopted by Nikolaj Volkov[28] and by Blok's biographers, V. Orlov and A. Pyman.[29]   There is nothing wrong with such readings, especially since the cycle is dedicated in the text to Voloxova ("Posvjaščaetsja N.N.V.") and since many details in SnM are lifted directly from real experience.   V.P. Verigina, one of the actresses in Voloxova's circle, relates that much of the imagery in SnM #17-#22 is taken from a masquerade party held to celebrate the premiere of Blok's play "Balagančik" (December 30, 1906).[30]   In her account the dialogue in SnM #19 ("Skvoz' vinnyj xrustal'") reproduces verbatim an exchange between Blok and Voloxova at this fete.[31]   Verigina adds that "in almost all the verses of 'The Snow Mask' are included real conversations and facts of that time."[32]   It is questionable, however, whether knowledge of biographical realia improves ones understanding of SnM as art. Ginzburg argues persuasively that

> this information is important for the creative history of "The Snow Mask," but it does not change our reception of this work.   The metaphoric structure of "The Snow Mask" does not become more concrete.   Before us is not the intrusion of the concrete world into the metaphoric element, but rather the reverse process—the projection of poetic symbolism onto life...[33]

Indeed even Verigina acknowledges that the actresses and the others who surrounded Blok in an admiring bevy during the staging of "Balagančik" (including the director Vsevolod Mejerxol'd) were drawn into a theatrical game of Blok's invention; the play itself and words from Blok's poetry served to a large degree as a scenario for life.[34]

Before considering other ways of summarizing the cycle's plot
it is worth noting a comment Blok made in May 1908 apropos of
his affair with Voloxova: "There was no love [ljubvi].   There was
infatuation [vljublennost']" (ZK, 108).   The distinction Blok draws
between *"ljubov"* and *"vljublennost"* is not irrelevant to SnM.
Nowhere in the cycle does the poet state explicitly that he "loves"
("ljubit") the Snow Mask.   In the first poem, for instance, the
words indicate the contrary:

> И вновь вдыхаю, <u>не любя</u>,
> Забытый сон о поцелуях,
> О снежных вьюгах вкруг тебя.   (SnM #1)

Of the four other occasions where the verb "ljubit" appears, three
are in utterances of the heroine, not the poet:

> Ты запрокинула голову в высь.
> Ты сказала: "Глядись, глядись,
> Пока не забудешь
> Того, что <u>любишь</u> ".
>
> И указала на дальние города линии,
> На поля снеговые и синие,
> На бесцельный холод.   (SnM #6)

> Не в земной темнице душной
>   Я гублю.
> . . . .
> Ты пойми душой послушной,
>   Что <u>люблю</u>.   (SnM #8)

> Я ль не пела, не <u>любила</u>,
> Поцелуев не дарила
> От зари и до зари?
> . . . .
> Я была тебе верна.
> Я была верна три ночи...   (SnM #30)

One will note that in SnM #6 the sense of "ljubiš" is ambiguous;
from the context it is unclear whether the verb's object is the
heavens (the world of the Beautiful Lady) or the "city," "fields"
and "cold" (images allied with the Snow Mask).   The very fact

that the heroine points alternately to these diametrically opposite symbolic universes suggests the confusion her gestures ("zaprokinula golovu v vys' . . . ukazala") engender in poet. In SnM #8 and #30, where the subject of "ljubit'" is the Snow Mask, the reader nevertheless finds cause in the immediate context (not to mention the context of the cycle as a whole) to doubt the sincerity of this sentiment. On the one occasion the poet himself uses the verb "ljubit'" in the first person, the direct object is clear grammatically, but not empirically:

> Ты ль нисходишь?
> Ты ль уводишь, —
> Ты, кого я <u>полюбил</u>? (SnM #12)

Every commentator of these lines has assumed that "ty" is the Snow Mask, but the word "nisxodiš'" suggests that "ty" may well be the Lady. In any case it is uncertainty about the identity of "ty" that stimulates the poet's question. When the poet speaks unambiguously of his feeling for the Snow Mask, the word he uses is "vljublennost'":

ВЛЮБЛЕННОСТЬ

> И опять твой сладкий сумрак, <u>влюбленность</u>
> И опять: "Навеки. Опусти глаза твои".
> И дней туманность, и ночная бессонность... (SnM #12)

From these lines it is apparent that "vljublennost'" carries more negative connotations than positive ones, but the word's implications are not fully manifest until we encounter the figurine of Cupid on the poet's bookshelf:

> "А в шкапу дремали книги.
> Там—к резной старинной дверце
> Прилепился голый мальчик
> На одном крыле. (SnM #17)

> —Посмотри, подруга, эльф твой
>   Улетел!
> . . . .
> И потеранный, <u>влюбленный</u>
>   Не умеет прицепиться
> Улетевший с книжной дверцы
>   Амур. (SnM #18)

This episode outlines the poet's predicament in microcosm. Cupid ("Amur"), the hero's alter ego, has "flown away" from the bookshelf door, which is a symbol of the old ideal (the epithet "*starinnaja* dverca" confirms this).[35]   In the condition of "infatuation" ("vljublennost'"), Cupid cannot reattach himself to the door, cannot reacquire what he has forfeited—hence the equivalency of "vljublennyj" and "poterjannyj." The word "vljublennyj" occurs once more in SnM #25, where it is allied with the spurious world of the masquerade:

> Странных очерков видений
> В черных масках танцевали —
> Были влюблены.   (SnM #25)

Thus it is clear that the images "ljubov'" and "vljublennost'" function contrastively in the cycle. This does not invalidate readings of SnM as "love story," but it does provide an interesting footnote to them.

II. *SYMBOLIC PASSAGE* (The lyric hero continually moves from the world of his former ideal to the world of the Snow Mask.)
    In her book *Lirika Aleksandra Bloka* Minc argues convincingly that SnM represents a history of the lyric hero's passage from "the world of the former 'I'" (or "the world of 'heaven's emissaries'") to "the blizzard world" of the Snow Mask. Much of her analysis is devoted to characterizing these two diametrically opposite realms, which correspond roughly to what I have called the "World of Ideal Faith" and the "World of Betrayal."[36]   The distinctions Minc makes can be summarized as follows:

The World of the Former "I"	*The Blizzard World of "You"*
Enclosed space ("dom," "xram," "komnata," "steny," etc.)	Open space ("bezdna," "propast'," etc.)
Motionlessness ("prostert," "stojat," "na straže")	Circular movement ("vixri," "v'juga," "vzvixrit'sja")
Normal spacial relationships (up=up, down=down, far=far, near=near)	Abnormal (reversed) spacial relationships (up=down, far=near, "oprokinut")
Warmth ("vesna," "solnce")	Extreme cold/heat ("led," "koster")

Light ("svetlyj," "zlatoverxij")	Darkness ("ten'," "mgla," "temnaja")
Good	Evil
Love-service ("rycar'," "paž")	Love-passion ("pocelui," "laski")
Fidelity	Infidelity

According to Minc, the hero's role in the plot is passive (it is the heroine who acts, drawing him out of the enclosed world of his past), although it is the hero's spiritual evolution that creates the cycle's plot movement (the heroine's spiritual character remains unchanged). This evolution progresses in three separate stages: 1) the "past" ("the world of the former 'I'"); 2) the "present" (an intermediate stage marked by the hero's exit from the home and his numerous meetings with the heroine on earth); and 3) the "future" (final passage to "the blizzard world" and ultimate "Meeting" with the heroine in her own domain). This linear sequence, however, does not correspond precisely with the presentation of these stages in the cycle itself—there are transpositions of story events in the discourse (what I called earlier "anachronies"). To account for these transpositions on the level of the cycle's macrostructure, Minc uses Blok's division of SnM into the sections "Snega" (poems #1-16) and "Maski" (#17-30), but proposes instead a tripartite segmentation: $Snega^1$ (#1-16), $Maski$ (#17-22), and $Snega^2$ (#23-30).[37] $Snega^1$ chronicles the hero's movement from the "past" to the "present"; $Maski$ is a temporary return to situations of the "past" (parodies of chivalric love for the Lady); $Snega^2$ traces the hero's movement to his "future" environment (the final "Meeting" and death).

Minc's study is painstakingly thorough, elegent in design and persuasive. With regard to plot its advantage lies in the way it accounts for the cycle's motivic diversity. Though Minc bases her analysis on a single leitmotif (the metaphor of "flight" or movement to the Snow Mask), she does not confine herself to this motif alone. By using the concept of different "worlds," understood as amalgams of symbolic attributes, she is able to consolidate the complex imagery of SnM into a coherent system.

The effort to systematize the imagery of SnM, however, occasionally results in a tendency to discount exceptions, to "round off" discrepancies. Of course, some of this is inevitable in any critical endeavor, but it is possible to make certain correctives to

Minc's analysis without detracting from its general thrust. Such correctives can even reveal further potential in her line of reasoning.

One can question, for instance, how true it is that the heroine's world represents "open (unenclosed) space." The exceptions to this rule cannot be entirely dismissed. While the heroine indeed promises escape from enclosure ("steny," "temnica") and passage to boundless expanses (*"beskrajnye* snega," *"otkrytye sinie bezdny"*), there are intimations that the world to which she leads the poet constitutes, paradoxically, a new form of enclosure. Minc herself points out that the poet's ultimate destination is the heroine's "lunar circle":

> Чтоб с тобою, сердцу милой,
> В серебристом лунном круге
> Вся душа изнемогла.   (SnM #12)

> Она
> Ты—в лунном круге...   (SnM #15)

She discounts this detail, however, arguing that "the 'circle' does not denote here the presence of a boundary, but the 'circular' (spherical) structure of the cosmos."[38] This explanation is plausible enough, except that the heroine's "circle" does indeed prove to be a symbol of enclosure:

> Нет исхода из вьюг
> И погибнуть мне весело.
> Завела в очарованный круг
> Серебром своих вьюг занавесила.   (SnM #28)

The verb "zanavesila" even connotes a residential *interieur*, not unlike the domicile from which the hero was earlier released ("Tixo vyvela iz komnat") (SnM #24). If we consider that the final "Meeting" with the heroine is death, it is not irrelevant that death itself is likened to a domicile ("obitel'") and possesses a definite metaphoric boundary ("dno"):

> Белой смерти предала...
> И в какой иной обители
> Мне влачиться суждено,
> Если сердце хочет гибели,
> Тайно просится на дно.   (SnM #27)

Я бросил сердце с белых гор,
  Оно лежит на дне!   (SnM #29)

The word "dno," of course, carries ironic implications, since the heroine originally evoked expectation of an "abyss" ("bezdna"). The conclusion to be drawn from this is not that Minc is wrong, but that her system fails to accommodate conflictual perceptions inherent in the hero's passage to the world of the Snow Mask. Certainly, SnM only gains in esthetic appraisal from acknowledgement that its denouement contains such a paradox.

Minc's observation that the lyric hero is "passive" (the object of the heroine's action) also requires scrutiny. Indeed along the coordinates "passivity vs. activity" it is possible to formulate a somewhat different version of the protagonists' relationship—one that undergoes a certain evolution. This evolution is the subject of the plot summary that follows.

III. *STRUGGLE FOR DOMINANCE* (The hero and the heroine struggle for dominance over each other; initially the hero is the successful party, but ultimately the heroine gains control over her rival.)

The relationship between the protagonists of SnM can be seen from the outset as an antagonistic one—a rivalry, in which the hero enlists the power of his verse to keep the heroine in submission, while the heroine draws upon her arsenal of natural elements (passion, the snowstorm) to escape this control and reverse the model of dominance. Moreover the pattern "hero dominant → heroine dominant" develops almost identically in each of the cycle's two sections, "Snega" (#1-16) and "Maski" (#17-30), with relatively few anachronies.

At the beginning of "Snega" the heroine is kept in check by the poet. She is the "captive" of his verse and has no existence apart from it ("Ty—stixov moix *plennaja vjaz*")(SnM #2). It is significant that at this point the poet is even in control of the Snow Mask's very element ("spletaja vjaz',/*Niti snežnye tku i pletu*"), and, ironically, the heroine's "cold" participates in her own confinement ("I *skovana l'dami* zlaja voda") (SnM #2). The poet, by contrast, is "free"—in control of his own fate:

Я — непокорный и свободный.
Я правлю вольною судьбой.   (SnM #4)

And it is he who holds sway over the heroine's heart:

> Ты дала мне в руки
> Серебряный ключик,
> И владел я сердцем твоим.   (SnM #7)

At the midpoint of "Snega," however, the heroine begins to assert her dominance ("*Ee* pesni": "Ty pojmi dušoj *polušnoj*,/Čto ljublju") (SnM #8). Moreover she expropriates the metaphor of "weaving" (or "braiding"), intimating that the power of the poet's verse may ultimately be relinquished to her:

> <u>Пряжей</u> спутанной кудели
>   <u>Обовью</u>.   (SnM #8)

In SnM #15 the poet has already succumbed to the Snow Mask and becomes her "captive." In part the reversal is signaled by the symbolic morpheme "*-kov-*," which denotes constraint; earlier (SnM #2) this motif was allied with the poet, but now it belongs solely to the heroine's element ("drema," "snega"):

> [Я] <u>Скован</u> дрёмой...
> . . . .
> На груди — снегов <u>оковы</u>,
> В ледяной моей пещере —
> Вихрей северная дочь.   (SnM #15)

In "Maski" the same pattern is repeated. At first the poet, now in the guise of "temnyj rycar'," snares the heroine in the intricate design of his "tales" ("skazki"):

> —Посмотри, как темный рыцарь
> Скажет сказки третьей маске...
>
> Темный рыцарь вкруг девицы
> <u>Заплетает</u> <u>вязь</u>.   (SnM #18)

The heroine is entrapped in a creation of the hero's poetic imagination, and it is this authority that he contemplates in SnM #20:

> Верь лишь мне, ночное сердце,
>   Я — поэт!
> Я какие хочешь сказки
>   Расскажу.
> И какие хочешь маски
>   Приведу.   (SnM #20)

It is not accidental that in this poem we find a metrical configuration (4-2 foot troche) identical to that in "Ee pesni" (SnM #8), suggesting that the hero is using words for their incantory effect, much as the heroine had earlier. This attempt at incantation, however, fails—in part because the poet himself becomes part of his "tale" ("vy sami v skazke, rycar'")(SnM #21), in part because he becomes confused and loses control over his own creation:

> Смотри: я спутал все страницы,
> Пока глаза твои цвели.
> Большие крылья снежной птицы
> Мой ум метелью замели.
>
> Как странны были речи маски!
> Понятны ли тебе? — Бог весть! (SnM #23)

Ironically, these lines seem to be a realization of the heroine's earlier threat ("Prjažej *sputannoj* kudeli/Obov'ju"). Thus again, roughly at the midpoint of "Maski," a reversal begins. The heroine's dominance becomes increasingly manifest, and the motif "-*kov*-" reappears as a sign of this trend:

> Ты свела меня сюда.
> Завела, сковала взорами
> И рукою обняла.   (SnM #27)

In the final poem the heroine's ascendancy over the poet is evident not only in that she presides over his crucifixion, but in that she usurps the authority of his verbal medium. She herself narrates the concluding episode, and her elements have now become the "spinners" of the poetic "thread":

> Равнодушны, снежнооки,
> Ходят ночи в высоте.
>
> Молодые ходят ночи,
> Сестры — пряхи снежных зим,
>
> И глядят, открывши очи,
> Завивают белый дым.   (SnM #30)

In the scenario just outlined the hero is far from passive. He sets the story in motion by creating the heroine and then attempts to control her by means of his poetic gift. The heroine, however, is endowed with powers that supersede and ultimately assimilate the creative design.

IV. *DRAMA OF RECOGNITION* (The image of the heroine is from the outset confused with the image of the former ideal beloved; the heroine compounds the confusion through her own deceipt; the hero strives to ascertain the heroine's true identity, in which effort he is ultimately successful.)

Virtually every previous discussion of SnM has operated from the premise that the Snow Mask is the antithesis of the Beautiful Lady.   Yet in the poet's eye the cycle's heroine embodies alternately (and sometimes simultaneously) the "World of Ideal Faith" and the "World of Betrayal."   Confusion of these two worlds in the heroine's image creates a dramatic conflict that is resolved in the cycle's denouement.   As is typical of Blok, however, this very resolution incorporates a paradox.   On one level the Snow Mask's deception is uncovered: she is recognized as distinct from the Lady and assigned beyond doubt to the "World of Betrayal."   On another level the betrayal itself and retribution for it are acknowledged as necessary stages on the path to the "World of Ideal Faith."

Uncertainty about the identity of "ty" is strongest at the beginning of each section, "Snega" and "Maski."   SnM #1, for instance, represents utter confusion of ideal love and demonic love:

СНЕЖНОЕ ВИНО

И вновь, сверкнув из чаши винной
Ты поселила в сердце страх
Своей улыбкою невинной
В тяжелозмейных волосах.

Я опрокинут в темных струях
И вновь вдыхаю, не любя,
Забытый сон о поцелуях,
О снежных вьюгах вкруг тебя.

И ты смеешься дивным смехом,
Змеишься в чаше золотой,
И над твоим собольим мехом
Гуляет ветер голубой.

И как, глядясь в живые струи,
Не увидать себя в венце?
Твои не вспомнить поцелуи

На запрокинутом лице?   (SnM #1)

Among the attributes of "ty" there are many which belong to the new or "evil" heroine ("iz čaši *vinnoj*," "v tjaželo*zmejnyx* volosax," "v *temnyx* strujax," "*zmeiš'sja*"), while others recall the ideal beloved of SPD ("*nevinnoj*," "v čaše *zolotoj*," "veter *goluboj*"). Certain details are ambiguous, but could conceivably be allied with the Lady also: "*strax*" (cf. "No *strašno* mne: izmeniš' oblik Ty"; "Na *strašnom*, na poslednem pire/Dlja nas gotovit vstreču bog"; "Mne *strašno* s Toboj vstrečat'sja") (SPD #21, #141, #163) (I, 94, 214, 237); "*snežnye v'jugi* vkrug tebja" (cf. "I nyne vsja ovejana *snegami*"; "Ty pesn'ju bez konca rastajala *v snegax*"; "Ty v beloj *v'juge*, v *snežnom* stone"; "Otošla ja v *snega* bez vozvrata,/No *xolodnye vixri* krutja...") (SPD #30, #36, #70, #140) (I, 103,109, 143, 213); "*smeeš'sja*" (cf. "*smejuščiesja* dali"; "Ona . . . na tom *smeetsja* beregu") (SPD #84, #131) (I, 157, 204); "*mex*" (cf. "Ee srebristo-černyj *mex*"; "On dumal o šubke s *mexom*") (SPD #147, #161) (I, 221, 235). The image of "*venec*" (line 14) is multivalent. It recalls on the one hand the imagery of the first volume, for example the "marriage crown" (cf. "toska po *bračnomu vencu*") (SPD #61) (I, 134) or the "crown" as a symbol of regency—whether the Lady's ("Tebja *venčala* korona") (SPD #122) (I, 195) or the poet's as the Lady's consort ("ja, mudryj *car*") (RAS #2) (I, 240). On the other hand, it signifies the "wreath of thorns" in the Gospel and prefigures the assumption of martyrdom by the poet later in SnM. All three associations are operative in this image. They are, moreover, not entirely alien to each other, since Christ is the Biblical "King of kings" as well as the "Bridegroom" of the Church, as mentioned in Chapter III. Finally, contributing to the impression that "ty" is not wholly separate from the ideal beloved of the first volume are indications that the meeting described in SnM #1 marks not a new but a renewed relationship ("I vnov'," "zabytyj son," "vspomnit'").

In SnM #2 certain phrasings evoke the image of the Lady, most notably the expression "(vse) to že":

Ты смотришь всё той же пленной душой
В купол всё тот же—звездный...
. . . .
И ты молчишь.
И в душе твоей безнадежной
Та же легкая, пленная грусть.   (SnM #2)

These words appear repeatedly in Blok's poetry (not to mention his
critical prose, correspondence and diaries) as an emblem of the
Lady's immutability ("Prošli goda, no ty—*vsë ta že:*/Stroga,
prekrasna i jasna"; "*Vsë ta že* ty, kakoj cvela kogda-to") (RazSt II
#56; RazSt III #4) (II, 101; III, 129).[39] The possibility of an
autoreminiscence is supported by two other details in SnM #2 that
recall the heroine of the first volume: "kupol" and "molčiš'." The
former brings to mind the scenario of meeting the Lady in or next
to a church; on one occasion the cupolas are identified with the
Lady's realm ("[My] postigli solnečnye volny/Vverxu—na temnyx
kupolax./I s ètoj vetxoj pozoloty,/Iz ètoj strašnoj glubiny/Na
prazdnik moj spustilsja Kto-to/ S ulybkoj laskovoj Ženy") (SPD
#87) (I, 160).[40] The latter brings to mind the Lady's "silence";
typically She was speechless ("Ona bez mysli i *bez reči*") (SPD
#131) (I, 204) and gave no response to the poet's prayers ("No i
noč'ju *net otveta,*/Ty ujdeš' v rečnoj kamyš"; "Na zare drugoj
vesny/*Net želannogo otveta*") (SPD #26, #78) (I, 99, 151).

In the section "Snega" the heroine continues to acquire
attributes associated with the "World of Ideal Faith," whether or
not they rightly belong to her. As mentioned earlier, she
expropriates the images "krest" and "korabl'," and in SnM #9
there are other verbal hints of the Lady's presence in the Snow
Mask's stormy element:

На небе — звездные дороги,
Среброснежные чертоги.

Сны метели светлозмейной,
Песни вьюги легковейной,
Очи девы чародейной.   (SnM #9)[41]

Confusion of the "ideal" and "evil" heroines in the figure of the
Snow Mask reaches its apogee in SnM #11-#12, where the hero
discerns in the distance her "pre-arranged sign" ("uslovnyj znak"):

На снежносинем покрывале
Читаю твой условный знак.   (SnM #11)

———

Сердце, видишь:
Кто-то подал знак,
Тайный знак рукой? (SnM #12)

One is likely to recall similar situations in SPD ("Ja tol'ko ždu *uslovnogo* viden'ja"; "A tam—odna čerta svetla,/I na čerte—*uslovnyj znak*") (SPD #15, #45) (I, 88, 118). It is significant that in SnM #11 the poet is unable to puzzle out the meaning of the "sign" ("znak") because he is as yet uncertain about the heroine's symbolic identity:

> Не разгадать живого мрака,
> Которым стан твой окружен.
> И не понять земного <u>знака</u>...   (SnM #11)

In SnM #10 he is still perplexed as to who gives the "sign" and then descends with the promise of upward flight:

> Ты ли? Ты ли?
> . . . .
> Ты ль нисходишь?
> Ты ль уводишь, —
> Ты, кого я полюбил?
>
> Над бескрайными снегами
> Возлетим!
> За туманными морями
> Догорим!   (SnM #12)

As mentioned earlier, the verb "poljubil" tends to link the image of "ty" with the Lady. Moreover the scenario depicted in these lines is reminiscent of situations in the first volume, namely—the Lady's descent to the poet ("Iz lazurnogo čertoga/Vremja tajne *snizojti*"; "Ty *sošla*, kosnulas' i vzdoxnula,—/Den' svobody zavtra mne?"; "Ja znal časy, kogda *sojdet*/Ona...") (SPD #55, #111, #147) (I, 128, 184, 221) and the poet's flight up to Her realm ("Ja *umcuš'* s ognevymi krugami/I nastignu Tebja v teremu"; "O, esli krylami vzmaxnes',/S toboj navsegda *ulečul*..") (SPD #47, #107) (I, 120, 180). The image "za tumannymi morjami" is also likely to evoke an association with the Lady (cf. the symbolism of seafaring in EP). Thus in many respects the events anticipated in SnM #12 correspond to the sacred Meeting as visualized in the first volume. At the same time, however, the poet cannot completely detach the image of "ty" from the "evil heroine" (note, for instance, the epithet "*temno*kryloj" in line 18).

At the end of "Snega" the Snow Mask's true identity is revealed. The baneful consequences of union with her become apparent in the loss of the "sword" ("Meč moj . . . utonul") (SnM #15), the sinking of the "ship" ("korabl' . . . tonet") (SnM #16) and the discovery of deceit ("I ja . . . Toboj obmanut") (SnM #16).

At the beginning of "Maski," however, the hero and heroine are placed in an environment where deception flourishes again, where "ideal love" and "betrayal" are again inseparable. In the setting of a costume ball the hero reacquires the chivalric accoutrements: the "sword" ("opersis' na meč") (#18), steel mail ("s temnymi cepjami/Na stal'nyx rukax") (#21), the faceplate ("pod zabralom") (#21) and the helmet ("vaš . . . šlem") (#21). He and the Snow Mask play out the roles of "knight" ("rycar'") (#18) and "mistress" ("Gospoža moja") (#19), although the charade is quite transparent (hence the repeated reference to "skazki"). In SnM #23 we find the first effort on the part of the hero to break out of this artificial, "fairy-tale" world and reestablish a distinction between the ideal beloved and the "evil heroine":

> Не будь и ты со мною строгой
> И маской не дразни меня,
> И в темной памяти не трогай
> Иного—страшного—огня.   (SnM #23)

The image "strašnyj ogon'" is undoubtedly connected with the idea of original, divine inspiration and seems to stand in contrast to inspiration by the Snow Mask—"Zolotistyj ugol' v serdce/Mne vožgla" (SnM #13). Both images, of course, can be traced back to Puškin's "Prorok." The admonition not to be "stern" ("strogoj") also serves to delineate the Snow Mask and the Lady, since "sternness" ("strogost'") was one of the Lady's attributes ("Dol'nemu stuku čuzda i *stroga*"; "Belaja Ty . . ./V žizni—*stroga* i gnevna"; "Ty smotriš' tixaja, *strogaja*") (SPD #1, #112, #123) (I, 74, 185, 196). In the latter half of "Maski" it again becomes apparent that the Snow Mask is only a counterfeit of the Lady. She is the agent of forgetfulness ("V'juga pamjat' poxoronit"; "Ja vsex zabyl, kogo ljubil") (#26, #29), sleep ("Spjat cari i geroi/Minuvšego dnja . . . O, Tvoi . . . snežnye žertvy") (#28) and death; moreover she is characterized once again as "neznakomaja" (#28). Even in the final scene, however, despite all indications to the contrary, the Snow Mask seeks to perpetuate her deception with mocking references to her "fidelity" ("Ja byla verna tri noči") and to the hero's "knighthood" ("rycar' milyj,/V snežnoj maske ty gori!") (#30).

Thus outlined, the plot of SnM traces a transformation from mistaken identity to proper identification of the heroine.[42]   To this summary, however, one must attach a paradoxical addendum. Although the Snow Mask is ultimately distinguished from the Lady and assigned to the "World of Betrayal," there are subtle indications that the "betrayal" itself and the retribution it entails constitute a necessary stage on the hero's path to the "World of Ideal Faith"—in a sense there is a certain justification or propriety to the confusion of their two images.   As noted earlier, the Snow Mask acts in alliance with the ideal world to the degree that she brings about the hero's death and fulfills the prophecy made near the beginning of the cycle ("I On potrebuet otveta") (#4).   Hence the image of the "cross" belongs equally to the "World of Ideal Faith" and the "World of Betrayal." The same can be said of the coordinate motif of "impaling" ("pronzit'," "raspjat'").   The verb "pronzit'," first evokes fear in the poet when its agency is attributed to "heaven's emissaries":

> Прочь лети, святая стая,
>
> . . . .
>
> Не <u>пронзить</u> меня Дарами
> И Причастием своим!   (SnM #13)

Ultimately, however, it is the Snow Mask who is the hero's "impaler":

> <u>Она</u>
> Тебя <u>пронзили</u> снежные иглы!   (SnM #15)

> <u>Пронзай</u> меня,
> Крылатый взор,
> Иглою снежного огня!   (SnM #29)

> И взвился костер высокий
> Над <u>распятым</u> на кресте.   (SnM #30)

There is a sense, therefore, in which the "evil heroine" is the instrument of "Ideal Faith," bringing about the humiliation and death of the hero as a necessary precondition to his resurrection (an eventuality realized not in SnM but in the third volume). This is why the episode of "betrayal" is seen from one perspective as something fated or predestined:

И твоя ли <u>неизбежность</u>
Совлекла меня с пути?   (SnM #26)

—————

. . . колеблемый вьюгами <u>Рока</u>,
Я взвиваюсь, звеня . . .   (SnM #28)

Thus one can interpret the lines "Put' otkryt naverno k raju/Vsem, kto idet putjami zla" (SnM #5) as both ironic and sincere—there is justification for both readings, though each logically excludes the other.   These words seem to confirm the apprehensions of the young Blok when he wrote already in 1902: "Is it really possible to reach 'the light' without first passing through 'the darkness'?" (VIII, 37).

As we have seen, the "snow threads" ("niti snežnye") of Blok's cycle are woven into an intricate and multilayered design ("vjaz'")—whether by the poet himself or by the Snow Mask and her elements, which progressively expropriate the weaving function. "Niti" is a metaphor for sequences of motifs, of words—or more generally, for poetic speech itself.   Blok used this metaphor on other occasions as well:

Совьются <u>нити</u> тонкие
Немеркнущих осенних слов.   (I, 537)

—————

Ребенком я любил играть,
    А юношей — бродить,
Ловить и долго развивать
    Одну и ту же <u>нить</u>.   (II, 412)

Nor is the metaphor Blok's alone; it occurs for instance in folk poetry:

Я частушку на частушку,
Как на <u>ниточку</u>, вяжу.[43]

At the same time these "threads" embody a story, they give an account of a crucial episode in the poet's fate—these "niti" are also "threads" of a life, of life seen as narrative or myth.   This metaphor too is common in poetry (e.g., Del'vig's "Genij-Xranitel'": "im vyprjast' *nit'* tvoej žizni") and goes back to the classical image of the Fates (or Parcae) who "spin the thread of human destiny."   This meaning was not unknown to Blok either:

Заплетаем, расплетаем

Нити дьявольской Судьбы.   (RazSt II #63) (II, 112)

In a most basic sense, SnM is about the inseparability of the two tenors in this bivalent metaphor. From the outset the poet recognizes the intimate connection between fate and the poetic word, and he strives to govern one by regulating the other. He attempts to control fate by controlling the verbal medium, he wishes to be only the weaver—not the thing that is woven. Ultimately, this effort fails—the words prove stronger than their maker, the poet is enveloped in his own creation and compelled to obey its internal laws. This was perhaps inevitable from the very conception of the work as an access route to Dionysus because the bacchant always becomes the instrument of his own unbridled impulse. The tragedy of SnM lies precisely in this lost boundary between created and creator, between art and life. In the cycles that follow there is in general a tendency to redefine this boundary, exert control over the creative medium again and reassert mastery over the lyric hero's fate.

"Faina," "Zakljatie ognem i mrakom," "Vol'nye mysli"

Besides SnM, three other cycles in the second volume contain a certain plot dynamic: "Faina" (F), "Zakljatie ognem i mrakom" (ZOM) (a subsection of F) and "Vol'nye mysli" (VM).

F is a companion to SnM in that it chronicles the poet's ongoing relationship with the Snow Mask's main biographical prototype, Natal'ja Voloxova. But whereas the story of SnM unfolds almost exclusively on a fantastic plane, F tells a story that incorporates the fantastic while still being firmly grounded in the real world. In F, for instance, there is an attention to the concrete realia of setting quite uncharacteristic of SnM; the setting of SnM is essentially a metaphoric cosmos, while the setting of F (for the most part) is specifically St. Petersburg with its Neva, its sphinxes, its canals, its theaters, even its pigeons and stray alley cats. Moreover unlike the Snow Mask, whom it would be difficult to describe concretely, the heroine of F has real physical features and apparel—her black curly hair, her alternately reddish ("ryžie") and dark ("černye") eyes,[45] her pale cheeks and swarthy shoulders, her weak and "slender" hands, her height, her narrow waist, her

black silks and tight belts.   She also has a certain social status
(she is a popular actress) and a complex personality—a curious
fusion of decorum and unbridled sensuality, modesty and arrogance,
kindness and sadistic cruelty.   It is not surprising that she elicits
such oxymoronic formulations as:

Нагло скромен дикий взор...   (F #1)

Мою прекрасную змею...   (F #13)

Ненавидя, кланя и любя...   (F #14)/(ZOM I)

Горят глаза твои, горят,
    Как черных две зари...   (F #15)/(ZOM II)

On the symbolic plane, as these quotations begin to suggest, the
heroine of F (like the Snow Mask) synthesizes the worlds of "Ideal
Faith" and "Betrayal," although ultimately she also demonstrates
her stronger and more basic allegiance to the latter.   For this
reason the heroine Faina, whose name means "radiant" ($\varphi\alpha\varepsilon\iota\nu\alpha$),
cannot be identified entirely with her namesake in Blok's "Pesnja
Sud'by" (1908), whose image at the end of the play is beneficent.

    The plot of F is less clearly defined than that of SnM, largely
because F was not initially conceived as a narrative nor even for
that matter as a cycle.   The title "Faina" in fact did not appear
until 1916, when roughly half of the cycle's poems were arranged
under this rubric in *Stixotvorenija* (Volume II); in *Zemlja v snegu*
(1908) and *Sobranie stixotvorenij* (1911-12) they had appeared
under various other headings ("Meščanskoe žit'e," "Pesnja sud'by,"
"Poslanija").   The concept of this grouping as a cycle, therefore,
evolved gradually and well after the poems had been written
(December 1906-November 1908).   In its final complement, F
contains thirty-one poems arranged chronologically to form a lyric
diary.   The only deviations from chronology are found in the
subcycle ZOM, which will be examined separately.

    In contrast to SnM, whose plot develops simultaneously (and
at different rates) along many motivical chains, the plot of F
unfolds essentially around a single theme that might be called
"dominance," "authority" or "superiority."   Through most of the
cycle the heroine exercises almost complete dominance over the
hero in their romantic relationship and relinquishes her superior
position only at the very end.   Thus in the first poem, which
narrates the heroine's appearance, the poet immediately assumes an
attitude of subservience, as symbolized by his entry into her

"circle":

> Вот явилась. Заслонила
> Всех нарядных, всех подруг,
> И душа моя вступила
> 4 В предназначенный ей круг.
>
> И под знойным снежным стоном
> Расцвели черты твои.
> Только тройка мчит со звоном
> 8 В снежно-белом забытьи.
>
> Ты взмахнула бубенцами,
> Увлекла меня в поля...
> Душишь черными шелками,
> 12 Распахнула соболя...   (F #1)

His helplessness is underscored by the verb "dušiš'" (line 11) and by the fact that the heroine directs their joint movement ("Uvlekla menja") (line 10). Subsequently the heroine's authority is suggested by her acquisition of regal and divine attributes. In F #2, for instance, she is surrounded by the "bright ring" of the footlights, which recalls the circle of fire around the goddess Brünnhilde in Wagner's *Ring of the Nibelung*:

> Живым огнем разъединило
> Нас рампы светлое кольцо,
> И музыка преобразила
> И обожгла твое лицо.   (F #2)

In F #3 Faina is depicted in "crown" or "wreath" ("v *vence* metelej"), behaving like a conqueror in a crowd of admirers ("I vse, kto vlasten i ničtozen,/Opustjat predo mnoj meči"), and in F #12 she accepts Petersburg as one might a regal offering ("I gorod moj železno-seryj/. . ./Ona, kak carvtvo, prinjala"). Accompanying these rather flattering images are indications of her despotism:

> И вот—меня цветистым хмелем
> Безумно захлестнула ты...   (F #25)

> ———
>
> Ступай—бичом хлестну!..
> . . . .
> Над вашей глупой головой—
> Свисти, мой тонкий бич!   (F #26)

By contrast the poet's demeanor is generally submissive, even servile:

> И я провел безумный год
> У шлейфа черного . . .   (F #13)

———

> И я, как темный раб . . .   (F #17)(ZOM IV)

———

> Рабом безумным и покорным
> До времени таюсь и жду...   (F #17)(ZOM IV)

Beginning in F #27 ("Vsju žizn' ždala..."), however, the poet assumes a different posture characterized on the one hand by anger and insubordination ("Ved' tol'ko ljudi govorjat,/Čto nado ždat' i byt' pokornym.../. . ./Nad liroj, gnevnoj, kak sekira") and on the other hand by compassion, which suggests the hero's moral equality if not superiority over the heroine:

> Когда вы стоите на моем пути,
> Такая живая, такая красивая,
> Но такая измученная,
> Говорите всё о печальном,
> Думаете о смерти,
> Никого не любите
> И презираете свою красоту —
> Что же? Разве я обижу вас?   (F #28)

On her part the heroine is now depicted with certain human weaknesses that remove her from the pedestal. These include self-abasement ("preziraete svoju krasotu") (#28), an almost pitiful clumsiness ("uronila na pol/Tolstyj tom xudožestvennogo žurnala/. . ./Vsë èto bylo . . . dovol'no nelepo") (#29) and emotional vulnerability ("Ee zalomlennye ruki/. . ./Vesennim livnem burnyx slez")(#30). The final, irreversible blow to her image is struck in the last poem—she is dethroned and "forgotten":

> Теперь, когда мне звезды ближе,
> Чем та неистовая ночь,
> Когда еще безмерно ниже
> Ты пала, униженья дочь,
>
> Когда один с самим собою
> Я проклинаю каждый день,

Теперь проходит предо мною
Твоя развенчанная тень...

С благоволеньем? Иль с укором?
Иль ненавидя, мстя, скорбя?
Иль хочешь быть мне приговором? —
Не знаю: я забыл тебя.   (F #31)

The verb "zabyl" signals a reversal of roles since the Snow Mask had prevailed upon the poet to "forget" past allegiances, as did Faina:

Воротясь, ты направишь копье полуночи
Солнцебогу веселому в грудь.
Я увижу в змеиных кудрях твои очи
Я услышу твой голос: "Забудь".   (F #5)

A similar reversal is suggested by the lines:

И стало всё равно, какие
Лобзать уста, ласкать плеча,
В какие улицы глухие
Гнать удалого лихача...   (F #31)

If earlier the heroine had surrounded herself with admirers, denying exclusivity to the hero, now the tables are turned. It is worth noting also that in contrast to the cycle's first poem, the carriage now moves at the behest of the hero, not the heroine.

Unlike F, of which it comprises roughly one third (F #14-#24), ZOM was conceived almost immediately as a cycle, even before all the poems in it were completed. On October 26, 1907, Blok wrote Brjusov requesting a delay in publication of "Snežnaja Deva" (F #12) because, as he explained, "[this poem] will grow into a whole cycle which I would like to send to you as soon as it is written."[46] Although "Snežnaja Deva" was not in fact included in ZOM, this remark suggests Blok composed the cycle as a work in progress rather than as an afterthought. On November 14, having finished the cycle, Blok dispatched it to Brjusov for publication in the journal *Vesy*, appending to it the following description: "Here is the new cycle of poems or a *poèma* that directly adjoins [neposredstvenno primykajuščaja] 'The Snow Mask'."[47] Brjusov was apparently persuaded by Blok's characterization of the cycle as a narrative work (*poèma*), because he announced the upcoming appearance of ZOM in the December issue of *Vesy* as follows: "Aleksandr Blok.   Zakljatie ognem i mrakom i pljaskoj metelej. *Poèma.*"[48]

Blok's observation that ZOM is a sequel to SnM has considerable justification. Even without knowing the biographical events underlying these two cycles, one can see that the Snow Mask and the heroine of ZOM are essentially the same symbolic persona. Indeed the latter is referred to as "maska" (ZOM VIII), "Deva Snežnaja" (XI), and her image elides with the night, the snowstorms and the whole "World of Betrayal" ("Vsë—viden'ja, vsë—*izmeny*") (VIII). In terms of its story, moreover, ZOM picks up in a sense where SnM left off. If SnM ends with the episode of confinement to the heroine's "circle" and crucifixion on her "cross," ZOM narrates the poet's effort to free himself from these constraints by means of "incantation." It will be recalled too that incantation plays an important role in SnM as well, and conjuring is reflected in the very instrumentation of the poems. As in SnM the hero of ZOM attempts to control the heroine's behavior with the poetic word:

> Пойми, в этом сумраке—магом
> Стою над тобою и жду...   (ZOM V)

And in ZOM incantory phrasing (word repetitions, internal rhymes, syllabic echoes) is quite conspicuous:

> Невозможное было возможно,
> Но возможное — было мечтой.   (III)

> Истоми ты истомой ресницы...   (VI)

> По улицам метель метет,
> Свивается, шатается.
> . . . .
> Течет она, поет она,
> Зовет она, проклятая.
> . . . .
> Там воля всех вольнее воль
> Не приневолит вольного,
> И болей всех больнее боль
> Вернет с пути окольного.   (VII)

С ума сойду, сойду с ума...   (IX)

———

Работай, работай, работай...

. . . .

Ах, сладко, как сладко, так сладко...   (X)

Despite these similarities, however, ZOM differs substantially from SnM. One will note, for example, that all incantory utterances above belong to the poet alone; the poet does not cede the conjuring power of the word to the heroine as he had done earlier with such baneful consequences. In SnM the heroine had expropriated the hero's medium, poetic speech, whereas in ZOM it is the hero who utilizes the heroine's elements ("ogon'," "mrak") to reverse, temporarily at least, the hold she has over him. It is significant also that while SnM focuses on the "passage," evolution or attitudinal change in the hero, ZOM deals with the evolution of the heroine, the transformation of her from a sophisticated urban tigress into a flirtatious country lass ("lixaja soldatka," "molodica") (X). This metamorphosis coincides with the migration of the hero and heroine from the city to the open expanses of the motherland—a movement that symbolizes the poet's desire to ally his own personal fate with that of the folk (narod). The same tendency is present in EP, as we have seen, as well as many other poems of the second volume, but ZOM marks the first occasion in which Blok manages to convey these aspirations cogently in cyclic form. SnM, which is by no means inferior to ZOM esthetically, nevertheless portrays romantic love in its most intimate aspect with no attention to issues of national or social import. Symbolically, it represents a perverted recrudescence of the chivalric, essentially Teutonic courtship of SPD. The Snow Mask, in playing the role of the Lady, surrounds herself with "pages," "knights," and "jesters" (SnM #21), and she is unable to speak Russian ("Vy ne znaete po-russki,/Gospoža moja...) (SnM #19). By contrast the heroine of ZOM, under the spell of the poet's incantation, ultimately finds herself in the company of country lads, singing folksongs and dancing in the round ("Ušla za selo, v xorovod") (ZOM X).

The plot of ZOM, like that of SnM, accumulates around a number of leitmotifs—primarily metaphoric ones. The plot is simpler, however, since such motif-accumulators are fewer and anachronies are virtually non-existent. In this respect ZOM is the more traditional episodic cycle.

The dominant plot motif in ZOM is the path (*put'*)— namely the path from enclosed space (symbolizing bondage and confinement) to open space (symbolizing freedom). Topographically, closed space is represented by the city (particularly the *interieur*), while open space is represented by rural landscapes (particularly the field or steppe). Excluding ZOM I, which is prefatory and does not participate in any plot sequence, we can discern the following distribution of symbolic space in the cycle: closed (II-VII), open (VII-X), closed (XI). This generalized scheme outlines the circular path traveled by the protagonists. One will note that ZOM VII occupies a pivotal position and marks a turning point in this plot line. It will be fruitful to examine precisely how this pattern manifests itself.

The dichotomy between bounded and unbounded space is established in ZOM I. The latter is the poet's emotional preference since it is allied with the maximally positive images "vesna" and "mečta" ("O, *vesna* bez konca i bez kraju —/Bez konca i bez kraju *mečta!*"); but the theme of the poem is acceptance of both categories:

> Принимаю пустынные веси!
> И колодцы земных городов!
> Осветленный простор поднебесий
> И томления рабьих трудов!   (ZOM I)

In poems II-VII the hero is located primarily within enclosed space, represented by interiors ("Ja zdes' v *uglu*.../Ja prigvožden *k stene*"; "Prislonennyx, kak ja, *u steny*") (II, VI), the city ("Ja budu zdes'. My vse sgorim:/Ves' *gorod* moj, reka, i ja") (II), the "dungeon" of erotic passion ("ty celueš' žadno/. . ./Xranja *v temnice* bezotradnoj/Menja, kak bednoe ditja") (IV) and the inaccessibility of the sky ("Ne smeja v *nebo* zagljanut'") (IV). The idea of enclosure is correlated with the theme of enslavement ("ja, kak temnyj *rab* . . ./. . ./*Rabom* bezumnym i *pokornym*") (IV). Movement between locations, which would normally signal freedom, is equated with continued confinement since the poet's destinations are identical and his path is bounded ("Perexožu ot kazni k kazni/Širokoj polosoj ognja") (IV). Poem VII marks the turning point; the poet moves from the world of enclosure (symbolized by the canal's constricting "granite") to the world of unbounded space (the "field"):

По удицам метель метет,
Свивается, шатается.
Мне кто-то руку подает
4 И кто-то улыбается.

Ведет — и вижу: глубина,
Гранитом темным сжатая.
Течет она, поет она,
8 Зовет она, проклятая.

. . . .
Бегу. Пусти, проклятый!
Не мучь ты, не испытывай!
Уйду я в поле, в снег и в ночь
24 Забьюсь под куст ракитовый!

Там воля всех вольнее воль
Не приневолит вольного,
И болей всех больнее боль
28 Вернет с пути окольного!   (ZOM VII)

Here the motif of the path, signaled by the words "begu" and "ujdu," is allied with the idea of escape—not only from the confining environments mentioned earlier, but from death (contemplation of the waters in the canal is associated with suicide).[49] This passage from closed to open space, anticipated in ZOM VII, is realized in ZOM VIII. The heroine's swirling "dance" beckons the hero into the snowy night and gives the promise of boundlessness:

Ты виденьем, в пляске нежной,
Посреди подруг
Обошла равниной снежной
Быстротечный
Бесконечный круг...   (ZOM VIII)

It is worth noting that even in an enclosed environment, the dance had earlier signaled disappearance of boundaries ("*V beskonečnoj dali* korridorov/Ne ona li tam *pljašet* vdali?") (ZOM VI). At the conclusion of ZOM VIII, as the hero's passage nears its end, there are suggestions that he has indeed escaped the world of confinement ("Ščemjaščie zvuki/I—*vol'naja* Rus'?"; "Zemlja ubegaet, *vskryvaetsja tverd*"). In ZOM IX-X, where the dance motif predominates, the hero is located in the symbolically "free," "open" environment, but he does not participate in the dance—he remains an observer, an outsider. At best he can only contemplate joining in (hence the subjunctive particle *by*):

> Ты знай про себя, что не хуже
> Другого <u>плясал бы</u> — вон как!
> Что мог бы стянуть и потуже
> Свой золотом шитый кушак!   (ZOM X)

This circumstance predicates the hero's regress into the world of confinement; in the cycle's last poem his path comes full circle—he finds himself once again in enclosure ("V . . . svoej temnice") and assumes a servile pose at the feet of the heroine:

> И я опять затих у ног —
> У ног давно и тайно милой...
> . . . .
> Но имя тонкое твое
> Твердить мне дивно, больно, сладко...
> И целовать твой шлейф украдкой,
> Когда метель поет, поет...   (ZOM XI)

Here the heroine has returned to the *interieur* and reacquired the aspect of an urban temptress ("tvoj šlejf"); the detail "zatix u nog" indicates not only the hero's renewed subservience, but also the fact that the liberating "dance" has ended. In ZOM, unlike SnM, the poet maintains his distance from the ecstatic, orgiastic experience into which the heroine beckons him; by doing so he preserves his life but sacrifices his freedom.

Another motif that acts as plot-accumulator is the flower. In ZOM V, before passage through the snowstorm begins, the poet dreams of "autumn roses" that appear hazily through the "darkness" and "frosts":

> И розы, осенние розы
> Мне снятся на каждом шагу
> Сквозь мглу, и огни, и морозы.
> На белом, на легком снегу.   (ZOM V)

After passing through the blizzard (ZOM VIII), the poet sees a multitude of flowers—not roses (which are allied symbolically with the world of first love) but wild flowers of the native Russian steppe:

Эй, желтенькие лютики,
Весенние цветки!
. . . .
Смотрою я — руки вскинула,
В широкий пляс пошла,
Цветами всех осыпала
И в песне изошла...   (ZOM IX)

In the cycle's last poem the image of the flower reappears, now as a symbol of death and frustrated anticipations:

Как будто, на средине бега,
Я под метелью изнемог,
И предо мной возник из снега
Холодный, неживой цветок...   (ZOM XI)

The development of the flower motif parallels closely that of the path—from hope of realizing a dream, to near fulfillment of it, and ultimately to disillusionment. Just as the path is not followed to the end (which would have entailed joining in the dance), so too the real flowers remain beyond the poet's reach and their substitute is only a painful reminder of failed anticipations.

Regardless of what motif is used to trace the plot of ZOM (and we have examined but two of many possible ones), its general outline is circular. In this respect it conforms to that elementary pattern Todorov claims is the basis of all plots: equilibrium → loss of equilibrium → new equilibrium.[50] To a degree, this circularity is reflected in the sequence of titles Blok invented for the poems in the cycle's first publication. Together they comprise what Blok called a single "incantory sentence":[51] "I Accept" (I), "In Fire" (II), "And in Darkness" (III), "Under Torture" (IV), "In the Snows" (V), "And in the Distant Rooms" (VI), "And at the Edge of the Abyss" (VII), "I Incant by Madness" (VIII), "In a Wild Dance" (IX), "And Again Submissive" (X), "I Surrender to You" (XI). In the "canonical" version of ZOM Blok discarded these titles, but the "emotional graph" they trace remained intact.[52]

"Vol'nye mysli" (VM), which follows immediately after F and closes out Blok's second volume, is not a plot cycle per se although each of the four vignettes it contains is a miniature narrative. The poems are unified rather by theme (urban social mores), setting (the environs of Petersburg), meter (blank iambic pentameter)[53]

and their realistic descriptive manner.[54]   The latter two features
have evoked comparison with Puškin,[55] although the cycle's title
was apparently borrowed from Apollon Grigor'ev.[56]   It is fitting
also to invoke the name of Nekrasov, in whom Blok had begun to
take an active interest at the very time he was writing VM
(summer 1907).   In tone and content VM comes close to
Nekrasov's cycles "Na ulice" and "O pogode," which belong to the
genre of the socio-ethnographic sketch.

The unifying compositional dynamic of VM is characterized
quite accurately by Pavel Gromov: "The logic of the cycle's
composition lies in the fact that the narrator moves more and
more from the role of observer to the role of participant in the
action."[57]   To Gromov's remark one should add that there is also
movement from emotional detachment to emotional involvement,
from objectivity to subjectivity.

In VM #1 ("O smerti") the poet narrates two deaths with
remarkable detachment.   In each instance he is an outsider—he
views a the jockey's death from outside the hippodrome fence, and
he does not join the gaping crowd that surrounds the drowned
dock worker.   He describes these scenes without satire or
commiseration and, after witnessing these events, moves on alone
("svoim putem"), engaging in introspection:

> Сердце!
> Ты будь вожатаем моим. И смерть
> С улыбкой наблюдай. Само устанешь,
> Не вынесешь такой веселой жизни,
> Какую я веду. Такой любви
> И ненависти люди не выносят,
> Какую я в себе ношу.   (VM #1)

Here the poet exhibits an almost frivolous indifference to the
tribulations of others, as if to say that the scenes he has just
depicted have no relevance whatsoever to his own experience.   VM
#2 ("Nad ozerom") opens with a similar attitude of contemplative
detachment.   The poet communes with nature and is completely
aloof from human affairs.   By increments, however, he becomes an
unwitting participant in the flirtation he witnesses at lakeside, and
near the end interferes in the lovers' tryst with childish
maliciousness:

> Я хохочу! Взбегаю вверх. Бросаю
> В них шишками, песком, визжу, пляшу

Среди могил — незримый и высокий...
Кричу: "Эй, Фёкла! Фёкла!".....   (VM #2)

In VM #3 ("V severnom more") loss of objectivity and increased emotional involvement are evident in the satirical tone of the sketch:

Что сделали из берега морского
Гуляющие модницы и франты?
Наставили столов, дымят, жуют,
Пьют лимонад. Потом бредут по пляжу,
Угрюмо хохоча и заражая
Соленый воздух сплетнями . . .   (VM #3)

Moreover, despite his cynicism, the poet joins the vacationers on a motor boat excursion around the bay. In VM #4 ("V djunax") there is no longer any pretense of disinterested observation—the poet is the protagonist (indeed, the villain) of his own vignette:

Я гнал ее далеко. Исцарапал
Лицо о хвои, окровавил руки
И платье изорвал. Кричал и гнал
Ее, как зверя, вновь кричал и звал,
И страстный голос был как звуки рога.   (VM #4)

So ends the path from detachment to involvement, from observer to participant—which, though not a plot, is nevertheless a graph of changing perspective. One can only wonder what purpose this conversion serves. Perhaps it serves none, and its very freedom from esthetic function becomes one justification for the epithet "Vol'nye" ("free") in the cycle's title. Or perhaps the aim of Blok's changing perspective is to bring the lyric subject into direct contact with the world around, with people in the real world. What the poet does might be compared to experimentation with a movie camera. At first the cameraman points the lens away from himself and perfects the machine's capacity to record external detail. By doing so he also validates the external, empirical world as esthetic object. Then gradually, hesitantly, he makes forays in front of the lens, relishing the new-found ability to become part of the objective reality that the camera sees. This would be in keeping with Blok's growing effort in these years to free himself from the solipsism of his lyric method.

    Another, more visceral rationale for the title "Vol'nye mysli" lies in the way Blok treats the theme of erotic love in the cycle.

Throughout VM Blok distinguishes between natural, uncivilized, "animal" love and a civilized, sophisticated love that conforms to accepted social norms.   The latter is repeatedly satirized, as for instance in the affected mannerisms of the officer on the beach ("on žmet ej ruku!.. smotrjat/Ego gljadelki v jasnye glaza!../. . ./I vdrug... protjažno čmokaet ee,/Daet ej ruku i vedet na daču!/. . ./. . . ne zabyvaja/Vixljat' provorno zadom") (#2) or in the ludicrous incongruity of the graffiti on the breakwater:

> Прочтя все надписи: "Навек с тобой",
> "Здесь были Коля с Катей", "Диодор
> Иеромонах и послушник Исидор
> Здесь были. Дивны божии дела"...   (VM #3)

Preference is given instead to love without artificial trappings and words of endearment:

> Всегда хочу смотреть в глаза людские,
> И пить вино, и женщин целовать,
> И яростью желаний полнить вечер...   (VM #1)

The poet himself, however, is not invulnerable to genteel expressions of affection, as is apparent at the end of VM #2:

> И в комнате моей белеет утро.
> Оно на всём: на книгах и столах,
> И на постели, и на мягком кресле,
> И на письме трагической актрисы:
> "Я вся усталая. Я вся больная.
> Цветы меня не радуют. Пишите...
> Простите и сожгите этот бред..."
>
> И томные слова... И длинный почерк,
> Усталый, как ее усталый шлейф...
> И томностью пылающие буквы,
> Как яркий камень в черных волосах.   (VM #2)

One familiar with Blok's second volume cannot fail to recognize here the image of Faina ("tragičeskoj aktrisy," "šlejf," "černyx volosax").   That the poet focuses his attention on her letter and is receptive to its pathos suggests that he is as yet not "free" of the sophisticated enslavement her love represents.   VM #4, however, indirectly (or perhaps more accurately—on a subliminal level) narrates the poet's emancipation from this relationship.   The poem opens with the cycle's most vivid contrast between "civilized" and "uncivilized" love—the first couched in phrases denoting both endearment and possession (hence "enslavement"), the second couched in an idiom unencumbered with these artificial accessories:

> Я не люблю пустого словаря
> Любовных слов и жалких выражений:
> "Ты мой", "Твоя", "Люблю", "Навеки твой".
> Я рабства не люблю. Свободным взором
> Красивой женщине смотрю в глаза
> И говорю: "Сегодня ночь. Но завтра —
> Сияющий и новый день. Приди.
> Бери меня, торжественная страсть.
> А завтра я уйду — и запою".   (VM #4)

The heroine of this vignette is a wild, untamed creature—though not coincidentally her features are reminiscent of Faina's:

> . . . . . И вот она пришла
> И встала на откосе. Были рыжи
> Ее глаза от солнца и песка.
> И волосы, смолистые как сосны,
> В отливах синих падали на плечи.
> Пришла. Скрестила свой звериный взгляд
> С моим звериным взглядом . . .   (VM #4)[58]

In the scene that ensues the poet hunts down the object of his passion, determined to force her into submission:

> . . . . . . Я не уйду отсюда,
> Пока не затравлю ее, как зверя,
> И голосом, зовущим, как рога,
> Не прегражу ей путь. И не скажу:
> "Моя! Моя!" — И пусть она мне крикнет:
> "Твоя! Твоя!"   (VM #4)

Here the poet immerses himself in an elemental, bestial urge without committing his spiritual sensibilities to it. He may say "Moja! Moja!" but he will not be enslaved by the lexicon of endearment. From her, however, he will extract the words ("Tvoja! Tvoja!") as a sign of her submission. Gromov is not entirely correct, therefore, when he says that "there are no internal connections" between ZOM and VM.[59] The heroine of ZOM is indeed present in VM (#2), and by means of a relationship with her surrogate (VM #4) the poet succeeds in reversing the model of subjugation that prevailed in ZOM.

Our discussion has not touched two major groupings of the second volume—namely "Puzyri zemli" (PZ) and "Gorod" (G), which are not plot cycles by any stretch of the imagination. What unifies PZ and G is a topographical principle—they belong, generally speaking, to the genre of "locale cycles" popularized in the late nineteenth century by such poets as Majkov, Polonskij, and Aleksej Tolstoj.   PZ is set in marshy grasslands resembling Neva estuary, and G is set in St. Petersburg.   These cycles, however, are not simply scenic descriptions—in each case the choice of locale is symbolic.   The bogs and swamps of PZ symbolize stagnation and decay, the waning of those heroic aspirations that inspired the lyric hero of the first volume; moreover the swamps are lowlands—the antithesis of the lofty climes inhabited by the Lady.   The city of G is the habitat of the Devil, the locus of corruption, deceipt and defiled beauty.
Although G itself does not contain a plot, it participates in a supracyclic narrative dynamic that spans the latter half of the second volume.   As we have seen, the cycles SnM, F, its subcycle ZOM and VM form a narrative-like sequence.   SnM charts a circular path from enclosure inside the domicile to exit or escape into boundless expanses and ultimately to renewed enclosure within the Snow Mask's icy realm.   ZOM narrates the lyric hero's unsuccessful attempt to liberate himself from this relationship via incantation, via transformation of the heroine into a different symbolic entity.   F, in the form of a lyric diary, recounts the lyric hero's ultimate emancipation from enslavement in more or less realistic terms.   And VM is a kind of epilogue that reaffirms the lyric hero's freedom from such binding romantic entanglements. The cycle G, which immediately precedes SnM, ends with a number of poems in which the poet retreats from the temptations of the city into the relative security of the domicile.   These poems, which are sometimes referred to by critics as Blok's "attic cycle" (e.g., "Xolodnyj den'," "V okjabre," "Okna vo dvor," "Na čerdake"), manifest the rudiments of a dramatic situation that prepares the episode of escape in SnM.[60]   In the poem "Na čerdake" (G #43), for instance, there are verses that prefigure SnM quite directly:

Что на свете выше

Светлых чердаков?
Вижу трубы, крыши
Дальних кабаков.

Путь туда заказан,
И на что — теперь?
Вот — я с ней лишь связан...
Вот — закрыта дверь...
. . . .
Ветер, снежный север,
Давний друг ты мне!
Подари ты веер
Молодой жене!

Подари ей платье
Белое, как ты!
Нанеси в кровать ей
Снежные цветы!   (G #43) (II, 205)

This imagery anticipates not only the stormy element of the Snow Mask and the episode of opening the "door" in "Vtoroe kreščen'e" (SnM #5), but also the confusion of the ideal and evil heroines at the outset of SnM.

Surveying the design of the second volume we find that its various sections and cycles are disposed to some degree chronologically: PZ (May 1904—October 1905), NF (November 1905—May 1906), RazSt II (January 1904—August 1908), G (February 1904—February 1908), SnM (December 1906—November 1908), VM (June—July 1907). One will note, however, that the dates overlap to some extent and that the particular sequence Blok chose is at least in part discretionary. G, for instance, contains some poems that antedate those in PZ, and F contains some that postdate those in VM. The section RazSt II, whose chronological parameters in effect span the entire second volume, could conceivably have been positioned virtually anywhere in the sequence. It is worth noting also that a number of poems within the cycles PZ and ZOM, judging from the dates subscribed beneath them, are out of chronological order. All of this indicates that the arrangement of cycles (and in certain instances the arrangement of poems within the cycles) is dictated not solely by chronology, but by some other principle as well.

In his landmark essay "Ideja puti v poètičeskom mire

Aleksandra Bloka" Maksimov argues that this other principle is a "supra-chronological [sverx-xronologičeskoj] sequentiality," a "well-defined evolutionary and logical development . . . *as if in time*".[61]   The arrangement of cycles represents "a series of milestones marking the different stages of the poet's [creative-spiritual] path."[62]   What Maksimov stops just short of saying is that the second volume contains a certain plot, although the concept of plot is subsumed in the notion of "development . . . *as if in time.*"

It is fruitful to view Maksimov's remarks in light of the distinction between *chronos* (passing time, simple succession) and *kairos* (the critical or proper time).   As Frank Kermode points out in *The Sense of an Ending,* "we associate 'reality' with *chronos*, and a fiction which entirely ignored this association we might think unserious or silly or mad."[63]   But in order to create plots "we need ends and *kairoi*. . . we look for a fullness of time, for beginning, middle, and end in concord."[64]

Blok's first volume adheres exclusively to *chronos*.   Each poem represents the lyric insight of a particular moment, and the order of these moments coincides with empirical reality.   As a result, the sense of plot is almost non-existent.   Life provides the raw material for narrative, but it does not in itself constitute narrative.   In the second volume, by contrast, Blok is already giving equal weight to *kairos*—he is making displacements in time that are necessary to create plot, to fashion from life (and from the lyrics that register moments in that life) the biography of a lyric hero.   In the third volume, as we shall see, such displacements become more pronounced.

V

CHAOS AND COSMOS:
"THE TERRIBLE WORLD" AND THE DESIGN
OF BLOK'S THIRD VOLUME

> Poetry is life at the remove of form and
> meaning; not life lived but life framed and
> identified.
> —R. P. Blackmur, "A Critic's Job of Work"
>
> Amorphousness is dangerous (a continuation of
> the antithesis . . .).
> —A. Blok, *Notebooks* (March 26, 1910)

In *L'Univers poétique d'Alexandre Blok* Sophie Bonneau writes that
Blok's life during the years 1908-1914 was immersed in "chaos":

> Retombé l'élan qui l'avait porté vers la Tempête
> de Neige Blok s'enfonce dans l'abîme tzigane, dont
> Volokhova, aussi bien, lui avait ouvert le seuil. Par
> delà son existence familiale qui n'est qu' apparence, que
> "masque," il entre, it vit dans le "chaos." Et dans ce
> chaos, il demeure du début 1908 au 31 août
> 1914. . . . . [1]

Though there is no easy scale by which to gauge "chaos" in a
person's life, one is inclined to agree with Bonneau on a number of
counts. There are Blok's innumerable sexual liaisons of the most
haphazard kind,[2] nightly perigrinations through the streets of
Petersburg (often in the company of prostitutes), chronic
drunkenness, growing alienation from literary circles, repeated
infidelities on the part of Ljubov' Dmitrievna, her prolonged
absences from the home, and finally the death of Blok's father and

infant son in 1909.   Beneath these visible signs is the spiritual
turmoil recounted with painful sincerity in Blok's diaries, notebooks
and of course in his lyric poetry, which remained as always
intimately confessional.

It is a measure of how art not only reflects life but also
restructures and compensates for it, however, that Blok's third
volume, whose dates (1907–1916) correspond roughly to the period
of which Bonneau speaks, adheres so firmly to principles of
order—cosmos rather than chaos.   In fact if there is one feature
that distinguishes the third volume from the first and second, it is
its elaborate cyclic architecture, its meticulous delineation and
careful balancing of different contextual framings.

Even a cursory survey of the third volume gives evidence of
its exceptional orderliness.   The total number of cycles (17) is more
than triple that in the first (5) and nearly double that in the
second (10), [3] despite the fact that the third volume is roughly
equal to the others in length.   At the same time, the number of
major segments in the third volume does not exceed that of the
second, so that the increase in the total number of cycles is
achieved largely via subordination and hierarchization of cyclic
context—certain cycles are placed *inside* others.   In this regard the
volume's four "macrocycles" (large cycles containing one or more
smaller groupings) are the dominant form of cyclic composition.
The macrocycles, together with the nine subcycles they contain,
account for more than half the poems and three quarters of the
cycles in the volume:

> "Strašnyj mir" (StM) (48 poems)
> > *Subcycles*
> > "Pljaski smerti" (PS) (5 poems)
> > "Žizn' moego prijatelja" (ŽMP) (8 poems)
> > "Černaja krov'" (ČK) (9 poems)
>
> "Ital'janskie stixi" (ISt) (24 poems)
> > *Subcycles*
> > "Venecija" (VEN) (3 poems)
> > "Florencija" (FLO) (7 poems)
>
> "Arfy i skripki" (AS) (72 poems)
> > *Subcycles*
> > "Tri poslanija" (TP) (3 poems)
> > "Mèri" (MÈR) (3 poems)

"Čerez dvenadcat' let" (ČDL) (8 poems)

"Rodina" (ROD) (27 poems)
Subcycle
"Na pole Kulikovom" (NPK) (5 poems)

If we posit the idea of framing or containment as one of the main compositional features of the third volume, it seems not incidental that the volume's smaller segments (excluding the subcycles) are placed namely *between* the macrocycles. Between StM and ISt are located two rather small groupings:

"Vozmezdie" (VOZ) (17 poems)
"Jamby" (JAM) (12 poems)

And between AS and ROD we find one small cycle and one short cycle-like narrative:

"Karmen" (K) (10 poems)
"Solov'inyj sad" (SS) (7 sections)

Only the diminutive cycle "O čem poet veter" (OČPV) (6 poems), which appears at the very end of the volume, is located outside the boundaries formed by the macrocycles. All in all, the layout of the third volume is extremely elaborate, but the hegemony of the four macrocycles lends it a certain balance and simplicity.

Contributing to the impression of orderliness is the degree of symmetry in the disposition of the volume's various segments. The section "Raznye stixotvorenija" (RazSt III) (25 poems), which differs from the other segments by being in effect non-cyclic, divides the volume into two more or less symmetrical halves. (In the second volume, by contrast, the placement of RazSt created two asymmetrical portions: PZ—NF—*RazSt II*—G—SnM—F—VM.) Each hemivolume, in turn, manifests a similar pattern with regard to the size and arrangement of its segments: large—small—small—large (StM—VOZ—JAM—ISt); large—small—small—large (AS—K—SS—ROD). One will note also that the larger macrocycles (StM and AS), both of which hold three subcycles, are located at the beginning of each hemivolume, while the smaller ones (ISt and ROD) are positioned at or near the end of their respective halves. Comparing the number of lines in each segment tends to confirm the impression that symmetry and balance are important features of the volume's organization:

1127—352—193—422;   1123—174—148—650.   It may help to
visualize these comparisons graphically:

StM	VOZ	JAM	ISt
(largest)	(small)	(small)	(large)
(3 subcycles)	(no subcycles)	(no subcycles)	(2 subcycles)
(1127 lines)	(352 lines)	(193 lines)	(422 lines)

//RazSt III//

AS	K	SS	ROD
(largest)	(small)	(small)	(large)
(3 subcycles)	(no subcycles)	(no subcycles)	(1 subcycle)
(1123 lines)	(174 lines)	(148 lines)	(650 lines)

//OČPV//

Admittedly, the patterns outlined above are based on rather
superficial criteria, but further analysis will show that they exist at
very deep levels of theme and structure.   As we shall see, the
overriding constructive principle of the third volume as a
synchronic system is precisely one of *binary symmetry*.   In essence,
the volume is designed according to a factor of *two* (not a factor of
three, as has been proposed elsewhere).[4]   Therefore the most
meaningful and conspicuous textual equivalencies tend to appear at
far poles of linear coordinates, at various perimeters—especially at
the perimeters formed by four macrocycles.   The first and last
poems of each macrocycle echo each other thematically and
lexically.   The macrocycles at opposite ends of each hemivolume
(StM—ISt, AS—ROD) are linked by prominant parallels and
contrasts.   The same is true of macrocycles that face each other at
coordinate ends of the two hemivolumes (StM—AS, ISt—ROD).
Finally, the interrelationship between StM and ROD, which mark
the far limits of the book, creates a dynamic which is absolutely
essential in the design of the volume.

Given the importance of the macrocycles in the design of the
third volume, it is fair to consider them the dominant cyclic
type—the more so because they contain 171 of the volume's 241
separate lyrics.   But to the degree that typology is a function of
tradition, there is no single cyclic dominant.   In the third volume
Blok has assembled a veritable museum of different cyclic types,

selected as if to illustrate the cycle's long and distinguished history. There are generic cycles reminiscent of the eighteenth and early nineteenth centuries (TP and the grouping "Poslanija" in RazSt III); episodic plot cycles in a fairly traditional (Brjusovian) mold (OČPV and especially ČK); a hybrid archetypal-episodic plot cycle (ŽMP); a "memory cycle" whose gross design is quite conventional (ČDL); locale cycles (VEN, FLO and ROD); a travel-diary type cycle not unlike those popularized by Apollon Majkov, Aleksej Tolstoj and Karolina Pavlova (ISt).[5]   StM is essentially a dramatic-situational grouping, and AS resembles the loosely integrated "mood cycles" of Fet and Bal'mont.   Certain other cycles represent a hybridization of the thematic-ideational and dramatic-situational types (VOZ, JAM, MÈR, and K).   By including such a wide array of cyclic genres Blok seems to acknowledge his debt to the tradition in which his lyric oeuvre so obviously participates.   At the same time he architects from these traditional types a contextual edifice unprecedented in the history of the lyric cycle.   It is arguable, therefore, that the entire third volume comprises a monumental cycle of the whole—the truest fulfillment of Blok's earlier claim to have "created a building" out of his "songs" ("Iz ètix pesen sozdal ja zdan'e") (RAS #43) (I, 283).[6]   Indeed there is a sense in which the volume revitalizes the common metaphor of an artist's creative "monument."   Its very form, however, seems to polemicize with the "Exegi monumentum" poems of his predecessors (e.g., Deržavin, Puškin): Blok's edifice, as we shall see, is not a tomb-like monolith but rather a "house" ("dom")—a "home" in which he plans to live and wait.

Given the meticulous care with which Blok crafted the third volume, one must ask, naturally, why he felt the need in this case to devise such elaborate cyclic contexts for his lyrics.   The answer to this question seems to lie in the apprehensions Blok began to have about the lyric mode in mid 1907, just a few months after completing SnM.   If in that cycle he had ridden the wave of an unbriddled Dionysian impulse, now he became troubled by what he saw as the lyric's dangerous tendency toward disorder, unpredictability and discontinuity.   In the preface to his Liričeskie dramy (August 1907) Blok wrote:

> In lyric poetry are rooted experiences of the soul,—a soul which in our time is of necessity isolated.   These experiences are usually complex, chaotic; to make sense

of them one must himself be "somewhat of the same fiber." But even he who makes sense out of the complex experiences of the contemporary soul cannot pride himself that he stands on a firm path . . . .

Lyric poetry offers up in elegant and varied form a whole wealth of refined and disconnected experiences. The most lyric poetry can do is enrich the soul and complicate feelings; by no means does it even always make them more acute, but to the contrary sometimes dulls them by heaping upon the soul an unimaginable chaos . . . .[7]

Echoing these concerns in a letter to Andrej Belyj from October 1907, Blok allied the lyric with the concepts of "decay," "decomposition" and expressed fear that "the rust of the swamp and the lyric will corrode the well-shaped columns and marble of life and tragedy" (VIII, 213). As these statements begin to suggest, Blok was disturbed by two aspects of the lyric which he linked under the concept of "chaos." On the one hand, each lyric poem originated in a chaotic feeling—it brought together a multitude of "disconnected experiences," and its very richness was proportionate to the number of contradictions inherent in the creative stimulus. On the other hand, each lyric, being a product of a separate inspirational "moment," tended to destroy the continuity of time he wished to discover in life and art. This is a problem that lay at the very core of the "trilogy": how was Blok as a poet to fashion a coherent "life" or "tragedy" for his lyric hero, if the content of each poem was spontaneous, unpredictable and did not necessarily jibe with the plan he had conceived early in his career? As he explained in 1910, when the idea of his "trilogy" was already concretely formulated, his principal goal as an artist was "to establish the internal linkage of events" (V, 426), whereas the lyric, so closely rooted in the anarchy and complexity of the momentary inspirational vision, drew one back into "those worlds where there is no cause and effect, no time and space, no corporeal and incorporeal—and these worlds are without number" (V, 433).

At this time Blok earnestly sought ways of putting limits on this lyric "chaos" and regulating what Jung aptly called "the terrible ambiguity of the immediate experience."[8] Moreover he believed that somewhere in art itself lay the mechanism which would make this possible. On September 3, 1909 he proclaimed in a letter to his friend Evgenij Ivanov:

> Art is only cosmos—the creative spirit which gives form to chaos (the emotional and corporeal world). There is no need to elaborate on the fact that the world of corporeal and emotional phenomena is *only* chaos—this must be known to the artist (as it was known to Aeschylus, Dante, Puškin, Bellini, Leonardo, Michelangelo and will be known to future artists). Our great writers (primarily I have in mind Tolstoj and Dostoevskij) built everything *on top of* chaos (they "valued" it), and therefore chaos emerged multiplied tenfold, that is, they were bad artists. One can build cosmos only *out of* chaos. (VIII, 293) [Blok's emphasis—D.S.]

Two days later he wrote in his notebook, more succinctly and eloquently: "The form of art is its shaping essence, its creative order. . . . I recognize as a *good artist* only one who out of a given chaos (and not *in* it and not *on* it) . . . creates cosmos" (ZK, 160). [Blok's emphasis—D.S.]

In December 1906, when Blok read *The Birth of Tragedy*, he copied out and underscored the sentence "Apollo could not live without Dionysus" (ZK, 79). At that time he gave priority to the latter diety, following Nietzsche's own bias; SnM (and more generally the poetry which was to comprise his second volume) were conceived as a path "to Dionysus" (ZK, 86). Blok was aware, however, that Nietzsche did not dismiss the role of Apollo. If "Apollo could not live without Dionysus," Dionysus' life was meaningless without the agency of Apollo; Nietzsche writes:

> Art owes its continuous evolution to the Apollonian-Dionysiac duality, even as the propagation of the species depends on the duality of the sexes, their constant conflicts and periodic acts of reconciliation.[9]

The more chaotic the Dionysian impulse, the harder Apollo had to work to mold and transfigure it. In this interaction Nietzsche saw the lesson of Hellenic culture for modern man:

> These two prime agencies must develop in strict proportion, conformable to the laws of eternal justice.

Whenever the Dionysiac forces became too obstreperous, as is the case today, we are safe in assuming that Apollo is close at hand, though wrapped in a cloud, and that the rich effects of his beauty will be witnessed by a later generation.

The reader may intuit these effects if he has ever, though only in a dream, been carried back to the ancient Hellenic way of life. Walking beneath high Ionic peristyles, looking toward a horizon defined by pure and noble lines, seeing on either hand the glorified reflections of his shape in gleaming marble and all about him men moving solemnly or delicately, with harmonious sounds and rhythmic gestures: would he not then, overwhelmed by this steady stream of beauty, be forced to raise his hands to Apollo and call out: "Blessed Greeks! how great must be your Dionysus, if the Delphic god thinks such enchantments necessary to cure you of your dithyrambic madness!"[10]

In composing his third volume Blok enlisted Apollo's "enchantments" more zealously than he had in either the first or the second. In those books life itself collaborated with the cyclist to help channel Dionysus' "dithyrambic madness" into a meaningful design; in each instance life provided a single love that helped organize time and focus the poet's lyric sensibilities. In the period of the third, by contrast, such collaboration is all but non-existent. Even the poet's consuming love for Ljubov' Andreevna Del'mas spanned but a brief period of time and produced only the diminutive cycle K and the short *poèma* SS, neither of which—unlike SPD and SnM—could serve as a volume's organizing center.

Paradoxically, the "central" cycles of the third volume, those that do most to organize the whole—StM and ROD—are located not at the geographical "center" of the book but at its perimeters.[11] What gives shape to the book as it unfolds in sequence ("as if in time") is the concept of the lyric hero's passage from the "terrible world" (or, just as accurately, *through* it) to the expanses of the motherland where he awaits his final destiny. This passage, however, has in fact little to do with Blok's real biography since Blok, in arranging the cycles, made virtually no effort to follow life's chronology. The very fact, for instance, that StM

(*1909*-1916) to a significant degree postdates ROD (*1907*-1916) would seem to militate for disposing these cycles in reverse order. In this respect the volume's design represents a victory of art's (the cycle's) "cosmos" over the "chaos" of life and lyric. The poet's passage or "path" is a pseudo-geographic, pseudo-temporal analogue to this victory.

This "path," however, resembles least a triumphant procession along some well-mapped parade route.[12] The cycles (and the *poèma* SS) that lie between StM and ROD chart a highly circuitous course—one that contains as many wrong turns and blind alleys as it does reliable roads and signposts. The lyric hero of StM already knows his ultimate destination but does not know the way to it. Hence in StM #2 ("Pod šum i zvon odnoobraznyj..."), the poem that most closely reproduces the conceptual outlines of the third volume in microcosm, the poet identifies the motherland as his goal but can only pray that his Muse will show him the path which will enable him to reach it:

Под шум и звон однообразный,
Под городскую суету
Я ухожу, душою праздный,
В метель, во мрак и в пустоту.

Я обрываю нить сознанья
И забываю, что и как...
Кругом—снега, трамваи, зданья,
А впереди—огни и мрак.

Что, если я, завороженный,
Сознанья оборвавший нить,
Вернусь домой уничиженный,—
Ты можешь ли меня простить?

Ты, знающая дальней цели
Путеводительный маяк,
Простишь ли мне мои метели,
Мой бред, поэзию и мрак?

> Иль можешь лучше: не прощая,
> Будить мои колокола,
> Чтобы распутица ночная
> От родины не увела?   (StM #2) (III, 9)

This is an unusual statement of faith in the power of art to regulate itself—especially in ways not fully comprehended by its creator.   The confusion, the loss of consciousness, the "chaos" at the beginning of the poem correspond to that condition Blok identified with poetic inspiration.   The alliance of "poetry" with "snowstorms," "darkness," and "delerium" in the fourth stanza makes this association very clear.   In both the third and the fifth stanzas, however, Blok attributes to his Muse (and to poetry) a compensatory "cosmic" capacity, a capacity to bring order to disorder and direction to an aimless path.   One is reminded that even in one of his most scathing attacks on the lyric ("O lirike," 1907) Blok had spoken about "a strange kinship between the poison of lyric and *its constructive force)*" (V, 132).

The design of Blok's third volume ultimately confirms the implications of this programmatic poem.   The orders in the book—even if they are imposed upon the lyric quite consciously and deliberately—remains orders of poetic form.   Cyclization allowed Blok to adjust the accidents of life and create plot where life provided none.   Moreover artistic intuition, which accompanied the creation of every individual poem, facilitated ahead of time the transformations that conscious effort was later able to effect. Blok's continual obsession with particular motifs and words, coupled with a certain consistency in their treatment, made it possible, post factum, to design the volume so that a "path" would become progressively more manifest and lead finally in the direction he wished his lyric hero to travel.

The present chapter has a binary focus.   It concentrates first on the macrocycle StM, which opens the volume, and second on the supracyclic design of the volume as a whole.   These two apparently separate objects of attention are in fact closely related. The very form of the macrocycle, for instance, with its internal contextual framings (cyclic context within a cyclic context) is in some sense a scaled-down model of the volume *in toto*.   Moreover StM itself is a crucial part of the larger structure: it poses a conceptual dilemma that the volume as a whole is enlisted to resolve. [13] The "terrible world" depicted in StM is the prime locus of chaos, a chaos that pervades every aspect of the poet's experience and threatens, as Blok feared, to destroy "the well-shaped columns" of life and art. The design of the third volume, as a monumental esthetic construct, countermands the dire auguries of StM and by its very configuration allows cosmos to burgeon and prevail.

Chaos and cosmos are not, strictly speaking, themes—or at least they are not *only* themes, no more than plot is the "theme" of a novel or harmonic counterpoint is the "theme" of a baroque concerto. They are rather constructive principles which manifest themselves both on a thematic level and on the level of compositional form—in the cycles' design and in the cycles' interrelationship. To the degree that chaos and cosmos are embodied thematically, they tend to crystallize around two polivalent semantic complexes—the "home" and the "path." To the connotative field of the "home" belong real dwellings, buildings, or indeed any bounded structure; the homeland; the symbolic world of "ideal love," which the lyric hero seeks to rediscover; and finally poetic structure itself. Similarly, the "path" has various manifestations: real paths, roads, streets and highways; the metaphoric "path" of empirical life; and finally the "path" of life as mythic (esthetic) construct. By virtue of their convergence in this last category (artistic form) the "path" and the "home" (in their multiple senses) become mutually signifying—the mythopoetic "path" of life and the poetic vessel which contains that myth are metonymically equivalent. The design of the third volume is a "home" in which the "path" is manifest, and, as we shall see, it is also the destination toward which the "path" is directed. Blok gave a clue to this when he wrote in 1908: "The Promised Land is a path" (ZK, 107).

Both the "home" and the "path," moreover, can be functions of either cosmos or chaos. The cosmic "home" is an ideal space with secure walls or boundaries; the chaotic "home" lacks secure walls and is the locus of a perverted ideal. Similarly, the cosmic "path" is straight, bordered, open, but ending-oriented;the chaotic "path" is circular, unbounded, blocked or unending—it is a "path" that defeats the purpose of any path, which is to reach some destination. The ongoing dialectic between chaos and cosmos, between the chaotic and the cosmic "homes," between the chaotic and cosmic "paths" is the dynamic which unifies Blok's third volume.[14]

"Strašnyj mir": *The Realm of Chaos*

StM belongs in a broad sense to the genre of the
dramatic-situational cycle, as its title suggests. The noun "mir"
("world") denotes an environment; the adjective "strašnyj"
("terrible" or "terrifying") denotes the lyric hero's attitude toward
this environment.

One must at the outset draw a distinction between the
"terrible world" as environment and StM the cycle. The
environment is a chaotic realm where cosmos appears only as a
grotesque perversion of itself. The cycle, by contrast, is an esthetic
artifact which contains many manifestations of cosmos, poetic order.
On the microstructural level the word, the lexeme is already a
cosmic entity. As Blok wrote in "O naznačenii poèta" (1921):
"The second requirement of Apollo is that sound, lifted up from
the depths and not originating from the empirical world, be
enclosed inside *the sturdy and tangible form of the word*" (VI, 163).
In his view the word, its very sound is the first manifestation of
cosmos in the creative process because it is the first created object;
before the poet utters the word, he is only a listener to the
formless sounds which emanate from what Tjutčev called "maternal
chaos" ("rodimyj xaos"). [15] The individual poems are also cosmic
structures, as are the subcycles and the macrocycle itself. In all of
these things one sees the presence of artistic design.

Roughly half the poems in StM are contained in subcycles
(22), while the other half belong to the unpartitioned "matrix"
(26). It is possible, however, to blind oneself temporarily to this
distinction and analyze the patterns of meaning that emerge at a
more rudimentary level. The present discussion aims to show how
the smallest units of poetic structure—seme, lexeme, word,
motif—formulate a coherent statement about the "terrible world"
and the lyric hero's place in it. Once again we are dealing with
the "migratory" integrators of Blok's poetic universe. At this level
one uncovers an extraordinarily rich network of recurring semantic
elements which, indifferent to the macrocycle's internal boundaries,
form their own "intricate weave" (V, 125). To a significant degree
the reader's image of the "terrible world" is derived from the
cumulative effect of these minute units, just as the image of the

lyric hero materializes from the pattern of tiny gestures that reveal personality.

Let us begin by examining semantic features which characterize the "terrible world" as a physical environment. Primary among these is *darkness*. The lexeme *"noč"* (noč', nočnoj, polnoč', nočevat') appears in twenty-two of the cycle's forty-eight poems. Other words from the same semantic field (mrak, mračnyj, sumrak; t'ma, temnyj, temnet', temnota; černyj, čern'; gasnut', gasit') occur in nearly every poem. The light that does exist in the "terrible world" is as a rule *dim* (especially as denoted by the lexeme *"bled-"*: "gorod blednyj," "blednoe nebo," "blednyj den'," "mesjac blednyj") and *artificial* (especially as evident in the leitmotif of the *streetlamp*: "odin fonar' kačaetsja," "na želtoj zare—fonari," "Noč', ulica, fonar', apteka," "pod fonarem belesym"). Light tends to be colored in hues which carry negative connotations, as for instance *yellow* (which in Blok signals death or decay) ("želtye dni," "želtyj zimnij zakat," "na želtoj zare")[16] or *violet* (a sign of the demonic) ("purpurovo-seryj . . . krug," "sumerki lilovye"). The *sun* is characteristically *absent* or *disappearing* ("solnce . . . zakatilos'," "Dnevnoe solnce—proč'," "solnce ne vstanet").

As might be expected in an essentially sunless world, the environment is cold. Words belonging to the semantic field *cold/winter* appear with exceptional frequency and in great variety (sneg, snegovoj, osnežennyj; metel'; v'juga; buran; xolod, xolodet', xolodnyj, xladnyj; stuža, ostudit'sja, prostyt'; zimnij; moroznyj; ledenit', led'janoj). The cycle's real setting is *northern* ("I kovarnee severnoj noči") and, more specifically, *Petersburg* ("Elagin most," "senat," "zasmotritsja stolica"). The image of the south appears once, but only as an imagined, not a real setting ("No za v'jugoj—solncem *juga*/Opalennaja strana"). The image of *intense heat* appears, but generally as a metaphor for destructive erotic passion ("Ty menja *obžigaes'* glazami," "Božestvenno-prekrasnym telom/Tebja ja stranno *obožgu*"). Moderate heat, warmth is non-existent. The word "koster" ("bonfire"), for instance, appears three times in the cycle, but only once as a real source of warmth and light; on that occasion the "bonfire" is inaccessible ("Gorodovoj . . . otgonit . . . *ot kostra*"). The lexeme "tepl-" ("warm") does not appear at all.

The "terrible world" is characteristically also *desolate, empty*; the lexeme *"pust-"* appears more often than in any other cycle of the volume and with a wider range of lexical variants: "*pustoj*" ("v vozduxe . . . pustom," "pustaja ulica," "pustaja/Vselennaja," "Pusto, tixo i temno"), "*pustota*" ("Ja uxožu . . . v pustotu," "I golos govorit iz pustoty," "Ty poletiš' . . ./V sijajuščuju pustotu"), "*pustynja*" ("veet veter iz pustyni," "v pustynju zovut," "Pustynej neba"), "*pustyr'*" ("s dalekix pustyrej"), "*opustelyj*" ("bereg opusteloj gavani"), "*pustynnyj*" ("Žizn' pustynna").[17] To the same semantic field belong the recurring motifs "*gluxoj*" and "*bezljudnyj*.."

Another attribute of the "terrible world" is its *antimusicality*. Its sounds are predominantly unmelodic, unharmonious; hence the recurrence of the motifs "vizg," "vopl'" and "skrip" ("vizg cyganskogo napeva," "vopl' tumannyj," "per'ja . . . skripjat"). Such dissonant sounds are balanced less by harmony than by utter *silence*; hence "*tix-*" is the cycle's single most prevalent auditory lexeme ("noč' tixo brodit," "Pusto, tixo i temno," "Tixo, xolodno, temno," "mesjac . . . /Nasylaet tišinu").

The condition of the hero within this environment is above all *alienation*. Things and people in the "terrible world" are repeatedly characterized by the epithet "*čužoj*," a word which appears with greater frequency in StM than in any other cycle of the third volume ("V *čužix* zerkalax otražat'sja/I ženščin *čužix* celovat'"; "ty, dal'naja, *čužaja*"; "ja—bludal sred' *čužix*; "s *čužim* naedine"; "Cto lezeš' ty v serdce "*čužoe*" "konvert . . . nadušennyj *čužimi* duxami").[18] The word "*drug*" and its cognates, if we exclude those instances where "drug" is merely a conventional form of address, always occur in contexts which indicate the absence or loss of of genuine friendship ("[Ja] . . . *družbu poterjal/* . . ./Potok neset *druzej* i ženščin *trupy*"; "Ja—ne muž, ne ženix tvoj, *ne drug!*"; "Vnov' *sdružus' s kabackoj skripkoj*"). Aside from the title of the subcycle ŽMP, the lexeme "*prijatel'-*" appears only once in an obviously ironic context ("On krepko žmet *prijatel'skie* ruki—/Živym, živym kazat'sja dolžen on!") (PS I). The image "*ljudi*" is almost universally negative. There is a tendency, for instance, to deanimate "ljudi" by equating "people" with things ("Angary, *ljudi*, vsë zemnoe—/Kak by pridavleno k zemle"; "zal *mnogoljudnyj* i mnogokolonnyj"); or the poet may question the word's applicability to human beings ("Ètix golyx risunkov žurnala/*Ne ljudskaja* kasalas' ruka.../ . . . /Razve tak suždeno mež *ljud'mi?*"). Contact with "ljudej" is, more often than not, unpleasant ("Kak tjažello xodit' sredi *ljudej*"; "Kak tjažko mertvecu sredi *ljudej*"; "soboju ty k *ljudjam* prideš',/A ujudeš' ot *ljudej*—ne soboj"). In the poem "Na ostrovax" the poet seeks out "bezljudnost'" (*"Bezljudnost'* nizkix ostrovov"). On only one occasion does he strive to make contact with "ljudi," and this effort fails:

> Идут часы, и дни, и годы.
> Хочу стряхнуть какой-то сон,
> Взглянуть в лицо людей, природы
> Рассеять сумерки времен...
>
> Там кто-то машет, дразнит светом
> (Так зимней ночью, на крыльцо
> Тень чья-то глянет силуэтом,
> И быстро спрячется лицо).
>
> (StM #16)(III, 16)

Not surprisingly, the word *"ljubov'"* appears almost exclusively in contexts involving depreciation, loss or irony (*"zabyl* ljubov'"; "ljubov' *projdet*"; *"Razve èto my zvali ljubov'ju?"*; *"Bessmyslennyj* vostorg živoj ljubvi"; "Ešče prosit *pytok* ljubvi"); the verb *"ljubit'"* does not occur in the cycle at all. This is not to say that the image of genuine love is entirely absent in StM but that its locus is beyond the boundary of the "terrible world" in a distant realm (*"dal'nej celi*/Putevoditel'nyj majak"; "O, *gde ty, Beatriče*?; "sinij *bereg raja*").

Minc writes that the "terrible world" is a place where all boundaries, all distinctions, all oppositions are removed,"[19] whereas the landscape is comprised mostly of enclosed spaces—buildings, rooms, houses, halls, restaurants, etc. Properly qualified, this observation is a key to understanding many aspects of the "terrible world" and the lyric hero's relation to it.[20]

On the one hand boundaries and bounded structures which organize space and provide protection from the entropy of the external elements frequently become dysfunctional. Compartmentalized space may suddenly turn into something entirely imaginary:

> Не сходим ли с ума мы в смене пестрой
> Придуманных причин, пространств, времён...
>
> (StM #25) (III, 41)

On the other hand boundaries which confine and restrict tend to

be immovable.   The chaos of the environment is counterbalanced
by an ironic, distorted kind of cosmos—one that reverses the
spiritual and esthetic satisfation one normally derives from
contemplation of form and order.

This paradox materializes largely at a semic level: words
denoting borders or walled structures are frequently used in
contexts that bring the dilemma to the fore.   Let us consider, for
instance, various occurrences of the lexeme -*dom*-.

(1)   В эти желтые дни меж <u>домами</u>
       Мы встречаемся только на миг.
       Ты меня обжигаешь глазами
       И скрываешься в темный тупик.   (III, 10)

———

(2)   С мирным счастьем покончены счеты,
       Не дразни запоздалый уют.
       Всюду эти щемящие ноты
       Стерегут и в пустыню зовут.

       Жизнь пустынна, <u>бездомна</u>, бездонна . . .
                                          (III, 22)

———

(3)   Разве <u>дом</u> этот—<u>дом</u> в самом деле?
                                          (III, 31)

———

(4)   Повеселясь на буйном пире,
       Вернулся поздно я <u>домой</u>;
       Ночь тихо бродит по квартире,
       Храня уютный угол мой.

       Слились все лица, все обиды
       В одно лицо, в одно пятно;
       И ветр ночной поет в окно
       Напевы сонной панихиды...   (III, 35)

In the first poem *dom* is allied with the concept of enclosure or
entrapment, as the noun *tupik* at the end makes clear.   In the
second, by contrast, the walls of the home offer no security from
the elements outside and, in a sense, evaporate; life within the
home is equated with "homelessness" ("bezdomna").   The idea of

the third passage is similar to that of the second. In the fourth, the walls of the home are simultaneously chaotic and cosmic (in the perverted sense). The presence of "night" as intruder suggests the ineffectiveness of the home's walls but the reference to the wind's funeral singing ("panixida") creates the obvious analogy between home and coffin, an impervious enclosure. It is significant that the same physical boundary, as for instance the walls of the domicile above, can be at once immaterial and impenetrable, dissappearing and permanently fixed—a symbol of exposure and at the same time a symbol of entrapment. Neither the home without walls nor the home which imprisons is an ideal space. Both are chaotic "homes" in that they reverse the basic symbolic meaning of the domicile as a place of shelter, security, and contentment.

Around words belonging to the same semantic field as *dom* (e.g., *zal*, *spal'naja*, *komnata*, *kabinet*, *ujut*, *dvorec*) there accumulate similar contextual implications. Boundaries tend to be either ephemeral or confining:

(В кабинете ресторана
За бутылкою вина).

. . . .

Взор во взор—и жгуче-синий
Обозначился простор.

. . . .

Веет ветер из пустыни . . .   (III. 11)

———

Передо мною бесконечный зал.   (III, 16)

———

Я обречен в далеком мраке спальной,
Где спит она и дышит горячо,
Склонясь над ней влюбленно и печально,

Вонзить свой перстень в белое плечо!   (III, 18)

———

Бессмысленность всех дел, безрадостность уюта . . .
     (III, 47)

———

Я завлек ее в мой дворец!
Три свечи в бесконечной дали.   (III, 57)

Other lexemes (e.g., *bereg*, -*d/o/n*-) contribute to the image of an environment where interior boundaries are non-existent, while outer boundaries are hopelessly impassable:

Из <u>бездн</u> ночных и пропастей туманных . . .

(III, 18)

Я пронесу тебя над <u>бездной</u>,
Ее <u>бездонностью</u> дразня.

(III, 60)

И один фонарь качается
На оснеженном <u>берегу</u>.

И матрос, на на борт не принятый,
Идет, шатаясь, сквозь буран.

. . . .

А <u>берег</u> опустелой гавани
Уж первый легкий снег занес...

(III, 19)

It is noteworthy that the word "*stena*" does not occur at all in StM, though it appears in every other cycle of the third volume. The uncertainty of most borders in StM suggests the absence of internal compartmentalization in the "terrible world," while the imperviousness of others suggests the permanence of its outer limits. In a sense the "terrible world" has order only at its very fringes: it is a vast "cosmic" container of chaotic space.

More generally chaos is manifest through invalidation of boundaries within many different semantic categories. This is especially true of *time*. Time, like space, can lose its internal "walls"—the divisions which differentiate its measurable units. Duration can become arbitrary—hours and years may become indistinguishable ("Prošli *časy*, ili *goda*"); one "night" may be equivalent to "centuries/ages" ("*Noč*'—kak *veka*"); "night" and "day" may coincide ("*Noč*', *den*' li tam v okne?"; "*Čem noč*' belee, tem černee zloba/ . . . /Mertvec ves' *den*' truditsja"); points in time may acquire duration ("Tak ètot *mig* nastal . . ./I mrak byl glux. I *dolgij* večer mglist./ . . . /No ne kljani povestvovanij strannyx/O tom, kak *dlilsja* neponjatnyj son"; "*korotkij mig*"). The boundaries separating past, present, and future , may be erased, creating a strange convergence of "first" and "last":

... застиг меня <u>последний</u> пир.

· · · · · · · · · · · · · · · · ·

Я ликованье <u>первое</u> постиг!

· · · · · · · · · · · · · · · ·

Я испустил <u>впервые</u> страстный крик!
(StM #6) (III, 16-17)

———

Зачем ты в небе был, отважный,
В твой <u>первый</u> <u>и</u> <u>последний</u> раз?
(StM #18) (III, 34)

Here the issue is not so much one of "time linkage" ("svjaz'
vremen")—the similarity of events separated by time—but one of
confused time frames, incompatible time scales superimposed upon
and invalidating each other, as for instance in "Golos iz xora":

Всё будет чернее страшный свет,
И всё безумней вихрь планет
<u>Еще века, века!</u>

И век последний, ужасней всех,
<u>Увидим и вы и я.</u>
(StM #48) (III, 62)[21]

In the "terrible world" normal sequentiality frequently becomes
inoperative. This is why the idea of senseless repetition (which
accumulates around the leitmotif *"vnov'"*/*"snova"*/*"opjat'"*) plays
such an important role in the cycle and becomes the temporal
analogue to spatial enclosure; to this issue we shall return in
analyzing the subcycle PS.

The problem of non-existent or unknown boundaries
insinuates itself upon virtually every semantic category. The
antithesis *"sound vs. silence,"* for instance, can become
dysfunctional (*"Gromovye raskaty v tiši"*; *"Voet veter*
ledenjaščij,/Pusto, tixo i temno"), as can the antithesis *"illusion vs.
reality"* ("Starejuščij junoša (Stranno, /Ne snilsja li mne on vo
sne?)"; "on byl, ili ne byl,/ètot večer"). Most disturbing is the
fact that ethical categories lose delineation. The Muse, for
example, as she is depicted in the cycle's opening poem ("K
Muze"), is ethically ambivalent: both sacred (*"v napevax tvoix
sokrovennyx"*) and blasphemous (*"prokljat'e zavetov svjaščennyx"*);

friend ("tvoix *uteśenij* prosil") and enemy ("Ja xotel, čtob my byli
vragami"); good and evil ("*Zla, dobra li?*—Ty vsja—ne otsjuda");
affectionate and sadistic ("I *kovarnee* severnoj noči/ . . . /Byli
strašnye *laski* tvoi").   Nowhere is the confusion of ethical
distinctions more evident than in the frequent perversions of ideal
models from the first volume.   StM #8 ("Na ostrovax"), for
instance, is constructed entirely on the principle of intertwining
motifs of ideal love from SPD and RAS (čislit', strogij, pokornyj,
obrjad, ženix, "pervaja") with motifs of impious love from SnM
and F (sani, plennaja, tonkij stan, lukavit', bal, "ne pervaja")—the
effect being that these two antithetical spheres become
undifferentiable.   Autoreminiscences from the first volume are
common in StM as they are throughout the third volume, but here
they occur almost exclusively in such "contaminated" contexts.

The concept of missing boundaries is relevant to the
predicament of the lyric hero as well.   His dilemma lies partly in
the fact that he misplaces the "boundary" of the self, the line
separating him from his environment.   One will note, for instance,
that the imagery of the type "*pustye oči,*" "*pogasśie oči,*" "*duša
černaja,*" "*duša gluxaja*"—which involves transfering attributes of
the "terrible world" (represented by the epithets) onto the physical
and spiritual world of the hero (represented by the nouns)—is
extremely prevalent in the cycle.   Without the boundary
"I"//"environment" the lyric hero internalizes much of what he
finds most loathsome in the "terrible world" and becomes in a
sense part of its landscape.   At the same time he projects his
inner, spiritual experience onto the environment, populating the
landscape with doubles and phantoms who are the incarnation of
his deepest fears.   This explains why the mirror motif, which
appears hardly at all in other cycles of the third volume, is so
prominant in StM (the words "*zerkalo,*" "*zerkal'nyj*" occur eight
times).   The mirror is the most typical "internal" boundary in the
"terrible world" because it does not organize real space but rather
contributes to its confusion, providing a false sense of depth.   At
the same time it is the most formidable "outer" boundary in that
it refocuses the soul back upon itself, enclosing it and confining it
to its own chaotic fantasies.

"Paths" and movement in StM, as Minc has pointed out, are
almost exclusively chaotic.[22]   If we trace the lexeme "*put-*"
through the cycle, for instance, we find that it is almost always
associated with loss of direction ("rasputica nočnaja"; "iskal *putej,*"

"utrativ pravyj *put'*," "Gde *sputnik* moj?") or movement toward death ("na poslednij *put'* vstupaja"; "Govorit Smert': A sam—k moej blaženuoj dveri/Otyskivaet vjalo *put'*"). Elsewhere movement tends to be either non-directed, "circular" (as evident in the recurring images "brodit'," "bluždat'," "skitat'sja") or directed *into* the "terrible world" in any of its various manifestations ("v metel', vo mrak i v pustotu"; "v sumrak perexod"; "v pustynju"; "v tu oblast' noči"). The lyric hero is depicted moving *away from* ideal space more often than toward it ("Ja uxožu [iz doma]"; "Iz sveta . . . perexod"; "Uxodi i ty [ot žizni]"); in this regard he continually relives the episode of betrayal and exit from the "home" dramatized in SnM. Return to the ideal "home" (which in StM is allied exclusively with the past) is contemplated repeatedly and crystallizes around the lexemic series *"vozvrat/vozvraščat'sja /vernut'sja"*:

> Что, если я, завороженный,
> . . . .
> <u>Вернусь</u> <u>домой</u> уничиженный...
>
> (StM #2) (III, 9)

Symbolically, virtually any "return" (whether the poet's or that of the beloved) resurrects the positive associations of the forfeited "home":

> (Так ранняя молодость снится.
> А ты-то, <u>вернешься</u> ли ты?)
>
> (StM #5) (III, 13)

———

> Хочу <u>вернуть</u> навек на синий берег рая
> Тебя, убив всю ложь и уничтожив яд...
>
> (ČK IV) (III, 55)

All these associations are operative even when "return" is used metaphorically, with no direct indication of a "path":

> "Но в старости—<u>возврат</u> и юности и жара..."
> Так начал я . . . .
>
> (StM #26) (III, 42)

The possibility of "return," however, is continually negated:

. . . . .Томиться должен ты
И по кругам скитаться <u>невозвратным</u>.

(StM #26) (III, 17)

———

"А отступлю в ту область ночи,
Откуда <u>возвращенья</u> <u>нет</u>...

(StM #15) (III, 28)

———

Ты изменил давно,
<u>Бесповоротно</u>.

(StM #10) (III, 23)

———

. . . . . но он настойчиво прервал:
"Она—всё та ж: Линор безумного Эдгара.
<u>Возврата</u> <u>нет</u>. —Еще? теперь я всё сказал".

(StM #26) (III, 42)

On only one occasion does the lyric hero actually "return" to the "home":

Повеселясь не буйном пире,
<u>Вернулся</u> поздно я <u>домой</u>;
Ночь тихо бродит по квартире,
Храня уютный угол мой.

(StM #19) (III, 35)

This event, however, is a perversion of the earlier wish ("Čto esli ja . . . vernus' domoj?..") rather than a realization of it; the loathsome element ("noč'") has invaded and desanctified the ideal space which the "home" once represented. All of the scenarios just outlined chart trajectories of chaotic "paths," none of which succeeds in penetrating the "terrible world's" outer boundary. Each confirms R.S. Spivak's observation that "the 'terrible world' is a static environment. It only simulates movement, depriving it of genuine momentum."[23]

The Subcycles of "Strašnyj mir": Latent Habitats of Cosmos

To this point our analysis of StM has concentrated on the smallest elements of the macrocycle's structure—word and motif—which, as we have seen, pattern a meaningful esthetic statement. This statement exists, however, regardless of how the poems are arranged—nothing in it would change if Blok were to have used any of the millions of possible sequences that forty-eight separate poems can generate.

The disposition of the poems, however, also carries esthetic information. All of the poems are dated in the text and all but two of the twenty-six poems in the matrix (i.e., those not in subcycles) are arranged in strict chronological order. This might not appear significant, but the fact that the poems' sequence does *not* suggest any change or development (i.e., plot) indicates that empirical time is a chaotic phenomenon: life does not arrange its own events in any logical succession. To the degree that esthetic time mimics empirical time, it too falls victim to the entropy of life and becomes chaotic. According to Blok "the crowning stage of the antithesis" (V, 430) occurred when life and art became indistinguishable: "What happened to us in the period of the 'antithesis'? Why did . . . the violet worlds gush forth and mix with this world, *producing chaos, making art out of life?*" (V, 433). Where life translates directly into art and imposes its own orders on the latter, the poet relinquishes control over his creation and defers to the authority of chance and chaos. Where the poet separates art from life and imposes his own purely esthetic orders on his creation, he serves design and cosmos.[24]

With the exception of StM #1 ("K Muze") and StM #48 ("Golos iz xora") chronology is violated only at points where the subcycles are introduced into the matrix:

StM #19   January 6, 1912

StM #20-24   ("Pljaski smerti")
    PS I   February 19, 1912   (EARLIEST)
    PS II   October 20, 1912
    PS III   October 1912
    PS IV   February 7, 1914   (LATEST)
    PS V   February 7, 1914

StM #25	July 2, 1912
StM #26	November 2, 1912
StM #27	December 18, 1913
StM #28	December 30, 1913
StM #29	February 21, 1914

StM #30-37	("Žizn' moego prijatelja")	
ŽMP I	February 11, 1914	
ŽMP II	December 30, 1913	(EARLIEST)
ŽMP III	December 30, 1913	
ŽMP IV	December 30, 1913	
ŽMP V	December 30, 1913	
ŽMP VI	May 24, 1914	
ŽMP VII	December 10, 1915	(LATEST)
ŽMP VIII	December 10, 1915	

StM #38-46	("Černaja krov'")	
ČK I	January 2, 1914	
ČK II	March 22, 1914	(LATEST)
ČK III	January 30, 1914	
ČK IV	February 1912	
ČK V	January 29, 1914	
ČK VI	January 2, 1914	
ČK VII	December 27, 1913	
ČK VIII	October 1909	(EARLIEST)
ČK IX	March 13, 1910	

StM #47	June 9, 1916

Chronology is followed within PS, but not within ŽMP and ČK. Even PS violates chronology in that PS II-V, on the basis of their dates alone, do not belong between StM #19 and StM #25. Moreover, judging from the earliest and latest poems of ŽMP and ČK, these two subcycles should be in reverse order. One must conclude that the subcycles of StM differ from the matrix in that chronology plays little or no role either in their internal ordering or in the location chosen for them in the macrocycle. Thus the subcycle is one important habitat of cosmos.

The subcycles are functions of cosmos in one other important respect: they impart order to the macrocycle by bringing into sharper relief issues apparent in the larger corpus but lacking there the same degree of resolution.

If contextual syntax emerges at the level of word and motif, it does so in the macrocycle at a necessarily slow rate, and it places extraordinary demands on a reader's retentive capacity. It is a syntax that risks becoming lost in the intertext. After all, no serious reader approaches a cycle of more than 1000 lines and reads it like a short story. Each poem is its own center of gravity, its own small context which must be read with care and patience. Edgar Allan Poe knew this when he wrote: "That degree of excitement which would entitle a poem to be so called at all, cannot be sustained throughout a composition of great length."[25] Blok was undoubtedly aware that cycles of great magnitude, whose poems are not born of one inspirational surge, risk crossing an invisible threshold beyond which apprehension of system may elude the reader and coherence may be lost. The subcycles of StM prevent this from happening. Each is a compact, tightly organized cyclic context that highlights and defines some important aspect of macrocycle: PS focuses on the "terrible world" as environment; ŽMP and ČK focus on the psyche of the lyric hero within this environment. Moreover, their particular sequence—PS// ŽMP//ČK—is meaningful: it defines a pseudo-narrative dynamic. All these features, however, are functions of cosmos on the level of *composition*—not theme. Hence the subcycles are *latent* rather than conspicuous habitats of the cosmic principle which will ultimately prevail in the volume thematically as well as structurally.

The discussion below will devote proportionally more attention to PS than ŽMP or ČK, because it is emblematic of StM's role in the design of the third volume.[26] PS presents most vividly the dilemma which the "terrible world" poses.

"Pljaski smerti" (PS) contains five poems cyclized for the first time in 1921, in the "canonical" edition of the third volume. The commonality of at least four of the poems, however, had been suggested earlier since Blok attached to each the title "Dance of Death" long before they were grouped together. PS I, II, and III appeared under the heading "Totentanz" in 1912 and 1914 , [27] and PS V was entitled "Pljaska smerti" when it first appeared in 1915.[28] The idea or theme of the "Dance of Death," therefore, must have been a crucial factor in bringing these poems together—not merely an impressionistic afterthought.

For this reason one must confront seriously the question of the cycle's title. The problem is by no means easily resolved because the motif of dancing appears explicitly only in PS I ("no vy ne priglašali/Na *val's* NN").

From the late Fourteenth Century the Dance of Death, which began flourishing at the time of the Black Death (1373),[29] has a long history in various art forms. We encounter it in drama, pictorial arts, sculpture, music and literature. Blok was drawing from this tradition when he composed PS.

In Blok scholarship the tendency has been to cite likely literary models for PS, especially from the nineteenth and twentieth centuries.[30] The parallels between PS and these sources, however, are either minor or so tenuous that one might just as well argue that Blok was drawing from a general thematic fund rather than individual works. Indeed, macabre depictions of life in death are so common in literature, especially during the first ten or fifteen years of the twentieth century, that searching out modern literary prototypes for Blok's conception turns into an unending and rarely fruitful pursuit.[31] Contemporary music and drama are not likely sources either. Blok heard Musorgskij's "Songs and Dances of Death" but apparently did not like them (VIII, 73). He was probably familiar with Strindberg's play "Dödsdansen" (1901), but this work offers no useful comparisons either.

To the degree that Blok followed any models in PS, they belong to the late Middle Ages and the Renaissance—namely the frescoes and etchings that depict Death as a skeleton or emaciated corpse engaging members of society in dance (or some other activity); participation in the "dance" represented allegorically the passage from life to death.[32] The best known representative of the genre are Hans Holbein's forty-one etchings (first printed in a Lyon edition of 1538). Holbein's drawings, however, only crown a tradition that dates back perhaps as far as 1312.

Blok was familiar with this tradition from the secondary sources he used in researching his play "Roza i krest," which is set in medieval France;[33] it is no accident that PS II and III were composed precisely at the time he was most actively writing this drama (fall 1912). Given his research for the play and given his life-long fascination with medieval and Renaissance art, Blok could hardly have been unaware that the pictorial genre of the Dance evolved from what was originally a continuous or mural-type design into a cyclic design. The earliest known murals of the

Dance, such as the ones at the Cemetery of the Innocents in Paris (1424), depicted a continuous chain of skeletons and mortals stretched hand-in-hand (rondelay-style). In renditions belonging for the most part to a later date, the chain or procession is broken into discrete scenes—each picture displays one skeleton standing beside one or more mortals. Apropos of the paintings at the Dominican convent in Berne, for example, James Clark writes: "The old conception of a procession is no longer in evidence. . . . The illustrations are almost independent of each other and some of them are more like separate groups."[34] Holbein's etchings are the most vivid example of this cyclic-type Dance: "Instead of a chain of figures or dancing pairs [Holbein] sketched a series of separate scenes, independent of one another and furnished with appropriate settings."[35]

This conspicuous cyclicality militates for the conclusion that Blok fashioned PS primarily after Holbein's Dances. Certain other parallels tend to corroborate this conclusion. It is worth noting, for instance, that the motif of dancing *per se* plays a negligible role in Holbein's drawings, just as it does in Blok's cycle; Holbein's skeletons assume a dance-like pose in only a few instances, and the human victims are not pictured in dance at all. In both cases dance has become only a vestige of the genre's original concept. What is more important is that Holbein, departing from tradition, has Death confront each of his victims in their customary social roles and settings—the king on his throne in the royal chamber, the lady in her sumptuous boudoir, the judge in his courtroom. Each setting is highly individuated and full of realistic detail. Blok also pays special attention to setting—although in a different way and for a different purpose.

Holbein's drawings are unified most conspicuously by the figure of personified Death who appears in each separate frame, wearing different clothing according to the exigencies of the occasion but always recognizable as the same persona. This figure is the only concrete invariable, while the living subjects and settings vary from frame to frame. As Leonard P. Kurtz writes: "'Death,' as interpreted from the woodcuts of Holbein, is a concept of a single individual who travels around, like a salesman, into the houses and life of man."[36]

In Blok's cycle, by contrast, the concept of peripatetic Death is all but inoperative (PS I being the only exception). The question arises, therefore, as to the cycle's unifying principle.

What feature or features are forefronted by the poems' interaction?

To answer this question one can begin by examining the poems at the most elemental structural level. It is apparent, perhaps even after the first reading of the cycle, that PS contains an extraordinary number of lexical or lexemic repetitions. If one studies the location of the repeated items, he sees that the majority of them are introduced in PS I and then re-echoed in PS III, IV, and V (line numbers are indicated parenthetically below):[37]

I	III	IV	V
mertvec (1, 5, 9, 15, 18)		mertvec (12)	
kak (1, 39, 40, 43)		kak (21)	
skryvat (4)			krovlja (3)
vstavat' (5)	privstat' (10)		
belyj (7)	belëjsyj (12)	belyj (7)	
černyj (7)	černyj (6)	černyj (3, 21)	černota (8)
zloba/zlost' (7, 41, 42)			zol (1)
per'ja		per'ja (11)	
skripet' (8)	skripučij (4)		
proxožij (14)		perexodit' (15)	
drugoj (15)	drugoi (9)	drugoj (6)	
frak (18)		frak (8)	
ulybka (19)			ulybat'sja (20)
xozjajka (20)	xozjajstvenno (4)		
zaglušon (22)		gluxo (14)	
liš' (25)		liš' (3)	
tam (33)		tam (3, 4)	
iskat' (33)	iskat' (6)		iskat' (12)

lico (35)		lico (11)	lico (13)
smotret' (39)			smotret' (4)
zvon (44)	zvjaknut' (7)	zvonok (13)	

Similarly PS II, despite its diminutive size (8 lines),[38] introduces a large number of words and lexemes that reappear in PS III-V. Prominent among them is the word "fonar'," which occurs in all four poems:

II	III	IV	V
ulica (1, 8)	ulica (12)		
fonar' (1, 8)	fonar' (12)	fonar' (2)	fonar' (16)
apteka (1, 8)	aptekar' (2, 8)		
svet (2)			svet (16)
vsě (4, 6)		vsě (11)	vsě (9)
net (4)		net (11)	
po<u>v</u>torit'sja		<u>v</u>to<u>r</u>oj (9)	
v<u>star</u>'		<u>star</u>yj (1)	
<u>led</u>janoj		<u>led</u>enjaščij (17)	

Other repetitions, not originating in PS I or II, occur between poems III-V:

III	IV	V
pustoj (1)	pusto (18)	pustyr' (15)
okno (1)	okno (19)	
son (2)	son (1)	
plašč (11)	plašč (7)	platok (18)
	<u>ten</u>' (5, 9, 24)	ot<u>ten</u>jat' (6)
	<u>tix</u>o (18)	ti<u>š</u>ina (5)

Between PS I and II links of this sort are not especially numerous:

I	II
kak (1, 39, 40, 43)	kak (6)
živoj (2, 5, 24, 36, 38)	žit' (3)
noč' (7)/polnoč' (31)	noč' (1, 7)
pro<u>xo</u>žij (14)	i<u>sx</u>od (4)
bessmyslennyj (36)	bessmyslennyj (2)

The outline above calls for two observations. First, such concentrated recurrence of the same lexemes is exceptional, even for Blok—the tiny cycle is virtually packed with "migratory words." What is remarkable, however, given the apparently close interrelationship of the poems, is that the word chains do not create plot, as we might expect; they establish bonds between the poems but not linear trajectories of thought—there is an uncharacteristically static quality in the words' interaction. Second, PS I and II function in a lexical sense as "parent" poems whose words ("genes") are inherited so to speak by three "offspring" (PS III-V). Pursuing the metaphor further, one could add that the "offspring" poems share more lexical similarities than do the "parent" poems; hence PS III-V form a more or less homogenous grouping, while PS I-II make a heterogenous pair.

Analyzing recurring motifs which do not necessarily appear as identical lexemes yields other information and helps isolate the cycle's dominant:

	I	II	III	IV	V
woman	x		x	x	
man	x		x	x	x
erotic love	x		x (?)	x	
bureaucracy	x				x
canal		x		x	
dim light		x	x	x	x
poison	x		x		
suicide		x	x (?)	x	

cold	x	x		x	
wind		x		x	
face			x	x	x
street	x	x	x	x	(x)
building(s)	x	x	x	x	x
city	x	x	x	x	x
night	x	x	x	x	x
darkness	x	x	x	x	x

Several of these motifs, unlike the recurring lexemes, appear in all five poems and therefore unify the cycle as a whole. Moreover all of the universal motifs are attributes of a setting: each poem is set at night on a city street, even where the street is depicted only briefly (PS I) and where its presence is only implied (PS V). In all but one poem (PS III) the city is clearly identifiable as Petersburg (the "senate" in I, the canal in II and IV, the tsar's palace in V).

It is apparent that Blok is departing from the pictorial Dance cycle in one important respect: in PS setting is the invariable factor, migrating from one poem to the next and creating the same kind of intracyclic bond that the figure of itinerant Death produces in Holbein's drawings. The nocturnal cityscape replaces the Dance's traditional protagonist; in a sense Petersburg becomes the cycle's "hero."[39]

The fact that setting is the cycle's dominant causes PS II to acquire special importance. PS II is the only poem that depicts only setting—no human figures, no "dancers":

> Ночь, улица, фонарь, аптека,
> Бессмысленный и тусклый свет.
> Живи еще хоть четверть века—
> 4 Всё будет так. Исхода нет.
>
> Умрешь—начнешь опять сначала,
> И повторится всё, как встарь:
> Ночь, ледяная рябь канала,
> 8 Аптека, улица, фонарь.   (PS II)(III, 37)

This poem has attracted much critical attention, but its role in PS (and StM more generally) has not yet been entirely accounted for. Andrej Kodjak is right that the poem's remarkable symmetry, evident in the near identity of the outer couplets (lines 1–2, 7–8) and the parallelism of the interior couplets (lines 3–4, 5–6), "seems to function as the structural kernel of the remaining four poems."[40] Indeed, as he indicates, lexical repetitions (or coordinate images) appear at or near the perimeters of the four other texts as well:

> Но надо, надо в общество втираться,
> Скрывая для карьеры лязг костей...
> . . . .
> В её ушах—нездешний, странный звон:
> То кости лязгают о кости.
>   (PS I)(III, 36–37)

> Пустая улица. Один огонь в окне.
> . . . .
> На улице, под фонарем белесым.
>   (PS III)(III, 38)

> Старый, старый сон. Из мрака
>   Фонари бегут—куда?
>   Там—лишь черная вода,
>   Там забвенье навсегда.
> . . . .
>   Как свинец, черна вода.
>   В ней забвенье на всегда.
>   Третий призрак. Ты куда,
> Ты, из тени в тень скользящий?
>   (PS IV)(III, 38–39)

> С кровель каменных громад
> Смотрит месяц бледный...
> . . . .
> Он—с далеких пустырей
> В свете редких фонарей
> Появляется.   (PS V) (III, 38)

To Kodjak's observations one should add that in PS IV the very rhyme scheme (abbb bbba // cbbb dddc // efff bbbe) and strophic configuration (indented interior verses) are also circular. Kodjak stops just short of explaining, however, what function such circular structures serve.

In addressing this question it is useful to consider that a circle in its basic, literal meaning is a spatial entity—it outlines a certain area on a geometric plane. In this regard it seems not accidental that the outer couplets of PS II (where the circle is represented most conspicuously) focus specifically on physical, concrete, *spatially* manifest topoi of the urban landscape ("ulica," "fonar'," "apteka," "kanal"). The inner couplets, by contrast, focus on what is manifest *temporally*, specifically the phenomenon of repetition ("opjat'," "povtoritsja," "kak vstar'") and a measured unit of time ("četvert' veka"). The dichotomy, however, is not complete in that the outer couplets contain the noun "noč'," a temporal concept, and the inner couplets contain the metaphor "Isxoda net," which denotes spatial confinement. The very incompleteness of the dichotomy in turn suggests the correlation, indeed the equivalency of spatial and temporal phenomena—location within a specific environment (the empirical city, Petersburg) and temporal enclosure (the senseless repetition of events, "eternal return"). Moreover, the poem reproduces this equivalency graphically, "iconically," as Lawrence Feinberg points out, by making verbal repetition (a feature of artistic time) function as structural circularity (artistic space).[41] Thus spatial and temporal categories become mutually signifying on various levels.

When circular structures reappear in the cycle's other poems, they re-evoke the conceptual associations with which they were allied in PS II, since PS II is the locus of the cyclic dominant. Indeed, examination of PS I, III, IV, and V indicates that these associations are quite relevant. Each in some respect involves pointless recurrence of events and reinforces the idea of time as a circular rather than a linear phenomenon. PS I chronicles a daily routine devoid of redeeming purpose, consisting entirely of ritualistic banalities ("k drugomu bezobraz'ju," "ot dnja činovnoj skuki," "uslovno-svetskimi rečami"). In PS III repetition is not an overt theme, but one must wonder why else the two female corpses ("dvum ženščinam beznosym") require a vial of poison except to re-experience death. PS IV fulfills the promise of its opening line ("Staryj, staryj son...")—by recreating a scene from the first volume:

Тень вторая—стройный латник,

Иль невеста от венца?
Шлем и перья. Нет лица.
Неподвижность мертвеца.

В воротах гремит звонок,
Глухо щелкает замок,
Переходят за порог
Проститутка и развратник...   (PS IV)

"Strojnyj latnik," "nevesta ot venca" recall the traditional roles of
the poet and the Lady; "v vorotax . . . zamok" redramatizes the
door scenarios of SPD; "nepodvižnost'" is an auto-reminiscence
from the 1905 edition of SPD, whose first section carried this exact
title.   Here, however, the familiar images participate in a sordid
perversion of the original archetype. Like defiled relics they are
retrieved now   only to ridicule their once sacred promise: they too
are artifacts of senseless repetition.   PS V is about the
immutability of social injustice:

Вновь богатый зол и рад,
Вновь унижен бедный...   (PS V)

The image of the dead tsar at the end of the poem alludes not
only to the strangulation of Pavel I in 1801[42] but more generally
to the recurring phenomenen of regicide in Russian history:

Он—с далеких пустырей
В свете редких фонарей
Появляется.

Шея скручена платком,
Под дырявым козырком
Улыбается.   (PS V)

These words, which Žirmunskij calls "prophetic,"[43] presage the
recurrence of this event in a new political context (PS V was
written on the eve of the World War I and the Revolution). At
the same time they suggest that such events are ineffectual as
agents of historical change.   History too is locked in a pattern of
meaningless repetitions.
     If temporal repetition invalidates distinctions between past,
present, and future, the spatial analogue to this is the
neutralization of physical boundaries as meaningful limits.   In PS
II, for instance, the boundary separating the poet from the waters

of the canal is rendered meaningless; there can be no purpose to suicide if another, identical life will follow death. In PS I the "coffin" is no impediment to the perigrinations of the corpse; he moves from grave to "court," to "senate," to ballroom like points on a conventional itinerary. In PS IV crossing the "threshold," an event of momentous importance in Blok's early poetry, now evokes only indifference ("Naverxu gorit okno. *Vsë ravno*"). And in PS V the walls of the "palace" define neither the locus of royal benevolence ("Tol'ko ne išči dvorca,/Dobrodušnogo lica") nor the actual location of the tsar ("On—s dalekix pustyrej/ . . . /Pojavljaetsja"). Thus PS recreates the image of the "terrible world" in microcosm—a chaotic environment without secure internal boundaries.

The medieval and Renaissance "Dances of Death" operate on the premise that the living and the dead are separated by a permeable but functional boundary. Death makes forays into the world of the living, and the living at his invitation cross over into the world of the dead. By differentiating these two conditions the traditional Dances impart significance to a point in time (the moment of physical death) and do not invalidate the distinctions between past, present, and future. In Blok's cycle, by contrast, the line between life and death is erased: past, present, and future become identical.

The central paradox of PS is that invalidation of boundaries in time and space brings about temporal and spatial enclosure: there can be no "escape" from an environment which lacks definite limits. This is why Holbein's drawings, though they are the principal model for the cycle, are probably not its only one. The entrapment that PS depicts recalls instead an earlier concept of the Dance: not a collection of separate scenes but a continuous mural of dancers hand-in-hand, whose roundelay the circular structures in PS seem to mimic.

Structure of any kind, however, does not "mean" anything until the text invests it with significance. Symmetry is not inherently good or bad—it is an elementary principle of artistic form without which art itself would be unthinkable. It is a manifestation of esthetic cosmos. Ironically, PS turns what is a cosmic entity on the level of composition into a sign of chaos (temporal circularity) on the ontological level. The challenge Blok faced in designing the third volume was to make symmetry function as a vehicle of cosmos on both levels.

The concept of plot, which subsumes a developmental aspect of time, is quite alien to PS; it is not surprising, therefore, that its "migratory" word-motifs, despite their abundance, group together in a curious nesting pattern of "parent" and "offspring" poems without becoming carriers of narrative momentum. ŽMP and ČK, by contrast, are unified largely by plot.

The narrative dynamic of ŽMP is complex in that it unfolds simultaneously in two different modes, creating an unusual hybridization of the archetypal (summational) and episodic (sequential) plot cycle. The summational mode operates *within* certain poems which narrate what is essentially a single life, a single spiritual biography; from these poems emerges a recurring archetypal pattern: 1) a period of ideal faith belonging to the distant past and characterized by spiritual animation; 2) a period from the more recent past when the ideal was lost (or forgotten), consciousness was impaired and spiritual torpor set in; 3) an effort to regain the ideal and the fervor it once engendered; 4) failure of this effort, followed by renewed disillusionment, resignation 5) spiritual death or anticipation of physical death. The episodic mode, on the other hand, operates via the strategic arrangement of the lyrics and can be said to manifest itself at the junctures *between* them; from one poem to another unfolds a progression of events illustrating the latter stages of the lyric hero's biography. These two modes coexist and reinforce each other without being textually separate, so that even the summational poems contribute in some respect to the episodic progression. In addition to these two modes, which are alike in that their time frame spans a whole life (or at least the larger portion thereof), we find a complementary dynamic manifest on a diurnal (or even shorter) time scale; those poems which treat the hero's daily routine outline an emotive trajectory from passivity to animation to renewed passivity that spans only a few hours of empirical time but re-enacts stages 2-4 of the biographical archetype. It will be useful to examine each narrative dynamic briefly.

The biographical archetype is reproduced via summation most compactly in ŽMP III:

```
      Всё свершилось по писаньям:
      Остудился юный пыл,
      И конец очарованьям
4     Постепенно наступил.

      Был в чаду, не чуя чада,
      Утешался мукой ада,
      Перечислил все слова,
8     Но—болела голова...

      Долго, жалобно болела,
      Тело тихо холодело,
      Пробудился: тридцать лет.
12    Хвать-похвать,—а сердца нет.

      Сердце—крашеный мертвец.
      И, когда настал конец,
      Он нашел весьма банальной
16    Смерть души своей печальной.    (ŽMP III)
```

Here it is not difficult to discern the various stages of the archetype 1) a period of youthful animation ("junyj pyl"); 2) a period of impaired awareness when the initial enthusiasm was lost ("Byl v čadu, ne čuja čada," "bolela golova," "konec očarovan'jam"); 3) a futile effort to rediscover the locus of that enthusiasm ("Probudilsja . . . /Xvat'-poxvat',—a serdca net"); 4) disillusionment, indifference ("On našel ves'ma banal'noj..."); 5) spiritual death ("smert' duši svoej pečal'noj"). Indeed the very concept of an archetypal model is contained in the poem's first line ("Vsě sveršilos *po pisan'jam*")—the hero's life unfolds as if according to a predetermined pattern. A similar conspectus of the hero's fate is outlined in ŽMP II, VII and VIII.

The cycle's episodic dynamic develops most vividly in the median poems (ŽMP II-V), where it crystallizes around the motif of the heart or soul:

```
      То, что было, миновалось,
      Ваш удел на все похож:
      Сердце к правде порывалось,
      Но его сломила ложь.              (ŽMP II)
```

Хвать-похвать,—а <u>сердца</u> нет.
<u>Сердце</u>—крашеный мертвец.
. . . .
Смерть <u>души</u> своей печальной.

(ŽMP III)

———

Когда невзначай в воскресенье
Он <u>душу</u> свою потерял,
В сыскное не шел отделенье,
Свидетелей он не искал.   (ŽMP IV)

———

Пристал ко мне нищий дурак,
Идет по пятам, как знакомый.
"Где деньги твои?"—"Снес в кабак".—
"Где <u>сердце</u>?"—"Закинуто в омут".
. . . .
И правда (ну, задал задачу!)
Гляжу—близ меня никого...
В карман посмотрел—ничего...
Взглянул в свое <u>сердце</u>... и плачу.   (ŽMP V)

If in II the "heart" is only "broken," debilitated (*"Serdce...slomila
lož'"*) and there is still an effort to salvage the positive value it
once sought (*"Serdce k pravde poryvalos'"*), in III the
"heart"/"soul" is lost (*"serdca net"*) or dead (*"Serdce*—krašenyj
mertvec," "smert' duši") and the loss is treated with a certain
reckless flippancy ("xvat'-poxvat," "banal'noj"). In IV the "soul"
is forfeited by negligence ("nevznačaj"), and the poet's attitude is
one of indifference ("V sysknoe ne šel otdelen'e"). In V the heart
is willfully disposed of ("Zakinuto v omut") and made hopelessly
irretrievable ("omut" being the deepest part of a lake or river).
The cycle's outlying poems fill out this progression: in I the hero
still seeks spiritual fulfillment, while in VI he deliberately rejects it.
In poems VII-VIII he yearns only for physical death.
     ŽMP I and VI deal with the poet's daily routine. In them it
is possible to chart an identical behavioral pattern: the poet is
mired in a senseless, boring existence; in an excited state he seeks
after a redemptive ideal; this ideal remains beyond reach; he

regresses into renewed passivity. In each instance this circular pattern takes on a spatial dimension: either physically or in thought the poet exits the home, the locus of all that is repugnant, and moves toward a symbolic destination outside the home, the locus of something maximally positive; ultimately his path is reversed short of its goal, leaving no alternative but return to the domicile. It is not difficult to recognize in this odyssey an attempt to escape from the "terrible world" which now resides *inside* the home. The home provides neither comfort nor security; nor does it really belong to the hero any more (VI depicts a houseful of unwanted guests). It is a "chaotic" place even in a quite literal sense. In VI everything in the home is characterized by disorder and confusion—from the random topics of conversation ("bolezni," "služba," "Xristos," "gazeta," etc.) to the poet's own "quiet insanity" ("v sumasšestvii tixom").

The path toward ideal space, whether in the quotidian poems or elsewhere in ŽMP, is also chaotic in that it always involves blocked passage or reversal. The pattern is established already at the end of ŽMP I:

> Ты вскочишь и бежишь на улицы глухие,
>> Но некому помочь...
>
> . . . .
> Городовой, чтоб не заснуть, отгонит
>> Бродягу от костра...
>
> И, наконец, придет желанная усталость,
>> И станет всё равно...
> Что? Совесть? Правда? Жизнь? Какая это малость!
>> Ну, разве не смешно?   (ŽMP I)

The vagrant's access to the "bonfire" ("koster") is cut off, as is the poet's access to "conscience," "truth" and "life." The poet and the vagrant are one, as are "life's" positive values and the "bonfire." The same pattern recurs again and again. Even when ideal space is re-conceived as Death at the end of the cycle, access to it is still blocked:

> ГОВОРИТ СМЕРТЬ:
>
> . . . .
> Он больше ни во что не верит,
> Себя лишь хочет обмануть,

А сам—к моей блаженной двери
Отыскивает вяло путь.

. . . .

Я отворю. Пускай немного
Еще помучается он.   (ŽMP VIII)

The "path" model in ŽMP can be represented graphically as
follows:

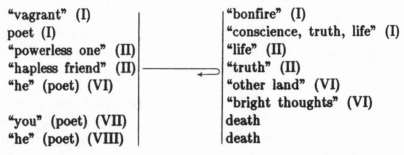

POET (OR POET SURROGATE)   IDEAL (OR IDEAL SURROGATE)

"vagrant" (I)   "bonfire" (I)
poet (I)   "conscience, truth, life" (I)
"powerless one" (II)   "life" (II)
"hapless friend" (II) ⟵   "truth" (II)
"he" (poet) (VI)   "other land" (VI)
                                "bright thoughts" (VI)

"you" (poet) (VII)   death
"he" (poet) (VIII)   death

As one can see, ŽMP dramatizes the poet's enclosure within the
"terrible world" no less vividly than PS.

In some respects ČK is a simpler, more conventional plot
cycle than ŽMP: in ČK plot development is purely episodic. The
action unfolds from poem to poem in linear sequence and, at least
on the surface, with almost boring predictability. The hero and
heroine meet and are immediately drawn to each other; at first
they resist their mutual attraction; eventually they surrender to
passion and make love; finally the affair ends and they go separate
ways. On the level of real, concrete events the story is no more
original than that of a dime novel. On the metaphoric and
symbolic level, however, ČK is far from simple. It contains in
essence two diametrically opposite plot lines (hero seduces heroine;
heroine seduces hero), one of which dominates, while the other
provides constant counterpoint. Like EP and SnM, ČK resists the
reader's desire for a single adequate plot summary.

As is true of virtually all Blok's plot cycles, the narrative
dynamic condenses around a number of leitmotifs, almost any one
of which could serve as a vehicle for summarizing the story. One
can trace the entire history of the liaison, for instance, by following
the motif of "eyes"/"glances":

Нет, <u>опустил</u> <u>я</u> напрасно <u>глаза</u>...
. . . .
<u>Ты</u>, и <u>не</u> <u>глядя</u>, <u>глядишь</u> на меня...   (ČK I)

—————

Я <u>гляжу</u> на тебя . . . . . .
. . . .
Нет! <u>Глаза</u> <u>отвратить</u>, и не сметь, и не сметь...
                                                (ČK II)

—————

Но, когда <u>ты</u> <u>сощуришь</u> <u>глаза</u> ...
. . . .
<u>Глаз</u> молчит, <u>золотистый</u> и <u>карий</u>...   (ČK III)

—————

Я <u>слепнуть</u> <u>не</u> <u>хочу</u>. . . . . . .
. . . .
Но ты меня зовешь! <u>Твой</u> <u>ядовитый</u> <u>взгляд</u>
Иной пропочит рай!—Я уступаю . . .   (ČK IV)

—————

В пустую грудь один, один <u>проникнет</u> <u>взгляд</u>...
                                                (ČK V)

—————

Тогда—<u>во</u> <u>взгляде</u> <u>глаз</u> <u>усталом</u>—
        Твоя в нем ложь!   (ČK VII)

—————

Буря спутанных кос, <u>тусклый</u> <u>глаз</u>...
. . . .
<u>Гаснут</u> свечи, <u>глаза</u>, слова ...   (ČK VIII)

—————

Ушла. <u>Оглянулась</u> пугливо...   (ČK IX)

The story is not difficult to follow: first there is glance avoidance (I-II); then her eye focuses on him long enough that its color can be discerned (III); the hero contemplates the danger of her glance (IV-V); after love-making her glance becomes weak and no longer threatening (VII-VIII); as the heroine leaves, she "glances back" (IX).

The central unifying plot motif, however, is the "home"

(understood both literally and symbolically). On one level (which may be considered dominant) ČK narrates the heroine's passage from her own "home" (a place of relative innocence) to the hero's "home" (a depraved abode, the residence of the poet–vampire):

ČK I   The heroine is located in *her* "home" environment, indicated metonymically by parental custody ("Mat' zapreščaet tebe podxodit'").

ČK III   The hero's invites the heroine to leave that environment ("Podojdi. Podpolzi.").

ČK V   The hero is in *his* "home" environment ("Vnov' u sebja").

ČK VI   The heroine is displaced, transported ("sxvačena, vlekoma") to an environment equivalent to the hero's "home" ("Kak èta komnata znakoma!").

ČK VIII   She is lured into his "home" proper ("Ja zavlek ee v moj dvorec").

ČK IX   She leaves his "home" ("Ušla. Ogljanulas' . . . na sizye okna moi").

On this level ČK is about the heroine's corruption by the hero. Consistent with her role as victim, the heroine is characterized as inexperienced, fearful, still capable of shame (I: "*Trepet* bežit po *drožaščej ruke*"; VI: "*Ispugom* sxvačena . . . *skryv lico* . . . *puglivyx* ruk"; VIII: "neponjatnyj *strax* . . . *pozor* moj"; IX: "ogljanulas' *puglivo*"). Her apparent innocence continually evokes in the hero recollections of ideal love (IV: "sinij bereg *raja*"; VIII: "o *nežnoj vesne*/Budet pet' tvoja krov' vo mne!"). At the same time, however, CK develops a secondary plot line which traces a diametrically opposite passage: the hero moves into *her* demonic space (I: "Širitsja *krug tvoego mne ognja*"; II: "*Každyj demon v tebe* . . . V ètu strašnuju propast' gljadet'"; IV: "*V ob'jat'ja strašnye* . . . No *ty menja zoveš'...tvoj zmeinyj raj*"); within this plot line the heroine emerges as a predatory and deceitful creature (VI: "Vop'etsja žadnyj vzgljad"; VII: "tvoja . . . lož'"). One can chart these two plot lines as follows:

Plot Line #1:

HEROINE'S "HOME"   HERO'S "HOME"
(RELATIVE INNOCENCE)   (DEPRAVITY)
heroine ——————————————→ (VAMPIRE'S "PALACE")

Plot Line #2:

HEROINE'S "HOME"	HERO'S "HOME"
(DEPRAVITY)	(RELATIVE INNOCENCE)
("SERPENTINE PARADISE") ◄———————	*hero*

These two plot lines coexist happily because they are symbolically
equivalent—each is simply the mirror image of the other.

More problematic is the inclusion of a third plot line that
runs counter to the implications of those above and involves
passage of both the hero and heroine to an ideal "home" identified
metaphorically with paradise *before* the Fall (*"Kak pervyj čelovek,
božestvennym sgoraja,/Xoču vernut'* navek na *sinij bereg
raja*/Tebja, ubiv vsju lož' i uničtoživ jad"*) (IV):

Plot Line #3:

Hero and heroine - - - - - >IDEAL (ORIGINAL) "HOME"
                              ("BLUE SHORE OF PARADISE")

This plot line is drawn tentatively (hence the dashes) because it
represents a potential rather than an actual scenario—it remains
unrealized in fact, yet it is sublimated symbolically and not
thoroughly expunged even in the cycle's finale. No matter how
depraved the heroine is (or becomes), she cannot help but evoke
the memory of Eve before the Fall. This is why the reappearance
of divine light at the end of VI resurrects the image of original
paradise ("utra *pervyj* luč"), and God's beatific gesture, while not
nullifying sin, leaves open the possibility of redemption ("I *čertit
bog* na tele spjaščej/Svoj svetovoj uzor"). The persistence of this
plot line helps explain the conflicting imagery in the cycle's last
poem:

> Над лучшим созданьем божьим
> Изведал я силу презренья.
> Я палкой ударил её.
>
> Поспешно оделась. Уходит.
> Ушла. Оглянулась пугливо
> На сизые окна мои.
>
> И нет её. В сизые окна
> Вливается вечер ненастный,

А дальше, за мраком ненастья,
Горит заревая кайма.

Далекие, влажные долы
И близкое, бурное счастье!
Один я стою и внимаю
Тому, что мне скрипки поют.

Поют они дикие песни
О том, что свободным я стал!
О том, что на лучшую долю
Я низкую страсть променял!   (ČK IX)

Here the heroine's virginal and demonic aspects are curiously
intertwined. In the first line she is "lučšee sozdan'e bož'e" — Eve
before the Fall; in the last line she is the purveyor of "nizkaja
strast'" — a corrupted Eve. The poet's ostensibly sadistic gesture
("ja palkoj udaril ee") chastises the former and exorcises the latter.
Ironically, having lured the heroine out from under the maternal
aegis (ČK I), the poet now performs the role of stern parent, a
belated guardian of her innocence. On a certain level the poet's
behavior is partial fulfillment of his desire to "return" her to the
"blue shore of paradise"; that endeavor too involved an act of
violence ("*ubiv* vsju lož'," "*uničtoživ* jad"). Given the ecstatic
mood of the poem, the sense of joy and liberation, one must
wonder also whether the coloration of the windows ("*sizye* okna")
does not contain a modicum of the divine "blue."[44]

The interrelationship between PS, ŽMP and ČK is
meaningful, and it seems no accident that these three subcycles are
arranged in this particular order. Judging from their chronological
dates, which overlap, Blok could have disposed them in virtually
any sequence.

PS poses the dilemma of existence inside a world that is not
a "home" in any genuine sense — the city is a chaotic space
wherein internal boundaries are meaningless and external boundaries
are impenetrableable. The only "path" one could possibly desire in
such an environment is escape, but escape (even in death) proves
impossible. The very absence of plot in PS is the compositional
analogue to the stasis that this environment imposes upon
everything within it.

ŽMP narrates various episodes of exit from a loathsome
"home" (in this case — the actual domicile) and depicts efforts to

discover some other, ideal space. All these efforts fail; no "path" is found which would allow the lyric hero to reach any goal whatsoever—even the "path" to death is blocked. The compositional analogue to the "path in ŽMP is a plot whose linearity is continually nullified by circular rhythms of behavior and thought, whether measured on the scale of a lifetime, a day or even a few seconds ("Volnueš'sja,—a v glubine pokornyj:/Ne vygorit—i pust'") (I).[45]

In ČK the *present* "home" (though not the past "home" and not necessarily the future "home") is the setting for a sordid liaison—whether this be the hero's "palace" or the heroine's "serpentine paradise." In ČK, however (and this is the principal difference between it and ŽMP), all "paths" are straight and open—they are genuine avenues for reaching destinations (even if the destination is demonic, morally repugnant). Straightness and openness, as mentioned earlier, are features of the *cosmic* "path"; this is why, it seems, ČK is one of the few places in StM where the lyric hero glimpses beyond the outer boundary of the "terrible world" into another, positive element burgeoning on the distant horizon ("za mrakom nenast'ja,/Gorit *zarevaja kajma*") (IX). The straightness and openness of the "paths" in ČK have their structural analogues in the linear sequentiality of its plot and in its open-ended denouement. ČK narrates the final episode of the romantic liaison in two different and logically incompatible ways: the heroine is murdered by the poet-vampire (VIII), the heroine is chastised and sent away by the poet (IX). It seems almost as if the plot (the "path") is so straight, so open that it need not stop at logical endings. This is a plot that declares the freedom of the artist to create as he pleases—something Blok saw as the essence of the "thesis":

> *The Thesis*: "You are free in this magical world full of correspondences." Create whatever you wish, because *this world belongs to you.* (V, 426) [Blok's emphasis.—D.S.]

The victory of *esthetic* freedom—the freedom to mold, shape, design and combine artistic things in whatever way the artist chooses—is perhaps the main idea of ČK's ending; and it is the idea that carries over into the rest of the volume.

The Design of the Third Volume: The Architecture of a Path

In designing the third volume Blok faced a formidable task, but one which afforded him considerable freedom. Of the 241 poems he elected to include in the "canonical" version fewer than one third were so closely interrelated that dispersing them was unthinkable. To this category of tightly bound poems one would have to assign those belonging to ISt, K, OČPV as well as those in PS, VEN, FLO, TP, MÈR, ČDL, and NPK; the same can be said, with some reservations, of the poems in JAM, ŽMP, and ČK. Still, well over half the poems (141) were independent enough that any number of different orderings and groupings would have been feasible. Such poems make up the bulk of the cycles StM, VOZ, AS, and ROD, not to mention the whole section RazSt III. Indeed the evolution of the third volume through its various editions (1912, 1916, 1921) indicates that these groupings underwent continual and rather dramatic changes: a good number of poems migrated between them with each reformulation of the book.[46] The core concept of each cycle was established early, but each was flexible enough to tolerate transpositions.[47]

What made Blok's task difficult was not that the migrating poems and others of the "loosely bound" category were unrelated, but that they were related in many different ways and on many different levels. Grouping certain of them together forefronted particular aspects of their interrelationship while deemphasizing others. Placing a given poem into a given cycle was an interpretive and creative act—it isolated aspects of the poem Blok deemed most important to the whole, and it affected, however, slightly, the very design of the whole. It was also an act of mythmaking since Blok, as editor of the volume, was capable of "narrating" the final stage of his lyric hero's biography in almost any way he saw fit. To appreciate this one need only imagine what shape the third volume would have taken had Blok arranged all the relatively independent poems (i. e., those not belonging to tightly bound groupings) solely according to chronology. The entire design of the volume would be lost. We would confront a body of poems which, with few exceptions, would tell no story at all—a diary devoid of plot but filled with brilliant moments of lyric insight.

For this reason the composition and placement of the macrocycles, which contain most of the "loosely bound" poems, was crucial to the book's design. It is significant in this regard that despite the internal changes Blok made in the macrocycles, he never changed their sequence in the volume:

1912	1916	1921
→ StM	→ StM	→ StM
VOZ	VOZ	VOZ
→ ISt	("Opjat' na rodine")[48]	JAM
→ AS	→ IS	→ ISt
→ ROD	RazSt	RazSt
	→ AS	→ AS
	K	K
	→ ROD	SS
	OČPV	→ ROD
		OČPV

This outline suggests that the macrocycles were always important "milestones on a path," as Maksimov tells us.[49] Their very titles (at least those of StM, ISt and ROD) recommend a kind of itinerary, inasmuch as they denote different topographical or pseudo-topographical locations: "terrible world"—Italy—Motherland. Significant too is the fact that when new cycles were added (with the exception of OČPV), they were always placed *inside* the macrocycles or *between* them, suggesting that the macrocycles were not only "milestones" but also indispensible bastions of the volume's architecture—they become containers, bounded and bounding structures. Hence in understanding the volume's design neither the metaphor of the "path" nor the metaphor of the "building" is adequate in isolation: the design incorporates both principles. Let us examine first the architectural metaphor, which in discussions of the third volume has received rather little attention.

The idea of poetry as edifice is common in literature, but it seems to have had special importance for Blok. The allusion to his songs as a "dungeon" (I, 197) or as a "building" (I, 283) is one indication of this, as is Blok's repeated usage of the metaphor of the "wall" ("stena") for poetic creation—an image prevalent throughout his career (e.g., "My, poèty, . . . na *stenax* čitaem sroki") (III, 90).[50]

Though not every building is symmetrical in an obvious way,

symmetries of some sort are evident in most if not all architecture. Certainly most residential homes are symmetrical in the sense that their opposite walls usually parallel each other. The question of symmetries was raised earlier, and it will be fruitful to return to it now. We shall be concerned, specifically, with symmetries manifest in the design and disposition of the macrocycles. Symmetry on the level of form alone is a function of cosmos, though as we saw in PS, it may on the ideational level become a sign of the chaotic ("eternal return"). The argument below aims to show that symmetry gradually asserts itself as a function of cosmos on *both* levels, and that it does so largely via the progressive emergence and ultimate validation of a cosmic "path"—a "path" with beginning and ending, a "path" that legitimizes itself by differentiating its departure point from its point of arrival.

Looking for symmetries in things can be an exercise of negligible value, as Jonathan Culler warns in his critique of Roman Jakobson;[51] with enough ingenuity one can find symmetrical structures in virtually anything. At the same time, where symmetry is abundant and where it has a clear rationale, it is foolish to blind oneself to its existence.

The symmetries in Blok's macrocycles belong to the latter category. Gerald Pirog demonstrates persuasively, for instance, that the perimeters of ISt are directly parallel. The epigraph at the beginning and the epitaph at the end are correlated, as are the first three poems of the cycle and the last three: together they form an elaborate compositional framing.[52] Ronald Vroon illustrates the "careful orchestration of beginning and end" in ROD, evident in the prosodic and thematic interconnection of "Ty otošla..." (#1) and "Koršun" (#27).[53] Pursuing this further, it is not difficult to see that StM #1 ("K Muze") and StM #48 ("Golos iz xora") depict, respectively, the anarchy prevailing in the most intimate sphere (the poet's inspiration) and in the most general sphere (the universe); it is fitting that Blok opens and closes the cycle with such bleak statements of its central theme. Even in AS, one of Blok's most diffuse cycles, the outlying poems (#1-2, #71-72) echo each other quite conspicuously as is apparent from the extraordinary concentration of shared lexemes (e.g., son/snit'sja; pet'/pesnja; vesna/vesennij, vešnij; zelenyj/zelen'; cvet/cvesti). In StM and ISt it was necessary to violate chronology to create such parallels; in AS, however, only a minor adjustment was needed, and in ROD—none at all. This suggests that Blok, like Baudelaire in preparing the 1861 edition of *Les Fleurs du Mal*, was composing some poems "expressly . . . so as to become part of an existing framework."[54]

Symmetries generated by relationships *between* the macrocycles are so numerous that it will be necessary to focus only on the most significant ones.   Moreover, since symmetry is most pronounced at opposite ends of linear coordinates, we shall concentrate on those manifest at opposite poles of each hemivolume (StM—ISt, AS—ROD), at coordinate poles of different hemivolumes (StM—AS, ISt—ROD) and at the far poles of volume as a whole (StM—ROD).

StM and ISt are so closely interconnected that the latter almost deserves to be called the Italian habitat of the "terrible world." Blok himself came close to saying this when he wrote his mother in 1909: "It is impossible to live in Italy. . . . There is no life, there is only art and antiquity."[55]   This remark captures the essential similarity of the two cycles and at the same time their inherent difference.   Like the environment of StM, contemporary Italy in ISt is a place of living death ("Doma i ljudi—vsë *groba*"; "Gondol bezmolvnye *groba*"; "O bella [Florencija], . . . /Gniloj morščinoj *grobovoju*/Iskaženy tvoi čerty"), but in the Italian landscape and in its art is preserved the immortal memory of an ideal past, especially the Renaissance.   Moreover Italy at least *has* an antiquity (Petersburg does not).   The very fact that the distinction "past vs. present" is imminent in ISt signals an essential difference between this cycle and StM, where time categories are undifferentiable.

Present-day Italy as discrete from its past, however, is a close facsimile of the "terrible world."   It is characterized by darkness ("*černoe nebo* Italii," "okrestnyj *mrak*," "mutnyj *mrak*") and emptiness ("vinogradnye *pustyni*," "v *pustynnom* pereulke").   It is an environment where the poet feels alienated ("na *čužoj* storone"), where people are equated with things ("doma i *ljudi*—vsë groba"; "dvorcy, kanaly, *ljudi*") and where the chance meeting of eyes can be fatal ("*Vzor* tvoj—*mečami pronzajuščij* vzor") (cf. "Tvoj *razjaščij*, tvoj *vzor*, tvoj *kinžal'*.") (StM #3).   It is a place too where what was once holy, especially the Virgin Mary, is continually desecrated.   From the poems "Glaza opuščennye skromno..." (IS #21) ("ona [Marija]... na *porugan'e* predana") and "Blagoveščenie" (IS #22) ("Temnolikij *angel* s derzkoj vetv'ju") one can draw clear parallels to StM, particularly

the poem "K Muze" ("prokljat'e zavetov svjaščennyx . . .
poruganie sčastija . . . *angelov* ty nizvodila/Soblaznjaja svoej
krasotoj").

   Moreover ISt, like StM, is primarily an urban cycle; Blok
focuses his attention on Italian cities, especially cities that remind
him of Petersburg.   This is true of Florence with its "wheezing
autos" ("*Xripjat* tvoi *avtomobili*") (FLO I) (cf. "*skrežeščuščij* . . .
taksomotor")(PS I) and its "streetlamps" ("*pod uličnyj fonar*")
(FLO VII) (cf. "Na *ulice, pod fonarem belёsym*") (PS III).   It is
even more true of Venice, about which Blok wrote Brjusov:
"Venice . . . is almost outside Italy; one can love it much the
same way one loves Petersburg; Petersburg's relation to Russia is
the same as Venice's to Italy" (VIII, 293).   The correlation
between Petersburg and Venice in Blok's mind helps explain the
remarkable parallels between the subcycles PS and VEN.   If one
reads the third volume in sequence, it is impossible to encounter
VEN II without recalling phrasings in PS:

> Холодный ветер от лагуны.
>
> . . . .
>
> Всё спит—дворцы, каналы, люди,
> Лишь призрака скользящий шаг,
> Лишь голова на черном блюде
> Глядит с тоской в окрестный мрак.   (VEN
> II)

One is reminded of PS I ("*Živye spjat*"); PS II ("*ledjanaja* rjab'
kanala");[56] PS V ("ne išči *dvorca*"); and especially PS IV ("Iz
mraka/Fonari begut—kuda?/Tam—*liš' černaja* voda/ . . . /Voet
veter ledenjaščij/ . . . /Tretij *prizrak*. Ty kuda,/Ty, iz teni v ten'
skol'zjaščij").   Moreover it hardly seems accidental that both PS
and VEN explicitly treat the theme of metempsychosis—albeit with
different implications.   In PS II reincarnation is a function of
repetition without change; there is no escape—even the setting
repeats itself.   In VEN III, by contrast, reincarnation effects
transport to a different time and place ("o žizni *buduščej*," "v
drugoj strane"); the poet's fantasy depicts his own rebirth in a new
age that may resurrect Italy's ideal legacy.   Herein lies one crucial
difference between StM and ISt: StM confuses past, present, and
future, while ISt preserves the past in dormancy—perhaps for
regeneration in some distant future.

   AS and ROD, which mark the perimeters of the second

hemivolume, are no less closely interconnected than StM and ISt.[57]
What links these two cycles most conspicuously is the
predominance in both of rural settings; it is worth noting in this
regard that the images "kovyl'" ("feathergrass") and "step'"
("steppe")—prominent leitmotifs in ROD—appear nowhere else in
the third volume except AS ("Ty li, žizn', moju gornicu
skudnuju/Ubirala *stepnym kovylem!*") (AS #21) (III, 176). The
significance of this detail will become more apparent later in our
discussion of the theme of the path; as we shall see, AS prepares
the lyric hero's passage through the native Russian landscape in
ROD. More generally, the switch from urban to rural settings is
meaningful because in Blok's conception the city represents a
demonic environment wherein ideal love is easily perverted,
confused with its opposite. In AS and ROD reminiscences of first
(ideal) love are abundant and they are virtually never
corrupted—they almost always appear under the same halo of
sanctity that graced them originally, in the period of the "thesis":

> Только <u>первая</u> снится <u>любовь</u>...
> (ČDL VIII)(III, 186)

> Я различаю на мгновенье
> За скрипами—иное пенье,
> Тот голос низкий и грудной,
>
> Каким ответила подруга
> На <u>первую любовь</u> мою.
> (AS #56) (III, 210)

> Россия, нищая Россия,
> Мне избы серые твои,
> Твои мне песни ветровые—
> Как слезы <u>первые любви</u>!
> (ROD #9) (III, 254)

> Хоть во сне твою <u>прежнюю милую руку</u>
> Прижимая к губам.
> (ROD #17) (III, 265)

The poet's attitude is not identical to that in SPD, but in these cycles we no longer find "the joy of trampling what was cherished and sacred" (StM #1) (III, 8).

In the treatment of love, however, there is an essential difference between AS and ROD, even as their titles suggest. AS ("Arf*y* i skripk*i*") is *plural* and contains *two* nouns: "Arf*y*" symbolizing the harmony of ideal, pure love; "skripki" symbolizing, in general, the dissonances of the "terrible world," unbridled and destructive passion.[58] ROD ("Rodin*a*"), by contrast, is a *singular* noun that carries exclusively positive connotations; it is, moreover, the only macrocycle in the third volume whose title contains just *one* word. Here grammar provides a clue to the cycles' interrelationship. AS deals specifically with the multiplicity of beloveds, whose images in time have become intertwined and thoroughly confused; the poet's dilemma is stated quite explicitly in AS #3:

И я любил. И я изведал
Безумный хмель любовных мук,
И пораженья, и победы,
И имя: враг; и слово: друг.

Их было много... Что я знаю?
Воспоминанья, тени сна...
Я только странно повторяю
Их золотые имена.

Их было много. Но одною
Чертой соединил их я,
Одной безумной красотою,
Чье имя: страсть и жизнь моя.

(AS #3) (III, 160)

The poet has "combined" all loves inside "one line," one circle. Put differently, the image of woman has become for him hopelessly chaotic—ideal and sinister love ("drug," "vrag") are no longer distinguishable. Once again boundaries have disappeared. AS chronicles the poet's effort to redraw these boundaries, to separate out the different images of romantic love in his past with the aim of delineating the sacred from the demonic. He does so with the aid of memory and "music," which in Blok's view had the capacity to transform the chaotic into the cosmic.[59] Hence AS depicts a wide variety of "loves"—prostitutes, unfaithful wives, gypsy singers,

femmes fatales, his adolescent love (Sadovskaja) (ČDL), country
girls, the faithful sweetheart of folk-tales (MÈR), and the Beautiful
Lady herself.   At the end of the cycle the last image prevails,
though it remains distant ("povtorjaja *dalekoe imja*") (AS #72)
(III, 226).   In ROD, by contrast, the dominant idea from the
outset is the singularity of the beloved, who represents a synthesis
of the homeland and the Lady ("Ty—rodnaja Galileja").   Even
where apparently different beloveds appear, they are assimilated
within the myth of "first love," as for instance the folk maiden in
ROD #2 ("Obnimet rukoj, opletet kosoj", "kust belyx roz") or the
poet's "friend" ("podruga na večernem pire") in ROD #12:

> Подруга, на вечернем пире,
> Помедли здесь, побудь со мной.
> Забудь, забудь о страшном мире,
> Вздохни небесной глубиной.
>
> . . . .
>
> И нам, как дым, струиться надо
> Седым туманом—в алый круг.
>
> (ROD #12) (III, 258)

One can hardly mistake the words "struit'sja... v *alyj krug*" as
anything except an autoreminiscence from SPD ("Ty otxodiš' v
sumrak alyj,/tajnyj *krug*...") (I, 81, 109).   Movement to the
"crimson circle" represents nexus with the Lady.   The Lady
remains sacred, but she has been humbled—she is no longer
untouchable, and her identity with the homeland makes her for the
first time truly accessible.

The two macrocycles that form the outer "walls" of Blok's
third volume—StM and ROD—are remarkably similar yet
significantly different.   In some respects the environment depicted
in ROD is a replica of that in StM.   It is *dark* ("v temnote,"
"pered Donom temnym," "gluxota i černota," "pod černoj tučej");
predominantly *nocturnal* ("pust' noč'," "nočnye pticy," "dolgix let
neskončaemoj noči"); and *barren, empty* ("ja v pustyne," "na
pustynnom prostore," "pustynnyj lug").   It is generally either *quiet*
("za tišinoju neprobudnoj," "pobeždaet tišina") or permeated with
disturbing sounds ("rokoty seči," "krikov vragov," "vzov'etsja
krikom voron'e"); for the most part, the homeland as depicted in
ROD is a non-musical or even anti-musical locale.   The natural
elements in ROD can be just as threatening as those in StM; this
is evident in the recurring motif of the storm clouds which

symbolize the impending Revolution ("ispugannye *tuči*," "byli
dymnye *tuči* v krovi").   Moreover the world depicted in ROD is
just as much a homeless environment as that in StM—the irony of
ROD is that the lyric hero passes through the "homeland" but
does not arrive at the cosmic "home."   The two images of the
home that conclude the cycle are extremely disquieting:

> Как не бросить всё на свете,
> Не отчаяться во всём,
> Если в гости ходит ветер,
> Только дикий черный ветер,
> Сотрясающий мой дом?
>
> Что ж ты, ветер,
> Стекла гнешь?
> Ставни с петель
> Дико рвешь?   (ROD #26) (III, 279-280)

> Чертя за кругом плавный круг,
> Над сонным лугом коршун кружит
> И смотрит на пустынный луг.—
> В избушке мать над сыном тужит:
> "На хлеба, на, на грудь, соси,
> Расти, покорствуй, крест неси". (ROD #27) (III, 281)

ROD #26 is reminiscent of StM: the poet sits alone in a house
whose boundaries provide hardly any protection from the elements
outside—the distinction "inside *vs.* outside" is extremely tenuous.
ROD #27 paints an equally ominous picture: the circling "kite"
("koršun") seems to anticipate a fresh supply of carrion, and the
mother's resentful nurturing creates a grotesque icon of Madonna
and Child.   Despite these parallels, however, ROD presents a
different and more optimistic picture of the world than StM.   The
image of "first love," repeatedly defiled in StM reappears in ROD
in its original sanctity and holds forth the promise of genuine
union with the Lady in the near future—hence the recurrence of
nuptial, fairy-tale and chivalric imagery familiar from the first
volume ("Tam menja *nevesta* ždet"; "*nevesta*, Rossija"; "O
zamorskoj, o *carevne*,/O *carevne*"; "ja ne predal *beloe znamja*";
"konik *v latax*"; "Ostri svoj *meč*").   This is not to say that the
Lady has remained identical in every way to her image in the first

volume.   Paradoxically, she has remained the same yet she has also changed:

А ты всё та же—лес, да поле,
Да плат узорный до бровей.   (ROD #9) (III, 254)

———

Ты всё та, что была, и не та,
Новым ты обернулась мне ликом...   (ROD #19) (III, 269)

———

А ты всё та ж, моя страна,
В красе заплаканной и древней.   (ROD #27) (III, 269)

The fact that ROD validates a time coordinate along which change can and does take place indicates that we are dealing with a concept of time quite different from that in StM.   StM is a world of "eternal returns," chaotic and senseless repetition; this is why the motif *opjat'/snova/vnov'* nearly always carries negative connotations in that cycle.   In ROD, by contrast, this same motif is predominantly positive ("*Opjat', kak v gody zolotye*"; "Vot ja *vnov'* nad tvoeju postel'ju/ . . . /Ja skvoz' temnye noči—*v vence*"; "prižimaju k gubam *tvoju prežnuju ruku/* . . . /Snitsja—*snova ja mal'čik i snova ljubovnik/* . . . /Gljanet *nebo opjat', rozoveja ot kraju do kraju*").   In ROD the poet envisions, primarily, not "*eternal* returns" but a *single* return that is simultaneously identified as something new.[60]   Circular time is a function of chaos, while linear time with its teleologic orientation is a function of cosmos; in ROD the latter establishes hegemony.

To illustrate this one need only compare PS and NPK ("Na pole Kulikovom"), subcycles of StM and ROD, respectively.   The parallels between these two groupings are striking, and it hardly seems accidental that Blok placed them at opposite perimeters of the third volume.   Both contain five poems and very nearly the same number of lines (109 in PS, 120 in NPK).   Both are unified by a common setting (Petersburg, the Kulikovo Field), and in both there is the motif of recurrence.   It is noteworthy, moreover, that both evoke contemplation of the fourteenth century (PS via depiction of the Dance of Death, inspired by the Black Death of 1373; NPK via depiction of Dmitrij Donskoj's battle with the Tatars in 1380).   In both the setting is nocturnal, and in both the poet contemplates death.   On the microtextual level both   are unified by an elaborate network of repeated lexemes, some of which are even shared by the two subcycles (drug-, tix-, noč'-, svet-). From here on the comparison becomes contrastive:

PS		NPK
"stronjnyj latnik," "šlem i per'ja" (perversion of chivalric model: prostitute and lover)	KNIGHTLY ACCOUTERMENTS	"kol'čuga," "ščit," "dospex," "meč" (original chivalric model poet and Lady)
"*Net lica*" "*ne išči*. . . Dobrodušnogo *lica*" (absence of face)	FACE	"Byl v ščite *Tvoj lik nerukotvornyj*" (presence of Lady's face)
"Il' *nevesta* ot venca?" (prositute)	BRIDE	"A Neprjadva ubralas' tumanom,/*Čto knjažna fatoj*" (the Lady)
"kanal," "černaja voda" (river as symbol of death)	WATER	"Don," "Neprjadva," "Za rekoj—poganaja orda" (river as symbol of marriage)
"bessmyslennyj i tusklyj svet," "fonar'" (weak, meaningless light)	LIGHT	"Ozarim kostrami/ Stepnuju dal'," "blesnet svjatoe znamja," "ty sošla v odežde svet strujaščej" (bright, fateful light)
"ulica" (short, urban path)	PATH	"Naš put'—stepnoj," "dolgij put'" (long, rural path)
"Smotrit *mesjac* blednyj,/ Nasylaet tišinu" (quiet)	MOON	"Razvjazany dikie strasti/ Pod igom uščerbnoj *luny*" (agitation)
"On šepčet ej *neznačaščie* reči" (voice of dandy–corpse)	SPEECH	"Slyšal ja *Tvoj golos* serdcem veščim" (Lady's voice)
"*on. . .pojavljaetsja/ Šeja skručena platkom*" (ghost of Pavel I)	VISITATION	"*Ty sošla. . .*" (the Lady alive)
Palace coup (murder of Pavel I and other tsars) (no change)	REBELLION	Popular uprising (overthrow of Tatar Yoke) (change)

"*Umreš'*—načneš' opjat' snačala" (to escape life) (not possible)	DEATH	"Za svatoe delo *mertvym* leč'" (to sanctify life) (possible)

There is a great difference between the senseless recurrence of events in PS (repetition which brings no change), and the fateful linkage of time Blok depicts in NPK. At the beginning of NPK there is indeed a suggestion of "eternal return" ("I *večnyj* boj!") (I), but the idea that prevails in the cycle is cosmic and teleologic ("*Ne vernut'sja*, ne vzgljanut' nazad") (II). The presence of plot movement in NPK (absent in PS) is further evidence of its linear orientation;[61] the end of NPK signals the beginning of a deferred denouement: "Teper' *tvoj čas nastal.*—Molis'!" (V). The very words "čas nastal" ("the hour has arrived") embody a time concept antithetical to that in PS; in NPK there is a cosmic sense of time that proves stronger than the chaotic—there are temporal boundaries, decisive moments that distinguish past from future.

As we have seen, a dialectic operates between the macrocycles at the far poles of the hemivolume (StM—ISt, AS—ROD) and the far poles of the whole volume (StM—ROD). These cycles are in a condition of dynamic equivalence (similarity and dissimilarity) which defines their different functions in design of the book. The same can be said for the macrocycles StM—AS and ISt—ROD. Between StM and AS the following equivalencies are significant:

StM	*AS*
forgetfulness	memory
urban	rural
dissonance/silence	music

Between ISt and ROD one can posit the following oppositions:

ISt	*ROD*
foreign land	native land
destiny belongs to past	destiny belongs to future
corrupted by modern civilization	untouched by modern civilization

break between past	linkage between past
and present	and present
desecration of what was holy	dedication to holy mission
defiled Virgin Mary	sanctified Lady

It seems significant too that Blok chose the titles "Ital'janskie stixi" (not "Italija") and "*Rodina*" (not "Russkie stixi"). The Italy Blok loved was preserved mainly in its art, whereas the potential of native Russia lay in the elements and the soil. It is no accident that Blok borrows the image of Bobrok listening to the ground from "Skazanie o Mamaevom poboišče" in NPK II ("k *zemle* sklonivšis' golovoju") or that he speaks of Russia's "underground Messiah" ("*podzemnaja* messija") in ROD #19 ("Novaja Amerika").

The constant tug and pull of such equivalencies creates the architecture of the whole and gives it a certain stability. Each of the macrocycles is in some respect equated with and at the same time counterpoised with the others. If StM poses the dilemma of chaos, each of the other macrocycles contains some cosmic principle to counterbalance it, yet none of the macrocycles in isolation represents a purely cosmic environment. For Blok, as we shall see, the only cosmic "home" in the absolute sense was the volume itself.

The "architecture" of the volume, however, is a metaphoric space without real dimensions; no one can inhabit such a space any more than he can inhabit a thought or a dream. Blok's lyric hero is concerned with *real* space—he lives in real environments, moves about real cities and through real landscapes, he sits in real apartments and eats in real restaurants. The real space that is charged with the greatest symbolic meaning for him, however, is the "home"—an actual abode which provides security, protection from the elements and human companionship.

The dilemma the lyric hero faces in StM is that the "home" in this genuine sense no longer exists—it has been forfeited. To understand this one need only recall the events of SnM—the door of his home is opened, the snowy elements enter and the poet himself, pursuing the Snow Mask, exits the home. In the myth of the "trilogy" this action constitutes the permanent loss of the original "home." The lyric hero can never return to it. His departure from the original "home" can be equated with the loss of innocence or virginity—the event is irreversible.

The situation is quite similar to that in Blok's play "Pesnja

Sud'by" (1908). German, the play's protagonist, hears the "song of fate" in the wind and rushes out of "his quiet white house" to follow this call, leaving behind his faithful wife Elena. The monk, a clairvoyant visiter who interprets the symbolic meaning of these events, tells Elena that "the white house will no longer be" and that German will never be able to return. At the end of the play German is abandoned and homeless, following the path of a wandering pedlar.

The dilemma of "Pesnja Sud'by," however, is not without potential solution. Indeed the lost home, in its original form, cannot be restored, but the path German takes is presented as a kind of compensation for the loss. If, as Elena says, "he has left everything here . . . all his books, all his things, . . . *His whole soul is here*," the Monk, nevertheless suggests that German can recover what he has forfeited. The Monk urges Elena to leave the "quiet house" and follow after German, saying: "Here is your white snowy road. The path is long. It will last many years. *And at the end of the path is German's soul*" (IV, 158). The path becomes the metonymic equivalent of the home inasmuch as it reconstitutes what the home once contained: German's soul. In a sense, movement along the path is synonymous with re-architecting the lost home.[62]

What Blok does in the third volume of his "trilogy" is precisely this—out of the raw material of his lyrics he architects a real path and at the same time a metaphoric home. And by virtue of the path's reality—the space it traverses in actuality—he allows the metaphor of the restored home to be realized (OČPV).

Whereas the metaphor of the "home," however, consists in the synchronic balancing of cyclic elements, the reconnoitering of the "path" occurs diachronically and depends—from the reader's perspective—on apprehending orders that emerge in sequence, from cycle to cycle.

In designing the third volume Blok seems to have been intent on having his lyric hero search out this path by degrees, forcing him to pass through purgatory like Dante in quest of Beatrice. In StM, as we saw, paths are predominantly chaotic; only the demonic path, taken by the hero of ČK, is straight (and in this sense cosmic), but it leads to a sinister "home." Simple "returns," shortcuts through the "terrible world" are impossible. The following cycle, "Vozmezdie" (VOZ), presents the prehistory of the dilemma but no resolution to it; as in StM the hero's movements lack direction (*"Skitalis' my"* *"prežnix xižin* *ne mogli najti,"* *"Naprasnye skitan'ja!"*), and the present environment still represents entrapment:

> Нет конца и нет начала,
> Нет исхода—сталь и сталь.
> Душу бедную обстала
> Прежде милая мне даль. (VOZ #17)(III, 84)

VOZ, however, despite its pessimism, prepares the volume's denouement by narrating also the heroine's exit from the original "home" ("No čas nastal, i *ty ušla iz domu . . . V syruju noč' ty iz domu ušla*"); the parallel between this event and Elena's departure after German in "Pesnja Sud'by" requires no comment. In the cycle "Jamby" (JAM) the theme of the path is less prominent; the function of JAM is not to give new direction to the hero but to rule out illusory "returns" to the world of "first love":

> . . . за тучкой легкопёрой
> Сквозит мне первая любовь...
>
> Забудь, забудь о страшном мире,
> Взмахни крылом, лети туда...
>
> Нет, не один я был на пире!
> Нет, не забуду никогда!   (JAM #8)(III, 92)

> Пускай зовут: Забудь, поэт!
> Вернись в красивые уюты!
> Нет! Лучше сгинуть в стуже лютой!
> Уюта—нет. Покоя—нет.   (JAM #11)(III,95)

It is significant that "return" here is conceived as flight "upward"; by implication the proper path (unlike Dante's) is specifically a horizontal and lowly one—a path along the earth (cf. "svoj *niščij put' vozvratnyj*") (VOZ #12) (III, 76). If anything, the proper path must mimic the peasant's, whose gait is listless but nevertheless has direction ("Mužik *poplelsja borozdoju*/Syroj i černoj") (JAM #8) (III, 92).

     In ISt the theme of the path is prominent and complex. There is, of course, the motif of an empirical journey over the Italian landscape which, interestingly enough, if mapped out geographically, traces a convoluted, basically circular path (the paradigm of chaos). Even without the aid of a map, however, it is apparent that the poet's route doubles back upon itself twice (ISt #3 and #23 carry the designation "Spoleto"; #7 and #22 are designated "Perugia"). If we treat the journey as a spiritual one, the dynamic is, as Pirog illustrates, essentially from hope to "disillusionment".[63] Moreover there is a growing sense of alienation from the landscape: "The peculiar ambivalence and pessimism that permeates *The Italian Poems* is precisely the result of a failure on the part of the modern poet to achieve a relationship with the landscape which was possible for the artist of the Renaissance."[64] To be sure, in fantasy and in art the poet can temporarily escape contemplation of this depressing circumstance—hence the recurring motif of departure ("S nej *uxodil* ja v more"; "O, sladko . . . *ujti* v tvoj drevnij znoj i v nežnost'"; "Goluboj večernij znoj/. . . /*Uneset* menja volnoj"; "Liš' v legkom čelnoke iskusstva/Ot skuki mira *uplyveš*"). Yet these momentary flights of fancy are recognized as impermanent and irrelevant to the more arduous task the poet has set for himself ("*Iskusstvo—noša na plečax*"). Present day Italy as depicted in ISt represents, ultimately, a dead end rather than a genuine "path."

In essence the cycles of the first hemivolume (StM—VOZ—JAM—ISt) provide only "negative" direction to the lyric hero—they rule out certain possibilities but offer no acceptable alternatives. In the second hemivolume, by contrast, the dominant idea is discovery of a "positive" direction, although here too there are unforeseen detours.

In AS the theme of the path is prevalent but not easily tractable. On the one hand there are abundant indications of aimlessness and enclosure characteristic of StM and VOZ ("*Nevernyj povorot rulja.../.../Bescel'nyj put', bescel'nyj* v'jun"; "mne *net isxoda*"; "*letet' bescel'no*/V sijajuščuju noč'!"; "*neizvestnost' puti*"). It is significant too that the cycle's first poem contains the image of the "green star" ("I angel podnjal v vysotu,/*Zvezdu zelenuju* odnu"), which in Blok's prose is associated with uncertainty of direction, circular movement without forward progress (V, 75, 82). The idea of discerning a path and a destination with the aid of memory (and sometimes sound), on the other hand, gradually emerges as the cycle's dominant:

Весь я—память, весь я—слух,
Ты со мной печальный дух,
Знаю, вижу—вот твой след,
Смытый бурей стольких лет.   (AS #28) (III, 182)

———

Что б ни было,—ты помни, вспомни что-то,
        Душа... когда? когда?
. . . .
Чтобы сквозь сны бытийственных метаний,
        Сбивающих с пути,
Со знаньем несказанных очертаний,
        Как с факелом, пройти.   (AS #45) (III, 198)

———

Ветр налетит, завоет снег,
И в памяти на миг возникнет
Тот край, тот отдаленный брег...
. . . .
Ночь, лес и снег. И я несу
Постылый груз воспоминаний...
Вдруг—малый домик на поляне,
И девочка поет в лесу. (AS #46) (III, 199)

"Path" and "memory" become equivalent ("Ty, vremja, *pamjat'* prituši,/A *put'* snežkom zaporoši") (AS #54) (III, 208). The goal of the path that holds the greatest appeal for the poet is quite clearly identified as the realm of first love; this is why AS is virtually saturated with reminiscences from SPD. In contrast to StM, VOZ and JAM, however, movement in the direction of this ideal world is no longer conceived as a "return"; in fact words related etymologically to the verb "vernut'sja" always (with only one exception) appear in constructions denoting negation: "Iz *nevozvratnogo* daleka" (III, 195), "*ne vernut'* tex neg" (III, 220), "te *nevozvratnye* dni . . . *nevozvratimo*" (III, 221). As a rule the paths in AS, even when they provoke fear or when they are uncertain, are nevertheless *straight* and *open* ("semafor . . . mne ukazal *svobodnyj put'*"; "*letiš' ty*, no—zarja v krovi"). And toward the end of the cycle the image of passing *through* the "terrible world" becomes quite prominent ("No žizn'— *proezžaja doroga*"; "Moj *poezd letit*, kak cyganskaja pesnja . . . *vse mimo, mimo*"; "I *skvoz' kružen'e* vixrevoe/ . . . /Vedet, uvodit v goluboe/Edva primetnaja *stezja*"). Rarely, in the latter half of AS, is the lyric hero's movement circular. All of this indicates that the cosmic path, which will prevail in ROD, has already acquired a certain hegemony in AS. In one instance in fact the poet already identifies his destination as the homeland:

> Тебя провижу, как изгнанник
> Провидит <u>родину</u> свою. (AS #60) (III, 214)

The cycle "Karmen" (K) and its companion piece "Solov'inyj sad" (SS), both of which were inspired by the actress and singer Ljubov' Andreevna Del'mas,[65] represent departures from the path discerned in AS. The heroine of K embodies a world of pure musicality and lyricism quite antithetical to the cosmic plan that had already begun to emerge in the second hemivolume:

> <u>Там</u>—дикий сплав миров, где часть души вселенской
> Рыдает, исходя гармонией светил.
> . . . .
> Всё—музыка и свет: нет счастья, нет измен...
> Мелодией одной звучат печаль и радость...
>
> (K #10) (III, 239)

Her image is incompatable with the concept of his own, earthly homeland (*"smyvaja pamjat' ob otčizne"*; "kak pamjat' ob *inoj otčizne*"). Passage to her world is tantamount to betrayal of his chosen fate. Hence Don Jose's plea to Carmensita to "leave this life" ("Ujdem, ujdem ot žizni,/Ujdem ot ètoj grustnoj žizni!") (K #6) carries different implications for the actor on stage and his counterpart, the poet in the audience. For Don Jose, Carmensita's willingness to "leave this life" is his only hope of salvation; for the poet it means immersing himself once more in a chaotic lyric impulse and abandoning that plan of "life" he had so painstakingly wrought in the third volume. The cycle's denouement, the poet's farewell to Karmen, measures the superior claim of this plan as esthetic imperative.

SS is a parable about the dangers contemplated in K. The "nightingale garden," like the realm of Karmen, is a locus of pure musicality alien to the "path":

> Наказанье ли ждет, иль награда,
> Если я <u>уклонюсь</u> <u>от</u> <u>пути</u>?

Наказанье ли ждет, иль награда,
Если я уклонюсь от пути?

                                                (SS III) (III, 242)

———————

Однозвучно запели ручьи,
Сладкой песнью меня оглуили,
Взяли душу мою соловьи.

. . . .
Я забыл о пути каменистом...

                                                (SS IV) (III, 243)

It is significant that when the hero leaves the "path" and enters
the garden he also forfeits the "home" ("Gde že dom?") (VII), thus
the equivalency "path=home" is made explicit.   Among the other
punishments   exacted   are   disorientation,   confusion   of   time
("Neizvestno kotorogo dnja") (VI), forgetfulness of direction ("Ili
vse ešče èto vo sne?") (VII).   One can hardly mistake these topoi
from StM; it is as if the prospector-hero finds himself in the
chaotic environment of the "terrible world."   In this respect SS
serves as allegorical warning to the poet–hero of the "trilogy."
     The path from which the protagonist of SS temporarily strays
is of course a metaphor for the routine of life, but more specifically
it represents the "life-myth" that Blok by now is so close to
concluding.   The fact that it is called a *stony* path ("O puti
kamenistom," "Put' . . . *kremnist*") (IV, VII) tends to confirm this
because   the   metaphoric   equivalency   "stone=poetic   word"   was
certainly known to Blok even in the period of the first volume:

            Ей в мире оставлю мою свечу,
            Оставлю мой камень, мой здешний звон.

            Поставлю на страже звенящий стих.
            Зеленый камень Ей в сердце зажгу.
            И камень будет Ей друг и жених,
            И Ей не солжет, как я не лгу.   (RAS #46) (I, 286)

It appears again   in an unfinished draft of the poem "Osennjaja
volja":

            В белый день в очах проснулась мгла
            И прильнула . . . . .
            И в камнях слова произнесла.   (II, 400)

The image of the "stony path" (or "stone path"), however, has
other relevant associations as well. "Stone roads," for instance, are
designated in the first volume as those which will lead ultimately
to the meeting with the Beautiful Lady:

> Тебя я встречу где-то в мире,
> За далью <u>каменных</u> <u>дорог</u>.
> На страшном, на последнем пире
> Для нас готовит встречу бог. (SPD #141) (I, 214) [66]

In the period of the second volume, moreover, the "stone path" is
associated with movement through the homeland, as for instance in
the essay "Bezvremen'e" ("*kamennyj put'* po beskrajnim ravninam
Rossii") (V, 73) or in the poem "Osennjaja volja":

> Выхожу я в <u>путь</u>, открытый взорам,
> Ветер гнет упругие кусты,
> Битый <u>камень</u> лег по косогорам,
> Желтой глины скудные пласты.
> . . . .
> Кто взманил меня на <u>путь</u> знакомый,
> Усмехнулся мне в окно тюрьмы?
> Или—<u>каменным</u> <u>путем</u> влекомый
> Нищий, распевающий псалмы?
>
> Нет, иду я в <u>путь</u> никем не званый,
> И земля да будет мне легка!
> <u>Буду</u> <u>слушать</u> <u>голос</u> <u>Руси</u> пьяной,
> Отдыхать под крышей кабака.   (RazSt II #36)(II, 75)

From the two poems just quoted it is apparent also that the
"stone path" is a final path, apparently a path leading to death
("Na strašnom, na poslednem pire...", "I zemlja da budet mne
legka!").   It is not implausible, therefore, to make the association
"kremnistyj put'=krestnyj put' = ternistyj put'," as does G.
Levinton; [67] this path is also in a sense the road to Calvary, the
path of Christ's martyrdom. The prominence of "thorns" at the
entrance to the nightingale garden" ("koljučie rozy," "šipy") lends
credence to this possibility.   One is tempted, therefore, to draw
an analogy between the brief detour from the "path" in SS and
Christ's visit to the Garden of Gethsemane.   In both cases there is
hesitation and reconsideration before continuing along the course
mapped out by fate and the word.

The theme of the path in ROD develops logically from its treatment earlier in the hemivolume. The image of the "stone path" reappears ("Na puti—gorjučij belyj *kamen"*), although its more common manifestation is the "highway" ("put' *šossejnyj*," "*šosse*"); a close analogue to the highway is the image of the railroad, which appears twice. What these and most other paths in ROD have in common are those features which gradually emerged as dominant in AS. They are *straight* ("Naš put' streloj..."*, "Ne vernut'sja*, ne vzgljanut' nazad"), *open* ("poezd v dal' umčalo," "My idem po žniv'ju, ne speša..."), *long* (and sometime difficult) ("doroga dolgaja," "v dali dorožnoj," "rasxljabannye kolei"). As in AS the idea of passing *through* the landscape becomes especially emphatic in the latter half of the cycle ("*Dal'še, dal'še...*"; "put' šossejnyj, probegaja *mimo,/Mimo* inoka, prudov i zvezd"; "*Mimo, mimo*, navsega/ . . . /I kogda projdet vse *mimo*..."); thus movement along the path develops a certain momentum, a certain propelling force. It is, specifically, a path through the *steppe* (the words "step'"/"stepnoj" appear seventeen times)—a detail which, coupled with its straightness, seems to recall Isaiah and the Gospel:

3   Глас вопиющего в пустыне: приготовьте <u>путь</u> Господу, <u>прямыми</u> <u>сделайте</u> <u>в</u> <u>степи</u> <u>стези</u> Богу нашему;

4   . . . <u>кривизны</u> <u>выпрямятся</u>, и неровные пути сделаются гладкими.

(Isaiah, 40:3-4)

3   Ибо он тот, о котором сказал пророк Исаия: "глас вопиющего в пустыне: приготовьте путь Господу, <u>прямыми</u> <u>сделайте</u> <u>стези</u> Ему".   (Matthew 3:3)

The fact that the poet identifies with Christ in the cycle's first poem ("Mne—nevoskresšemu Xristu") and his words are indeed spoken by "a voice . . . in the wilderness" ("i ja v *pustyne*") make this subtext all the more relevant.

The poet's intended destination is very clearly some locus of meeting with the Lady whether in death ("Ta, kogo ljubil ty mnogo,/Povedet rukoj ljubimoj/V Elisejskie polja"), in marriage ("Tam menja nevesta ždet") or simply at the crossing of paths ("Da, nočnye puti, rokovye,/Razveli nas i vnov' sveli"). The last scenario was predicted in "Pesnja Sud'by" by the departure of

Elena in pursuit of German. In the third volume it is prepared by
the beloved's exit from the "home" in VOZ. In ROD discovery of
the cosmic "path" is already no longer at issue. The dialectic
between chaos and cosmos manifests itself rather in the problem of
arriving at a destination, a restored "home"—a path without end
is still a function of chaos. This is conveyed quite vividly in NPK
I:

Река раскинулась. Течет, грустит лениво
    И моет берега.
Над скудной глиной желтого обрыва
    В степи грустят стога.

О, Русь моя! Жена моя! До боли
    Нам ясен долгий путь!
Наш путь—стрелой татарской древней воли
    Пронзил нам грудь.

Наш путь—степной, наш путь—в тоске безбрежной,
    В твоей тоске, о, Русь!
И даже мглы—ночной и зарубежной—
    Я не боюсь.

Пусть ночь. Домчимся. Озарим кострами
    Степную даль.
В степном дыму блеснет святое знамя
    И ханской сабли сталь...

И вечный бой! Покой нам только снится
    Сквозь кровь и пыль...
Летит, летит степная кобылица
    И мнет ковыль...

И нет конца! Мелькают версты, кручи...
    Останови!
Идут, идут испуганные тучи,
    Закат в крови!

Закат в крови! Из сердца кровь струится!
    Плачь, сердце, плачь...
Покоя нет! Степная кобылица
    Несется вскачь.

The first stanza depicts an ordered, bounded world. The river flows within its borders ("moet berega"); hay is gathered neatly into stacks ("stoga"); a ravine demarcates the landscape ("obryv"). The image of the "path" in the second through fourth stanzas disturbs the serene quiet of the preceding scene, but in the treatment of the "path" there is still a sense of ordering space—the "path" is clear ("jasen"), straight ("streloj"); it cuts through the unbordered steppe without yielding to its entropy; and it will come to an end ("Domčimsja"). Despite the poet's agitation he has no fear ("ja ne bojus'"). The mood of the last three stanzas is dramatically different. The assurance of boundaries is suddenly lost—blood gushes from the heart ("iz serdca krov' struitsja") unlike the water contained within the riverbanks in stanza I; the poet and his environment become one ("zakat v krovi"); the discreteness of the road is replaced by the unbridled mare trampling the steppe grass (compare "stoga"); the road and time are deprived of end ("I večnyj boj," "I net konca"). The verb "Ostanovi!", unlike "Domčimsja" earlier, conveys a desperate plea for an end rather than faith in its inevitability.

This same desperation is evident repeatedly in ROD:

> Только ль страшный простор пред очами,
> Непонятная ширь <u>без конца</u>?
> . . . .
> Путь степной—<u>без конца, без исхода</u>,
> Степь, да ветер, да ветер . . .
>
> (ROD #19) (III, 268-269)

———

> <u>Безысходна</u>, величава,
> <u>Бесконечна</u>...Что <u>ж, конец</u>?
> Нет... еще леса, поляны,
> И проселки, и шоссе . . .   (ROD #21)(III, 273)

It is significant that here, as in StM, boundlessness and enclosure are equated, and their continued alliance undercuts whatever solace location within the homeland tends to offer. In a sense, the landscape of ROD is still part of the "terrible world," and only the straight path that traverses it gives hope that the chaotic environment will eventually be left behind. The thought that this path may have no end, no destination is a perpetual source of anxiety.

A sense of uneasiness carries through to the cycle's conclusion.

As we saw, the last two poems of ROD are set in "homes" that can hardly be called cosmic. Sitting alone in a house whose shudders are torn asunder by the wind or reincarnate as a child whom the circling predator waits to attack, the lyric hero is given little peace at the end of his path. As the artist who shaped that path, Blok, however, was free to do as he pleased. And Blok gave his hero peace.

"O čem poet veter": The Cosmic "Home"

"O čem poet veter" (OČPV), a grouping of six poems written in October 1913, is the most neglected and perhaps the least understood cycle in Blok's third volume. In discussions of Blok's poetry it is customary to skip directly from ROD to the *poèma* "Dvenadcat'" (which is not part of the "trilogy"), apparently because both deal with history and the Revolution. When OČPV is mentioned, it is invariably seen as a pessimistic piece.[68] Rarely is there any effort to account for its location at the very end of the third volume. Gorelov's comment that it is "tacked on as an afterthought" ("primostivšegosja na otšibe") says little for Blok's diligence as a cyclist.[69] Maksimov makes a more serious attempt to explain its location, pointing to Blok's apparent concern that "light" and "dark," "personal" and "national" sentiments be dispersed more or less evenly throughout the volume; the "gloomy" and intimate statement Maksimov sees in OČPV is deemed to balance out the uplifting mood and social content of ROD.[70]

This explanation, however, also misses the mark. If one reads OČPV in the context of all that precedes it, this small cycle is a perfectly conceived ending to the third volume specifically and the "trilogy" as a whole. Though not exactly optimistic, OČPV is beatific in that it grants peace simultaneously to the lyric hero and to his maker, the poet. Moreover it brings to a close the ongoing dialectic between chaos and cosmos.

To understand this it is useful to recall Tjutšev's poem "O čem ty voeš', vetr nočnoj?..." from which Blok derived the title of his cycle. Tjutčev's lyric—one of Blok's favorites—is about the chaos that inhabits the natural elements and the human soul, bringing them together in a common, indissoluble bond:

О чем ты воешь, ветр ночной?

О чем так сетуешь безумно?..
Что значит странный голос твой,
То глухо жалобный, то шумно?
Понятным сердцу языком
Твердишь о непонятной муке—
И роешь и взрываешь в нем
Порой неистовые звуки!..

О, странных песен сих не пой
Про древний хаос, про родимый!
Как жадно мир души ночной
Внимает повести любимой!
Из смертной рвется он груди,
Он с беспредельным жаждет слиться!..
О, бурь заснувших не буди—
По ними хаос шевелиться!

Chaos is terrifying because it abhors all boundaries and survives only by rupturing or erasing them. Cosmos, though not mentioned in the poem, is obviously embodied by the boundaries themselves. For Tjutčev, chaos (symbolized by the sound of the wind) is the stronger force; the human soul finds the attraction of this kindred element irresistible—hence the poet's desperate plea for the wind to stop singing.

For Blok, by contrast, cosmos proves to be the superior force, and OČPV narrates its victory over the opposite element. It does so, moreover, in two different ways, on two different planes simultaneously. For the lyric hero and his beloved the cycle's plot unfolds on a real (and symbolic) plane; for the poet and his muse the cycle's action is allegorical. All four actors are brought together in OČPV for the final resolution of their "life drama."

For the lyric hero and his beloved OČPV realizes the metaphor on which the third volume is based—it makes the architecture of the volume into a real home with four walls that provide the security, the protection from the elements and the companionship that was forfeited when the ideal home was abandoned. In a sense, it allows the path, which was indeed traveled to the end, to become that home it was intended to restore. This is not hard to understand if one considers that the hero and his beloved, for the first time in the third volume, are pictured together inside a cosmic environment—a warm and cozy house ("v teple," "v . . . teplom uglu," "vozle mirnogo ognja")

(#1, #3). The fact that it is called a "quiet" place ("tixon'ko," "v ètom tixom dome") recalls the tranquil home from which they once exited. The poet, however, has devised for his hero one final trial, one final conflict with the chaotic elements—as if to test the soundness of the new walls. Once again a storm begins to rage outside the house. The wind howls. The hero contemplates committing suicide by running out into the snowstorm. And then the cosmic environment begins to disintegrate. Fever grips the hero, and the home is invaded again by threatening visitors—first Azrael, the angel of death, and then the cold wind and Eros, who wounds the hero with his arrow. But finally we are told that all of this was just a fantasy; it occurred elsewhere ("Bylo to v temnyx Karpatax,/Bylo v Bogemii dal'nej") (#6). The home is secure, the walls are safe, and the hero lulls his beloved off to peaceful sleep. Read this way, on this level, OČPV is a story about a real home and its real inhabitants.

On another level it can be read as an allegory about the poet and his muse. Here again there is a struggle between chaos and cosmos, but now the two forces are manifest, respectively, as a new lyric impulse and an already established artistic design. The lines of the conflict are already drawn in the opening poem:

За окном, как тогда, огоньки
6   Милый друг, мы с тобой старики.

. . . .
Смотришь, точно ты хочешь прочесть
10   Там какую-то новую весть?

. . . .
Только стены, да книги, да дни.
14   Милый друг мой, привычны они.

. . . .
Только, вот, принялась ты опять
18   Светлый бисер на нитки низать,

Как когда-то, ты помнишь тогда...
. . . .
24   Так возьми ж и теперь попестрей,

Чтобы шелк, что вдеваешь в иглу,
26   Побеждал пестротой эту мглу.

(OČPV #1) (III, 282-283)

There may appear to be nothing allegorical here, but the equivalency "*steny*, da *knigi*, da *dni*" (line 13) must raise an eyebrow. Could not the "walls" represent the architecture of the volume (or the "trilogy") and the "days" represent the life-myth that is incorporated within it? Why else would the "threading" of colorful "beads" (line 18) tend to subvert the order that the "walls" symbolize? It will be recalled from our discussion of SnM in the preceding chapter that "threading" can be a metaphor for poetic speech ("*Niti* snežnye tku i pletu"). It can be noted also that the image of "beads" ("busy," "biser") or "pearls" is not uncommonly associated in Blok with the sounds of the muse, the poetic word:

> Понемногу он погружается в синеву воспоминаний.
> По их <u>нити</u> он уходит в глубокую ночь. . . .тут
> же—<u>жемчужные</u> <u>речи</u>, бормочущие. . . .
>
> (ZK, 173)

> Скоро для поэзии наступят средние века. Поэты . . .
> Вернутся к самому обаятельному источнику поэзии,
> снижут <u>нити</u> из всех <u>жемчугов</u>—морского дня, и го-
> рода, и <u>ожерелья</u> девушек каждой страны.[71]

> Зачем она приходит
> Со мною говорить?
> Зачем в иглу проводит
> <u>Веселенькую</u> <u>нить</u>?
> Зачем она роняет
> <u>Веселые</u> <u>слова</u>?   (G #39) (II, 200)

> Ветер, снежный север,
> . . . .
> Подари ей зори,
> <u>Бусы,</u> жемчуга!   (G #43) (II, 205-206)

Nor does this association belong to Blok alone; consider, for instance, Gumilev's poetic collection *Zemčuga* (1910), the cover of which depicts a multitude of pearl necklaces, or Axmatova's *Četki* (1914). Might not the suggestion to take more colorful threads ("voz'mi . . . *popestrej*") (line 24) also allude to the "colors" of lyric (cf. "perelivčatyx *krasok* i *slov*"; "*Poju* ja, seryj *solovej*,/V moej temnice *mnogocvetnoj*") (I, 186, 197)?

In OČPV #2 the theme of lyric poetry is made explicit; the sounds of the "wind" and the "lyre" are one ("I *lira*/Poet nam sneg/Sedoj zimy"). The "wind," the "lyre" and indeed the unnamed muse are allied as if in conspiracy against the order that the cozy home represents. This is why the poet, as he becomes more enamored of the sound, is tempted to race out of the home into the stormy elements ("Tuda, tuda,/Na snegovuju grud'..."). In poem #3 the bounds of the home are already violated by Azrael, who situates himself, not surprisingly, directly behind the muse:

> За твоими тихими плечами
>   Слышу трепет крыл...
> Бьет в меня светящими очами
>   Ангел бури—Азраил!   (OČPV #3) (III, 286)

The reference to the poet's "fever" earlier in the same poem "*Lixoradka* b'et menja") can also be interpreted as a metaphor for inspiration; compare Mandel'štam's "*gorjačka solovjnaja*"[73] or an image from Axmatova's poem "Muza" ("Tajny remesla"): "[Muza] Žestče, čem *lixoradka*, ottreplet."

OČPV #4 apparently describes a fireworks display occurring outside the poet's window:[73]

> Из ничего—фонтаном синим
>   Вдруг брызнул свет.
> . . . .
> Зеленый, желтый, синий, красный—
>   Вся ночь в лучах...
> И, всполошив ее напрасно,
>   Зачах.   (OČPV #4) (III, 287)

Reading these lines, one is naturally reminded of Blok's attacks on lyric poetry in 1907-1908:

> [Lyric poets] possess immeasurable wealth, but to you, people, they will give nothing except *momentary colorful splashes*...
>
> (V, 132)

In every contemporary man are implanted *lyric fireworks which . . . explode suddenly and disappear without a trace.*

(V, 229)

> The fact is that the demand for works of art can indeed
> ignite *sparks of inspiration*, in fact *fleeting sparks* which are
> never destined to turn into a great flame. . . . Hundreds of
> young people have suddenly become artist (NB: these are
> almost without exception *lyric poets* . . .).

(V, 235)

These remarks recall Blok's statements in the preface to *Liričeskie dramy*, and their gist is the same: every lyric immersed the poet in a chaos of unregulated associations. For the architect of the "trilogy" each new creative impulse threatened to disrupt the carefully wrought plan.

OČPV #5 and #6 provide an ingenious solution to this dilemma and a fitting denouement to the allegory. In #5 the lyric is disarmed by its own means—the poet uses a lyric "fairy-tale" ("skazka") to lull his muse to sleep. In #6, the last poem, he refuses to become an actor in the "fairy-tale," he separates himself from the "tale's" protagonist and his own life from events in the "tale":

> Это—отрывок случайный,
> Это—из жизни <u>другой</u> мне
> Жалобный ветер напел...   (OČPV #6) (III, 290)

This is the antithesis of what happened in SnM, where the poet lost himself in "tales" of his own creation ("Ax, *vy sami v skazke, rycar'!*"), and it reverses the predicament in which he found himself at the beginning of third volume ("*strašnyj mir,/Gde ja brodil slepoj, kak v dikoj skazke*")("Pesn' Ada"). To become part of the "tale" means to render up life to the wind's chaotic melodies, to sacrifice the design of the "poet" to the spontaneous visions of "singer." In OČPV Blok resists this urge and keeps the walls of his house intact against the entropy of the wind. Unlike Tjutčev, however, he does not attempt to silence wind's song:

> Жди, старый друг, терпи, терпи,
> Терпеть недолго, крепче спи,
>   Всё равно всё пройдет,
>
> Всё равно ведь никто не поймет,
> Ни тебя не поймет, ни меня,

Ни что ветер поет
  Нам звеня...   (OČPV #6)(III, 290)

These the final words of the "trilogy" cap the lyric impulse but do
not check the source of its power. The elements are banished
from the home, but they continue "ringing" ("zvenja..."). The
poet cannot stifle the wind, but he can hold his own silence. As
Blok wrote at the time he conceived the "trilogy": "Having
established the inner linkage of events, I shall consider it my duty
to become silent" (V, 426).

At the beginning of this chapter I quoted Sophie Bonneau's
remark that Blok's life in the period of the third volume was
"chaotic."   Bonneau herself, as she acknowledges, borrowed this
observation from an essay by the poet   Georgij Čulkov, Blok's
personal acquaintance. She quotes, however, only part of Čulkov's
statement.   Indeed Čulkov speaks of "chaos," Blok's "terrible
stranger," but he also says something else: "The more tempestuous
and painful Blok's inner life was, the more insistently he strove to
create coziness and order in his home. Blok had two lives—one
routine, domestic, quiet; the other erratic, unsettled, intoxicated.
In Blok's home there was order . . ."[74] One can draw an analogy
between life and art. Just as in life Blok existed in two
antithetical spheres, so too in poetry he served two competing
idols—chaos and cosmos. Whereas in life, however, he could keep
the two spheres discrete, in poetry the conflicting forces had to be
reconciled to some degree—even if complete reconciliation was
impossible. To make lyric conform neatly to a pre-conceived
scheme was to rob lyric of its spontaneity. To allow each lyric to
be an entirely separate imprint of inspiration's momentary flight,
on the other hand, was to ignore the linkage of time and sacrifice
the "life drama" to the inarticulate harmonies of the wind. The
vehicle the mature Blok found to preserve the tension between
these forces and make their interaction esthetically meaningful is
the design he conceived for the third volume.

VI

CONCLUSION

Жизнь—без начала и конца.
Нас всех подстерегает случай.
. . . .
Но ты, художник, твердо веруй
В начала и концы. . .
—A. Blok, Prologue to "Vozmezdie"

Их давит власть бездонных слов...
—N. Gumilev, "Proroki"

Osip Mandel'štam wrote that Blok was "a man of the nineteenth
century" and that his "fate was linked most intimately with
nineteenth-century Russian poetry."[1] In Mandel'štam's view,
however, Russian symbolism, which Blok embodied more fully than
any other poet, was "the womb of all modern Russian poetry"; "all
contemporary Russian poetry emerged from the native womb of
symbolism."[2] There is no real contradiction in these statements.
In essence Mandel'štam is saying that Blok's poetic legacy spans
the gap between two centuries and epitomizes their interconnection.
The key to understanding this lies to a large degree in Blok's use
of the lyric cycle and in the concept of his lyric "trilogy."

There is no need here to reiterate all that was said in
Chapter 2 about Blok's kinship with the nineteenth-century poetic
tradition. It will suffice to recall that Blok was raised in an
environment where old-fashioned literary tastes prevailed, where
Baudelaire (1821-67) was considered very nearly an avant-garde
poet. In childhood he was exposed primarily to poetry of the early
and mid-nineteenth century, to which he developed a life-long
attachment. Familiarity with the bulk of Vl. Solov'ev's poetry
came only in 1901; genuine acquaintance with Bal'mont and
Brjusov *as cyclists* occurred only in 1903. Blok's earliest lessons in

the contextuality of separate lyrics came from Žukovskij, Grigor'ev, Apuxtin, Polonskij, Fet, probably Heine and perhaps Baudelaire.

That Blok cited Žukovskij as his "first inspiration" (VII, 12) is hardly incidental to the contextuality characteristic of Blok's earliest lyrics and to the ultimate unification of his lyric oeuvre into a "trilogy of incarnation." Žukovskij was the first Russian poet to cultivate the image of a lyric hero and amalgamate a body of poetry into something resembling "a novel of the soul" (Gukovskij). Žukovskij's poetry initiated a phenomenon in Russian literature which Jurij Lotman characterizes quite accurately in his biography of Puškin:

> The idea that a poet's life, his personality and fate merge with his creative work, creating for the public a certain unified whole, belongs to the period of Romanticism.
>
> First pre-romanticism and later romanticism saw in the poet above all a genius whose unique and independent spirit was manifest in the originality of his work. A poet's collected work began to be seen as a single huge autobiographical novel in which his separate poems and poetic narratives formed chapters, while his biography served as its plot.[3]

In a very real sense Blok's "trilogy" represents the culmination and fulfillment of this inclination on a much larger scale than was envisioned by his predecessors. It emerges, most basically, from the tendency of the romantic poet to see his collective lyric output as a kind of "history of my passions" (Batjuškov), "a whole tale of your fate" (Puškin on Jazykov's elegies), or "songs in which my life is reflected" (Baratynskij).

In formulating his "trilogy," however, Blok faced a more formidable task than his early nineteenth-century antecedents—in part because he was more prolific as a lyric poet than most of them, in part because the idea that a poet's collected lyrics comprised a single "tale" or "history" was for his romantic counterparts a vague, or at best an embryonic metaphoric concept that carried few concrete obligations and was actualized literally only on a relatively small scale (in a few short collections or in cycles containing an archetypal plot). Blok, by contrast, adopted the idea as a binding esthetic imperative and attempted to realize it on a grand scale. No poet of the nineteenth century ever insisted, as Blok did, on fashioning a coherent biography for his lyric hero out of 765 poems (and two *poèmy*) written over a span of 19 years.

In doing so Blok followed Brjusov's model to some extent (the preface to *Urbi et Orbi*), but more meaningful ultimately are the "trilogy's" ties with *Evgenij Onegin*. One will recall that the preface and notes to the first edition of the "trilogy" contained direct reminiscences from Puškin's "novel in verse": "Vsju trilogiju ja mogu nazvat' *'romanom v stixax'*"; "Četvertaja glava (1901) . . . est' tot *'magičeskij kristall'*, *skvoz'* kotoryj ja *različil vpervye*, xotja i *'nejasno'*, vsju *'dal' svobodnuju* [in Puškin: 'svobodnogo'] *romana'"* (I, 559-560) (cf. *Evgenij Onegin*, VIII.1).

The conceptual parallels between these two works are striking despite their obvious differences in form and content. To begin with, the very prominence of the lyric strain in Puškin's novel gives it a certain kinship with Blok's "trilogy." By this I have in mind first of all the abundance of digressions in *Evgenij Onegin*, which continually focus the reader's attention on the poet as personality, his views on subjects from wines to literary currents, his evolving self-image. Indeed there is much validity to the view that the novel's central concern is the spiritual and literary development of the narrator, and on a certain level even the protagonists function as allegorical projections of his biographical concerns (Onegin's identification with "prose," Lenskij's with romantic poetry, and Tat'jana's with the Muse). Beyond this there is the novel's "lyric disorder" and fragmentation. Written over a span of eight years (1823-30) and published intermittently (a complete text appeared only in 1833), the novel was plagued by inconsistencies and contradictions which, in Lotman's view, Puškin exploited to esthetic ends:

> Both publication of the text in installments and the fact that in the course of the novel's creation the author changed, the reader changed, the epoch changed, were to a significant degree circumstances extraneous to Puškin's original conception of the work. Specific characteristics of the novel took shape spontaneously and were motivated only subsequently by the poet as a conscious principle. . . . What appeared on occasion accidentally [*slučajno*] was turned into a deliberate compositional idea.

In the mind of the author a creative concept was
formulated according to which contradiction in the text
became an asset as such. Only an internally
contradictory text was perceived as adequate to the
depiction of reality.[4]

The dynamic of Blok's "trilogy" is similar. The individual lyric,
born of a separate creative experience, is "accidental" (*"slučajno"*)
in the sense that it does not conform ostensibly to the design of
the whole. Yet the presence of "chance" (*"slučaj"*) mimics the
unpredictability of real life and therefore contributes to the
impression of verisimilitude. The grand scheme of the "trilogy"
with its relentless movement from beginning to middle to end in
pseudo-chronological sequence ultimately gains preponderance over
individual inconsistencies and subordinates them to the overall
pattern of inevitability. "Chance" is a category that is
progressively transmuted by the category of necessity and fate. As
Maksimov observes, Blok's "trilogy" "elevated 'the accidental' to
the level of 'the inevitable'."[5]

There is another meaningful similarity. In *Onegin*, as
Bočarov pointed out, author (creator) and hero (created) converge
within the same plane of reality—"the depiction of life has been
mixed with life itself."[6] In Blok's "trilogy" too the boundary
between empirical life and life represented in art is mobile—the
poet-author is both separate from and at the same time one with
his lyric hero. The paradox is signaled by the fact that Blok
subscribed every poem in the "trilogy" with its date of
composition. On one hand, dating symbolized the distance
separating the author from his hero in that the sequence of
creative events—the chronology of writing—did not coincide
entirely with the sequence of events "as if in time" in the life of
the lyric hero. Significantly, the two "chronologies" become
increasingly disparate from volume to volume: in the third
displacements of empirical time reach their apogee, suggesting that
the final stage in the biography of the lyric hero bears the least
resemblance to the biographical reality of the author. In this
respect the "trilogy" confirms a remark Blok recorded in
Čukovskij's journal on March 13, 1919: "Art cannot be reconciled
with life."[7] On the other hand, dating each poem within the text
registered the act of creation simultaneously as empirical and
esthetic fact. The experience recorded in any given poem was not

only an event in the life of the lyric hero, but a spiritual event in the life of the author inasmuch as it is ascribed to a specific point in real time. Thus during the act of creation the persona of the author-poet and the persona of the hero converged. For Blok, as for Puškin, this periodic convergence carried in fact extra-literary significance. The biography narrated in the "trilogy" belonged no less to Blok as author than it did to his lyric hero as protagonist.[8] Indeed the life Blok lived vicariously through his lyric hero in many ways made more sense than his own, and it compensated psychologically for the despair that rarely left him in his later years.

If the "trilogy" was allied to nineteenth-century tradition and to one of its major literary landmarks, it also epitomized the new attitude toward the poetic word epoused by the second generation of symbolists at the beginning of the twentieth century. The two principal mottoes of this generation were formulated by Vjačeslav Ivanov: 1) "A symbol is a genuine symbol only when its meaning is inexhaustible and boundless"; 2) "From symbol is born myth."[9]

From the very outset of his career, in his *Verses about the Beautiful Lady*, Blok discovered the dynamic that fulfilled Ivanov's first dictum—although Blok did so, it seems, independently and without any effort to follow a specific theoretical precept. The principle that any word carries as part of its semantic potential the implications it acquires in "migrations" through other texts in effect made the poetic word "inexhaustible," "boundless" in its possible meanings. In Blok's first volume the denotative function of many key words (e.g., "belyj," "stupeni," "dver'," "pyl'") is diminished or even eclipsed; the word begins to serve as an index of its other usages. This phenomenon, as we saw, had the effect of secreting the poetic message and drawing the reader (as well as the poet) deep into the fluctuating medium of the intertext. Anyone who reads Blok's early poetry and attempts to master its complex code can appreciate from experience the wisdom of Paul Valéry's observation in "Man and the Sea Shell" (1937): "Leaf through a dictionary or try to make one, and you will find that every word covers and masks a well so bottomless that the questions you toss into it arouse no more than an echo."[10]

In the second volume Blok enlists the cycle to regulate the verbal dynamic he uncovered in the first and gradually lost control over, wandering in the echo chamber of his own early verse. The smaller cycles of the second volume focused the contextual interaction of his poetry and confined the "bottomless" word to a narrower field of signification. Words still served a deciphering function, but their "migrations" were limited to a smaller body of texts. Moreover the introduction of plot, especially in "Snežnaja Maska," made the word into a mytheme; thus cyclization realized Ivanov's maxim "from symbol is born myth."

Blok's third volume is more accessible than the first or the second. Most of it can be understood without knowledge of the earlier poetry because words function largely denotatively and with connotative associations not necessarily specific to the "trilogy." Nevertheless reading it with an awareness of a given word's (or motif's) history in Blok's mythology greatly enhances one's appreciation of almost any particular lyric. By example one could cite the famous poem "Noč', ulica, fonar', apteka..." from the cycle "Pljaski smerti." There are different ways of approaching this poem, depending on whether one considers it in isolation (as a "closed" text) or with a view toward the various cyclic framings that contain it. Reading it in isolation gives access to a certain level of meaning—there is nothing especially cryptic in its symbolism. Reading it as part of the subcycle PS and the macrocycle "Strašnyj mir" already adds other levels of meaning —the landscape becomes a symbolic analogue to the lyric hero's predicament in the "terrible world." If we read the poem as part of its larger contextual framework, however, it acquires much more resonance; almost every word-motif in the poem explodes with implications derived from its previous (and future) "migrations" through Blok's "novel in verse." Almost every word signals some aspect of the myth that unifies the "trilogy." It is impossible of course to itemize all these associations, but if we consider just the first three words in the first line, it becomes apparent how much information the broader context has encoded in them. "Noč'" carries associations that go back to the first volume (e.g., "Noč'ju sumračnoj i dikoj...") (I, 85), but it harks back more directly to the poet's romance with the Snow Mask in the second ("Kubok dolgoj strastnoj noči") (II, 222); it recalls in general the dilemma of the lyric hero in the third volume (e.g., "tropoj podzemnoj noči," "Ja brosil v noč' zavetnoe kol'co") (III, 15, 64) and prepares for the reaffirmation of faith in the cycle "Rodina" ("Pust' noč'. Domčimsja...") (III, 249). "Ulica" evokes the theme of the "path," which is crucial in the design of the third volume; as an intra-city and short thoroughfare, the "street" stands in apposition to the road through the steppe in ROD ("dolgij put'," "put' stepnoj")—a contrast that underscores the sense of enclosure in the poem. Nor is it irrelevant to trace the leitmotif of the path back to the first and second volumes, even where the comparison may be contrastive (e.g., "Tebja ja vstreču gde-to v mire/*Za dal'ju kamennyx dorog*"; "Vyxožu ja v *put' otkrytyj vzoram*") (I, 214; II, 36). *"Fonar"* carries sinister connotations that originate in the cycle "Gorod" (as for instance in the poems "Petr," "Legenda," "Nevidimka"), and as a form of weak, artificial illumination it an inadaquate substitute for the radiance that re-emerges late in the third volume (*"Ozarim kostrami*/Stepnuju dal'"; "Ty sošla, *v odežde svet strujaščej*")("Na pole Kulikovom").[11]   This is not to say that one must read the poem with these associations in mind, but it is apparent that the "trilogy," as a monumental cycle, forefronts and actualizes meanings that are not evident in the immediate context.

The poetic schools which eclipsed symbolism in the second decade of the twentieth century reacted vehemently against the semantic multivalence that was essential to Blok's cyclic method. Virtually every acmeist manifesto attacked the investment of the word with new meanings.   Nikolaj Gumilev complained about the "instability" of the symbolists' "words" ("zybkost' slov");[12] Sergej Gorodeckij and Mandel'štam developed this objection at some length:

> Symbolism tried to utilize the *word's fluctuations* [tekučest' slova]. . . . One and the same image means different things not only to different people but to the same person at different times.   The symbolists consciously set as their aim to exploit . . . these *fluctuations*, amplifying them in every possible way. . . . Forcing words to enter combinations not on one level but on many in unpredictable ways, the symbolists built their monument in violation of the laws of equilibrium. . . . For the acmeists a rose is again beautiful in and of itself, with its petals, its fragrance and color, and without its resemblance to mystical love or anything else. (Gorodeckij)[13]

> Let's take as an example a rose and the sun, a dove and a girl.   For the symbolist none of these images is interesting in and of itself, but rather a rose is the likeness of the sun, the sun is the likeness of a rose, a

dove is the likeness of a girl, a girl is the likeness of a dove.   Images are gutted like museum animals and stuffed with some other content.   Instead of a forest of symbols we have a taxidermist's workshop.

This is the point to which professional symbolism has led us. . . .   There is nothing real, nothing genuine left.   Just a terrifying contredanse of "correspondences" nodding to each other, an endless winking at one another.   Not a single clear word—only suggestions, unfinished statements. . . .   Acmeism arose as a counteraction: "Away with symbolism! Long live the real rose!"—such was its initial slogan. (Mandel'štam)[14]

The futurists also spoke out against the symbolists' use of language. In "Slovo kak takovoe" (1913) A. Kručenyx and V. Xlebnikov attacked Blok directly: "Recently some have tried to turn woman into the eternal feminine, the beautiful lady, and in the same way a skirt has become something mystical . . . . We believe that language ought to be above all a language and if it must remind one of something, then better it be a saw or the poisoned arrow of a savage."[15]   To be sure, there were certain points of agreement between the symbolists and futurists, but the futurist manifestoes contained little to suggest that the word ought to be used as Blok used it, as an integrator of a cyclic universe.   In Majakovskij's post-mortem tribute to Blok, one can detect a certain irony in the way he speaks about "Blok's word": "Some to this day cannot escape the charm of his enchanting verses—taking one of Blok's words they elaborate on it for whole pages, building on top of it all their poetic riches."[16]

There is nothing in the acmeist or futurist manifestoes to indicate a bias against cyclization per se, but in general the cycle was a less essential device for most poets of the immediate post-symbolist era than it had been for the symbolists.   It is difficult to make generalizations because the great poets whose careers began either just before or just after 1910—Osip Mandel'štam, Anna Axmatova, Vladimir Majakovskij, Boris Pasternak, Marina Cvetaeva—were quite divergent in creative method from the outset and, moreover, the poetic technique of each evolved with time.   It may be said, however, that with certain exceptions cyclization continued after 1910 largely by inertia and to the degree that it persisted, it was based for the most part on principles of contextuality quite different from those that were operative in Blok's lyrics.

There is a good deal of truth in D. Maksimov's observation that "the separate poems of the acmeists were as if emancipated from the sovereignty of the whole; each solidified within itself... The acmeists in contrast to the symbolists, no longer thought in terms of cycles."[17] Indeed, the major representatives of acmeism were not inherently cyclic poets, at least not early in their careers. Gumilev's poetic collections are rather weakly and impressionistically unified, although there are indications in his later books (*Koster, Ognennyj stolp*) that he might have developed into a more contextual poet had he lived beyond 1921. Axmatova's early collections have a certain contextuality based on an embracing dramatic situation and sometimes even plot, but their unity is not derived from the close linguistic interaction of separate texts; hers is a kind of contextuality reminiscent of the novelistic-diaristic formulations of Ogarev and Grigor'ev in the mid-nineteenth century. There is much substance to Boris Èjxenbaum's observation that Axmatova's early collections, read in sequence, have the quality of "a complex lyric novel" whose theme is the heroine's tragic, unrequited love.[18] But this unifying principle is not manifest, as certain scholars have argued, at the level of "symbols" or recurring words which acquire contextual meaning.[19] The separate lyrics of early Axmatova are not mutually informing in the same sense as Blok's. The poetry of the late Axmatova (from the late 1930's on) is a different matter.[20] In her *Sed'maja kniga* (1936-60), which appeared as part of the collection *Beg vremeni*, the interrelationship between separate lyrics is tighter, and we find a genuine interpenetration of meaning at the most elemental textual level rather than simply an all-embracing general concept; the groupings "Tajny remesla," "Šipovnik cvetet" and "Luna v zenite," for instance, are finely honed pieces of cyclic integration.[21] Axmatova's greatest cyclic achievement, however, is undoubtedly "Rekviem" (1935-43), wherein recurring motifs and lexemes suggest meaningful ways of realigning and juxtaposing dispersed textual segments—much as they do in the best cycles of Puškin and Blok.

Notwithstanding his remark about words becoming "stuffed museum animals," Mandel'štam came closer than any poet after Blok to reproducing the verbal dynamic which was the key to Blok's cyclicality. In Mandel'štam's poetry a number of leitmotifs (e.g., "lastočka," "soloma," "černyj," "suxoj," "dyšat'") acquire contextual associations which go beyond the bounds of the individual lyric and are often essential for deciphering the imagery in a particular poem.[22] Ginzburg is correct that "the meaning of Mandel'štam's images is determined by their concrete ties with context. . . . [Separate] lyrics . . . provide a key to each other's meaning. Each of them is a separate unit, and at the same time they are unified by recurring symbols that pass through all of Mandel'štam's poetry."[23] There is justification, therefore, in seeing his entire lyric oeuvre (and not only his lyrics) as "one entity, one large form."[24] Nevertheless the contextuality of Blok's poetry and that of Mandel'štam's are by no means identical. Taranovskij ascertains one essential difference when he points out that "in Blok single poems (and whole cycles and poèmy, as well) reveal various aspects of a symbol, and only the totality of all aspects gives a symbol its complex figurative meaning," whereas in Mandel'štam the meaning of recurring symbols "varies within rather narrow limits" that can be identified without allusion to every occurrence of an image.[25] The meaning of Mandel'štam's symbols can usually be paraphrased, whereas Blok's defy translation into abstract language. Another difference lies in the unrelenting self-consciousness of Blok as a cyclist and the zealousness with which he composed his collections. Blok was, on the whole, a more deliberate architect of cycles than Mandel'štam—though it may well be that the circumstances under which Mandel'štam lived and wrote made it impossible for him to follow Blok's example even if he had wished to. *Kamen'* (1913) and *Stixotvorenija* (1928) are indeed well-constructed collections in which the poems' disposition is far from arbitrary, but *Tristia* (1922) and *Vtoraja kniga* (1923) are haphazard formulations (though not entirely through the fault of the author).[26] The precise composition of *Voronežskie tetradi* (1934-37), which may well be Mandel'štam's crowning achievement as a cyclist, remains in doubt.[27] Ultimate evaluation of Mandel'štam's contribution to cyclization, therefore, must await the work of textologists, but from available evidence he does not appear to have been a poet for whom the cycle was an essential tool. For him contextuality derives basically from the interaction of individual poems that form "internal cycles" whose precise composition was not generally specified by the poet himself; this is especially true of his "twin-poems" ("dvojčatki"), as for instance "Aja-Sofija" and "Notre Dame" or "Iz omuta zlogo i vjazkogo..."

and "V ogromnom omute prozračno i temno...".[28]

Majakovskij, though a reformer of poetic technique, was by no means an innovator when it came to the lyric cycle. The collection of his works he prepared just before death (published 1927-33)[29] represents in part a return to the generic cyclization of the eighteenth century ("Satira," "Lirika," "Agitstixi," "Reklama"), in part a reliance on conventional grouping by theme ("Revoljucija," "Byt," "Iskusstvo kommuny"), locale ("Zapad," "Stixi ob Amerike") or chronology. There are indeed a number of cyclic gems ("Ja" and "Vojna" for instance in the first volume), but Majakovskij was not by nature a poet for whom cyclicality or even the contextuality of separate lyrics played an especially important role. As for Blok's influence in this regard there is hardly any useful avenue of comparison.

By contrast Pasternak, who was allied with Majakovskij early in his career, has a certain kinship with Blok in the domain of cyclization. *Sestra moja—žizn'* (1922), as Katherine O'Connor demonstrates, is a richly integrated collection that resembles in some respects a novel—the book's ten cycles function as chapters of an unfolding narrative.[30] The structural principle of *Tema i variacii* (1923) is more that of a musical composition, as its title suggests. Here Pasternak comes very close to Blok's technique in that repeated words (e.g., "skala," "pesok," "pustynja"), particularly in the section "Tema s variacijami," unify the poems on the microstructural level and acquire contextual meaning that carries from one lyric to another. This same principle is operative in "Stixotvorenija Jurija Živago" (1946-53), where certain leitmotifs (e.g., the road, the sky, life, the seasons) are meticulously and meaningfully orchestrated; the cycle is so well-integrated that it can be read and appreciated independently from the novel to which it is appended. There is reason to agree, therefore, with Ginzburg's observation that "Russian poetry, as it took shape after the symbolists and in reaction against the symbolists, nevertheless could not forget what they had discovered—the associative intensity of the poetic word, its new semantic multivalence, multilayeredness."[31] This is true for poets like Axmatova, Mandel'štam and Pasternak—but not at the very beginning of their careers. These poets only gradually rediscovered the verbal potential that the symbolists (and Blok in particular) had revealed to them.

After Blok there is no Russian poet for whom the cycle was a more intrinsic means of expression than Marina Cvetaeva. In 1933 she remarked about her own method: "I almost do not write [separate] verses—they emerge for me in families, in cycles, like funnels or even whirlpools into which I fall."[32] As the metaphor of "falling" into a "whirlpool" suggests, Cvetaeva usually wrote each of her cycles with the intensity of a sustained creative impulse, much as Blok wrote "Snežnaja Maska" and "Dvenadcat'." Her cycles were rarely the product of post factum editing.

As a rule Cvetaeva's cycles are unified by a dramatic situation that modulates from poem to poem, sometimes with the effect of generating a certain plot. In this respect her technique is not unlike Blok's, but there are also substantive differences. All of Blok's poetry in essence develops a single myth of the author's own creation—the ongoing saga of his relationship with the Lady. To some degree every poem reaches back beyond its own bounds and beyond the bounds of the cycle that contains it to this central, invariable mythic construct. Cvetaeva, by contrast, utilizes a wide variety of different myths (broadly understood), each of which is borrowed and each of which is specific to a given cycle alone. Taking a dramatic situation from folklore, literature or history, Cvetaeva uses it to convey her own spiritual experience and to transform biographical reality into something mythic. In "Stixi k dočeri" (1916-19), for instance, Cvetaeva superimposes the biographical reality of her relationship with her daughter onto the borrowed mythic situation of the Virgin Mother's love for the Christ Child. In "Marina" (1921), which is about her attitude toward the Revolution, the mythic situation is Marina Mnišek's role in the Time of Troubles.[33] In "Georgij" (1921), which deals with her husband's participation in the Civil War, the borrowed myth is the legend of St. George, the dragon slayer. In "Stixi k Bloku" (1916-21) the biographical reality is Cvetaeva's desire to commune with Blok as a man and poet, while the borrowed situation is the very myth of Blok's "trilogy" in its various component scenarios.[34] The fact that on every occasion Cvetaeva focuses on a separate myth gives each of her cycles a more self-enclosed quality than we find in most of Blok's.

Cvetaeva, like Blok, wrote cycles that are integrated at the most minute level of textual structure, not just by an embracing concept as in those of early Axmatova. Separate poems tend to echo each other—not only in the recurrence of motifs and lexemes but in the very acoustic formulation of the text. The cycle

"Razluka" (1920), for example, encodes the sound of its title as an
anagram in its component lyrics:

I   У̲зких подошв—сл̲ед.
           Точно ру̲кой
           Сброшенный в ночь...

II   У̲роненные та̲к давно
      Взы̲маю ру̲ки.
      В пустое черное окно
      Пу̲стые ру̲ки
      Бросаю в полу̲ночный бой..

III   Всё кру̲че, всё кру̲че
      За̲ламывать ру̲ки!
      Меж нами не версты
      Земные,—Разлу̲ки
      Небесные ре̲ки, лазу̲рные земли...
      · · · · · · · · · · · · · · · ·
           Я ру̲к не л̲омаю!
           Я тол̲ько тяну их—
           Бе̲з зву̲ка!

V   Тихон̲ько
      Ру̲кой осторожной и тон̲кой
      Ра̲спутаю пу̲ты:
      Рученки̲,—и, ржанью
      Посл̲ушная, зашелестит амазон̲ка
      По звон̲ким, пустым ступеням ра̲сставанья.

VI   На всю твою му̲ку
      Раз̲зор—плач:
           —Брось ру̲ку!

VII   Ро̲стком серебряным
      Рвану̲лся ввысь.
      Чтоб не узр̲ел его
      Зевес—
      Мол̲ись!

The same phenomenon is quite pronounced in "Sugroby" (1922)
and some other groupings from the 1920's.   Such acoustical
resonances reduce the sense of the poems' discreteness and tend to

make many of Cvetaeva's cycles seem like extended lyric improvisations.

It is perhaps this very continuity of the lyric sequence that distinguishes Cvetaeva most from Blok. Progress through Blok's "trilogy" charts a graph of increasing disparity between life chronology and the arrangement of separate lyrics. If the first volume is a chronological diary about life's day-to-day experience, the third represents a consistent effort to redispose the sequence of events in life so as to fashion a satisfactory biography for the lyric hero. By contrast Cvetaeva's collections, as Simon Karlinsky points out, "constitute an uninterrupted lyrical diary of her experience and emotions between 1908 and 1925."[35] On the few occasions Cvetaeva adjusts life's chronology, she feels the need to explain, one might even say apologize to the reader for doing so, as for instance when she displaces the third poem in the cycle "Sivilla" (*Posle Rossii*): "The poem is transposed here from the future by virtue of its intrinsic kinship [with the other poems]."[36] Such a comment only underscores Cvetaeva's insistence elsewhere that the clock of art and the clock of life be synchronized, as if to suggest that there exists between them an inviolable correspondence.

Undoubtedly, both Cvetaeva and Blok experienced life in two different ways concurrently—as concrete existence and as poetic fantasy. Whereas Cvetaeva, however, continually reconciled the two by keeping them in constant synchronic balance, Blok was able to do so only after the fact—by making life lived reformulate itself into life as esthetic construct. His "trilogy" is, in essence, a monumental testimony of faith in the artist's ability to effect such things.

NOTES

PREFACE

[1]D.M. Pocepnja, *Proza A. Bloka: Stilističeskie problemy* (L: Izd. LGU, 1976), 134.

[2]Edward Stankiewicz, "Centripetal and Centrifrugal Structures in Poetry," *Semiotica*, No. 3/4 (1982), 231.

[3]Stankiewicz, 240.

CHAPTER ONE

[1]Helen M. Mustard, *The Lyric Cycle in German Literature* (New York: King's Crown Press, 1946), 1.

[2]V.A. Sapogov, "Liričeskij cikl i liričeskaja poèma v tvorčestve A. Bloka," in *Russkaja literatura XX veka (Dooktjabr'skij period)* (Kaluga: Tul'skij gos. ped. inst., 1968), 178.

[3]*Kratkaja literaturnaja ènciklopedija* (M:"Sovetskaja ènciklopedija," 1962–78), VIII, 398.

[4]Joachim Müller, "Das zyklische Prinzip in der Lyrik," *Germanisch-Romanische Monatsschrift*, XX, No. 1/2 (1932), 6–7.

[5]Müller, 7–8, 15.

[6]Müller, 2.

[7]Müller, 2, 13.

[8]L.K. Dolgopolov, *Poèmy Bloka i russkaja poèma konca XIX–načala XX vekov* (M–L: "Nauka," 1964), 13–14.

[9]Quoted by Gérard Genette, *Narrative Discourse: An Essay in Method*, trans. Jane E. Lewin (Ithaca, N.Y.: Cornell University Press, 1980), 149.

[10]While it might appear that such an interest falls victim to the so-called "intentional fallacy," one should not overlook that critical judgements about any work assume some level of intentionality. It would be an idle exercise to analyze *Crime and Punishment*, for instance, if we could not assume that the author intended the chapters contained therein to be part of the same novel. Here I am saying only that when a poet creates a cycle he intends the poems he includes to comprise a specific grouping, he outlines a context within which the poems are to be read. Once created, of course, the cycle may be interpreted in different ways, and the reader is at liberty to infer meanings which the author did not necessarily intend.

[11]F.G. Welcher, *Der epische Cyclus oder die homerischen Dichter*, Part I (Bonn: Eduard Weber, 1865), 4–7.

[12]The "closeness of joins" between these epic fragments is discussed by Albin Lesky, *A History of Greek Literature*, trans. James Willis and Cornelis de Heer (New York: Thomas Y. Crowell Co., 1966), I, 83.

[13]As Jonathan Culler writes: "the task of structuralist poetics . . . would be to make explicit the underlying system that makes literary effects possible," not to define the effects themselves; see his *Structuralist Poetics: Structuralism, Linguistics and the Study of Literature* (Ithaca, N.Y.: Cornell University Press, 1975), 118.

[14]Michael Riffaterre, *Semiotics of Poetry* (Bloomington: Indiana University Press, 1978), 72.

[15]On this point see Umberto Eco, *The Role of the Reader: Explorations into the Semiotics of Texts* (Bloomington: Indiana University Press, 1979), 23. Compare also A.F. Losev, *Znak, simvol, mif: Trudy po jazykoznaniju* (M: Izdatel'stvo Moskovskogo Universiteta, 1982): "Every sign acquires its full meaning only in the context of other signs. . . . It is impossible to imagine any sign in an absolute semantic vacuum" (59).

[16]Eco, *The Role of the Reader*, 35.

[17]Jerrold J. Katz calls these "primitive semantic markers" in his *Semantic Theory* (New York: Harper and Row Publishers, 1972), 38; V.G. Gak calls them "differentiating semes" in his "K dialektike semantičeskix otnošenij v jazyke," in *Principy i metody semantičeskix issledovanij* (M: "Nauka," 1976), 87.

[18]Barbara Herrnstein Smith, *On the Margins of Discourse: The Relation of Literature to Language* (Chicago: University of Chicago Press, 1978), 36.

[19]Tzvetan Todorov, *The Poetics of Prose*, trans. Richard Howard (Ithaca, N.Y.: Cornell University Press, 1977), 240.

[20]In *The Role of the Reader* Eco writes: "The form of the work of art gains its aesthetic validity precisely in proportion to the number of different perspectives from which it can be viewed and understood. These give it a wealth of different resonances and echoes without impairing its original essence. . . . Every reception of a work of art is both an *interpretation* and a *performance* of it, because in every reception the work takes on a fresh perspective for itself" (49).

[21]Jurij Lotman, *Struktura xudožestvennogo teksta* (Providence: Brown University Press, 1971), 102. Compare also Stankiewicz, "Centripetal and Centrifugal Structures in Poetry": "Each resemblance implies the presence of difference, and each difference compels us to look for hidden resemblances. The poetic text is thus a process that transcends the either/or oppositions of the linguistic code" (220).

[22]Lotman, 142.

[23]Eco writes: "Since the semantic encyclopedia is in itself potentially infinite, semiosis is unlimited, and from the extreme periphery of a given sememe the center of any other could be reached, and vice versa . . . . Since every proposition contains every other proposition . . . a text could generate, by further semantic disclosures, every other text" (*The Role of the Reader*, 24).

[24]N.V. Izmajlov, "Stixotvorenie Puškina 'Mirskaja vlast'" (Vnov' najdennyj avtograf)," *Izvestija AN SSSR, Otdelenie literatury i jazyka*, 13 (1954), 553. Ultimately, Izmajlov disavowed part of his original thesis, discarding "Ja pamjatnik sebe vozdvig..." from the initial position and suggesting in its stead the poem "Strannik" ("Odnaždy stranstvuja sredi doliny dikoj..."); see his "Liričeskie cikly v poèzii Puškina konca 20–30-x godov," in his *Očerki tvorčestva Puškina* (L: "Nauka," 1975), 258.

[25]N.L. Stepanov, *Lirika Puškina: Očerki i ètjudy* (M: "Xudož. lit.," 1959), 32.

[26]Rolf-Dietrich Keil, "Zur Deutung von Puškins 'Pamjatnik'," *Die Welt der Slaven*, 6 (1961), 219.

[27]M.P. Alekseev, *Stizotvorenie Puškina "Ja pamjatnik sebe vozdvig...": Problemy ego izučenija* (L: "Nauka," 1967), 124. Alekseev also cites the wrong page number from Keil's article. It is unclear why Izmajlov did not discover and correct these errors.

[28]V.P. Stark demonstrated that poems II, III and IV are arranged so as to conform to the liturgy of the Orthodox Church on the days immediately preceding Easter; see his "Stixotvorenie 'Otcy pustynniki i ženy neporočny...' i cikl Puškina 1836 g.," *Puškin: Issledovanija i materialy*, 10 (1982), 200.

[29]Stark, 198.

[30]In 1836 Puškin was out of favor with the public, and his new journal *Sovremennik* was the constant brunt of insidious attacks by the rival press. At the time Puškin had ample reason to feel abandoned and betrayed by his former literary allies. Izmajlov discusses this in his "Liričeskie cikly v poèzii Puškina konca 20–30-x godov," 248.

[31]Among the different explanations of this scene, Stark's is the most plausible: "There is usually no crucifix at all in an Orthodox church, but once a year it is brought into the church and placed in the center. This occurs on Thursday of Holy Week. . . .   On Good Friday it is replaced by a symbol of death, the shroud of Christ, which remains in the church until Easter Sunday. On these three days (Thursday, Friday, Saturday), when the church is filled with more worshipers than at any time, the presence of sentries in the church is required as a 'custodial guard,' which apparently was stationed in Kazan Cathedral beside both the cross and the shroud"; see Stark, 202.

[32]In poem I Puškin continues the tradition of adapting Horace's ode "Exegi monumentum..." cited in the epigraph; the best known translations or paraphrases of this ode before Puškin belonged to Lomonosov and Deržavin. Poem II reproduces Efrem Sirin's prayer, as mentioned earlier. "Podražanie ital'janskomu" (III) freely renders sonnet by the poet-improviser Francesco Gianni (1760–1822); see B. V. Tomaševskij, "Istočnik stixotvorenija 'Kak s dreva sorvalsja predatel' učenik'," *Puškin i ego sovremenniki*, No. 38–39 (1930), 78–81. And although the title "Iz Pindemonti" was thought to be only a ruse to placate censors, M.N. Rozanov demonstrates that this poem indeed mimics phrasings of Ippolito Pindemonte (1753–1828); see his "Ob istočnikax stixotvorenija Puškina 'Iz Pindemonte,'" *Puškin: Sbornik vtoroj* (M–L: Gosudarstvennoe izdatel'stvo, 1930), 126–137.

[33]According to Eco every work of art is to some degree "closed" in that it will not support every interpretation, however implausible, and to some degree "open" in that it permits a breadth of interpretive freedom to the

reader. Medieval allegory is a relatively "closed" text because "the meaning of allegorical figures and emblems which the medieval reader is likely to encounter is already prescribed by his encyclopedias, bestiaries and lapidaries." Nineteenth century symbolism, by contrast, was oriented toward the "open" text, wherein "the important thing is to prevent a single sense from imposing itself at the very outset of the receptive process." See his *The Role of the Reader*, 51, 53.

[34]Stankiewicz's remark to this effect was quoted in the preface. M. L. Rosenthall and Sally M. Gall call the "modern poetic sequence" (that is, the modern lyric cycle) "the crucial genre of modern poetic art . . . the modern poetic form within which all the tendencies of more than a century of experiment define themselves and find their aesthetic purpose"; see their *The Modern Sequence: The Genius of Modern Poetry* (New York: Oxford University Press, 1983), vii.

[35]Numbered and unnumbered lists of poems compiled by Puškin in preparation for publication can be found in *Rukoju Puškina: Nesobrannye i neopublikovannye teksty* (M-L: Academia, 1935), 225-263.

[36]Fedor Sologub, *Stixotvorenija* (L: Sovetskij pisatel', 1975), 578.

[37]I have expropriated this phrase from Šestov's "Tvorčestvo iz ničego," *Mosty*, 5 (1960), 121-150; this essay originally appeared in *Načala i koncy* (1908).

[38]Riffaterre, *Semiotics of Poetry*, 150 .

[39]In one instance, however, a student decided that a cycle I had composed by leafing through old issues of the journal *Bajkal* was not only a "real cycle" but an impressive artistic achievement. When he learned how the cycle came into being, he was surprised and genuinely disappointed. Here "interpretation" is indistinguishable from pure creativity.

[40]Umberto Eco, *A Theory of Semiotics* (Bloomington: Indiana University Press, 1976), 271.

[41]Jonathan Culler, "Literary Competence," in *Reader-Response Criticism: From Formalism to Post-Structuralism*, ed. Jane P. Tompkins (Baltimore: The Johns Hopkins University Press, 1980), 102.

[42]Mustard, *The Lyric Cycle in German Literature*, 102.

[43]L. Ljapina, "K voprosu tipologii liričeskix ciklov (liričeskij cikl v poèzii Bal'monta)," *Materialy XXVI naučnoj studenčeskoj konferencii* (Tartu: TGU, 1971), 61-62.

[44]Here "plot" is understood to mean simply "the event dimension" of any narrative, as Seymour Chatman puts it in his *Story and Discourse: Narrative Structure in Fiction and Film* (Ithaca, N.Y.: Cornell University Press, 1978), 42. No effort will be made here to explore the maze of other definitions sometimes applied to this controversial term; anyone wishing to do so may begin by consulting Kieran Egan's excellent survey "What is Plot?," *New Literary History*, No. 3 (Spring 1978), 455-473. Nor will any attempt be made to clarify the terms "fabula" and "sjužet," which are still embroiled in a seemingly endless debate; see S. Vajmin, "Vokrug sjužeta," *Voprosy literatury*, No. 2 (1980), 114-134. It must be emphasized, however, that I do *not* adhere to Paul Goodman's definition of plot: "Any system of parts that carries over, continuous and changing from the beginning to the end"; see his *The Structure*

of Literatura (Chicago: University of Chicago Press, 1954), 16.   Using
Goodman's definition one could find "plot" in every literary work and perhaps
even in a telephone book; while it cannot be rejected outright, this definition
would obviously render the present typology meaningless.

[45]Mustard, 7, 37; Müller, 6–7, 15–17.

[46]For a survey of how the term "liričeskaja poèma" has been used in
literary scholarship and for a discussion of its relation to lyric cycles see
Dolgopolov, 8–46.

[47]It is difficult to agree with Efim Ètkind that Blok's "Karmen" is only
a "liričeskaja poèma," not a "cycle"; see his "'Karmen' Aleksandra Bloka:
Liričeskaja poèma kak antiroman," in Aleksandr Blok Centennial Conference,
ed. Walter N. Vickery (Columbus, Ohio: Slavica Publishers, 1984), 138.
Ètkind, moreover, is not consistent. He calls "Karmen" a "cycle" at least a
dozen times in this article.

[48]Here I have in mind no special type of ending, only the fact that all
narrative, as Frank Kermode writes, "presupposes and requires that an end
will bestow upon the whole duration and meaning"; see his The Sense of an
Ending: Studies in the Theory of Fiction (New York: Oxford University Press,
1967), 46.   On the teleological directedness of narrative see also Paul Ricoeur,
"The Narrative Function," Semeia, No. 13 (1978), 182; and Louis O. Mink,
"Everyman His or Her Own Annalist," in On Narrative, ed. W.J.T. Mitchell
(Chicago: University of Chicago Press, 1981), 238.

[49]This cycle was first published in Brjusov's Polnoe sobranie sočinenij i
perevodov, I (1913), although the poems in it are contemporaneous with those
in Chefs d'oeuvre (1895).

[50]Dologopolov, 20.

[51]Chatman, 28–29.

[52]Chatman, 30–31.

[53]Vladimir Propp, Morfologija skazki (L: Academia, 1928), 29.

[54]Chatman, 31–32.

[55]Kermode, 18.

[56]Here "archetype" is used in its most basic sense: "an original pattern
from which copies are made or an idea of a class of things representing the
most essential characteristic elements shared by members of a class"
(Princeton Encyclopedia of Poetry and Poetics, 48).   This usage conforms with
Lotman's: "The term 'archetype' and those similar to it ('archeschema,'
'archestructure'). . . are used to mean the aggregate of differentiating features
common to two elements at a given level" (p. 368).   I am interested
specifically in a pattern or model that can be abstracted from separate poems
in a lyric cycle; I am not concerned necessarily with those universal literary
and cultural patterns that are the focus of so-called "archetypal critics" (e.g.,
Northrop Frye, Maud Bodkin, Clyde Kluckhorn), anthropologists and
mythographers.   Cyclic plot archetypes may indeed reproduce patterns found
in man's intercultural experience, but this issue is irrelevant to a theoretical
typology of the cycle.

[57]In a letter to N.N. Straxov (April 23, 1876) Tolstoj remarked: "If I

wanted to say in words all that I had in mind to express by my novel, I should have to write the same novel which I wrote all over again"; see Leo Tolstoj, *Anna Karenina* (New York: W.W. Norton and Co., 1970), 750–751.

[58]See Chatman, 45–47; and Tzvetan Todorov, "Structural Analysis of Narrative (1969)," in *Modern Literary Criticism 1900–1970*, ed. Lawrence I. Lipking and A. Walton Litz (New York: Atheneum, 1972), 440.

[59]For some reason commentators usually refer to Propp's analysis of "100" folktales. Propp, however, states specifically that he used as his sampling tales No. 50–151 in Afanas'ev's anthology; see Propp, *Morfologija skazki*, 33.

[60]The fact that Propp's study aimed to determine the essential constituents of a particular kind of folktale and made no pretense of being a theory of *all* narrative was overlooked by Claude Lévi–Strauss, whose critique of *Morfologija* faulted Propp for not simplifying his "functions" further. It is gratifying that Propp's eloquent rebuttal of Lévi–Strauss sets the record straight; see Propp, "Structure and History in the Study of Folktales (A Reply to Lévi–Strauss)," *Russian Literature*, 12 (1982), 11–31.

[61]Andrej Belyj, *Zoloto v lazuri* (M: Skorpion, 1904), pp. 1–59. The version in *Stixotvorenija i poèmy* (M–L: Sovetskij pisatel', 1966) is incomplete, containing only 19 of the cycle's 37 poems.

[62]Vjačeslav Ivanov, *Po zvezdam: Stat'i i aforizmy* (Pb: "Ory," 1909), 243.

CHAPTER TWO

[1]L.K. Dolgopolov, *Poèmy Bloka i russkaja poèma konca XIX—načala XX vekov* (M–L: "Nauka," 1964), 12.

[2]Dolgopolov, 14.

[3]Dolgopolov, 47.

[4]V.A. Sapogov, "Poètika liričeskogo cikla A. Bloka" (Avtoreferat dissertacii na soiskanie uč. step. kand. filol. nauk) (M: Moskovskij ped. institut im. Lenina, 1967).

[5]Sapogov, 7.

[6]Sapogov, 6.

[7]Sapogov, 4–5.

[8]Sapogov, 5–6.

[9]See, for instance, S.A. Fomičev, "'Podražanija Koranu': Genezis, arxitektonika i kompozicija cikla," *Vremennik puškinskoj komissii*, No. 16 (1978), 22–45; N.V. Izmajlov, "Liričeskie cikly v poèzii Puškina konca 20–30–x godov," in his *Očerki tvorčestva Puškina* (L: "Nauka," 1975), 213–269; V.B. Sandomirskaja, "Iz istorii puškinskogo cikla 'Podražanija drevnim' (Puškin i Batjuškov)," *Vremennik puškinoj komissii*, No. 13 (1975), 15–30; E.V. Slinina, "Liričeskij cikl A.S. Puškina 'Stixi, sočinennye vo vremja putešestvija' (1829)," *Puškinskij sbornik: Sbornik naučnyx trudov* (L: Ped. institut im. A.I. Gercena, 1977), 3–15; V.P. Stark, "Stixotvorenie 'Otcy pustynniki i ženy neporočny...' i cikl Puškina 1836 g.," *Puškin: Issledovanija i materialy*, No. 10 (1982),

193–203. See also my article "Pushkin's 'Lyric Cycle of 1836' and the Lessons of Izmailov's Hypothesis: Some Notes on the Semiotics of Cycles," *Ulbandus Review* (forthcoming).

[10]The date which marks the beginning of modern Russian poetry is debatable. Trediakovskij's tract, which introduced the principle of syllabo-tonic versification, is usually cited as the earliest landmark, although 1739 (the year Lomonosov composed his "Oda na vzjatie Xotina" and "Pis'mo o pravilax rossijskogo stixotvorstva") is also frequently suggested. Aleksandr Levitsky, in my personal conversations with him, proposed 1743 as the most appropriate date because in this year Trediakovskij, Lomonosov and Sumarokov committed themselves *jointly* to the new syllabo-tonic system by publishing their three renditions of Psalm 143 under one cover. Ideally, a history of cyclization would begin in the pre-modern era with the various collections of Simeon Polockij (*Rifmalogion, Vertograd mnogocvetnyj*) and Kiril Trankvilion Stravroveckij (*Perlo mnogocennoe*), but since the focus of this book is Blok, who was at best only marginally familiar with these poets, I have elected to begin no earlier than the eighteenth century.

[11]Aleksander Levitsky, *Russian Sacred Verse from Polockij to Deržavin* (Chapter 2, Part 1), 41; this excellent book is presently still in manuscript.

[12]*Sobranie raznyx sočinenij v stixax i proze M. Lomonosova* (SPb: 1751), I, 5–34.

[13]The theme of persecution by "enemies," which is so strong in the cycle's median poems, undoubtedly reflects Lomonosov's real situation in the 1740's (and perhaps the early 1750's, depending on how the psalm transpositions are dated); during this time he was falsely accused by envious colleagues at the Academy of Sciences and temporarily placed under house arrest by state authorities.

[14]Levitsky's interpretation of this cycle is quite similar to mine, although we arrived at our views independently. He suggests in addition that the arrangement of poems may be modeled after the "xrija," an eight-part syllogistic argument Lomonosov discusses in *Ritorika*. This is very persuasive, but I find it difficult to agree with Levitsky's opinion that Lomonosov may have intended to include his unfinished paraphrase of Psalm 103 (not included in the cycle) in the eighth position, following Psalm 145. It is clear that Lomonosov elected not to violate the psalms' Biblical sequence, hence he would have had to place it in the sixth position (between Psalms 70 and 143). This, however, would have disrupted the conceptual unity of one intracyclic grouping (poems Nos. 3–6); the tone and content of Lomonosov's translation of Psalm 103 is consonant with the cycle's last three poems (celebration of nature) but inconsistent with the poet's accusatory stance in the median poems.

[15]V.K. Trediakovskij, *Sočinenija i perevody, kak stixami tak i prosoju* (SPb: Pri Imperatorskoj Akademii nauk, 1752), II, 63–152. The source for poem No. 14 is given incorrectly in this edition; it should read "Avvakum glava 9.".

[16]*Ežemesjačnye sočinenija* (September 1755), 251–261. For more on this grouping see Levitsky, 96–98 (Chapter 2, Part 3).

[17]*Tri ody parafrastičeskija psalma 143, sočinennyja črez trex stixotvorcev, iz kotoryx každoj odnu složil osoblivo* (SPb: 1744). This booklet actually

appeared in August 1743.

[18]V.A. Zapadov writes: "When in 1798 the first (and only) volume of Deržavin's unfinished collection of poetry appeared in print, the poet was so dissatisfied with the mistakes in the text that he even asked that F.N. Golicyn, curator of Moscow University, to whose press the book was submitted, to order the destruction of all copies, but then changed his decision. The reasons for the poet's dissatisfaction with the book are summarized by him in 'Warning to the Reader,' which was placed at the beginning of this edition. Deržavin complained that . . . the wrong poems had been included, not the ones which were intended for it; [and] that *the poems were not arranged in the order indicated by the author* "; see Zapadov, "Neizvestnyj Deržavin," *Izvestija otdelenija literatury i jazyka AN SSSR*, No. 1 (1958), 45–46.

[19]*Sočinenija Deržavina*, I (SPb: V tipografii Šnora, 1808), iv.

[20]The dating and psalm sources are given according to the notes of Ja. Grot; see *Sočinenija Derežavina. 2-e akademičeskoe izdanie* (SPb: V Tipografii Imperatorskoj Akademii Nauk, 1868), I.

[21]L.G. Frizman makes this point in his *Žizn' liričeskogo žanra: Russkaja èlegija ot Sumarokova do Nekrasova* (M: "Nauka," 1973), 9, 22.

[22]V.K. Trediakovskij, *Izbrannye proizvedenija* (M-L: Sovetskij pisatel', 1963), 395–396; the elegies themselves are on pages 397–402.

[23]G.A. Gukovskij, *Russkaja poèzija XVIII veka* (L: "Academia," 1927), 53.

[24]A rearrangement in the 1769 edition explains why my numbering is not identical to that discussed by Gukovskij, although he also discerns a common "lyric situation." Gukovskij uses an earlier edition of the elegies. His numbering (in Roman numerals) corresponds to mine (in Arabic) as follows: I (#3), II(#4), III(#5), IV (#6), V (#7), VI (#8), VII (#9), VIII (omitted in 1769), IX (#1), X (#2), XI (#10). See Gukovskij, *Russkaja poèzija XVIII veka*, 54–59.

[25]*Raznye stixotvorenija Aleksandra Sumarokova* (SPb: Pri Imperatorskoj Akademii Nauk, 1769), 183–224.

[26]*Sočinenija Karamzina*, I (M: v tipografii S. Selivanovskogo, 1803).

[27]*Stixotvorenija Barona Del'viga* (SPb: v tipografii Departamenta Narodnogo prosveščenija, 1829) is not divided into sections in the text at all; the table of contents, however, lists the poems under the following genre headings: "Idillii," "Pesni i romansy," "Sonety," and "Rasnye stixotvorenija."

[28]*Stixotvorenija N. Jazykova* (SPb: v tipografii vdovy Pljušar s synom, 1833) has one exception: a grouping of three poems under the heading "Elegii" (entitled "Tri èlegii" in the table of contents).

[29]G.A. Gukovskij, *Puškin i russkie romantiki* (M: Xudož. lit., 1965), 85.

[30]Quoted in R.V. Iezuitova, "Poèzija russkogo romantizma načala XIX veka," in *Istorija russkoj poèzii*, I (L: "Nauka," 1968), 231.

[31]The term "lyric hero" was introduced by Jurij Tynjanov to characterize the image of the poet in Blok; see his *Arxaisty i novatory* (L: "Priboj," 1929), 513.

[32] L.Ja. Ginzburg, "Puškin i liričeskij geroj russkogo romantizma," in *Puškin: Issledovanija i materialy*, IV (1962), 141–144.

[33] Ginzburg, 144.

[34] Ginzburg, 141.

[35] *Puškin i russkie romantiki*, 139.

[36] B. Èjxenbaum, "Ot voennoj ody k 'gusarskoj pesne'," in Denis Davydov, *Polnoe sobranie stizotvorenij* (L: Izdatel'stvo pisatelej v Leningrade, 1933), 42.

[37] Puškin's choice of the word "elegy" ("I svod *èlegij* dragocennyj") is not to be taken completely literally. Already in 1823 Orest Somov wrote in his article "O romantičeskoj poèzii" "all genres of poetry have now almost fused under the heading of the elegy alone." Puškin himself wrote in an unfinished review of Baratynskij's *Stizotvorenija* (1827): "the pure elegy almost does not exist in our poetry"; see his *Sobranie sočinenij v 10-i tomax* (M: Xudož. lit., 1974–78), VI, 241. Moreover, Jazykov himself used the word quite freely, calling civic odes and drinking songs "elegies," even though they had nothing in common with the genre as commonly understood; on this point see Vladimir Orlov, *Puti i sud'by: literaturnye očerki* (L: Sovetskij pisatel', 1971), 247, 251.

[38] *Rukoju Puškina: Nesobrannye i neopublikovannye teksty* (M–L: Academia, 1935), 230. Compare also a remark made in the preface to *Sočinenija i perevody v stixax Pavla Katenina*, cašt' pervaja (SPb: V tipografii vdovy Pljušara, 1832): "To account for the vivid quality of Mr. Katenin's poetry one should also point out its *variety*; each poem almost seems to belong to the pen of a separate author." (viii).

[39] This section contains the following poems: 1) "Toska po milom"; 2) "Mal'vina"; 3) "Cvetok"; 4) "Pesn' araba nad mogiloj konja"; 5) "Dobraja mat'"; 6) "Plovec" ("Vixrem bedstvija gonimyj..."); 7) "Pesnja" ("Sčastliv tot, komu zabavy..."); 8) "Pesnja" ("Moj drug, xranitel'-angel moj..."); 9) "Pesnja" ("O milyj drug! teper' s toboju..."); 10) "Žaloba" ("Nad prozračnymi vodami..."); 11) "Pevec" ("V teni derev, nad čistymi vodami..."); 12) "Putešestvennik"; 13) "Sirotka"; 14) "Želanie"; 15) "Uznik k motylku, vletevšemu v ego temnicu"; 16) "Èlizium"; 17) "Mečty"; 18) "Pesn' russkomu carju ot ego voinov."

[40] In those cases where the protagonist of a lyric poem is not the same as the customary image of the poet or author (e.g., Puškin's "Gusar"), N.L. Stepanov proposes the term "lyric character" (liričeskij personaž); see his *Lirika Puškina* (M: Xudož. lit., 1974), 99–100. V. Gippius suggests the term "role lyric" (rolevaja lirika); see his "Nekrasov v istorii russkoj poèzii XIX veka," *Literaturnoe nasledstvo*, Nos. 49–50, pp. 39–40.

[41] Iezuitova, 232.

[42] "O napravlenii našej poèzii, osobenno liričeskoj, v poslednee desjatiletie," in *Xrestomatija po istorii russkoj žurnalistiki XIX veka* (M: "Vysšaja škola," 1969), 33–34. This article originally appeared in the miscellany *Mnemozina*, Part 2 (1824), 29–44.

[43] The exact composition of the section "Èlegii" is reproduced in K.N.

Batjuškov, *Opyty v stixax i proze* (M: "Nauka," 1977), pp. 260–284. Although Nikolaj Gnedič edited *Opyty* and had final say in ordering the poems, Batjuškov apparently determined which poems would be included in each section, at least as regards "Élegii." This seems apparent from his letter to Gnedič dated September 15, 1816: "The section of elegies will be the best. I shall send you the whole box [of them]"; and also from the letter dated October 28–29, 1816: "I shall send off first the book of elegies." See *Sočinenija K.N. Batjuškova* (SPb: Tipografija (byvšaja) Kotomina, 1886), III, 400, 409.

[44]On this account Iezuitova writes: "The elegy in Batjuškov, despite a certain conventionality . . . is more directly connected with reality"(232).

[45]One indication of this is that he began to revise the composition of the cycles as he prepared for a second, unrealized edition of his works; see I.M. Semenko, "Batjuškov i ego 'Opyty'," in *Opyty v stixax i proze* (1977), 483–484.

[46]The first five poems in the section "Liričeskie, didaktičeskie i drugie stixotvorenija" are: 1) "K Provideniju"; 2) "Arfa Davida"; 3) "K drugu" ("Kogda krugom..."); 4) "K nemu že" ("Kogda iz glubiny..."); and 5) "Prijutino"; see *Stixotvorenija N. Gnediča* (SPb: v tipografii Imperatorskoj Akademii Nauk, 1832).

[47]These are 1) "Poètu" ("Kogda s toboj..."); 2) "Podražanie psalmu XIV"; 3) "K muze" ("Moj Angel milyj..."); 4) "K A.A. Voejkovoj"; 5) "Ručej"; 6) "Trigorskoe"; 7) "Rodina"; 8) "Dve kartiny"; 9) "Élegija" ("Skaži, vorotiš'sja..."); and 10) "Élegija" ("Ne uletaj...").

[48]*Stixotvorenija Denisa Davydova* (M: V tipografii Avgusta Semena, 1832): 1) "V al'bom" ("Na v'juke, v šorokax..."), 2) "Borodinskoe pole," 3) "Partizan (Otryvok)," 4) "Gusar (1802)," 5) "Pesnja (1815)" ("Ja ljublju krovavyj boj..."), 6) "Burcovu" ("Burcov, era, zabijaka..."), 7) "Burcovu" ("V dymnom pole..."), 8) "Gusarskoj pir," 9) "Pesnja starogo gusara," 10) "Polu–soldat (1826)," 11) "Gusarskaja ispoved'."

[49]N.V. Izmajlov, "Liričeskie cikly v poèzii Puškina 30–godov," *Puškin: Issledovanija i materialy*, II (M–L: AN SSSR, 1958), 8.

[50]Izmajlov, 10.

[51]*Rukoju Puškina*, 231.

[52]*Rukoju Puškina*, 232–234.

[53]S.A. Fomičev suggests the same when speaks of "the constant juxtaposing of separate poems onto each of which falls the reflection of the others and the combined whole"; see his "'Podražanija Koranu': Genezis, arxitektonika i kompozicija cikla," *Vremennik puškinskoj komissii*, No. 16 (1978), 43.

[54]On the sources of Puškin's cycle see K.S. Kaštaleva, "'Podražanija Koranu' Puškina i ix pervoistočniki," *Zapiski Kollegii vostokovedov pri Aziatskom muzee AN SSSR*, No. 5 (1930), 243–270.

[55]According to Fomičev, the cycle "did not come easily to the poet"; this may be why Puškin halted work on it at the end of 1824 (34).

[56]Fomičev, 42.

[57]*Rukoju Puškina*, 228–234.

[58]*Rukoju Puškina*, 260.

[59]Izmajlov, 11; this list can be found in *Rukoju Puškina*, 260.

[60]This list is given by Izmajlov, 40–41.

[61]Mixail Lermontov's *Stixtvorenija* (SPb: V tipografii Il'i Glazunova, 1840), the only collection published during his lifetime, contains no cycles; the twenty–eight poems in it are arranged rather haphazardly, so there are hardly any grounds for speaking of Lermontov as a cyclist. As for Fedor Tjutčev, see below, p.

[62]The section "Èlegii" in *Stixotvorenija Evgenija Baratynskogo* (M: v tipografii Avgusta Semena, 1827) contains the following: *Kniga pervaja*—"Finljandija," "Vodopad," "Istina," "Mogila" ("Usopšij brat..."), "Rim," "Rodina," "Dve doli," "Burja"; *Kniga vtoraja*—"Razluka," "V al'bom" ("Tebe na pamjat', v knige sej...") [Later the first line of this poem was changed to "Zemljak! v strane čužoj, surovoj..."], "Leta," "Ropot" ("On blizok..."), "Unynie," "Razmolvka," "Bdenie," "Razuverenie," "Padenie list'ev," "Ot"ezd"; *Kniga tret'ja*—"Utešenie," "Poceluj," "Èlizejskie polja," "Delii," "Opravdanie," "Dogadka," "Ožidanie," "Vozvraščenie," "K...nu" ("Pora pokinut'..."), "L. P–nu" ("Pover', moj milyj!.."), "Èpilog."

[63]It is difficult to agree with E.N. Kuprejanova, who characterizes the first part of this edition as "something resembling a lyric autobiography"; see her notes to E.A. Baratynskij, *Polnoe sobranie stixotvorenij* (L: Sovetskij pisatel', 1958), 331.

[64]Kuprejanova, 37.

[65]Among the other episodic plot cycles of this period it is worth mentioning Majkov's "On i ona (Četyre kartiny)" (in *Stixotvorenija*, 1858): 1) "Davno l' byla ona maljutka...", 2) "Gremit orkestr; vino sverkaet...", 3) "On snes udar sud'by...", 4) "Kak pereletnyx ptiček staja..."; and also Polonskij's "Sny" (in *Polnoe sobranie sočinenij*, 1885): 1) "Zatvoreny dušnye stavni...", 2) "Mne snilos, legka...", 3) "Už utro!—No, Bože moj...", 4) "Podsolnečnoe carstvo," 5) "Tiš i mrak."

[66]In its original publication this cycle had six poems, although the "Biblioteka poèta" edition gives it in a later version with seven poems; see A.N. Apuxtin, *Stixotvorenija* (L: Sovetskij pisatel', 1961), 83–87.

[67]In 1875 Turgenev wrote: "Who doesn't know that right now Heine is just about the most popular foreign poet in Russia"; see Genrix Gejne, *Stixotvorenija, Poèmy, Proza* (M: "Xudož. lit.," 1971), 742.

[68]One indication of this is that the word "cikl" is not widely used in Russia before mid–century when Heine's popularity was greatest. (Heine had used the subtitle "Zyklus" in *Buch der Lieder*.) The word does not appear in Puškin at all. The oldest use of "cikl" I have encountered is in a letter from Ogarev to T. M. Granovskij, dated January 1847; see N.P. Ogarev, *Izbrannoe* (M: "Xudož. lit.," 1977), 403.

[69]Dolgopolov, 11–13.

[70]On this point see my article "The Author's Digressions in Ševčenko's 'Hajdamaky': Their Nature and Function," *Harvard Ukrainian Studies*, No. 3 (September 1978), 315–316.

[71]Dolgopolov, 13.

[72]See A.G. Cejtlin, *Masterstvo Turgeneva-romanista* (M: 1958), 10–11.

[73]A. Slonimskij, *Masterstvo Puškina.* 2-e izdanie (M: Xudož. lit.," 1963), 311.

[74]K.G. Isupov's "O žanrovoj pirode stixotvorenogo cikla," *Celostnost' xudožestvennogo proizvedenija i problemy ego analiza* (Doneck: Doneckij gos. universitet, 1977), 163–164.

[75]It is clear from the preface to *Stixotvorenija F. Tjutčeva* (SPb: V tipografii Eduarda Praca, 1854) that Tjutčev left the choice and arrangement of poems entirely up to his editors; outside of giving his permission, Tjutčev took no part in their publication.

[76]A.A. Fet, *Večernie ogni* (M: "Nauka," 1971), 240, 242.

[77]This preface, entitled "Iz zapisnoj knižki (1899)," appeared only in the second edition of *Gorjaščie zdanija* (1904); see K. Bal'mont, *Sobranie stixov*, tom 2 (M: Skorpion, 1904), 1–2.

[78]Andrej Belyj, *Stixotvorenija i poèmy* (1966), 544.

[79]Valerij Brjusov, *Sobranie sočinenij* (M: "Xudož. lit.," 1973–1975), I, 604–605.

[80]*The Genesis of Secrecy* (1979), 17.

[81]D.S. Merežkovskij, *Polnoe sobranie sočinenij*, XV (M-SPb: 1912), 250.

[82]Merežkovskij, 252.

[83]Merežkovskij, 287.

[84]Brjusov, *Sobranie sočinenij*, VI, 27.

[85]Brjusov, *Sobranie sočinenij*, VI, 30.

[86]Brjusov, *Sobranie sočinenij*, VI, 45–46.

[87]*Gornye veršiny. Kniga I. Iskusstvo i literatura* (M: Grif, 1904), 77.

[88]Z. Gippius, *Sobranie stixov. 1889–1903 g.* (M: Skorpion, 1904), iv.

[89]Sologub's attitude toward cyclization was ambivalent. He fastidiously preserved the composition of some smaller cycles, such as "Zvezda Mair" and "Sobornyj blagovest," but in preparing his *Sobranie stixov* (M: Skorpion, 1904) he gave Brjusov authority to "arrange the poems in whatever order you find best." After a single effort at continuous cyclization (*Plamennyj krug*, 1908), he abandoned cycles entirely in the first volume of *Sobranie sočinenij* (SPb: Šipovnik, 1909). There he attached the following comment, which sounds like a parody of Symbolist prefaces: "For several reasons I have decided not to arrange these poems in chronological order and have not divided them into sections; I limited myself to arranging them in such an order that will not seem arbitrary to the attentive reader" ("Ot avtora," no page number).

[90]Brjusov, *Sobranie sočinenij*, VI, 258.

[91]Aleksandr Blok, *Sobranie sočinenij v 8-i tomax* (M-L: "Xudož. lit.," 1960–63), V, 374. Subsequently all references to this edition will be given parenthetically in the text; references to his *Zapisnye knižki 1901–1920* (M: "Xudož. lit.," 1965) will be given the same way, preceded by the initials ZK.

[92]Innokentij Annenskij, *Knigi otraženij* (M: "Nauka," 1979), 330.

[93]K. Bal'mont, *Sobranie stixov*, I (M: Skorpion, 1905), vi.

[94]Bal'mont generally referred to *Pod severnym nebom* (1894) as his "first book"; he committed his *Sbornik stixotvorenij* (1890) to oblivion.

[95]Vi. Orlov, *Pereput'ja: Iz istorii russkoj poèzii načala XX veka* (M: "Xudož. lit.," 1976), 227.

[96]I cannot agree with I. Mašbic-Verov, who disputes Bal'mont's summary; see his *Russkij simvolizm i put' Aleksandra Bloka* (Kujbyšev: Kujbyševsk. knižn. izdatel'stvo, 1969), 39–46. He argues that Bal'mont remains incorrigibly individualistic in all his collections and that the poetry of his apparently "sunny" collections is insincere. The first objection misinterprets Bal'mont's statement (Bal'mont claims to become more optimistic, not more socially oriented); the second is irrelevant to judicious literary criticism.

[97]Bal'mont's concept of poetic creativity is best conveyed in his fable "Bezumnyj časovščik." There the hero, an inspired watch–maker, loses control over the mechanism he created and can do nothing to stop it; it continues to spew forth chaotic agglomerations of sound, which echo the natural elements.

[98]Brjusov's inclination toward "schemata" and "logical formulae" is noted also by D.E. Maksimov, *Brjusov: Poèzija i pozicija* (L: Sovetskij pisatel', 1969), 73.

[99]V. Brjusov, *Urbi et Orbi: Stixi 1900–1903 g.* (M: Skorpion, 1903). This version is considerably different from the one in *Sobranie sočinenij*, I, 267–366.

[100]This may not be the only occasion Brjusov borrowed cyclic titles from his predecessors. *Tertia Vigilia* contains the cycle "Ljubimcy vekov," which may be a reminiscence of Majkov's "Veka i narody"; *Vse naprevy* contains the grouping "Mgnovenija," a title used by both Majkov and Slučevskij; the section "Sovremennost'" in Brjusov's *Stephanos* seems to recall the grouping "Sovremenniki" in Nekrasov's *Poslednie pesni* (1877).

[101]Brjusov, *Sobranie sočinenij*, I, 605.

[102]It is interesting that in 1905 Blok called Brjusov "a gifted poet of the Alexandrian period of Russian literature"; see *Literaturnoe nasledstvo*, 92, I (1980), 391.

[103]Nikolaj Gumilev, in his review of Brjusov's *Puti i pereput'ja* (volume II), which contained a revised version of *Urbi et Orbi*, commented: "Above all one is struck by the unity of the plan. . . . Brjusov is concerned with only two magnitudes—'I' and 'the world'—and in his strict patterns, devoid of anything incidental, he gives different possibilities and interrelationships"; see his *Sobranie sočinenij*, IV (Washington, D.C.: Victor Kamkin, Inc., 1968), 199.

[104]*Literaturnoe nasledstvo*, 92, I (1980), 382.

[105]V. Brjusov, *Puti i pereput'ja* (M: Skorpion, 1908–09), I, vii.

[106]Victor Erlich, "The Maker and the Seer: Two Russian Symbolists," in his *The Double Image: Concepts of the Poet in Slavic Literatures* (Baltimore: The Johns Hopkins Press, 1964), 68–119.

[107]Maksimov, *Brjusov: Poèzija i pozicija*, 59.

[108]On the importance of this idea, especially for the "younger generation" see D. Maksimov, *Poèzija i proza Al. Bloka* (L: Sovetskij pisatel', 1981), 86.

[109]In *Po zvezdam: Stat'i i aforizmy* (SPb: Izdatel'stvo "Ory," 1909) Vjačeslav Ivanov distinguished the "older" and "younger" symbolists precisely on this basis. The former, he said, saw everything "in the evanescence of self-sufficent 'moments', in 'instantaneousnesses' [mgnovennostjax] that had their own inherent value and basis"; the latter developed 'the cult of eternity and pan-unity in the multicolored reflections ('im farbigen Abglanz', as Faust says) of instants" (242).

[110]Brjusov, *Sobranie sočinenij*, VI, 91.

[111]Vladimir Solov'ev, *Sobranie sočinenij* (SPb: Izdatel'stvo tovariščestva "Obščestvennaja pol'za," 1901-1907), III, 175.

[112]*Po zvezdam*, 248.

[113]*Po zvezdam*, 274-275.

[114]*Po zvezdam*, 218, 285-286.

[115]*Po zvezdam*, 243-244.

[116]Andrej Belyj, *Simvolizm. Kniga statej* (M: Musaget, 1910), 440.

[117]Z.G. Minc, "O nekotoryx 'neomifologičeskix' tekstax v tvorčestve russkix simvolistov," *Blokovskij sbornik III* (Tartu: TGU, 1979), 77; published as No. 459 of *Učenye zapiski* TGU.

[118]Pavel Gromov makes this point also in his *A. Blok: Ego predšestvenniki i sovremenniki* (M-L: Sovetskij pisatel', 1966), 267.

[119]Gromov, 271.

[120]Annenskij, *Knigi otraženij*, 332-333.

[121]*Po zvezdam*, 284-285.

[122]*Po zvezdam*, 284.

[123]Edward Stankiewicz, "Centripetal and Centrifugal Structures in Poetry," *Semiotica*, volume 38, No. 3/4 (1982), 217.

[124]A. Blok, *Stixi o Prekrasnoj Dame* (M: Grif, 1905); in fact this book appeared in October 1904.

[125]Ivanov makes this statement in a letter to Brjusov, who had commissioned him to write a review of Blok's collection for the journal *Vesy;* quoted by Z.G. Minc and Ju. P. Blagovolina, "Perepiska Bloka s V.Ja. Brjusovym (1903-1919)," *Literaturnoe nasledstvo*, 92, I, 468.

[126]A. Blok, *Sobranie stixotvorenij* (M: Musaget, 1911-12); *Stixotvorenija* (M: Musaget, 1916); the "canonical" version appeared variously as follows: Volume I—*Sobranie sočinenij* (Pb: "Alkonost," 1922), Volume II— *Stixotvorenija: Knigi 1-2* (Pb: "Zemlja," 1918), Volume III—*Stixotvorenija: Kniga 3* (Pb: "Alkonost," 1921).

[127]The task of determining "influences" on Blok will become easier when the complete inventory and description of his Petersburg library is published. At this writing, only the first volume of this long awaited addition to Blok scholarship has appeared in print: *Biblioteka A.A. Bloka:Opisanie*, I (L: Biblioteka Akademii Nauk, 1984).

[128]Recently S.A. Nebol'sin, citing parodies of decadent literature Blok wrote in 1895 for his manuscript journal *Vestnik*, questions the validity of the

poet's assertion that he did not know the "new" poetry before autumn 1898; see his "V pervyx stolknovenijax s dekadentami," in *A. Blok i sovremennost'* (M: Sovremennik, 1981), 227–240. Nebol'sin's argument is persuasive, yet there is still no evidence that Blok knew the decadent poets *as cyclists* before the turn of the century.

[129]M. A. Beketova, "Aleksandr Blok i ego mat'," in *Aleksandr Blok v vospominanijax sovremennikov* (M: "Xudož. lit.," 1980), I, 68.

[130]In Blok's Petersburg library there is a copy of Heine in I. Semenov's translation (G. Gejne, *Stixotvorenija*, 1858), which Blok may have read at this time also; see *Biblioteka A.A. Bloka*, I, 207.

[131]That Blok may have read Heine in the original in these early years is suggested by a remark in his notebooks from December 8, 1918: "All day I read Heine to Ljuba in German—and felt young again" (ZK, 439).

[132]In a letter to N.A. Nolle–Kogan from February 1919, Blok thanks her for a copy of Heine's *Buch der Lieder* (the Elster edition) and remarks that he already has a copy, given him by his mother in 1908; see *Literaturnoe nasledstvo*, 92, II, 358.

[133]Knipovič, "Blok i Gejne," 177–178.

[134]A. Grigor'ev, *Stixotvorenija* (M: Izdatel'stvo K. F. Nekrasova, 1916).

[135]A.A. Blok, "Iz primečanij k 'Stixotvorenijam Apollona Grigor'eva'," *Sobranie sočinenij*, XI (L: Izdatel'stvo pisatelej v Leningrade, n.d.), 360–361.

[136]Blok, "Iz primečanij...", 363.

[137]P. Gromov, "Apollon Grigor'ev," in *A. Grigor'ev, Izbrannye proizvedenija* (L: Sovetskij pisatel', 1959), 75.

[138]Vladimir Solov'ev composed a cycle of forty-two poems inscribed in an album and addressed to C.A. Martynova, his last love. The grouping was never published and the album has been lost, so that its existence is known only from a list made in 1913 by M.A. Petrov and reproduced by Z. G. Minc in "Iz rukopisnogo nasledija Vl. Solov'eva poèta," *Učenye zapiski TGU* No. 358 (1975), 382–383. This is an extremely well–formulated episodic plot cycle, as suggested by Solov'ev's subtitles, under which the various poems are grouped: "Prolog," "Zavjazka," "Kollizija," "Razvjazka.".

[139]Z.G. Minc, "Simvol u A. Bloka," in *V mire Bloka: Sbornik statej* (M: Sovetskij pisatel', 1981), 179–180.

[140]Solov'ev, *Sobranie sočinenij*, III, 322.

[141]Solov'ev, *Sobranie sočinenij*, III, 35–36.

[142]Minc, "O nekotoryx 'neomifologičeskix' tekstax," 85–87.

[143]On these and other annotations the young Blok made in his copies of Solov'ev see D.E. Maksimov, "Materialy iz biblioteki Al. Bloka (K voprosu ob Al. Bloke i Vl. Solov'eve)," *Učenye zapiski* (Leningradskij gos. ped. institut), No. 184 (1958), 368–369, 375.

[144]Solov'ev, *Sobranie sočinenij*, VIII, 249.

[145]*Literaturnoe nasledstvo*, 92, I, 532.

[146]*Literaturnoe nasledstvo*, 92, I, 352–353.

[147] Already in February 1903, Blok was finding this quality in Fet's poetry (and perhaps his own); he writes A.V. Gippius: "There are no changes. All is the same, 'unity in multiplicity' (ἕν ἐν ὁμοιῷ) . . ." See *Literaturnoe nasledstvo*, 92, I, 442.

[148] There is no question that Brjusov's preface to *Urbi et Orbi* was the model for these lines because Blok quotes it verbatim on the cover leaf of the complimentary first volume he sent Brjusov in May 1911; see *Literaturnoe nasledstvo*, 92, III, 40.

[149] See for instance Joan Delaney Grossman's interesting and informative article "Blok, Brjusov, and the *Prekrasnaja Dama*," in *Aleksandr Blok Centennial Conference* (Columbus, Ohio: Slavica Publishers, 1984), 159–177.

[150] *Literaturnoe nasledstvo*, 92, I, 410.

[151] *Sobranie sočinenij* (1960–63) dates this review "the end of 1903" (V, 530), but it is possible to be more precise. It was written, undoubtedly, in the first half of November, when Sergej Solov'ev visited Blok and reported seeing him hard at work on *Budem kak solnce* and *Tol'ko ljubov'*; see *Aleksandr Blok v vospominanijax sovremennikov*, I, 117. At the beginning of December Blok wrote his friend, "Brjusov has been tormenting me approximately since your departure [November 16, 1903], because at that time I began reading his book"; see *Literaturnoe nasledstvo*, 92, I, 352. It is unlikely that Blok returned to work again cn Bal'mont at this time since he can speak only of Brjusov from mid November to the end of December; moreover, the review of Bal'mont's collections already appeared in the January issue of *Novyj put'*.

[152] *Literaturnoe nasledstvo*, 92, I, 472.

[153] Minc and Blagovolina remark that in contrast to Brjusov's lyrics, "the most strikingly innovative quality in Blok's lyrics is hidden in the poetic semantics"; see their "Perepiska Bloka s V.Ja. Brjusovym," 467.

[154] This cycle contained the following poems: 1) "V polnoč' gluxuju roždennaja..." (I, 71); 2) "Ty otxodiš' v sumrak alyj..." (I, 81); 3) "Noč'ju sumračnoj i dikoj..." (I, 85); 4) "Odinokij, k tebe prixožu..." (I, 93); 5) "Sny razdumij nebyvalyx..." (I, 164); 6) "Ja prosypalsja i vsxodil..." (I, 85); 7) "Tam—v ulice stojal kakoj-to dom..." (I, 192); 8) "Po gorodu begal černyj čelovek..."; 9) "Doma rastut, kak želan'ja..." (I, 238); 10) "Sbežal s gory i zamer v čašče..." (I, 206); 11) "Svet v okoške šatalsja..." (I, 210); 12) "Ja byl ves' v pestryx loskut'jax..." (I, 277); 13) "Mne strašno s Toboj vstrečat'sja..." (I, 237); 14) "Den' byl nežno–seryj, seryj, kak toska..." (I, 284); 15) "Vot oni—belye zvuki..." (I, 529). In the letter accompanying these poems Blok asked S. A. Sokolov, the editor, to keep the arrangement intact if possible, because "I would like to give a range of varied anticipations (1–6), which merges with cold personal terror (7–13) and which is resolved only halfway by the stifling air before the storm (14) and all the way at dawn in the echoes, in the reflections of the departing storm clouds (15)"; quoted in *Literaturnoe nasledstvo*, 92, I, 528–529.

[155] *Literaturnoe nasledstvo*, 92, I, 467.

[156] Brjusov, *Sobranie sočinenij*, VI, 509.

[157] *Literaturnoe nasledstvo*, II, 9. .

[158] Kornej Čukovskij, *Kniga ob Aleksandre Bloke* (Berlin: "Epoxa," 1922);

V.M. Žirmunskij, *Poèzija Aleksandr Bloka* (Pb: "Kartonnyj domik," 1922), 64–65.

[159]Lidija Ginzburg, "Nasledie i otkrytija," in her *O lirike* (M–L: Sovetskij pisatel', 1964), 255–329; below I will cite the second, expanded edition: "Nasledie i otkrytija," *O lirike* (L: Sovetskij pisatel', 1974).

[160]Ginzburg, *O lirike* (1974), 260–261.

[161]Ginzburg, *O lirike* (1974), 267.

[162]E.M. Meletinskij, *Poètika mifa* (M: "Nauka," 1976), 172–173.

[163]Solov'ev, "Duxovnye osnovy žizni," *Sobranie sočinenij*, III, 334–335. Blok read these pages in early November 1903, leaving copious marginalia; see Maksimov, "Materialy iz biblioteki," 371–372. It is significant that Blok first mentions "vočelovečenie" in his correspondence with Belyj, a fellow disciple of Solov'ev (VIII, 250).

[164]When told this interpretation of his "trilogy" by V. V. Gippius, Blok is reported to have said: "At least its good that one can discuss this in a popular vein"; see V.V. Gippius, *Ot Puškina do Bloka* (M–L: "Nauka," 1966), 335.

[165]Z.G. Minc, "Iz poètičeskoj mifologii 'Tret'ego toma'," in *Tezisy I vsesojuznoj (III) konferencii "Tvorčestvo A.A. Bloka i russkaja kul'tura XX veka"* (Tartu: TGU, 1975), 47; the idea of the "path" is borrowed from D.E. Maksimov.

[166]The poet Georgij Čulkov expressed a similar idea: "In essence, if one reads Blok's first book carefully, it is not difficult to find in it all the motifs which were subsequently more fully developed in *Nečajannaja radost'* and *Snežnaja noč'* [These are the titles of volumes II and III in the first version of the "trilogy."—D.S.]; see G. Čulkov, "Aleksandr Blok i ego vremja," in A. Blok, *Pis'ma Aleksandra Bloka* (L: "Kolos," 1925), 95.

[167]This is in answer to Anton Del'vig's "Vdoxnoven'e (Sonet)."

[168]Of this poem Maksimov writes: "[Blok] foretold the changes of his inner life that awaited him in the future"; see his *Poèzija i proza A1. Bloka* (1981), 7.

[169]In the 1911–12 redaction of the "trilogy," "Snežnaja maska" was located at the beginning of Volume III.

[170]Vladimir Solov'ev, *Sobranie sočinenij*, II, 28. Blok read this at the end of 1901 or the beginning of 1902, leaving copious notes in the margins; see Maksimov, "Materialy iz biblioteki," 371.

[171]Aleksandr Blok and Andrej Belyj, *Perepiska* (M: 1940), 34.

[172]S. Bočarov, "'Forma plana' (Nekotorye voprosy poètiki Puškina)," *Voprosy literatury*, No. 12 (1967), 117–118.

[173]Bočarov, 129.

CHAPTER THREE

[1]Quoted in *Russkaja literatura konca XIX – načala XX v.: 1901–1907*

(M: "Nauka," 1971), 391. This review, written by V.P. Burenin, appeared in the newspaper *Novoe vremja* (April 25, 1903).

[2] Quoted by Vl. Orlov, *Gamajun: Žizn' Aleksandra Bloka* (L: Sovetskij pisatel', 1980), 152.

[3] L.I. Timofeev, *Aleksandr Blok* (M: Izd-vo MGU, 1957), 19.

[4] Anat. Gorelov, *Groza nad solov'inym sadom: Aleksandr Blok* (L: Sovetskij pisatel', 1970), 68.

[5] K. Čukovskij, *Kniga ob Aleksandre Bloke* (Berlin: "Èpoxa," 1922), 15–18.

[6.] *Paul Valéry: An Anthology* (London: Routledge & Kegan Paul, 1977), 109.

[7] Quoted by Gorelov, 84.

[8] The image of Aleksej Alekseevič Bessonov, who appears on the opening pages of the novel, is a thinly veiled pasquil of Blok.

[9] In a letter to his fiancee from June 1903, for instance, he characterizes his Muse as one "who offered and continues to offer me *that which I cannot make any sense out of at all*" (*Literaturnoe nasledstvo*, 89 (1978), 147). In a somewhat earlier letter he is at a loss to identify the spectre that had begun to make frequent appearances in his poetry; he only guesses that it might be "the Devil" (*Literaturnoe nasledstvo*, 134). In his correspondence with A. Belyj, which often has the same cryptic character as his verse, he admits "*I don't understand my words* when there are many of them. It's better when there are few" (October 13, 1903) (VIII, 67).

[10] Ljubov' Dmitrievna Mendeleeva–Blok points out that Blok confused the summers of 1899 and 1900 (VII, 341): see her *Byli i nebylicy* (Bremen: Verlag K Presse, n.d.), 21. At another point Blok attributes the first capitalized "Ty" to summer 1901 (VII, 350); in fact "Ty" is first capitalized in SPD #9 ("Sbylos' proročestvo moe...") (March 9, 1901) (I, 82).

[11] K. Močul'skij, *Aleksandr Blok* (Paris: YMCA Press, 1948), 67.

[12] A. Turkov, *Aleksandr Blok* (M: "Molodaja gvardija," 1969), 30.

[13] The first volume went through five printed editions: 1) *Stixi o Prekrasnoj Dame* (M: "Grif," 1905) (appeared October 1904); 2) *Sobranie stixotvorenij* (M: "Musaget," 1911); 3) *Stixotvorenija* (M: "Musaget," 1916); 4) *Stixotvorenija. Kn. 1 (izd. 4-e)* (Pb: "Zemlja," 1918) (this is essentially a repeat of the 1916 edition); 5) *Sobranie sočinenij* (Pb: "Alkonost," 1922). It is indicative of Blok's obsession with the first volume that he began preparing a fifth (unrealized) edition already in August 1918, before he had any contractual agreement for its publication—something he never did with either of the other volumes. It is in this connection that the Dante–style commentaries were initiated. Blok labored intermittently on the first volume (still with no contract) from August 1918 to April 1920, as numerous entries in his notebooks attest (ZK, 421,424, 426, 445, 462, 490). Blok cherished the first volume above the others, though he apparently felt it was artistically the weakest. He inscribed the copy he gave the poet Georgij Čulkov as follows: "with the request that you learn also about this, the *better part of my soul*"; see *Literaturnoe nasledstvo* 92, III, 139. Vladimir Pjast reports that Blok once told his mother: "You know, I wrote only the first volume—all the rest are trifles"; see Pjast, "O pervom tome Bloka," in *Ob Aleksandre Bloke* (Pb: "Kartonnyj domik," 1921), 213. Blok's dislike for the second volume is

well–documented.   Pjast reports Blok saying "I can't stand people who like the second volume most"; Pjast, 213–214.   He had the habit of calling this book not "Nečajannaja Radost'" (Unanticipated Joy), as it was entitled in the 1907 and 1911 editions, but rather "Otčajannaja Gadost'" (Desperate Repulsiveness); see V. P. Verigina, "Vospominanija ob Aleksandre Bloke," *Učenye zapiski TGU*, No. 104 (1961), 332.   The German translator Friedrich Fiedler writes that Blok told him in April 1912: "I will not send you the second volume separately because I don't like it at all"; see *Literaturnoe nasledstvo*, 92, III, 837.   Blok's attitude toward the third volume, which is universally acknowledged as his best, can be ascertained from the following anecdote.   On April 7, 1918, Blok was telephoned and asked to make a selection of his own verses for translation into Polish; the woman who made the request suggested lyrics from the second volume; Blok, however, chose fifteen poems—all from the third (ZK, 398).

[14]It is interesting that in *La Vita Nuova* Dante also gives quotations and cites their source (e.g., Homer, Ptolemy).

[15]The term "integrator" is borrowed from D. E. Maksimov; see below, p.   .

[16]Edward J. Brown, *Mayakovsky: A Poet in the Revolution* (Princeton, N.J.: Princeton University Press, 1973), 6.

[17]Simon Karlinsky writes: "The view of the world reflected in the writings of Marina Cvetaeva is one of the most personal ever recorded in literature.   Except for her ethical–philosophical essays, the autobiographical element played a major role in everything she wrote"; see his *Marina Cvetaeva: Her Life and Art* (Berkeley: University of California Press, 1966), 8.

[18]B.M. Èjxenbaum, "Sud'ba Bloka," in his *Skvoz' literaturu* (L: "Academia," 1924), 218.

[19]Ju. Tynjanov, "Blok," in his *Arxaisty i novatory* (L: "Priboj," 1929), 513.

[20]Many Blok scholars refer to the first volume (or SPD in the "canonical" version) as a lyric or poetic "diary"; see, for example, Močul'skij (66), Timofeev (26), and Maksimov, *Poèzija i proza A1. Bloka* (1981) (98). Blok himself wrote that his poetry, from 1897 on, "can be considered a diary" (VII, 15).

[21]N. Gumilev, *Sobranie sočinenij v 4-x tomax* (Washington, D.C.: Kamkin, 1962–68), IV, 303–304.

[22]Čukovskij, *Kniga ob Aleksandre Bloke*, 40.

[23]*Literaturnoe nasledstvo*, 89, 123.

[24]Z.G. Minc, "Funkcija reminiscencij v poètike A. Bloka," *Učenye zapiski TGU*, No. 308 (1973), 390.

[25]On the topography of Boblovo and, specifically, the "jagged–edged wood" see Vl. Orlov, "Istorija odnoj ljubvi," in his *Puti i sud'by: Literaturnye očerki* (L: Sovetskij pisatel', 1971), 666; and also V. Dement'ev, "'O, Rus' moja!..'," in *A. Blok i sovremennost'* (M: Sovremennik, 1981), 103.

[26]Avril Pyman, *The Life of Aleksandr Blok. Volume I* (Oxford: Oxford University Press, 1979), 98–99.

[27]T.S. Eliot's remark about efforts to decipher Mallarmé are noteworthy

in this connection: "One of the more obscure of modern poets was the French writer Stéphane Mallarmé, of whom the French sometimes say that his language is so peculiar that it can be understood only by foreigners. The late Roger Fry, and his friend Charles Mauron, published an English translation with notes to unriddle the meanings: when I learn that a difficult sonnet was inspired by seeing a painting on the ceiling reflected on the polished top of a table, or by seeing the light reflected from the foam on a glass of beer, I can only say that this may be correct embryology, but it is not the meaning." See his essay "The Music of Poetry," in *Selected Prose of T.S. Eliot*, ed. Frank Kermode (New York: Harcourt Brace Jovanovich, 1975), 111.

[28]Minc, *Lirika Aleksandra Bloka (1898-1906)* (Tartu: TGU, 1965), 7.

[29]Gorelov, 43.

[30]Most notable among the many articles on this subject are those by Minc: "Blok i Puškin," *Učenye zapiski TGU*, No. 306 (1973), 135-296; "Blok i Gogol'," *Blokovskij sbornik II* (Tartu: TGU, 1972), 122-205; "Blok i Tolstoj," *Učenye zapiski TGU*, No. 119 (1962), 232-278; "Blok i Dostoevskij," *Dostoevskij i ego vremja* (1971).

[31]It is tempting to speak of "conscious" *vs.* "unconscious" reminiscences, but rarely is it possible (nor is it always relevant) to determine the author's conscious intent. In Blok's case we know for certain that some reminiscences of other texts were unconscious. Apropos of RAS #53 ("Sižu za širmoj. U menja...") (I, 294), for instance, Blok wrote Belyj that the image of the poem's protagonist was inspired by Belyj's description of Immanual Kant in *Dramatičeskaja simfonija*, but that he realized this only subsequent to writing it ("kak okazalos' vposledstivii") (VIII, 69); for further discussion of this reminiscence, see Minc, "A. Blok v polemike s Merežkovskimi," *Blokovskij sbornik IV, Učenye zapiski TGU*, No. 535 (1981), 140. On inadvertent reminiscences in Blok V.N. Toporov writes: "One must remember the peculiarities of Blok's creative memory and the principles of its utilization—a profound . . . reworking of 'others" words up to the point of . . . forgetting their geneology"; see his "Blok i Žukovskij: K probleme reminiscencij," *Tezisy I vsesojuznoj (III) konferencii "Tvorčestvo A.A. Bloka i russkaja kul'tura XX veka"* (Tartu: TGU, 1975), 85.

[32]Minc, "Funkcija reminiscencij," 388.

[33]Kiril Taranovsky, *Essays on Mandel'štam* (Cambridge: Harvard University Press, 1976), 18.

[34]For pointing out the above reminiscences I am indebted to Minc, "Blok i Puškin," 142, 155; and Toporov, "Blok i Žukovskij," 87.

[35]Močul'skij, 37-38.

[36]This term was first used by V. Žirmunskij, *Drama Aleksandra Bloka "Roza i krest"* (L: LGU, 1964), 78. For a more detailed discussion of "poligenesis," see Minc, "Funkcija reminiscencij," 402-409.

[37]The connection with Puškin is noted by Minc, "Blok i Puškin," 142, and by Orlov in his commentaries to *Sobranie sočinenij* (I, 579), although both quote Puškin inaccurately.

[38]Minc, "Blok i Puškin," 164.

[39]Kiril Taranovsky, "Certain Aspects of Blok's Symbolism," *Studies in Slavic Linguistics and Poetics in Honor of Boris O. Unbegaun* (New York: New

York University Press, 1968), 251.

[40] Avril Pyman, "Aleksandr Blok and the Merežkovskijs (New Materials and General Survey)," in *Aleksandr Blok Centennial Conference*, ed. Walter N. Vickery and Bogdan B. Sagatov (Columbus, Ohio: Slavica Publishers, 1982), 245–246.

[41] Pyman writes that "it seems fairly doubtful that he [Blok] was ever a member of this circle," and that when he first visited the Merežkovskij home he was "forearmed . . . by his own deliberate adogmatism"; see her "Aleksandr Blok and the Merežkovskijs," 238, 245.

[42] Lidija Ginzburg, *O starom i novom: Stat'i i očerki* (L: Sovetskij pisatel', 1982), 35.

[43] V. Žirmunskij, "Poèzija A. Bloka," in *Ob Aleksandre Bloke* (Pb: "Kartonnyj domik," 1921), 126–127.

[44] This quotation is taken from a later version of the 1964 article: "Nasledie i otkrytija," *O lirike. Izdanie 2-e, dopolnennoe* (L: Sovetskij pisatel', 1974), 267–268.

[45] D.E. Maksimov, "Kritičeskaja proza Bloka," in *Blokovskij sbornik I* (Tartu: TGU, 1964), 28–97. A fuller version of this essay can be found in his *Poèzija i proza Al. Bloka* (1981), 184–520; on "polisemantism" see p. 310.

[46] Minc, "Poètičeskij ideal molodogo Bloka," in *Blokovskij sbornik I* (1964), 172–225.

[47] Maksimov, "Ideja puti v poètičeskom soznanii Aleksandra Bloka," in *Blokovskij sbornik II* (Tartu: TGU, 1972), 25–121. Later this essay was renamed "Ideja puti v poètičeskom mire Al. Bloka" and appeared in his *Poèzija i proza Al. Bloka* (1981), 6–151.

[48] See his "Ideja puti" (1981), 41.

[49] Z. G. Minc et al., "Častotnyj slovar' 'Stixov o Prekrasnoj Dame' A. Bloka i nekotorye zamečanija o strukture cikla," in *Učenye zapiski TGU*, No. 198 (1967), 209–316; Z.G. Minc and O.A. Šiškina, "Častotnyj slovar' 'Pervogo toma' liriki A. Bloka," in *Učenye zapiski TGU*, No. 284 (1971), 310–332.

[50] Z.G. Minc and Ju. M. Lotman, "O glubinnyx èlementax xudožestvennogo zamysla: K dešifrovke odnogo neponjatnogo mesta iz vospominanij o Bloke," in *Materialy Vsesojuznogo simpoziuma po vtoričnym modelirujuščim sistemam*, I (5) (Tartu: TGU, 1974), 173–174.

[51] D.M. Pocepnja, *Proza A. Bloka: Stilističeskie problemy* (L: Izd-vo LGU, 1976), 134.

[52] This remark is reported by Paul Valéry: "The great painter Degas often repeated to me a very true and simple remark by Mallarmé. Degas occasionally wrote verses, and some of those he left were delightful. But he often found great difficulty in this work accessory to his painting. . . . One day he said to Mallarmé: 'Yours is a hellish craft. I can't manage to say what I want, and yet I'm full of ideas....' And Mallarmé answered: 'My dear Degas, one does not make poetry with ideas, but with *words*'"; quoted in *Paul Valéry: An Anthology*, 147.

[53] *Literaturnoe nasledstvo*, 89, pp. 54, 80.

[54] The correlation between colors and words played an extremely

important role in Blok's creative consciousness throughout his career. Of this correlation he speaks, directly or indirectly, in the essays "Kraski i slova" (1905) (V, 19–24), "Pamjati Vrubelja" (1910) (V, 421–424) and "O sovremennom sostojanii russkogo simvolizma" (1910) (V, 425–436). The idea is also evident in his early poetry: "Ljubil ja nežnye *slova.*/Iskal tainstvennyx *socvetij*" (I, 230); "Nežno *belymi slovami*/Klikal brata brat" (I, 319); "V ščite moem kamen' *zelenyj* zažžen/.../Ostavlju moj kamen', moj *zdešnij zvon* /. . .zvenjaščij stix*" (I, 286).

[55]N.S. Gumilev, *Pis'ma o russkoj poèzii* (Pg: Izd-vo "Mysl'," 1923), 133.

[56]Much of the imagery in SPD #51 is remarkably similar to that in Baudelaire's "Correspondances.".

[57]*Kniga ob Aleksandre Bloke,* 29.

[58]Regrettably, Z. Minc, one of the best Blok scholars, who has contributed as much as anyone to the study of Blok's poetry over the last twenty years, is sometimes guilty of just this sin. In her effort to systematize the semantic values of Blok's imagery she occasionally tries to force Blok into a mold which does not quite fit. One might recall the humerous gibe Blok aimed at critics in 1905: "Critics walk circles around the artist, sizing him up from all sides, tugging now and then on his clothing; sometimes they begin doing something already quite gauche, something forgivable perhaps only in the most ancient of times: if the suit doesn't fit the artist, they cut off his legs, his hands, or—what is quite scandalous—his head" (V, 19–20). Minc of course does not go this far, but given her meticulous approach, it is surprising to find a certain overzealousness in making Blok's poetry adhere to the patterns she has discerned. In "Poètičeskij ideal molodogo Bloka" for instance (all examples below will be taken from this article), her aim is to demonstrate that Blok's Ideal (construed as synonymous with the Lady) is a semantically identifiable category containing the semes "isolation from the 'crowd'/from 'people'," "tenderness", "affectionate", "beauty", "bliss", "joy" "spring" "(harmonious) sounds," "colorfulness," "living," "holy," etc. By contrast into the negative category (synonymous with all that is antithetical to the Ideal, to the Lady) are placed such semes as "death," "colorlessness," "'crowd'/'people'" (this part of the antithesis does not receive so much attention). Essentially, Minc strives to categorize the semantic–connotative values of Blok's words according to this binary opposition. This model is valid, of course, so long as it is not treated as something absolutely unassailable, so long as it does not lay claim to absolute infallibility. In practice, however, Minc often attributes to her system a certain incorrigibility and makes sweeping generalizations to support it. For example she writes that "in the period of SPD . . . *there is no theme* of suffering people" (p. 197); to accept this statement at face value means excluding outright a goodly number of poems from the cycle, including for instance SPD #5 ("Duša molčit. V xolodnom nebe...") (I, 78), SPD #82 ("Ja šel—i vsled za mnoju šli...") (I, 155), SPD #128 ("Probivalas' pevučim potokom...")(I, 201) and SPD #129 ("Na smert' deda")(I, 202). Another hyperbolic generalization is that "*everything* 'bright' [i.e., positive] . . . is associated with antipathy for the 'crowd'" (p. 197); again, to accept this means to disregard a number of poems in SPD, among them SPD #110 ("Kto plačet zdes'? Na mirnye stupeni...") (I, 183), which contains a most ecstatic invitation for everyone to join in a gesture of reverence: "Vsxodite vse—v otkrytye vrata./Tam—v glubine—Marija ždet molenij,/Obnovlena roždeniem Xrista." To substantiate

such claims , Minc sometimes uses quotations which, when extracted from the poems, do indeed seem to support her point, but when returned to the context of the poems from which they were taken, are irrelevant or even contradictory to her argument.   Minc writes, for example that "Her [the Lady's] arrival is announced by 'a wonderous angel'" (p. 208) (this quotation is taken from SPD #6, "Nyne, polnyj blaženstva..."); but when we examine the poem, we find no mention at all of "*Her* arrival" ("*Ždu prekrasnogo angela*/S blagovestnym mečom..."). Minc writes that "the 'lofty' image of "bliss' [blaženstvo]. . . adjoins the image of 'laughter'" (p. 208) and then cites verse from SPD #152 ("On vxodil prostoj i skudnyj..."); but in the poem itself, which depicts entry of a phantom-like visitor, the "laughter" ("*Smejalsja* glaz") is sinister and grotesque—there is no intimation of "bliss." There are even instances (undoubtedly from carelessness) where Minc alters the text of the poems or attributes quotations to texts which in fact do not contain them (she uses, for example, quotations from AL #59 and RAS #20 to illustrate features of SPD).   All of this may sound like quibbling, but these errors point to a basic danger in Minc's approach.   In the interest of making Blok conform to a rigid model, Minc sometimes oversimplifies the verbal–semantic dynamic of his poetry, attributing to it an almost sterile regularity.   What makes the word powerful in Blok is not its docile membership to one half of a binary construct, but its ability to shift categories unexpectedly while   still carrying the memory of its primary associations.   Indeed, Minc provides the grounds for such a view, but she betrays too great an enthusiasm for abstract systems and forgets at times that the poetic word comes alive only when it is situated inside the poem.

[59] Orlov, *Gamajun*, 145.

[60] Minc, "A. Blok v polemike s Merežkovskimi," 135–137.

[61] Pyman is probably right also in doubting Blok's claim that this poem was inspired by Dostoevsky; see her *The Life of Aleksandr Blok*, I, 124.

[62] B. Ja. Brajnina's reading of the poem's last two lines is quite implausible: "The girl–bride who appears in the doorway of the restaurant makes the drunken idlers [spivšixsja guljak] 'start quietly weeping' [tixo zaplakat']"; see her "Pravo na žizn' (Pervaja kniga Aleksandr Bloka)," in *O Bloke* (M: "Nikitinskie subbotniki," 1928), 298.   The poem tells us that the other patrons "*heard* weeping sounds," not that they produced them. Moreover the words "tixo zaplakat'," which Brajnina offers as a quotation, do not appear in the poem.

[63] In Blok's diaries the poet interprets this crime as "murder," referring to "*ubijca*–dvojnik" and "učastie v *ubijstve*" (VII, 19).   This may well have been a rationalization, however, since even murder of the Lady was in some respects less frightening an idea than spoiling Her virginity.   In the mythology of the "trilogy" death of the Lady was by no means cataclysmic, since Her essential purity remained uncompromised and various scenarios (the Sleeping Beauty, the Second Coming) could reverse this tragic episode.   It is interesting that in a somewhat later poem ("Ne znaju tebja i ne vstreču...") (I, 509), which was not included in the "canonical" first volume, Blok apparently did contemplate the prospect of "deflowering" the beloved: "I legče tebja obescvetit'."

[64] "Častotnyj slovar' 'Pervogo toma' liriki A. Bloka" (p. 315) indicates six occurrences of the word "zver'" because it includes in its calculations poems

not belonging to the "canonical" first volume—those, for instance, which are uncyclized and those which appear in the cycle "Za gran'ju prošlyx dnej" (ZGPD).

[65]One way of interpreting the title of the cycle "Rasput'ja" is that the "crossroads" are *a place where one meets other people*, especially strangers. It worth recalling Matthew 22: 9, the only verse in the Gospel that contains the word "rasputie": "Itak pojdte na *rasputija* i vsex, kogo najdete, zovite na bračnyj pir" ("Go ye therefore into the highways, and as many as ye shall find, bid to the marriage") (Christ's words).

[66]Boris Solov'ev, *Poèt i ego podvig: Tvorčeskij put' Aleksandr Bloka* (M: Sovetskij pisatel', 1968), 67.

[67]Christ, of course, rides a horse in the Revelation (19: 11, 21). It is worth noting also a remark Blok made to Belyj in a letter from June 5, 1904: "V prošedšie gody izredka mel'kal v gorax Kto-to, Komu ja sklonen minutami skazat': zdravstvuj. Čašče vsego—èto byl *vsadnik v golubom*. Inogda xotelos' prinjat' ego za Xrista" (VIII, 103) (The emphasis is Blok's).

[68]See also the poems RAS #26 ("zaaleet pyl'")(I, 265), RAS #71 ("aloj pyl'ju") (I, 313) and RAS #76 ("V zakatno–rozovoj pyli")(I, 317).

[69]*Literaturnoe nasledstvo*, 89, p. 59.

[70]Frank Kermode, *The Genesis of Secrecy: On the Interpretation of Narrative* (Cambridge: Harvard University Press, 1979), 2.

[71]Kermode, 27–28.

CHAPTER FOUR

[1]Blok himself was in agreement with Sergej Solov'ev about the "diffuseness" ("rasplyvčatost'") of his early verse: "vo mne vsë to že, čto v prežnem 'rasplyvčatom'" (VIII, 97).

[2]L. Ginzburg observed that "in unbroken cyclization there was much that was irrational, at times even artificial. . . . The section 'Miscellaneous Poems' strengthened the efficacy of [Blok's] cycles by freeing them of poems which had been included with some strain"; see her *O lirike* (1974), 263. The section "Raznye stixotvorenija" first appeared in *Stixotvorenija* (1916) (Volumes II–III).

[3]Minc discusses the "plot" ("sjužet") of SPD at some length in her *Lirika Aleksandra Bloka*, I (1965), 16–29 *passim*. She admits that it does not unfold consistently in linear sequence: "In the 'lyric plot's' movement it is possible to isolate several clearly distinct stages. Nevertheless, the concept 'stage' here is more typological than chronological (in the actual fabric of the cycle typically different motifs and their resolutions are in fact present in each of the [cycle's six] sections)" (p. 24). She traces the "plot" of SPD through the following stages: 1) initial situation (poet anticipates union with the divine heroine); 2) heroine's unresponsiveness, indifference to the poet; 3) poet's doubts about the heroine's nature (beginning of ambivalence towards her); 4) heroine takes on a demonic, evil or earthly aspect; 5) hero and heroine both begin to merge with their earthly milieu. According to Minc,

this outline of events can be traced from the "first sections" (I–III?) to the "last sections" (IV–VI?). But in order to illustrate this "movement" she performs some questionable transpositions. At one point, for instance, illustrating "the third stage," she says the image of the city is "completely absent in the first sections of the cycle" (p. 27), neglecting the presence of the city in two poems of section II ("Ne ty l' v moix mečtax..."; "Za gorodom v poljax...")(I, 109–110).

[4]See, for instance, Pavel Gromov, *A. Blok: Ego predšestvenniki i sovremenniki* (M–L: "Sovetskij pisatel'," 1966), 102–117; Dolgopolov, *Poèmy Aleksandra Bloka* (1964), 49–52; Minc, "Simvol u Bloka," in *V mire Bloka: Sbornik statej* (M: "Sovetskij pisatel'," 1981), 181–183. It should be noted, however, that Minc, while ostensibly analyzing the 1905 edition (see her footnote on p.176), uses as illustrations many poems that do not appear in it. She includes, for example, "Duša molčit. V xolodnom nebe..." (I, 78), "Vnemlja zovu žizni smutnoj..." (I, 106), "Večerejuščij sumrak, pover'..." (I, 149), "Noč' na Novyj god" (I, 154) and "Probivalas' pevučim potokom..." (I, 201)—none of which were in Blok's first collection. She also makes the statement that "Blok dates all the texts of the cycle and arranges them in strict chronological order" (p. 181); this is true of the "canonical" first volume, but not the 1905 edition.

[5]Curiously, this characterization belongs to Minc, "Poèma A.A. Bloka 'Ee pribytie' i revoljucija 1905 g.," *Učenye zapiski TGU*, No. 139 (1963), 178.

[6]V.A. Sapogov, "'Snežnaja Maska' Aleksandra Bloka," *Učenye zapiski Moskovskogo gos. ped. instituta*, No. 255 (1966), 6.

[7]Valerij Brjusov, *Sobranie sočinenij v 7-i tomax* (M: "Xudož. lit.," 1973–75), VI, 330.

[8]D.E. Maksimov itemizes several "summational" poems from Blok's third volume, but none from the second; see his *Poèzija i proza Al. Bloka* (1981), 111–112.

[9]Blok expressed his intention to "abandon the *poèma*" and "break it down into separate poems" in a letter to Belyj from December 23, 1904 (VIII, 115).

[10]D.E. Maksimov, "Aleksandr Blok i revoljucija 1905 g.," in *Revoljucija 1905 g. i russkaja literatura* (M–L: AN SSSR, 1956), 257–259; Minc, (see note No. 5 above); Dolgopolov, *Poèmy Aleksandra Bloka*, 53–54; P. Rudnev, "Opyt semantičeskogo analiza monometričeskix i polimetričeskix stixovyx struktur na metričeskom urovne," *Učenye zapiski TGU*, No. 306 (1973), 306–311.

[11]Seymour Chatman, *Story and Discourse: Narrative Structure in Fiction and Film* (Ithaca: Cornell University Press, 1978), 63.

[12]Gérard Genette, *Narrative Discourse: An Essay in Method*, trans. Jane E. Lewin (Ithaca: Cornell University Press, 1978), 39–40.

[13]Maksimov, "Aleksandr Blok i revoljucija 1905 g.," 257–259.

[14]K was written between March 4 and March 31, 1914. Čukovskij reported that Blok wrote "Dvenadcat'" "in two days" (apparently January 27–28); according to Orlov's estimate, most of the work on the *poèma* was indeed completed in two days (III, 626).

[15]Apropos of SnM Vjač. Ivanov wrote Brjusov early in 1907: "This is the apogee of our lyric poetry's approach to the musical element. For the

first time, and moreover in a new way, Blok reveals himself completely as a poet of genuinely Dionysian, demonic and deeply occult experience"; see *Literaturnoe nasledstvo*, No. 85 (1976), 496-497.

[16]Sapogov points out that the plot of SnM develops on the level of certain repeated "key words" ("opornye slova"), but he does not analyze this dynamic; see his "'Snežnaja Maska' Aleksandra Bloka," 12-13.

[17]On this point see Chatman, 48.

[18]See Genette, 113-116. For present purposes I have provided only three of the five types of "frequency" itemized by Genette, since two are not relevant to my discussion.

[19]"Kryl'ja" (SnM #9) can be read either as the heroine's utterance (presumably the second of her "songs," mentioned in the title of SnM #8, "Ee pesni") or the hero's. Minc apparently holds the former view; see her *Lirika Aleksandra Bloka*, II, 6, 20, 41. Irene Masing argues the later view; see her *A. Blok's "The Snow Mask": An Interpretation* (Stockholm: Almquist and Wiksell, 1971), 30-31. Nikolaj Volkov also reads this as the hero's utterance; see his *Aleksandr Blok i teatr* (M: Gos. akademija xuduž. nauk, 1926), 81.

[20]Brjusov, VI, 330-331.

[21]Another "unstable" motif which passes from the "World of Ideal Faith" into the "World of Betrayal" is the color "white" ("belyj"); originally allied with the Lady's purity, it later becomes a symbol of death in the Snow Mask's domain.

[22]This idea is captured in the frontispiece to the original edition of SnM (appeared April 1907); the illustration depicts the poet racing out of the home into the snowy landscape after the Snow Mask.

[23]Tzvetan Todorov, *The Poetics of Prose*, trans. Richard Howard (Ithaca: Cornell University Press, 1977), 120.

[24]Tzvetan Todorov, *Grammaire du Décaméron* (The Hague: Mouton, 1969).

[25]Masing, 87.

[26]Masing, 88,.

[27]According to V.P. Verigina, "Blok's 'Snow Maiden'...existed not only in N.N. Voloxova but to a certain degree in all of us" (by which she means all the actresses involved in the staging of Blok's Play "Balagančik" at Vera Kommissarževskaja's theater that winter); see her "Vospominanija ob Aleksandre Bloke," in *Aleksandr Blok v vospominanijax sovremennikov v 2-x tomax* (M: "Xudož. lit.," 1980), I, 430.

[28]Nikolaj Volkov, "'Snežnaja maska'," *Aleksandr Blok i teatr*, 77-85.

[29]Vl. Orlov, *Gamajun: Žizn' Aleksandra Bloka* (L: "Sovetskij pisatel'," 1980), 308-314; Avril Pyman, *The Life of Aleksandr Blok*, I, 270-279.

[30]Verigina, 426-433.

[31]Verigina, 432-433.

[32]Verigina, 433.

[33]Ginzburg, *O lirike* (1974), 283.

NOTES

[34]Verigina, 430, 437.

[35]On the epithet "starinnyj" in Blok see Minc, *Lirika Aleksandra Bloka*, IV, 25.

[36]*Lirika Aleksandra Bloka*, II, 5–75. I provide a rather detailed summary of Minc's view because the book is not readily available (the copy I used was bound in typescript). Minc offers a similar description in her "Struktura 'xudožestvennogo prostranstva' v lirike A. Bloka," *Učenye zapiski TGU*, No. 251 (1970), 255–269.

[37]Minc, however, is not entirely consistent in these groupings. At times she includes SnM #23 ("Oni čitajut stixi") in *Maski*, at times in $Snega^2$. At times the examples she chooses to illustrate these groupings do not in fact appear in them.

[38]"Struktura 'xudožestvennogo prostranstva'," 259.

[39]For use of the phrase "vsë tot že" in this sense see Blok's essay "Solnce nad Rossiej" (1908) (V, 301) and his letter to Belyj from August 15–17, 1907 (VIII, 203).

[40]Compare also the poem "Ja dolgo ždal—ty vyšla pozdno..." (SPD #70): "I v večnom svete, v večnom zvone/Cerkvej smešalis' *kupola*" (I, 143). Fascination with the cupola had a biographical subtext; compare the following excerpt from an unsent letter to Ljubov' Dmitrievna: "In the cathedral there was hardly anyone. You were taken aback by the loftiness. . . . We went farther inside, stood next to a column and looked up at the slender threads of the staircase railings. The stairs lead up into the *cupola*" (August 29, 1902) (VII, 56).

[41]Minc fails to take into account the image "*svetlozmejnoj*" when she remarks that the heroine's world is either "dark" ("temnyj") or "white" ("belyj"), "but not 'light' ['svetel']." "Svetlyj," she writes, is an attribute that belongs solely to the "world of 'heaven's emissaries'"; see her *Lirika Aleksandra Bloka*, II, 41.

[42]This comes close to that type of plot Norman Friedman calls "affective": "There is a change in attitude or belief. . . . The problem in this type [of plot] is to come to see other person in a different and truer light than before"; see his *Form and Meaning in Fiction* (Athens, Georgia: University of Georgia Press, 1975), 90–91.

[43]Quoted by Edward Stankiewicz, "Centripetal and Centrifugal Structures in Poetry," *Semiotica*, No. 3/4 (1982), 225.

[44]*Bulfinch's Mythology* (New York: The Modern Library, n.d.), 13.

[45]The explanation for this unusual characteristic is found in Blok's play "Pesnja Sud'by," whose heroine is also modeled after Voloxova: "Look closer: these are dark [černye] eyes at night, while in the daytime they are reddish [ryžie]. Do you see... reddish?" (Scene 7) (Faina's words) (IV, 162).

[46]"Perepiska Bloka s V. Ja. Brjusovym," *Literaturnoe nasledstvo*, No. 92, I (1980), 505.

[47]"Perepiska Bloka s V. Ja. Brjusovym," 509.

[48]When ZOM appeared in the March 1908 issue of *Vesy*, however, the subtitle "*poèma*" was absent. The subsequent history of the cycle is quite erratic. It did not appear in the collection *Zemlja v snegu* (1908), though

poems from it were dispersed under various cyclic headings. In Volume III of *Sobranie stixotvorenij* (1912) it was reconstituted in its original form but disbanded again in *Stixotvorenija* (Volume II) (1916). In the "canonical" version of the second volume Blok restored the cycle to its full complement but shortened the title ("i pljaskoj metelej" was dropped).

[49]The canals of Petersburg are associated with suicide elsewhere in literature (Dostoevskij, *Crime and Punishment*; Černysevskij, *What is to be Done?*). Compare also Blok's poem "Noč', ulica, fonar', apteka..." (III, 37); on the link between these two poems see K.F. Taranovskij, "Zelenye zvezdy i pojuščie vody v lirike Bloka," *Russian Literature* VIII (1980), 368–369.

[50]Tzvetan Todorov, "Structural Analysis of Narrative," in *Modern Literary Criticism 1900-1970* (New York: Atheneum, 1972), 440.

[51]Apropos of ZOM Blok wrote Brjusov: "Together the titles comprise a single incantory sentence"; see "Perepiska Bloka s V. Ja. Brjusovym," 509.

[52]Helen Muchnic writes that Blok's "incantory sentence" "draws the emotional graph, the rise to the limit of ecstatic torment and the descent to acceptance and humility, which charts the emotional and musical pattern of *The Snow Mask* as well as this smaller cycle [ZOM]"; see her *From Gorky to Pasternak: Six Writers in Soviet Russia* (Toronto: Random House, 1961), 140–141.

[53]The dominant meter in VM is five-foot iambic, although there are isolated instances of four-, three- and six-foot verse.

[54]On the realistic manner of VM see N. Gubko, "A. Blok. 'Vol'nye mysli'," *Učenye zapiski Leningradskogo gos. ped. instituta*, No. 129 (1958), 223–231.

[55]See Ginzburg, *O lirike* (1974), 272.

[56]In the poem "Vopros" Grigor'ev writes: "novyx myslej, vyčitannyx v novom/Romane Sanda (*vol'nyx*, strannyx *myslej* . . .)." Blok commented on this poem in an early notebook entry (June 5–6, 1902) (ZK, 28); much later (March 1915) he records the phrase "vol'nye, strannye mysli" in connection with preparation of an edition of Grigor'ev's poetry (ZK, 259).

[57]Gromov, 261.

[58]Compare: "I *ryžij* sumrak *glaz* tvoix" (F #4) (II, 258–259); "*Na pleči volosy* tekut/Vol'noj *svinca — černee mraka*" (F #13) (II, 269–271).

[59]Gromov, 262–263.

[60]Blok's "attic cycle" is connected biographically with his move (together with his wife, Ljubov' Dmitrievna) from his mother's home to a new apartment on the fifth floor of a building on Laxtinskaja Street (St. Petersburg). For more information on this move and important insights into the "attic cycle" see Orlov, *Gamajun* (1980), 235–237.

[61]D. E. Maksimov, *Poèzija i proza Al. Bloka* (1981), 99–100.

[62]Maksimov, 98.

[63]Frank Kermode, *The Sense of an Ending: Studies in the Theory of Fiction* (New York: Oxford University Press, 1967), 50.

[64]Kermode, 58.

CHAPTER FIVE

[1]Sophie Bonneau, *L'Univers poétique d'Alexandre Blok* (Paris: Institut d'études slaves de l'Univ. de Paris, 1946), 129.

[2]The following entry appears in Blok's notebook from May 29, 1916: "I have had not 100—200—300 (or more?) women, but there are only two: one is Ljuba, the other is all the rest, and they are all different" (ZK, 303).

[3]In these calculations "Raznye stixotvorenija" and the unentitled subdivisions of SPD in the first volume were not counted.

[4]Efim Ètkind proposes a tripartite breakdown (StM—VOZ—JAM //ISt—RazSt—AS//K—SS—ROD). See his article "'Karmen' Aleksandra Bloka: Liričeskaja poèma kak antiroman," in *Aleksandr Blok Centennial Conference* (Columbus, Ohio: Slavica Publishers, 1984), 117.

[5]In his *Aleksandr Blok's "Ital'jaskie stixi": Confrontation and Disillusionment* (Columbus, Ohio: Slavica Publishers, 1983) Gerald Pirog writes that ISt is not "a travelogue" or "a loosely structured travel diary" (p. 44) inasmuch as the arrangement of poems does not reproduce Blok's real itinerary through Italy. I agree that the cycle is not "loosely structured," but the poems are grouped by locales designated in the text and their order traces a *possible* itinerary. It is fair to say, therefore, that ISt belongs to the genre of the travelogue-type cycle, while not being a biographical travel diary.

[6]E. Xomutova discusses the theme of the "home" and the metaphor of poetry as "building" in Blok, and her views coincide on several points with those expressed in this chapter; see her "'Revnost' po domu'," *Literaturnoe obozrenie*, No. 11 (1980), 27–31.

[7]Aleksandr Blok, *Teatr* (L: "Sovetskij pisatel'," 1981), 413.

[8]Quoted from Jung's *Psychology and Religion* by R. P. Blackmur, "The Dialectic of Incarnation: Tolstoi's *Anna Karenina*," in Leo Tolstoy, *Anna Karenina* (New York: W.W. Norton & Co., 1970), 899–900.

[9]Friedrich Nietzsche, *The Birth of Tragedy and the Geneology of Morals*, trans. Francis Golffing (Garden City, N.Y.: Doubleday & Co., 1956), 19.

[10]Nietzsche, 146. (I have adjusted the spelling of "Dionysus" and "Delphic" to conform to more common usage; Golffing's translation contains the spellings "Dionysos" and "Delic." —D.S.).

[11]Critics differ as to which of these two cycles is dominant. Vl. Orlov, for instance, calls StM "the central lyric cycle of the mature Blok"; see his *Puti i sud'by: Literaturnye očerki* (M-L: "Sovetskij pisatel'," 1963), 379. Whereas Z. Minc designates ROD as "the central cycle of the 'third volume'"; see her "Perepiska s Vl. Pjastom," *Literaturnoe nasledstvo*, 92, II (1981), 190.

[12]D. Maksimov is right to criticize "pretensions of seeing Blok's development as something resembling a victorious processional ascent to regions known to him ahead of time"; see his *Poèzija i proza Al. Bloka* (1981), 141–142. A. Gorelov makes a similar warning: "It is easy to fall prey to the temptation of straightening out the poet's path . . . and without justification turning his biography into a heroic epic"; see his *Groza nad solov'inym sadom* (1970), 314.

[13]Maksimov makes a similar observation in his *Poèzija i proza Al. Blok:* "In 'The Terrible World,' the opening cycle of the volume, there emerges a frightening vision of that reality which in the design of the volume is intended to be the background against which the other cycles–sections are perceived" (p. 139).

[14]R.S. Spivak treats the dialectic between chaos and cosmos in Blok's late poetry in her thoughtful and interesting book *A. Blok: Filosofskaja lirika 1910-x godov* (Perm': Permskij gos. univ., 1978). My own views on this topic are generally in accord with Spivak's; below I shall refer to her monograph where appropriate.

[15]In this connection Blok is reported to have told Vs. Roždestvenskij: "When I am haunted persistently by a certain idea, I tortuously search for that resonance in which it must take shape. At long last I hear a certain melody, and only then do the words come. I must be sure that they conform precisely to the tonal motif and do not contradict it in any way. Every poem is first of all a thought. Without thought there can be no creativity. But for me, for some reason, [the thought] first takes form in some resonance. Apparently, I am a musician *manqué*, except that my music is not in abstract sounds but in the intonation of the human voice." —reported in Vs. Roždestvenskij, *Stranicy žizni: Iz literaturnyx vospominanij* (M: "Sovremennik," 1974), 207.

[16]On the symbolism of the color yellow in Blok one may consult L. Krasnova, *Poètika Aleksandra Bloka: Očerki* (L'vov: Izd-vo L'vovskogo univ., 1973), 165–176.

[17]One can derive a cyclic "frequency quotient" for this or any other lexeme, word or semantic field by dividing the number of times a given item appears in a cycle by the total number of lines in the cycle and multiplying by a factor of 100. This figure will indicate the number of occurrences per 100 lines of verse. For "*pust-*" the frequency quotient in StM is 1.69, that is, this lexeme occurs slightly less than twice per 100 lines of text; in the third volume this frequency is approached only by the cycles ROD (1.53), VOZ (1.42) and the poèma SS (1.36).

[18]The frequency quotient for the word "*čužoj*" in StM is .62 (per 100 lines); this is higher than all the other cycles in the third volume, although one occurrence of the word in the short poèma SS gives it an inflated quotient there of .68.

[19]Z.G. Minc, "Struktura 'xudožestvennogo prostranstva' v lirike A. Bloka," *Učenye zapiski TGU*, No. 251 (1970), 275.

[20]There are in fact just as many exterior scenes in StM as interiors, and to say that "all" boundaries and distinctions are removed is hyperbole.

[21]In discussing this poem K. Taranovsky calls the phenomenon "a two–fold time guage"; see his "Certain Aspects of Blok's Symbolism," in *Studies in Slavic Linguistics and Poetics in Honor of Boris O. Unbegaun* (New York: NYU Press, 1968), 254.

[22]Minc, "Structura 'xudožestvennogo prostranstva'," 272 and 279; see also her *Lirika Aleksandra Bloka* (Tartu: TGU, 1965-75), II, 137.

[23]Spivak, 44.

[24]Spivak makes this point quite cogently: "In Blok life turned into art

(chaos) is the antithesis of art reworking life creatively (cosmos)" (p. 32).

[25]"The Poetic Principle," in *The Complete Tales and Poems of Edgar Allan Poe* (New York: The Modern Library, 1938), 889.

[26]Anyone who wishes a more detailed analysis of ŽMP and ČK may consult my articles "The Cyclical Dynamics of Blok's 'Žizn' moego prijatelja'," *Aleksandr Blok Centennial Conference*, 321–343; "Aleksandr Blok's Cycle 'Black Blood': An Interpretive Analysis," *Russian Literature*, XVIII, No. 3 (1985), 207–240.

[27]PS I carried the title "Totentanz" in *Sovremennik*, No. 11 (1912); PS II and III appeared together under this title in *Russkaja mysl'*, No. 3 (1914); see Blok, III, 507.

[28]*Russkaja mysl'*, No. 12 (1915); see Blok, III, 507.

[29]Chronicle sources from the Fourteenth Century suggest that the folk custom of dancing over the graves of the dead may have existed before the 1373 epidemic of the Black Death, but that the epidemic itself was instrumental in popularizing this ritual; on this point see Florence Warren, *The Dance of Death* (London: Oxford University Press, 1931), xiii–xiv.

[30]Among the possible literary models for Blok's cycle (or individual poems within the cycle) the following have been cited in critical literature: 1) A. Odoevskij's poem "Bal"; 2) Baudelaire's "Danse macabre" in *Fleurs du mal*; 3) Dostoevskij's short story "Bobok"; 4) Turgenev's prose poem "Čerepa"; 5) Brjusov's "Zamknutye"; 6) Belyj's "Maskarad." To this list I could add two more that Blok was undoubtedly familiar with: Heine's cycle "Traumbilder," where the image of the living or dancing corpse continually reappears, and Bal'mont's cycle "Danses macabres" in *Budem kak solnce*. Scholars have also called attention to isolated textual echoes in PS from sources not related to the Dance of Death. Orlov, for example, compares the line "Kak na plečo sklonilas' golova" (PS I) with the line "K pleču slegka tvoja sklonilas' golova" from Fet's poem "Včera, uvenčana dušistymi cvetami..."; see Blok, III, 507. Minc points out that the line "I ostryj jad privyčno–svetskoj zlosti" (PS I) echoes *Evgenij Onegin* ("Vot krupnoj sol'ju svetskoj zlosti/Stal oživljat'sja razgovor") (VIII. 23); see her "Blok i Puškin," Učenye zapiski TGU, No. 306 (1973), 241. To these textual reminiscences I would add two of my own. The opening lines in PS I ("Kak tjažko mertvecu sredi ljudej/Živym i strastnym pritvorjat'sja!") seem to recall verses from Puškin's "Kavkazskij plennik" ("Kak tjažko mertvymi ustami/Živym lobzan'jam otvečat'"). I would suggest too that certain phrasings in PS I ("Živye spjat. Mervec vstaet . . . On krepko žmet prijatel'skie ruki . . . 'Da, no vy ne priglašali/Na val's NN'") can be fruitfully compared with Gončarov's *Oblomov* (Part II, chapter 4): "Vse èto mertvecy, spjaščie ljudi. . . . My na bale u knjazja N. . . . Razve èto živye, nespjaščie ljudi? . . . Začem tak krepko žmut drug drugu ruki?".

[31]To be convinced of this one need only read Kornej Čukovskij's amusing essay "Veseloe kladbišče" (1911), which describes the morbid fixation of Russian writers near the turn of the century with the theme of "living death." Citing works by writers as diverse as Remizov and Sergeev–Censkij, Čukovskij provides a travel–guide through what he calls "the cemeterial period of life and literature"; see his *Sobranie sočinenij v 6-i tomax* (M: "Xudož. lit.," 1965–69), VI, 264. Blok's PS is indicative of this decadent trend and may in fact be a commentary on it, but his cycle is not derived from it in any but the most general sense.

[32]The parallel between PS and the Dance of Death drawings (or paintings) has been noted by M.N. Rozanov, "Motivy 'mirovoj skorbi' v lirike Bloka," in *O Bloke* (M: "Nikitinskie subbotniki," 1929), 246; and by Pavel Gromov, *A. Blok: Ego predšestvenniki i sovremenniki* (M-L: "Sovetskij pisatel'," 1966), 461. Rozanov and Gromov, however, only mention the connection without investigating it further.

[33]Žirmunskij provides a list of the sources Blok used for his play in *Drama Aleksandra Bloka "Roza i krest"* (L: Izd-vo Leningradskogo univ., 1964).

[34]James M. Clark, *The Dance of Death by Hans Holbein* (London: Phaidon Press, 1947), 74–75.

[35]*Ènciklopedičeskij slovar'* (Pb: 1898), XXIII, 943.

[36]Leonard P. Kurtz, *The Dance of Death and the Macabre Spirit in European Literature* (New York: Gordon Press, 1975), 194.

[37]In his article "O poètike liričeskogo cikla," *Filologičeskie nauki*, No. 4 (1982), I. V. Fomenko points out that this cycle is structured around certain "key words" ("opornye slova"), but focuses his attention on the colors "rozovyj" (PS I), "alyj" (PS IV) and "zolotoj" (PS V) rather than the shared lexemes (p. 39–40); he suggests that these colors are strategically placed so as to symbolize a progression from "hope" to "betrayal" to "entrapment.".

[38]It is interesting that PS II comes close to reproducing the strophic configuration of the verse texts that generally accompanied pictorial renditions of the Dance. These followed a dramatic format consisting of Death's dialogue with each of his victims: the invitation to dance alternated throughout with the victim's reply. To each speaker is alotted an eight-line strophe with cross rhyme (ababcbc); in PS II Blok also uses cross rhyme although the pattern is not identical (abab cdcd).

[39]I am grateful to Professor Taranovsky for pointing this out to me in conversation. Since that time I have come across two remarks in Boris Pasternak's "Autobiographical Sketch" which support this reading. Apropos of Blok's poetry Pasternak writes: "It is as if not a person is telling about what is happening in the city, but the city itself through the lips of a person is making a statement about itself." Later Pasternak adds that "the city in Blok's verses [is] the main hero of his story, of his biography." See Pasternak, *Proza 1915-1958* (Ann Arbor: The University of Michigan Press, 1961), 15–16.

[40]Andrej Kodjak, "Aleksandr Blok's Circular Structure," *Aleksandr Blok Centennial Conference*, 203.

[41]Lawrence E. Feinberg, "Poem as Such: Three Lyrics by Blok," *International Journal of Slavic Linguistics and Poetics*, No. 23 (1976), 121.

[42]Blok was familiar with Merežkovskij's drama "Pavel I," whose final scene depicts the strangulation of the tsar by means of a scarf (cf. "Šeja skručena platkom" in PS V); he alludes to this play in a diary entry from January 1913 (VII, 201). It should be noted that the image of the "dead king" was a standard fixture in almost all the early manuscripts and drawings of the Dance (though he is absent in Holbein's sketches); he always appears at or near the end of the sequence, as he does in PS.

[43]Žirmunskij, "Anna Axmatova i Aleksandr Blok," *Russkaja literatura,*

No. 3 (1970), 68.

[44]Note that Blok could have used "serye okna" instead of "sizye okna" without changing the metrical structure of lines 6-7.

[45]This instance illustrates the very accurate observation Lawrence Feinberg makes about the merger of linear and circular patterns in many of Blok's mature lyrics; see his "Of Two Minds: Linear vs. Non-Linear in Blok," *Aleksandr Blok Centennial Conference*, 153.

[46]The problem of cycles' evolution in Blok has not yet been adequately studied, although there are two generally reliable analyses of the changes undergone by StM and ROD. These are: I. Pravdina, "Istorija formirovanija cikla 'Strašnyj mir'," in *V mire Bloka: Sbornik statej* (M: "Sovetskij pisatel'," 1981), 209-244; and also by Pravdina, "Iz istorii formirovanija 'Tret'ego toma' liriki A. Bloka" [mainly about ROD], *Tezisy I vsesojuznoj (III) konferencii "Tvorčestvo A.A. Bloka i russkaja kul'tura XX veka* (Tartu: TGU, 1975), 38-43.

[47]As an example of migration between cycles one could cite the poem "Na železnoj doroge" (III, 260-261), which appeared first in StM (1912), then in RazSt III (1916), before moving to ROD in the "canonical" edition. The poem "Pozdnej osen'ju iz gavani..." (III, 19) likewise moved from AS to RazSt III to StM. Each of the macrocycles evolved in this way toward its final configuration.

[48]"Opjat' na rodine," a cycle of translations from Heine, was omitted in the "canonical" text of the "trilogy."

[49]Maksimov, *Poèzija i proza Al. Bloka* (1981), 139.

[50]Other poems in which the image of the "wall" is allied with poetic creativity are "Razgorajutsja tajnye znaki..." (I, 236), "V uglu divana" (II, 240), and "Vse na zemle umret..." (III, 189).

[51]See Jonathan Culler, *Structuralist Poetics* (Ithaca: Cornell Univ. Press, 1975), 55-74.

[52]Pirog, 47-49.

[53]Ronald Vroon, "Cycle and History: The Case of Aleksandr Blok's 'Rodina'," *Slavic and East European Journal*, No. 3 (Fall 1984), 353.

[54]Alan S. Rosenthal, "The Stategic Position of 'Obsession' in *Les Fleurs du Mal*," *Romance Notes*, No. 1 (1974), 3.

[55]*Pis'ma Aleksandra Bloka k rodnym* (L: "Academia," 1927-32), I, 268.

[56]It is worth noting that the word "kanal" appears only twice in the entire volume: PS II and VEN II.

[57]One historical indication of their linkage is the fact that the subcycle "Mèri" (MÈR) migrated from ROD in the 1912 edition to AS in "canonical" edition.

[58]This is an intentional oversimplification. There is also in Blok the image of harmonious, "other-worldly violins" (III, 192), although it is less common—hence the modicum of ambiguity in the title "Arfy i skripki." On the image of the "violin" in Blok one may consult D.M. Pocepnja, *Proza A. Bloka* (L: LGU, 1976), 63.

[59]This is evident from an entry Blok made in his *Notebooks* (June 29,

1909): "Music creates the universe. It is the spiritual body of the universe
. . . . One can listen to music only by covering his eyes and face (turning
oneself into only ears and a nose), that is, by creating the stillness and
darkness of night—"primordial" conditions. Under these conditions of night's
non-being the hitherto formless and non-existent chaos begins to mold itself
and take on forms—it begins to become cosmos" (ZK, 150).

[60] On this point I disagree with Vroon. I believe the problem with his
line of thinking is the supposition that every sign of circularity or symmetry
(whether structural or semantic), every sign of recurrence is a symbol of
"eternal returns." It is unclear why circling birds or passage to the "crimson
circle" (which implies fulfillment of the poet's most sacred wish) are
interpreted as symbols of senseless repetition. Moreover many indications of
forward movement in space and time are overlooked.

[61] For "plot summaries" of NPK see N.N. Evreinova, "Cikl stixov A.
Bloka 'Na pole Kulikovom' i ego istočniki v drevnerusskoj literature," in
Russkaja sovetskaja poèzija i stixovedenie (Materialy mežvuzovskoj konferencii)
(M: Mosk. obl. ped. in., 1969), 154–155. .

[62] The connection between architecture and the path had been made by
Blok also in an earlier play, "Korol' na ploščadi" (1906). One will recall that
the architect ("Zodčij") is the only character in the play who "clearly sees
[his] blue path" (Teatr, 98).

[63] Pirog, 52.

[64] Pirog, 41.

[65] That Del'mas was the inspiration for K has always been common
knowledge. As for SS this is apparent from the inscription Blok wrote to
Del'mas in a separate publication of SS: "To the woman who sings in the
nightingale garden"; see Literaturnoe nasledstvo, 92, III (1982), 65.

[66] The Lady's association with "stones" is apparent also in the poems
"Priznak istinnogo čuda..." ("Mglistyj mrak i kamnej gruda,/V nix goris'
almazom ty") (SPD #43) (I, 116) and "Neotvjaznyj stoit na doroge..." ("Tam,
gde kamnej vzdymaetsja gruda,/Golubaja carica zemli") (SPD #74) (I, 147).

[67] G. Levinton, "Dve zametki o Bloke," Tezisy I vsesojuznoj (III)
konferencii "Tvorčestvo A.A. Bloka i russkaja kul'tura XX veka," 72–73.

[68] Minc, for instance, places OČPV along with StM and VOZ into a
category of cycles about environments "governed by the universal laws of
'Hell'"; see her "Struktura 'xudožestvennogo prostranstva' v lirike A. Bloka,"
275.

[69] A. Gorelov, Groza nad solov'inym sadom (L: "Sovetskij pisatel'," 1970),
241.

[70] Maksimov, Poèzija i proza Al. Bloka (1981), 141–142.

[71] Blok makes this statement in a letter to Sergej Solov'ev from
December 20, 1903; see Literaturnoe nasledstvo, 92, I (1980), 356.

[72] This image appears in Mandel'štam's poem "Čto pojut
časy-kuznečik..." ("I ničem nel'zja pomoč',/Čto v gorjačke solov'inoj/Serdce
teploe ešče").

[73] According to Orlov, the imagery in this poem was inspired by a
fireworks spectacle Blok witnessed during his stay in southern France during

the summer of 1913; the more important subject of this poem, however, is not real fireworks but the metaphoric "fireworks" of lyric poetry.

[74]Georgij Čulkov, "Aleksandr Blok i ego vremja," in *Aleksandr Blok v vospominanijax sovremennikov* (M: "Xudož. lit.," 1980), I, 363. Čukovskij also commented on the "terrifying neatness" ("strašnyj porjadok") in Blok's apartment; see his *A. Blok kak čelovek i poèt* (Pg: A. F. Marks, 1924), 40–41.

CHAPTER SIX

[1]O. Mandel'štam, *Proza* (Ann Arbor, Michigan: Ardis, 1983), 75, 111.

[2]Mandel'štam, 146–147.

[3]Ju. M. Lotman, *Aleksandr Sergeevič Puškin* (L: "Prosveščenie," 1981), 53–54.

[4]Ju.M. Lotman, *Roman v stixax Puškina "Evgenij Onegin"* (Tartu: TGU, 1975), 8, 31.

[5]D. Maksimov, *Poèzija i proza Al. Bloka* (1981), 47. Compare a statement made by Blok to Belyj in 1907: "I go consciously along the path that is destined for me, and I must move along it without deviation. I am convinced that even a lyric poet, who is subjected to accidents [slučajnostjam], can and must have an awareness of responsibility and seriousness. And I have this awareness" (VIII, 184).

[6]S. Bočarov, "'Forma plana'," *Voprosy literatury*, No. 12 (1967), 118.

[7]*Čukokkala* (M: Iskusstvo, 1979), 212.

[8]I am not advocating here a crude biographical approach to literature. But nor is the image Blok projects in his poetry totally divorced from the real man. In Blok's view part of a poet's soul is contained in the lyric. To confirm this one can cite any number of remarks made to this effect during the course of his career: 1) "A writer . . . is placed in this world *in order to bare his soul* to those who have a spiritual hunger" ("O teatre") (V, 246); 2) "*The emotional [duševnyj] make-up of a genuine poet is expressed in everything*, right down to marks of punctuation" ("Sud'ba Apollona Grigor'eva") (V, 515); 3) "Requesting that you come to know also *this the better part of my soul*" (Inscription on the copy of *Stixi o Prekrasnoj Dame* given to Georgij Čulkov) (*Literaturnoe nasledstvo*, 92, III, 139). In his notes to the 1916 edition of A. Grigor'ev's poetry we read: "Almost all A. Grigor'ev's translations as well as his original verses *comprise a part of his soul*"; in A. Blok, *Sobranie sočinenij* (L: Izd-vo pisatelej v Leningrade, n.d.), XI, 361. Apropos of this edition Blok wrote N.S. Ašukin, secretary to the publishing house of K.F. Nekrasov: "I implore you and Konstantin Fedorovič not to divide Grigor'ev's verses into two volumes. . . . Dividing it would not be just a 'formality', it would affect the very substance of the matter. Of course I cannot prove this, but I have the feeling what this would be a wonderful, heavy (perhaps even physically heavy) book. *This is, after all, his whole life* (although it is not a complete edition of his poetry). A single book would be impressive, while two in my opinion would have a dampening effect; I would even say that *this might have an effect on his fate, and after his death he would remain the same*

unlucky person he was in life. Grigor'ev the poet, in my opinion, *is indivisible,* like Tjutčev. . . ." (VIII, 441–442). It is apparent that in Blok's view a book of poetry is equivalent to a poet's life, his fate and indeed the very persona of the poet.

[9]Vjač. Ivanov, *Po zvezdam* (SPb: "Ory," 1909), 39, 243.

[10]Paul Valéry, *An Anthology* (London: Routledge & Kegan Paul, 1977), 108–109.

[11]The fourth word in the line, "apteka," appears only twice in the "trilogy"—both occasions are in this poem. The very absence of internal associations ("migrations") allied with this word tends to enhance the sense of blocked movement that it conveys. After three words that generate an almost endless stream of reminiscences from elsewhere in the "trilogy," the reader encounters a word that has no resonance of this kind at all, that lands like a dull thud at the end of the path traced by the eye as it reads the first line.

[12]N. Gumilev, "Nasledie simvolizma i akmeizm," *Apollon*, No. 1 (1913), 41; for a translation of this essay see *Russian Literature Triquarterly*, No. 1 (Fall 1971), 141–144.

[13]S. M. Gorodeckij, "Nekotorye tečenija v sovremennoj russkoj poèzii," *Apollon*, No. 1 (1913), 46–48.

[14]Mandel'štam, "O prirode slova," *Proza*, 67–69.

[15]*Literaturnye manifesty: Ot simovolizma k Oktjabrju*, I (M: 1929), 81.

[16]V. Majakovskij, "Umer Aleksandr Blok," *Sobranie sočinenij v 8-i tomax*, II (M: "Pravda," 1968), 459; this essay was originally published in the newspaper *Agit-Rost* (August 10, 1921).

[17]Maksimov, 106.

[18]Quoted in A.I. Pavlovskij, *Anna Axmatova: Očerk tvorčestva* (L: Lenizdat, 1966), 27. Compare also the observation of Sam Driver: "The generalization made by Georgy Chulkov in 1915 on the basis of *Rosary* holds true though the next four collections: 'there is one single theme: a strange daydream about a secret lover who had abandoned his beloved'"; see his *Anna Akhmatova* (New York: Twayne Publishers, 1972), 55.

[19]V.V. Vinogradov and Eži Farino advance the hypothesis that·words in Axmatova's poetry, even in the earliest collections, acquire contextual meaning and function throughout her work as "symbols" or "coded" utterances. As much as I have tried to follow the logic of these arguments, I do not find them persuasive. See Vinogradov, "O simvolike A. Axmatovoj (Otkryvki iz raboty po simvolike poètičeskoj reči)," *Literaturnaja mysl'. Al'manax I* (Pg: "Mysl'," 1922), 91–138; Farino, "Kod Axmatovoj," *Russian Literature*, No. 7/8 (1974), 83–102.

[20]V.M. Žirmunskij notes the particular attention Axmatova pays to cyclization in her late period; see his *Tvorčestvo Anny Axmatovoj* (L: "Nauka," 1973), 118.

[21]For an interesting and thoughtful analysis of "Tajny remesla" see Eži Farino, "'Tajny remesla' Axmatovoj," *Wiener Slawistischer Almanach*, No. 6 (1980), 17–81.

[22]On the general phenomenon of contextual meaning in Mandel'štam see Omri Ronen, "Leksičeskij povtor, podtekst i smysl v poètike Osipa

Mandel'štama," *Slavic Poetics: Essays in Honor of Kiril Taranovsky* (The Hague: Mouton, 1973), 370–371. On the images of the swallow, hay, black, yellow, dry and breathing in Mandel'štam see Kiril Taranovsky, *Essays on Mandel'štam* (Cambridge: Harvard University Press, 1976), 10–14, 26–27, 54–59, 74, 77–79, 147.

[23] Quoted by Taranovsky, 26–27.

[24] Taranovsky, 7.

[25] Taranovsky, 29.

[26] Of *Tristia* (1922), Nadežda Jakovlevna Mandel'štam (the poet's wife) writes: "*Tristia* itself has a haphazard composition. It was made up of a pile of disorganized manuscripts taken abroad by the publisher without the author's knowledge"; see her *Vospominanija* (New York: Izd-vo im. Čexova, 1970), 200. She also reports that *Vtoraja kniga* (1923) was "ruined by the censors" (p. 200). According to G.P. Struve and E.M. Rajsa, "Mandel'štam did not consider [*Vtoraja kniga*] an organically unified work"; see Mandel'štam, *Sobranie sočinenij v 3-x tomax* (Washington, D.C.: Inter-Language Literary Associates, 1967), 372.

[27] Jennifer Baines provides what she calls the "definitive" list of poems in the first *Voronež Notebook*, in the order indicated to Nadežda Jakovlevna by Mandel'štam himself; see her *Mandelstam: The Later Poetry* (Cambridge: Cambridge University Press, 1976), xiv and 241. According to Baines' own admission, however, the first poem in her list ("Tvoim uzkim plečam...") was unknown to Nadežda Jakovlevna until after Mandel'štam's death, when it was brought to her attention by N.I. Xardžiev. One is at a loss to know how Baines could determine that this poem belonged first. Moreover the lists Baines provides do not coincide with the formulation of the *Notebooks* in *Voronežskie tetradi* (Ann Arbor, Michigan: Ardis, 1980); Viktorija Švejcer, the editor of this edition, comments: "You have in your hand the *Voronež Notebooks* . . . a book which is being issued now for the first time *in approximately the same form* as it was made by the author himself" (p. 133). The task of textology here is obviously formidable; the *Notebooks* themselves are not available, and speculation about their composition is based on the memory and knowledge of Nadežda Jakovlevna, which seem to be less than infallible.

[28] For a discussion of the second pair see Taranovsky, 51–54.

[29] The first eight volumes of this edition, which curiously has no title (M-L: Gos. izd., 1927-33), were formulated by Majakovskij himself. The last two were put together by the editors. It seems odd that in subsequent editions of Majakovskij's works the arrangements contained in volumes I–VIII, which obviously represent the author's last will, are never again reproduced. Beginning with *Polnoe sobranie sočinenij* (1934-37), most of the cycles Majakovskij formed are dispersed under chronological or other editorial rubrics.

[30] Katherine Tiernan O'Connor, "Boris Pasternak's *My Sister— Life:* The Book Behind the Verse," *Slavic Review*, No. 3 (1975), 399–411.

[31] Lidija Ginzburg, *O starom i novom* (L: "Sovetskij pisatel'," 1982), 333.

[32] Quoted by Vl. Orlov, "Marina Cvetaeva," in his *Pereput'ja* (M: "Xudož. lit," 1976), 288.

[33] On this cycle and on Cvetaeva's identification with Marina Mnišek see

Margaret Ann Troupin, "Marina Cvetaeva's *Remeslo*: A Commentary" (Doctoral Dissertation: Harvard University, 1974), 111–117.

[34]On this point see my "'Stixi k Bloku': Cvetaeva's Poetic Dialogue with Blok" in *New Studies in Russian Language and Literature* (Columbus, Ohio: Slavica Publishers, 1986), 258–270.

[35]Simon Karlinsky, *Marina Cvetaeva: Her Life and Art* (Berkeley: University of California Press, 1966), 8–9.

[36]Marina Cvetaeva, *Posle Rossii. 1922–1925* (Paris: no pub., 1928), 26.